Welfare States and Immigrant Rights

Welfare States and Immigrant Rights

The Politics of Inclusion and Exclusion

Diane Sainsbury

OXFORD
UNIVERSITY PRESS

Great Clarendon Street, Oxford, OX2 6DP,
United Kingdom

Oxford University Press is a department of the University of Oxford.
It furthers the University's objective of excellence in research, scholarship,
and education by publishing worldwide. Oxford is a registered trade mark of
Oxford University Press in the UK and in certain other countries

© Diane Sainsbury 2012, except chapter 6: Diane Sainsbury and Ann Morissens 2012

The moral rights of the authors have been asserted

First Edition published in 2012
Impression: 1

British Library Cataloguing in Publication Data
Data available

Library of Congress Cataloging in Publication Data
Data available

ISBN 978–0–19–965477–2
ISBN 978–0–19–965478–9

Printed in Great Britain by
MPG Books Group, Bodmin and King's Lynn

In memory of Robert Brewster and my parents, G. Forrest Sainsbury and Mary C. Sainsbury

Contents

Acknowledgments

This book has been long in the making, and I have accumulated many debts of gratitude along the way. My first debt of gratitude is to Welat Songur. When his thesis advisor moved to another university, I hopped in as his new advisor because of my knowledge of welfare states. Our many discussions about immigrants and welfare states made me realize what an exciting area this was, and they sparked the idea that this topic deserved a book.

I am deeply grateful to the Rockefeller Foundation for a fellowship at the Bellagio Study Center in the spring of 2003 and the Woodrow Wilson International Center for Scholars for a fellowship during the academic year of 2003–4. I received both fellowships to work on this book, and I owe thanks to John D. Stephens and Robert E. Goodin for their support of my research proposal. The Woodrow Wilson Center provided an ideal research environment, and my research intern, Natasha Heffinck, was outstanding. The year was a wonderful beginning and a source of inspiration to persevere and complete the book.

My colleagues at the Department of Political Science, Stockholm University, have offered constructive comments. They include Maritta Soininen, Kristina Boréus, Drude Dahlerup, Andreas Duit, Jouni Reinikainen, and Christofer Lindgren. Ann Morissens, who is co-author of Chapter 6, deserves special thanks. Over the years we have collaborated on several publications, and in the process have become more than just colleagues. In writing the chapter, we have drawn upon our earlier article, Ann Morissens and Diane Sainsbury, "Migrants' Social Rights, Ethnicity and Welfare Regimes," *Journal of Social Policy*, Volume 34 (4), pp. 637–60 (2005) © Cambridge University Press, reproduced with permission. I am especially grateful to Barbara Haskel, McGill University, for her critical comments. During the summer of 2010 she went through an unwieldy draft of the manuscript, interrogating every section. Our discussions greatly improved the book. In the final stages, Susanna Lindberg helped to compile the manuscript for submission to the publisher. I thank Susanna for her assistance and impeccability in carrying out the task. Thanks are also due to the publisher's two anonymous reviewers for their useful comments. Finally I am indebted to Dominic Byatt of Oxford University Press for his enthusiastic support of this project.

List of Tables and Figures

Tables

Figures

1

Welfare States and Immigrant Rights

Despite the growth of global migration, the arrival of immigration and immigrant integration onto the policy agenda, and claims that huge numbers of immigrants receive welfare benefits, comparative welfare state researchers have largely neglected the situation of immigrants and immigrant rights. Instead they have concentrated on the impact of immigration and ethnic/racial diversity on the welfare state. As early as the mid-1970s, scholars comparing the growth of welfare states argued that immigration and ethnic diversity inhibited welfare state expansion. Social heterogeneity heightened internal cleavages, undermining solidarity. Decentralization in combination with social heterogeneity further retarded growth (Wilensky 1975: 53, 57–8). Immigration also fragmented the working class and weakened the labor movement, which was seen as the prime motor of welfare state expansion (Stephens 1979). An extension of this argument was the claim that immigration would lead to the Americanization of European welfare state politics by reducing the political clout of working-class organizations and eroding the political consensus and solidarity necessary for generous welfare state policies (Freeman 1986: 60–1).

After a decade and a half in limbo, this sort of theorizing gained new momentum in the 2000s. Likewise speculations that the US experience is crucial in understanding the relationship between immigration, ethnic diversity, and welfare state change have resurfaced (Alesina and Glaeser 2004; Schierup et al. 2006; Castles and Schierup 2010: 287). Increasingly researchers have viewed migration, immigrants, and ethnic diversity as challenges to the welfare state or threats to existing welfare arrangements.

A major worry concerns the impact of immigration on the legitimacy and popular support of the welfare state. Ethnic and especially racial diversity caused by immigration, it is argued, weakens popular support for public provision of welfare (Alesina and Glaeser 2004). Although empirical studies find evidence that this is the case, these studies are limited primarily to the United States with its history of troubled race relations (Banting and Kymlicka

2006; Hero and Preuhs 2006). Evidence from the European countries so far is inconclusive. Attitudinal data reveal that the mass public in many European countries questions immigrants' deservingness to receive social benefits (van Oorschot and Uunk 2007), while other opinion surveys register fairly strong popular support for equal social rights of legal immigrants and citizens (Eurobarometer 2004; Mau and Burkhardt 2009: 218). Gradually analysts have called attention to other factors that influence welfare state support and counter the possible corrosive effects of ethnic diversity. Among the factors are the strength of left parties, the type of welfare state, multiculturalist policies promoting mutual respect and social trust, and national identity (Taylor-Gooby 2005; Crepaz 2008; Mau and Burkhardt 2009; Johnston et al. 2010).

Scholars have also highlighted that specific types of welfare states are especially vulnerable to the effects of immigration. One of the first discussions on immigration and the European welfare state in a comparative perspective (Banting 2000) concluded that expansive welfare states based on social insurance schemes were less vulnerable than slim welfare states that rely heavily on means-tested schemes. Social insurance and means-tested benefits create different political dynamics of inclusion. The very opposite argument has also been made: welfare states providing employment-based benefits and financed by work-related contributions—the basic construction of social insurance schemes—experience "the potentially most serious challenge from immigration" (Menz 2006: 394). Since a prerequisite of this type of welfare state is a high level of labor market participation, the welfare state is undermined if immigrants are not incorporated in the workforce. Lastly, the universal welfare state has been claimed to be most vulnerable (Nannestad 2004). Universalism assures the availability of benefits to immigrants; benefits constitute a barrier to employment, exacerbating the fiscal problems of the welfare state. In short, researchers argue that the welfare state, regardless of its type, is under serious strain because of immigration.

The impact of welfare states on immigrants

My focus is completely different. In fact, it is the reverse. This book deals with the impact of welfare states on immigrants' social rights, economic well-being, and inclusion. The current debate about immigration's impact on the welfare state has diverted attention away from immigrants, and much of the comparative scholarship on welfare states during the past decade has continued to ignore immigrants (Pierson 2001; Esping-Andersen et al. 2002; Castles 2004; Taylor-Gooby 2004; Armingeon and Bonoli 2006; Seeleib-Kaiser

2008). A major aim of this book is to fill this void in the comparative welfare state literature.

Immigrants' social rights (legal access to social benefits) are a critical issue for at least three reasons. First, the share of the foreign born in the population has increased in countries with established welfare states (OECD 2010: 299), and the children of immigrants usually represent a larger proportion of the population under 21 years of age than immigrants' overall share of the population. For example, in 2008 the foreign born and their children comprised nearly one-fifth of the German population, whereas the children of immigrants were approximately one-third of the population under 21. Immigrant children were an even larger percentage of the children living in low income families (BBMFI 2010: 37, 223, 576). In other words, although immigrants remain relatively small minorities, their growing numbers, especially among young people, make it imperative to include them in the analysis.

Second, the raison d'être of the welfare state has been the satisfaction of basic needs conceptualized either in terms of risks or rights. Conceiving of needs as risks has promoted the view of the welfare state as a system of social protection against sickness, disability, unemployment, and old age. A more comprehensive view of needs informs T. H. Marshall's concept of social citizenship where rights are an integral component. He defined social citizenship as a range of rights extending from "the right to a modicum of economic welfare and security" to the right of full social inclusion (1950: 72). Since immigrants have seldom been the focus of comparative analyses, there is little information about how welfare states meet the basic needs of immigrants. Are they protected from social risks to the same degree as citizens? And do they enjoy social rights to the same extent as citizens?

Third, the social inclusion of new residents can combat the emergence of permanent social and political divisions in society, which weaken the functioning of democracy. It is crucial to see that newcomers and their children, as potential citizens, do not suffer lasting effects of the harm and injustice of exclusion. In fact, analysts point out that an ethnicization and racialization of social exclusion has occurred across countries (Schierup et al. 2006; Castles and Schierup 2010). In combating social exclusion, welfare state policies are fundamental, and they are of utmost importance to immigrants who often are very vulnerable during the first years after their arrival. Furthermore, as cogently observed by T. H. Marshall, social policies are enabling; they furnish resources for individual development, and they enhance capabilities essential to exercising political rights. In this respect, social rights can aid in the political incorporation of immigrants.

Immigrants' social rights

While immigrants' social rights have long been a neglected topic in comparative welfare state research, immigrant rights have figured more prominently in international migration and ethnic relations studies. The interest in rights grew out of the shift from studying migration patterns and admission policies to analyzing immigrants in their new societies and settlement policies, and researchers began to distinguish between immigration policies and immigrant policies (Hammar 1985; Brubaker 1989, 1992; Layton-Henry 1990; Castles and Miller 1993; Baldwin-Edwards and Schain 1994; Koopmans and Statham 2000; Koopmans et al. 2005). Initially the focus was on membership rights related to nationality, but eventually attention turned to social rights (Baldwin-Edwards 1991; Soysal 1994: 120; Faist 1995a, 1995b; Dörr and Faist 1997). In an important comparative analysis on immigrant rights, Virginie Guiraudon (2000a, 2000b) puzzled over the different trajectories of immigrants' social and political rights in Germany, France, and the Netherlands. Contrary to T. H. Marshall's scheme of rights acquisition from civil rights to political rights and then social rights, immigrants acquired social rights before they gained political rights. She also underlined that the extension of social rights to immigrants or non-citizens has meant that legal residence has displaced nationality as the basis of social rights.

The analysis of immigrants' social rights in the international migration literature has been marred, however. A fundamental difficulty is the view that legal residence or the territorial principle is the foundation of social rights, which has led to the assumption that the social rights of legal alien residents are no different from those of citizens in a particular country. This assumption has gained credibility because of the failure to distinguish between the effective and formal rights of legal immigrants and citizens, that is, substantive rights as distinct from legal rights. Much of the literature has been limited to a discussion of formal rights across countries (Hammar 1985; Soysal 1994; Guiraudon 2000a, 2000b, 2002; Kondo 2001; Aleinikoff and Klusmeyer 2002). An additional shortcoming was that immigrant rights were long analyzed in terms of a generic immigrant and not in terms of the differentiation of rights caused by entry categories, such as family members, asylum seekers, refugees, or undocumented immigrants. A further weakness was a preoccupation with the extension of rights rather than their contraction (Soysal 1994; Jacobson 1996; Joppke 1999; Guiraudon 2000a, 2000b, 2002). Lastly, and perhaps most important, the assumption of no differences between citizens' and non-citizens' social rights has rendered immigrants' social rights irrelevant for analysis. It is symptomatic that an extensive study of immigrant and minority rights failed to examine social rights (Koopmans et al. 2005), and that the Migrant Integration Policy Index (MIPEX 2011) omits social security and social rights. A recent effort to bring social welfare policies into the comparative analysis of migrant integration uses the type of social welfare model as a proxy for the character of the welfare system (Papadopoulos 2011: 39), but this provides little leverage because how different types of welfare states influence immigrants' social rights is not systematically compared. The analysis in this book seeks to remedy these shortcomings.

To study immigrants' social rights I develop an analytical framework that combines insights from comparative welfare state studies and the international migration literature. The point of departure is Gøsta Esping-Andersen's influential welfare regime typology. However, immigrants' social rights are also shaped by both entry categories and a country's incorporation or integration regime regulating the inclusion or exclusion of immigrants. It is necessary to look at the dynamics between a country's welfare state regime, entry categories, and the incorporation regime in patterning immigrant rights.

The first major aim of this book is to compare immigrants' social rights by examining rights extension and contraction. The second aim is to move beyond a description of policy differences and similarities across countries to an analysis of the politics behind the policies—or what I call the politics of inclusion and exclusion. Rights are a prerequisite of inclusion. The politics of inclusion and exclusion involves the politics of the extension and the contraction of rights respectively.

The organization of the book

This book is divided into two parts. Part I presents the framework used to analyze immigrants' social rights. The analysis maps out the development of immigrants' social rights from the early postwar period to around 2010 in six countries representing different types of welfare states: the United States, the United Kingdom, Germany, France, Sweden, and Denmark. Three issues are addressed in Part I. The first is how inclusive or exclusionary the welfare state is in relation to immigrants, and especially how the type of welfare state and features of the incorporation regime affect their social rights. The second issue concerns changes in immigrant rights and the direction of the change: rights extension versus rights contraction. A third issue is immigrants' social rights in relation to those of citizens. How do immigrants, compared to citizens, fare in these welfare states?

Part II shifts from policies affecting formal and substantive rights to the politics of the policies. In analyzing the politics of inclusion and exclusion I focus on (1) the politics of social rights extension and contraction and (2) changes in the incorporation regime that impinge on immigrants' social rights. Again drawing on the comparative welfare state literature and the international migration literature, my analytical framework highlights (1) issue framing, (2) policy venues and institutional arrangements, (3) the territorial dimension, (4) political parties, and (5) immigrant mobilization and penetration of the political process. Through process tracing the chapters analyze the politics of inclusion and exclusion in each of the six countries, and the concluding chapter compares the importance of the components of the analytical framework across the countries. It also discusses the extent to which the analysis confirms earlier research or calls for revisions and new interpretations.

Parts I and II together fill two major gaps in our knowledge of welfare states and immigrant rights. Part I offers the first systematic comparison of immigrants' social rights across types of welfare states, investigating both the formal and substantive rights of immigrants. Part II breaks new ground in combining an analysis of the politics of rights extension and rights contraction.

In sum, the book analyzes current policies and politics and those of the recent past, but it is also of importance to the future. The analysis of social policy over time, as Hugh Heclo (1974: 10) remarked, is about "tracking the intractable." The enterprise here is further complicated by examining the interface between social policies and immigration policies to elucidate immigrants' social rights. Because social and immigration legislation is constantly changing, today's policy descriptions may be quickly outdated. Even with new developments, this book has major relevance since its time perspective is several decades; it covers critical periods of policy formation and reorientation that help us to understand today's policies and politics; it reveals the roots of current policy variations across the countries.

The book has significant implications for the future since issues involving immigrant rights and integration are now at the top of the political agenda. These issues mean that it is high time to turn around the comparative analysis of welfare states and immigrants by focusing on the impact of welfare states on immigrants instead of the effects of immigration and ethnic diversity on welfare states. Failure to do so is likely to result in overlooking key policies that facilitate or hinder immigrants' economic, social, and political incorporation. This in turn has momentous repercussions for the functioning of our societies and polities as they become ethnically and racially more diverse.

Part I

Immigrants' Social Rights in Comparative Perspective

2

Introduction to Part I

Immigrants' social rights in a comparative perspective constitute the focal point of Part I, and the analysis centers on three sets of questions. What are the differences and similarities in immigrants' social rights and entitlements across welfare states? And how does the type of welfare state shape their inclusion and exclusion? A second set of questions deals with changes in immigrant rights over time and the direction of the change. This involves an examination of the formal incorporation of immigrants into the welfare state, the effects of welfare state retrenchment and restructuring during the past decades on their rights, and efforts to restrict newcomers' access to benefits. Is there a general trend in rights extension or rights contraction across countries? The third set of questions interrogates the assumption that there are virtually no differences between the social rights of legal resident aliens and citizens. To answer this question we must look at both formal and substantive rights.

The framework used to analyze immigrants' social rights builds upon the insights and theories produced by comparative welfare state research and the literature on international migration and immigrant rights. The first body of scholarship has theorized important variations in social provision across countries by constructing models of social policy and welfare state typologies (Titmuss 1974; Korpi 1980; Esping-Andersen 1990, 1999; Leibfried 1992; Castles and Mitchell 1993; Ferrera 1996; Korpi and Palme 1998; Goodin et al. 1999; Scharpf and Schmidt 2000; Huber and Stephens 2001; Arts and Gelissen 2010). Underlying my analytical framework is the thesis that the type of welfare state affects immigrants' social rights. Equally important, however, the analysis of immigrants' social rights remains incomplete if examined only through the lens of social policy. A fuller understanding of immigrants' social rights requires that we also analyze the impact of the forms of immigration or "entry categories" and the type of incorporation regime.

Welfare state regimes

Among the most influential contributions in comparative welfare state analysis is Gøsta Esping-Andersen's welfare regime typology (1990), and this typology serves as the point of departure here. Four principal dimensions of variation underpin his typology. Most central to his typology are variations in decommodification, which refers to the ability to enjoy an acceptable standard of living independently of market participation (p. 37). This notion is used as a yardstick of the quality of social rights. The second dimension of variation consists of the stratifying effects of social policies. The third dimension is the relationships between the state, market, and family in social provision. The fourth dimension is the dynamics between the welfare state and the structure of employment. Using these dimensions, he constructs three types: the liberal regime, the conservative corporatist regime, and the social democratic regime.

Esping-Andersen's typology identifies crucial welfare state variations, but its relevance to immigrants' social rights is not immediately clear. The typology's dimensions of variation do, however, generate interesting empirical research questions. Do the social rights of immigrants have the same decommodification levels as the social rights of citizens? And do the regimes produce the same stratifying effects for immigrants and citizens? In other words, an examination of immigrants' social rights offers an additional test of the typology's robustness.

An important criticism of the typology is that it conflates *explanans* (explanatory factors) with *explananda* (outcomes) (Korpi and Palme 1998: 665–6). Both decommodification and stratifying effects are outcomes, while variations in the nexus between state, market, and family are characteristics of the regimes that can explain the varying degrees of decommodification and stratification. To solve this problem I distinguish between variations that are regime attributes and those that are outcomes.

Regime attributes and immigrants' social rights

The focus on regime attributes opens up new perspectives in theorizing about the effects of regime types on immigrants' social rights. Table 2.1 lays out the major attributes of each regime type in schematic form. It needs to be stressed that the three regimes are ideal types, and as such simplifications of reality, but they aid in specifying crucial differences. Several regime attributes promote inclusion and/or exclusion, with differing implications for the social rights of immigrants.

Table 2.1. Three welfare state regimes

Regime attribute	Liberal	Conservative corporatist	Social democratic
Basis of entitlement	Need	Work	Citizenship/residence
Main beneficiaries	The poor	Earners	All citizens/residents
Benefit construction	Flat rate	Earnings related	Flat rate/earnings related
Type of funding	Taxation	Contributions	Taxes/contributions
Sources of funding	State/market	Earner/employer/state	State
Caring and social services	Family/market	Family/intermediary groups	Family/state
Objective	Poverty alleviation	Income maintenance	Equality/income maintenance

Source: Adapted from Scharpf and Schmidt (2000: 11).

BASIS OF ENTITLEMENT

The three main bases or principles of entitlement discussed in the welfare state literature are need, work, and citizenship; and these principles rest on different notions of deservingness. The principle of need assumes that to uphold human dignity the individual is entitled to a social minimum, and that social benefits provide a safety net for those without adequate resources. The principle of work underlines that work is a major contribution to society. It rewards individuals engaged in the production of goods and services by protecting them for loss of earnings. The principle of citizenship emphasizes the rights of all citizens to a socially acceptable standard of living.

In most countries, social provision is not based on a single claiming principle. Instead policy makers have combined the three principles so that each country has its own specific mix. However, in this typology each regime is associated with one of the principles of entitlement because it plays a much stronger role in social provision than in the other two regimes. The liberal regime distinguishes itself by the prominence of entitlements based on need, the conservative corporatist regime by entitlements based on work, and the social democratic regime by entitlements based on citizenship or residence.

These three bases of entitlement have different impacts on the social rights of immigrants. Entitlements based on need should in principle encompass many immigrants since they, as newcomers, often lack resources and are typically vulnerable to poverty during their first years in the country. Two variations are important in shaping how exclusionary or inclusive the principle of need is, and their influence affects the entitlements of both immigrants and citizens. The first concerns the breadth or specificity of needs that provide benefits. The major distinction here is between general assistance schemes that provide benefits to all persons with insufficient resources to meet a standard minimum and categorical programs aimed at specific groups, such as the needy disabled or children in need. The second is how the means test is constructed: whether it is a poverty test to restrict benefits to the very needy or an affluence test to exclude the wealthy (Eardley et al. 1996a: 2–3).

Work as a basis of entitlement seems to dovetail neatly with labor migration. Foreign workers have usually had almost immediate access to benefits under the same conditions as citizen workers—and several benefits have been exportable. For immigrants, the major disadvantage is when this basis of entitlement involves rigorous work tests, such as lifetime earnings and full time employment. Even less severe tests, like minimum earnings or working hours, can have exclusionary effects. An additional shortcoming of this claiming principle is that it excludes those who are not in the workforce and often those in precarious employment.

Finally, entitlements based on citizenship appear to be a direct negation of immigrants' social rights since immigrants as a rule are non-citizens in their new country of residence. In many instances, however, rights accorded to citizens have been extended to permanent residents and thus generally include immigrants. Nevertheless, residence can pose at least three sorts of obstacles to immigrants' social rights. First, if rights depend upon the length of residence, immigrants will be disqualified from benefits until they meet the residence requirement. Second, if a permanent residence permit is the key to social benefits, the ease or difficulties in fulfilling permit requirements can have inclusive or exclusionary effects. Third, the criterion of residence can impede the exportability of benefits; changing country of residence affects entitlement.

MAIN BENEFICIARIES

The bases of entitlement determine who the main beneficiaries are. When need is the claiming principle, the circle of main beneficiaries consists of the poor or the less well-off, and its scope is much smaller than all residents in the social democratic regime or the working population and workers' families in the conservative corporatist regime.

BENEFIT CONSTRUCTION

The construction of benefits has different consequences for distributional outcomes. Flat-rate benefits that are typical of the liberal regime entail equal benefits to all recipients, with equalizing effects. An immigrant receives the same benefits as everyone else. In the conservative regime cash transfers are overwhelmingly earnings-related benefits. They mirror earnings and perpetuate income inequalities; the higher the earnings, the higher the benefit amount. This benefit construction tends to disfavor immigrants who generally have poorer earnings than citizen workers. The social democratic regime combines flat-rate and earnings-related benefits. Intuitively the combination of flat-rate benefits and earnings-related benefits would seem to have weaker equalizing effects than flat-rate benefits because it includes unequal benefits. Upon closer inspection, however, this combination does have important equalizing effects that flat-rate benefits on their own often lack. The earnings-related component reduces inequalities between beneficiaries and the working population, whereas the income gap widens if beneficiaries only have access to flat-rate benefits (Korpi and Palme 1998). The combination of both types of benefits means that immigrants get the same flat-rate benefits, which provide a basic income floor. If they also receive earnings-related benefits, they might be lower than those received by non-immigrants, but their basic income is topped up. They are generally better off than if they only received either flat-rate benefits or earnings-related benefits.

TYPE OF FUNDING

The type of funding also serves as a mechanism of inclusion or exclusion. Taxation tends to be more inclusive. Seldom have benefits been contingent upon payment of general taxes, whereas benefits funded by contributions, or in US parlance social security taxes, are limited to persons with a sufficient contribution record. Often funding through contributions has been accompanied by the principle of equivalence prescribing that benefits should be equivalent to contributions. In other words, persons who pay higher contributions and/or have a longer contribution record receive higher benefits. Ceilings on contributions operate to the disadvantage of groups whose earnings are under the limit; they pay a larger proportion of their income in contributions than do earners above the ceiling. All these features can easily disadvantage immigrants, and funding through general revenues tends to be less of a hindrance to inclusion than contributions.

The predominance of taxation in funding social provision in the liberal regime is reflected in the scope of means-tested programs and non-contributory benefits, which varies substantially across liberal welfare states. General taxes fund means-tested benefits, but both the UK and the US have extensive insurance schemes, funded by contributions. The conservative corporatist regime stands out through its heavy reliance on contributions to finance benefits, but an important variation is the share of contributions paid by workers and employers respectively. In the social democratic regime, despite ambitious social insurance schemes, contributions by the insured have tended to play less of a role in the funding of social provision, especially in Sweden and Denmark. Modest contribution requirements enhance immigrants' inclusion.

SOURCE OF FUNDING

In the liberal regime the preference for private solutions has an impact on funding. The market assumes significance through occupational or employer sponsored welfare schemes as well as individual schemes based on savings and often promoted by tax breaks. In the conservative regime countries the two major sources of funding are the earners and employers, with state funding limited to public assistance, social services, and family benefits. The state is a main source of funding in the social democratic regime. The source of funding has implications for immigrants' social rights, and the source of funding is especially important in the liberal regime because private welfare arrangements often curtail immigrants' access to benefits and services. Access to occupational welfare schemes generally reflects the job hierarchy, rewarding long-term service and those in the upper and middle echelons. Private schemes assume substantial means, and the tax advantages offered by these schemes favor individuals in high income brackets. These features tend to exclude many immigrants, along with others in low paying and part time jobs.

CARING AND SOCIAL SERVICES

Although the family is a major source of care in all three regimes, social benefits and the type of service provider impact on the family's care giving tasks. In the liberal regime the importance of the market as service provider has two major repercussions for immigrants' social rights. Immigrants are employed as care givers often in the informal sector with no social benefits. At the same time market services often have a high price tag and may not be an affordable option, resulting in reliance on the family and ethnic networks and organizations. In the conservative corporatist regime the principle of subsidiarity dictates limited state delivery of services. The principle holds that the state should only intercede when the family or civil society have exhausted their possibilities to provide welfare. The state is involved in funding but services are provided by intermediary groups, which can lead to a differentiated access to services for immigrants but also pave the way for the involvement of immigrant and ethnic organizations. A centerpiece of the social democratic regime has been publicly funded services available to all residents and delivered by local and regional governments, which has promoted immigrants' access to services.

MAIN OBJECTIVE

The overarching objectives of policies in the three welfare regimes are also dissimilar.[1] The policies of the liberal regime have been designed primarily to alleviate poverty. To the extent that immigrants are prone to poverty, this

---

[1] It should be underscored that, as in the case of the basis of entitlement, the regime objective is a matter of emphasis. A major pitfall of this formulation is that it rivets attention on a single goal for each regime, while the goals may not be mutually exclusive. Maintaining the standard of living and equalitarian distribution may be more effective in combating poverty than measures designed specifically to relieve poverty.

policy objective should lessen their economic hardships. The policies of the conservative corporatist regime have put a premium on income maintenance or maintaining the standard of living of the worker and his or her family in spite of loss of earnings. The focus of this goal has been on the earner, and especially the male breadwinner. As long as immigrants are earners, the main policy objective of the regime includes them. They are marginalized when they are outside the labor market, along with other persons without paid employment. The distinctive policy objective of the social democratic regime has been equalitarian redistribution, and this objective should benefit immigrants. However, it should be emphasized that the goal fulfillment of each regime type and the inclusion of immigrants are empirical questions that will be addressed as the chapters of this book unfold.

Forms of entry

Theorizing about the implications of welfare regime attributes for the social rights of immigrants gives us a new lens and substantial leverage. Nevertheless the welfare regime typology needs to be complemented in order to analyze the situation of immigrants (Sainsbury and Songur 2001; Songur 2002). International migration researchers provide two necessary complements. The first is the form of immigration, and in particular the "entry categories" associated with various forms of immigration (Morris 2002: 19; Geddes 2003a). These categories involve specific rights and restrictions that can influence immigrants' access to social benefits. The most important entry categories for the analysis here are: labor migrants, refugees and asylum seekers, family members, ethnic "citizens" or co-ethnic immigrants, colonials and ex-colonials, and undocumented immigrants. For the European countries, two entry categories of increasing importance are: (1) citizens of member states of the European Union (EU) and (2) non-EU nationals, so called third country nationals (TCNs) residing in the EU.

To illustrate the importance of entry categories, we can take the case of refugees with convention status. The 1951 United Nations Convention relating to the Status of Refugees lays down the obligation to accord refugees the same treatment as nationals with respect to public assistance and social security benefits (Articles 23 and 24). Ethnic "citizens" refer to immigrants of the same ethnic stock as the citizens of the country of settlement; this category, together with ex-colonial immigrants, often enjoyed citizen or near citizen status in the past. Immigrants who are EU citizens have gradually gained rights, approaching and in some cases exceeding the rights of co-ethnic immigrants and immigrants from former colonies. At the other extreme, asylum seekers and undocumented immigrants have minimal claims to entitlements.

In other words, entry categories stratify the social rights of immigrants, but the pattern of stratification is quite different from the stratifying effects conceptualized in the welfare state regime typology and potentially they can cut across regime types.

Incorporation regimes

An additional necessary complement is the notion of the immigration policy regime (Baldwin-Edwards 1991; Faist 1995a) or the incorporation regime (Soysal 1994) that regulates and facilitates immigrants' inclusion in or exclusion from society. The terms "immigration policy regime" and "incorporation regime" have been used similarly, and often interchangeably. However, the idea of an immigration policy regime is problematic. As a term it highlights immigration policy. As a concept, it encompasses immigration policy whose main focus is admissions, involving restrictions and controls, and settlement policies. In other words, it compounds the useful distinction made by Tomas Hammar (1985: 8–10) between immigration policy and immigrant policy. Furthermore, countries that pursue inclusive immigrant policies do not necessarily have open and generous immigration policies. For example, Australia and Canada are often pointed to as countries with strong multicultural policies, but at the same time both countries employ an elaborate point system that excludes many immigrants, especially the poor and uneducated. The simultaneous pursuance of expansive immigrant policies and a restrictive immigration policy complicates the classification of a country's immigration policy regime.

Since my focus is on policies affecting immigrants after their arrival in the country and not on immigration policy per se,[2] I have chosen to use the term "incorporation regime." More precisely, the incorporation regime *consists of rules and norms that govern immigrants' possibilities to become a citizen, to acquire permanent residence, and to participate in economic, cultural and political life* (Sainsbury 2006). The main policy dimensions of the incorporation regime used in the analysis here are:

- citizenship acquisition,
- the residence and work permit system,

---

[2] It is not always possible to separate the two as neatly as suggested by the distinction of immigration and immigrant policies because of overlap and the dynamics between the two types of policy. For example, policies on family reunification and the resident and work permit system involve both types of policy. Furthermore, entry policies can affect immigrants' rights once they are in the country, and settlement policies can give rise to demands to restrict admissions either generally or for specific entry categories (Tichenor 2002: 35). Likewise discourses on immigration policy can influence discourses on immigrant policies (Mörkenstam 2010).

- family reunification,
- special reception measures and settlement programs directed to newcomers,
- anti-discrimination legislation with respect to national origins, ethnicity, race, or immigration status, and
- granting or limiting non-citizens' participatory rights.

These policy dimensions impinge on immigrants' social rights in a variety of ways. Historically, the incorporation regimes of many countries required newcomers to have sufficient means to support themselves and their families as a condition to remain in the country. Becoming a pauper or a public charge has been grounds for removal. Economic self-sufficiency and non-utilization of public assistance or other benefits have been requirements for granting family reunification, permanent residence status, and in several countries for becoming a citizen. The permit system, as we shall see, has served as a vehicle for regulating immigrants' social rights and also the rights of specific entry categories. Settlement programs for newcomers can provide social benefits and also affect their future entitlements. It is counterintuitive that settlement programs and integration measures can negatively affect immigrants' social rights or serve as a mechanism of exclusion. However, the social rights of newcomers in reception programs have often been separated from mainstream social provision, and proof of integration has been increasingly tied to the granting of a permanent residence permit and naturalization. Anti-discrimination legislation can enhance their social rights by prohibiting unequal treatment on the labor market, housing, education, and public and private services more generally. The granting of participatory rights offers the possibility of influencing one's social rights.

Rather than classifying incorporation regimes in terms of ideal types or national models, which entails several disadvantages (Freeman 2004), I assess the policy dimensions of the regime using the continuum of inclusion versus exclusion. Of primary interest is how inclusive the regime is and who are included—and conversely who are excluded and through what controls and restrictions. By analyzing the policy dimensions in these terms, I can determine the inclusive or exclusionary nature of a country's incorporation regime and the direction of change over time.

This conceptualization of the incorporation regime has several merits compared to similar analytical constructs. Several scholars have given much emphasis to citizenship acquisition as the fundamental component of what I propose to call the incorporation regime (Castles and Miller 1993: 39, 223–8; Baldwin-Edwards and Schain 1994: 11–12; Williams 1995). They have highlighted significant distinctions regarding conceptions of the nation and citizenship as the bases of inclusion and exclusion. A drawback, however, has been the focus on the main principle of citizenship acquisition, but for the foreign born, naturalization rules are decisive to inclusion. A key distinction is whether naturalization is granted as a right upon fulfillment of specific requirements or at the discretion of the state. On the basis of this difference Rogers Brubaker distinguishes between the as-of-right model and the discretionary model of naturalization (1989: 109). This distinction can also be fruitfully applied to the residence and work permit system. The as-of-right model works in the direction of inclusion, while the discretionary model lends itself to exclusion.

Building on the citizenship regime literature and as a critical response, Ruud Koopmans and Paul Statham have proposed a framework based on two dimensions of citizenship—the basis of the political community and the range of cultural rights—and they have developed several empirical indicators of immigrant rights (Koopmans et al. 2005). Notably, their analysis does not deal with immigrants' social rights, which they view as basically invariant across countries (p. 31); they only discuss utilization of social benefits as an obstacle to naturalization. Nor do they deal with the residence and work permit system. In large measure, their framework concentrates on rights, with the exception of social rights, and it glosses over controls and restrictions. The focus on rights also has major implications for their conclusions about the direction of change in citizenship regimes across countries (pp. 72–3).

A major difficulty of the earliest models, as noted by Fiona Williams (1995), has been that they pertain mainly to a single policy dimension, citizenship acquisition, and they fail to take into full account other policies that are central to immigrants' inclusion. The inclusion of several policy dimensions avoids this shortcoming. As distinct from the framework devised by Koopmans and his colleagues, my framework pays attention to both rights and restrictions. The inclusion of both provides a better leverage in assessing change in immigrant rights.

The three components of my framework offers a stronger handle in analyzing immigrants' social rights compared to previous research, because the framework calls for simultaneous examination of welfare state regimes, forms of entry, and incorporation regimes in shaping immigrants' social rights. The framework also opens the way for investigating the interface between social and immigration policies. Lastly it allows us to study the dynamics between welfare and incorporation regimes, whether the interplay is characterized by conflicting logics or complementary logics, and the impact of the regime dynamics in patterning inclusion and exclusion.

A further advantage of my approach is that it does not assume that a particular welfare state regime is associated with a particular type of incorporation regime. In fact, the selection of countries explores the opposite possibility. Nor does the approach conceptually conflate the welfare state regime with the incorporation regime.

Selection of countries

The choice of the six countries in this study has been dictated by theoretical considerations as well as the availability of micro data on immigrants and ethnic groups to analyze their social rights. Of theoretical importance, the countries represent different welfare regimes and incorporation regimes. I have selected two countries as representatives for each welfare regime: the United States and the United Kingdom represent the liberal regime, France and Germany the conservative corporatist regime, and Sweden and Denmark the social democratic regime. Within each welfare regime I have picked countries that represent different incorporation regimes (Table 2.2).

The selection of these countries raises two intriguing questions and important caveats. The first question is: Do the two countries in each pair represent the same welfare regime? Many researchers would probably have no difficulty in accepting Sweden, Germany, and the United States as exemplars of each of the three regime types, but some might balk at the choices of Denmark, France, and the United Kingdom. Indeed, there are many social policy differences between the countries representing the same welfare regime. However, the point of the typology has been to identify crucial differences between regime types, and my empirical analysis illuminates social policy differences between the two countries representing each type of welfare regime and the implications of the differences for the social rights of immigrants.

The second question is whether the two countries in each pair represent different incorporation regimes. The literature has underscored differences in citizenship and nationhood between Germany and France (e.g. Brubaker 1992), and Germany has been held up as archetypal of the ethnic regime and France of the republican regime. Likewise the United States can be categorized as an example of the republican regime, whereas the United Kingdom represented the imperial regime and now a postcolonial regime. Originally,

Table 2.2. Welfare and incorporation regimes by country

Country	Welfare regime	Incorporation regime
United States	Liberal	Inclusive
United Kingdom	Liberal	Restrictive
France	Conservative corporatist	Inclusive
Germany	Conservative corporatist	Restrictive
Sweden	Social democratic	Inclusive
Denmark	Social democratic	Restrictive

the greatest doubts revolved around Sweden and Denmark, whose classification was not directly apparent. Moreover, the two countries have had similar nationality laws, in part because of Nordic cooperation and deliberate efforts of legal harmonization. However, as we shall see, their incorporation regimes have largely moved in opposition directions during the past two decades. In sum, my choice of countries is primarily based on theoretical considerations and the existing classifications in the literature, and the empirical analysis reveals the merits and shortcomings of the classifications.

Comparative strategy

The comparative strategy in this book is initially based on paired comparisons organized by welfare regime type, and eventually the comparative analysis is broadened to include all six countries. This strategy grows out of a central concern of the book: to understand the importance of welfare state variations for immigrants' social rights. It is based on the premise that newcomers' or immigrants' access to social protection systems depends upon the type of welfare state. The paired comparisons also shed light on social policy differences between countries representing the same type of welfare state— dissimilarities that the welfare regime typology obfuscates. In other words the paired comparisons maximize the possibility to assess welfare state variations by considering both intra-regime and inter-regime differences and their impact on immigrants' social rights as well as the importance of the incorporation regime.

Delimitations and caveats

A first delimitation is that my analysis of social rights deals primarily with entitlements to cash transfers as well as tax benefits that substitute for allowances and less with benefits in kind. There are two reasons for this emphasis. Many existing studies have concentrated on access to education, medical care, and decent housing (e.g. Freeman 1979; Miller and Martin 1982; Hammar 1985; Borevi 2002; Alber and Gilbert 2010). Ironically, much less attention has been given to income maintenance policies. Most important, these policies in the form of insurance and assistance schemes are critical in achieving a fundamental component of social citizenship—the right to a social minimum defined as an adequate standard of living. Moreover, such benefits contribute to the ability to participate in educational and training programs, receive medical care, and obtain decent accommodation. Furthermore, an adequate standard of living is a prerequisite for self-development and human dignity.

The benefits are especially important for the children of immigrants in combating childhood economic deprivation, which can affect their health and development with lasting consequences. It is also worth noting that this definition of social rights differs from the one used by Esping-Andersen; he is reluctant to include assistance benefits based on means testing as social rights.

Second, I do not chronicle the six countries' patterns of immigration. Instead emphasis is on immigrants and immigrant rights. I only present the broad contours of immigration for each of the countries. The reason for this is that my cases suggest that neither the volume nor ethnic/racial composition of immigration is decisive to immigrant rights. Although spikes in immigration have often produced restrictions, and at times a contraction of rights, the volume of immigration as measured in the proportion of foreign born in the population appears to have little influence. Three of the countries—the US, Germany, and Sweden—have similar proportions of foreign born, but restrictions on immigrants' social rights vary hugely between these countries. Nor do countries with low proportions of newcomers necessarily display more generous stances on immigrant rights.

Third, although a racial and ethnic dimension has been largely missing in comparative welfare state research,[3] this book does not seek to remedy this shortcoming. The focus is instead on immigrants and how immigration status affects the social rights of newcomers. The reason is that immigration status has increasingly been viewed as a legitimate basis for a differentiation in social entitlements (Engelen 2003), and thus requires careful analysis. Furthermore, there has been a tendency to conflate race/ethnicity with immigration status. A focus on immigration status is an initial step in disaggregating the two.

A final delimitation is that the book focuses on nation-states, and the European Union only enters the analysis obliquely. This focus is justifiable given that both welfare state policies and the policy dimensions of incorporation regimes, such as citizenship acquisition, the permit system, and settlement policies, have continued to be the prerogatives of the member states. There is little evidence in social policy convergence in the EU (e.g. Montanari 1995; Montanari et al. 2008; Nelson 2008), and surveys of integration policies in the EU 27 member states indicate far-reaching diversity (Bauböck et al. 2006; Guild et al. 2009; Carmel et al. 2011; MIPEX 2011). Nevertheless the EU has increasingly exerted influence especially over the immigration policies of the member states through harmonization and directives, and policy borrowing among member states has been on the rise. So far, however, the EU has

---

[3] Important exceptions that have incorporated the ethnic/racial dimension in the comparative analysis of welfare states are Ginsburg (1993); Lieberman (2005); Schierup et al. (2006); and Castles and Schierup (2010).

concentrated on immigration controls and admission policies, with the major exceptions of racial and ethnic anti-discrimination and the rights of third country nationals. The growing literature on EU immigration policies and politics (e.g. Koslowski 1998; Guiraudon 2003; Lahav 2004; Luedtke 2006; Geddes 2008; Menz 2009; Boswell and Geddes 2011) makes my contribution to this endeavor less urgent.

Overview of Part I

The coming chapters of Part I deal with the extension and contraction of immigrants' social rights. The chapters examine how the type of welfare state, forms of entry, and the incorporation regime have patterned immigrants' formal social rights across the six countries, looking first at the liberal welfare states in Chapter 3, then the corporatist conservative welfare states in Chapter 4, and finally the social democratic welfare states in Chapter 5. A central question is: To what extent are distinctive patterns and sequencing of immigrants' social rights across the countries associated with the type of welfare state, entry category, and incorporation regime?

The three chapters outline immigrants' formal inclusion in the social provision systems of the six countries during the postwar period, the impact of welfare state retrenchment and restructuring, and the eventual tightening of eligibility requirements. Very briefly, the trajectory of immigrants' social rights has tended to follow the vicissitudes of postwar welfare state expansion and contraction. The growth of entitlements generally benefited immigrants, while available evidence suggests that they disproportionately bore the brunt of welfare state crisis and economic downturns in the 1980s and 1990s. Taken together, the three chapters map out the balance sheet of immigrants' formal social rights as reflected in the rival trends of improved and restrictive access to social benefits.

Moving beyond formal entitlements, Chapter 6 deals with the effective or substantive social rights of immigrants compared to those of citizens across the six countries. Substantive rights are operationalized as participation in programs and the actual receipt of benefits. The quality of social rights is measured in terms of decommodification levels, benefit utilization in relation to needs, and the stratifying effects of benefits. By comparing these indicators, we can identify commonalities and dissimilarities across the countries. The comparison also allows us to assess the performance of the welfare systems, not only pinpointing strengths and weaknesses but also emerging problems.

3

Liberal Welfare States and Immigrants' Social Rights

The liberal welfare state regime derives its name from classic or laissez-faire liberalism that has influenced the regime's defining properties. According to Esping-Andersen (1990), these are a heavy reliance on means-tested programs and a strong preference for market solutions. Means-tested benefits are targeted to a limited clientele of the needy, and social insurance schemes provide fairly modest benefits. The state encourages market solutions both passively and actively. Its passive support involves guaranteeing only a bare minimum, which is lower than the wages of the working poor. Through subsidies the government actively supports private welfare arrangements. Social policies stratify the population into the poor and non-poor, and their decommodifying effects are minimal.

The central questions of this chapter are: How has the liberal welfare regime shaped the social rights of immigrants? What has been the impact of dissimilar incorporation regimes and contrasting immigration policies? And, finally, what influence has the form of immigration or entry categories had on immigrants' social rights? To answer these questions, the analysis turns first to the United States and then to the United Kingdom. For each country, I initially present the main features of its welfare and incorporation regimes, and this is followed by a discussion of the evolution of immigrants' social rights. Subsequently, I examine the impact of policy responses to the welfare state crisis on immigrants' social rights. Thus the focus is on both the extension and contraction of immigrants' entitlements during the postwar period. In discussing policy responses to the welfare state crisis, I distinguish between retrenchment and restructuring. "Retrenchment" refers to cuts in existing policies and programs that primarily result in downsizing the welfare state, whereas the term "welfare state restructuring" is reserved for reforms that fundamentally alter the nature of social provision. The chapter concludes by comparing the similarities and differences of the two countries' welfare and incorporation regimes and their importance for immigrants' social rights.

The United States: liberal welfare regime—inclusive incorporation regime

The United States has been seen as the epitome of the liberal welfare state regime where means-tested benefits and market solutions are of key significance. The first major federal programs of social provision, introduced by the Social Security Act of 1935, were characterized by a bifurcation. One tier consisted of means-tested assistance programs, commonly referred to as "welfare"; the second tier of programs were social insurance schemes, in popular parlance known as "social security." Programs in both tiers have expanded over time. The original national contributory old-age insurance scheme was extended to cover survivors (1939), disabled workers (1956), and medical benefits for retired persons (1965). Similarly the first assistance programs to aid the needy aged, blind, disabled, and poor children with an absent breadwinner were later complemented by means-tested medical benefits (Medicaid) in the 1960s, the expansion of food subsidies (Food Stamps) in the 1970s, and a variety of social services. Thus public provision displays a bifurcation that has made old age, disability, and medical benefits available through both insurance and assistance schemes. Importantly, and contrary to the countries representing the conservative corporatist or the social democratic welfare regimes, social insurance schemes have not crowded out means-tested benefits.

That means-tested benefits have figured prominently in US social provision is revealed by expenditures on this type of benefit and the proportion of the population receiving them. In the early 1990s spending on means-tested benefits in the United States constituted 40 per cent of expenditures on income maintenance programs (Eardley et al. 1996a: 38), the largest proportion among the six countries in this book. A decade later the percentage was roughly the same (calculated from SAUS 2006: 358, 361). Likewise a fairly large share of the population—slightly less than 30 per cent—received means-tested benefits in the late 2000s (SAUS 2011: 354). Despite this pattern of expenditure and utilization, the US distinguishes itself from the other countries here by not providing minimum income protection to the entire population. Only the deserving poor—the elderly, the blind and disabled, and children—qualify for assistance benefits. As a result, every year many persons in households whose income is under the official poverty level have not received any cash assistance payments (SAUS 1985: 358; 1997: 376; 2006: 360). Finally, many means-tested programs have offered meager benefits, usually below the official poverty line (Eardley et al. 1996b: 439; GB 2004: 3–36). The inadequate benefit levels of assistance programs have contrasted with more generous insurance benefits whose effectiveness in lifting beneficiaries over the poverty line has outstripped the poverty reduction effectiveness of means-tested schemes (GB 2004), contributing to a stratification between the poor and the non-poor.

An additional feature of public provision in the United States is its incomplete nature, compared to most other affluent countries, and the exceptional role of private welfare arrangements. Most notably, the US has lacked national health insurance providing sickness and medical benefits to the entire population. Nor are family allowances, maternity, and parental benefits publicly provided. Several public services and goods (housing) have been programs limited to the needy. The extraordinary scope of market solutions is underlined by the ratio of private to public welfare expenditures. In a comparative perspective the ratio is truly unique—roughly 1:2—and private spending has grown slightly faster than public spending during the postwar period (Hacker 2002: 15, 20).

Private welfare arrangements have primarily taken the form of employer sponsored benefits and tax benefits, and both underline the importance of the market and being employed. Nowhere is this more evident than in the case of medical benefits. The lack of a public health insurance covering the entire population has made it crucial to have job where the employer provides medical benefits. Several million people have been without coverage, and their numbers have steadily inched upwards since the late 1980s—from approximately 30 million to 48 million in the late 2000s. Besides medical and dental insurance, employers have been responsible for sickness, disability, and maternity benefits. Employer sponsored benefits and individual private savings plans comprise a major source of retirement income. Again coverage has been incomplete, and this is because of the programs' voluntary nature. The state has not mandated coverage but rather it has encouraged employers to provide health insurance, pensions, and other benefits and then has regulated their funding and administration (Hacker 2002: 35; Howard 2007: 207).

Tax benefits have further strengthened the significance of the market because they often require that the beneficiary have a market income. The dramatic expansion of tax expenditures—a fourfold increase from the mid-1960s to the mid-1990s—has also reinforced their importance. These benefits come in many forms but three are particularly critical as welfare policies: (1) tax benefits replacing cash transfers, (2) tax credits for low income workers, and (3) tax deductions or rebates to encourage private provision.

All three have been prevalent in the US. Tax benefits have often substituted for cash transfers and even for the payment of services. Fairly generous tax exemptions for children have compensated for the absence of child allowances, and in 1997 the Child Tax Credit also became available to middle and upper middle income families with children. Similarly tax deductions for the costs of child care were converted into a non-refundable tax credit in the mid-1970s, and the conversion eliminated the income ceiling so that the credit could be claimed by all earning parents. One of the fastest growing programs in terms of beneficiaries and expenditures has been the Earned Income Tax Credit (EITC), introduced in 1975 and aimed at low income families. The EITC (now EIC) has been widely acclaimed as the US's largest anti-poverty program. Very few tax benefits, however, have been targeted to the poor or near poor; and they have constituted a tiny faction of all tax expenditures (Howard 1997: 32; 2007: 41, 43, 85, 98–100). The largest tax expenditures have instead underwritten private benefits provided by employers, thus promoting private provision. In the late 1990s favorable tax rules allowing deductions for employer sponsored medical insurance and employer pensions totaled nearly $200 billion—roughly the amount spent on Medicare, the social security program providing medical benefits to senior citizens (Hacker 2002: 11). Much smaller tax benefits have acted as incentives for employers to provide child care and hire disadvantaged groups and for landlords to make housing available to low income individuals and families.

The heavy reliance on private welfare arrangements has important distributional consequences. Because provision of programs has been voluntary, private benefits exacerbate the incomplete nature of public provision. For example, the increases in tax expenditures for employer sponsored pensions over the years have not been matched by an expansion in coverage. Instead coverage has hovered around 50 per cent since the 1970s. To make matters worse, low income groups have been much less likely to receive employer sponsored benefits of all sorts. Both with regard to coverage and benefit levels, employer schemes have been skewed in favor of high income employees. In other words, private benefits have generally replicated the hierarchy of occupational rewards (Hacker 2002: 36–9; GB 2004: 3–13).

Tax benefits have favored persons in the high income brackets in several ways. Most basically, low income groups may be too poor to take advantage of tax benefits, such as deductions for contributions to charity or home mortgages. Typically, persons with low or modest incomes have claimed only a small portion of tax benefits, whereas taxpayers with incomes between $50,000 and $100,000 have claimed roughly half of the total tax relief. Because the amount of money devoted to tax benefits has been only slightly less than the spending on means-tested benefits, much of the redistribution achieved by traditional anti-poverty programs has been canceled out (Howard 2007: 205–6).

An inclusive incorporation regime

The United States, whose development as a country has depended upon immigration, has encouraged permanent settlers, recruiting immigrants as new members of the nation. The incorporation regime can be classified as a republican type that emphasizes that the nation is a political rather than an ethnic community. Citizenship has been based on birthplace (*ius soli*), and the US has subscribed to an unadulterated version of *ius soli* rather than a limited one. Accordingly, children born in the United States irrespective of their parents' nationality and immigration status have been automatically citizens from their birth. Naturalization has been relatively easy, and historically the naturalization rates of immigrants have been high.

The approach to settlement has been laissez-faire, decentralized, and fragmented, relying primarily upon the efforts of immigrants themselves, their families and ethnic community organizations, local initiatives and voluntary agencies (Fix and Zimmermann 1994: 251). Because of the limited involvement of the federal government, apart from aiding refugees, much responsibility has devolved to the state and local levels, resulting in sizable policy variations in immigrant policies across the country.[1]

On the other hand, the US has been a pioneer in anti-discrimination legislation; the 1964 Civil Rights Act prohibited discrimination on the basis of race, ethnicity, and sex. In the mid-1980s the ban on discrimination was extended to immigration status. The 1965 Voting Rights Act also sought to advance the participation of minorities in elections. As new ethnic groups gain access to the policy process and political office, there has been speculation that the incorporation regime is moving toward a multicultural regime through the increased recognition of the value of plural cultures.

Furthermore, since 1965 the immigration acts passed by Congress have reinstated the United States as a land of "open" immigration, leading to new waves of immigrants from Asia and Latin America; family immigration has also become increasingly important. The number of newcomers accelerated during the 1990s and the 2000s, when between 750,000 and 1,000,000 legal immigrants entered the country annually (Schuck and Munz 1998: viii; SAUS 2011: 46). Simultaneously, lengthy porous borders have permitted the entry of undocumented immigrants. Their growing numbers have been viewed as a vexing problem, eroding support for legal immigration and immigrants generally. In sum, the predominant form of immigration consists of permanent settlers; the main entry categories have been labor immigrants, refugees and asylum seekers, family members, and undocumented immigrants.

---

[1] For an analysis of immigrant policies at the state level illustrating the extent of variation, see Wendy Zimmermann and Michael Fix's (1994) discussion of Massachusetts and Texas in the early 1990s.

The evolution of immigrants' social rights

Immigrants' access to social security benefits, like the rest of the population, has depended upon their labor market participation, sector of employment, and payment of social security taxes. Initially the insurance scheme introduced by the Social Security Act of 1935 covered only workers in manufacturing and commerce. Eventually coverage came to include agriculture, domestic workers, the self-employed, the public sector, and non-profit organizations. Certain groups of immigrants have been employed in sectors with delayed coverage, notably shopkeepers and other small businesses, farm laborers, and domestic workers.

ACCESS TO SOCIAL SECURITY BENEFITS

Immigrants have been less likely to have social security retirement benefits and if they have them, their benefits on average have been less than those of the native born (Parrott et al. 1998: 19). Principal difficulties have been a work test and the treatment of years without earnings. As the social security system matured, the work test increased to 35 years of employment to the detriment of immigrants entering the country in mid-life or later. Of further disadvantage to newcomers, years with zero earnings have been factored into the benefit calculation, reducing benefits. In the late 1990s the average number of years with no earnings was much higher for other ethnic and racial groups than for white and African American workers. Although social security retirement benefits are frequently described as universal, approximately 8 per cent of the elderly white population, 12 per cent of the elderly African American population, and a much larger percentage of Hispanics did not have social security benefits (Hendley and Bilimoria 1999: 62). There has also been a substantial gap in citizens' and non-citizens' access to Medicare. In the late 1990s only 80 per cent of elderly non-citizens had Medicare compared to 99.2 per cent of native born citizens, and over 15 per cent of non-citizens aged 65 and older had no medical insurance at all (CPR 2002: 11).

Social security disability benefits have also involved a work test. For older workers it has consisted of five years out of the last ten years, while the period has been shorter for younger workers. Policy analysts, looking at the composition of beneficiaries, have concluded that social security disability benefits have served minorities since they are well represented. A different picture emerges if one examines the recipiency rates of disabled persons. A smaller proportion of African Americans and an even smaller share of Hispanics who are disabled have received social security benefits compared to white disabled persons (SAUS 2011: 362).

The average social security benefits of African Americans and Hispanics, irrespective of type of benefit, have been consistently lower than those of whites (SSB 1995: 211–12; 2007: 5.1–5.24; 6.5–6.). Likewise the poverty rates of elderly persons receiving social security benefits have been higher for African American and Hispanic men and women compared to their white counterparts (Hendley and Bilimoria 1999: 61–2). Nevertheless, the benefit formula has favored earners in low income brackets and in this way has frequently worked to the advantage of minorities and foreign born beneficiaries (Parrott et al. 1998; Martin 2007).

ACCESS TO PRIVATE BENEFITS AND TAX BENEFITS
Many immigrants and ethnic minorities also have poor access to benefits provided by employers. Health insurance coverage provides a telling example. Despite immigrants' high labor market participation rate, a much larger proportion was without health insurance compared to US citizens. In the late 1990s, 56.3 per cent of legal permanent residents were uninsured, compared to 31.6 per cent of US citizens (Fix and Passel 2002: 192). Newcomers and ethnic minorities were also less likely to receive employer sponsored retirement benefits compared to white workers. The disparity is likely to continue because coverage has dropped since the 1970s, and the decline has been sharper for ethnic minorities (Hendley and Bilimoria 1999: 60–1).

Nor does it seem that immigrants have taken advantage of tax benefits on the same scale as citizens, and especially the Earned Income Tax Credit—America's most important anti-poverty scheme. In the early 2000s relatively few immigrant families reported receiving EITC, around 15 per cent compared to nearly 60 per cent of native born families (Gelatt and Fix 2007: 78). At the same time immigrants have represented a large share of the working poor, given their high labor market participation rates and low wages. Utilizing tax benefits is a complicated process often requiring tax expertise, and this can act as a barrier to newcomers claiming tax credits.

ACCESS TO WELFARE BENEFITS
With poorer access to social security and private benefits as well as lower benefits, the welfare tier of benefits has often been crucial to immigrants' economic well-being. Historically, however, immigrants' access to "welfare" benefits has been restricted. In 1882 immigration law prohibited the entry of persons "likely to become public charges," and such persons became subject to deportation in 1891 (Tienda and Liang 1994: 332). In this spirit, poor relief and public assistance, long the responsibility of local and state governments, frequently barred aliens from receiving benefits. Even when the New Deal introduced the first federal assistance programs, they retained the traditional features of poor relief. They were administered locally, and eligibility criteria were stringent. Thus the New Deal had little impact on immigrants' social rights in the welfare tier.

Instead immigrants gained access to "welfare" in the early 1970s when the Supreme Court ruled that state governments could not deny welfare benefits to legal resident aliens. As a result, state assistance programs removed restrictions on non-citizens' eligibility. When Congress adopted the Supplemental Security Income Program (SSI), which transformed the federal-state programs for the aged, blind, and disabled into a national welfare program in 1972, immigrants became eligible (Parrott et al. 1998: 4, 28). This legislation also paved the way to other benefits in the welfare tier since SSI beneficiaries also qualified for programs, such as Food Stamps and Medicaid.

The 1980s witnessed a continued expansion of immigrants' social rights but also the introduction of restrictions. Court decisions lay behind the main extensions. In 1982 the Supreme Court overturned a Texas statute that denied free public education to the children of illegal immigrants. A lower court ruling also expanded non-citizen eligibility in the SSI program by ruling that non-citizens whose presence was tolerated by the immigration authorities were eligible for benefits (Parrott et al. 1998: 6). Signaling the trends of the coming decade, Congress in 1986 enacted a mandatory written declaration of an individual's citizenship or alien status for all applicants and recipients of family assistance benefits and federal welfare programs (Fix and Passel 1994; SSB 1995: 121).

Entry categories and social rights

The social rights of refugees exemplify the importance of entry categories. Refugees' social rights have followed quite a different trajectory. Initially on an ad hoc basis, refugees who were victims of communist persecution received resettlement assistance. The first major federal program provided cash, medical, and educational assistance to primarily Cuban refugees in the early 1960s. The next large-scale venture to aid refugees was the Indochina Migration and Refugee Assistance Act of 1975. Ultimately the 1980 Refugee Act fully institutionalized domestic resettlement assistance for refugees (Tienda and Liang 1994: 337–8). The Act also changed the definition of refugees to be in accord with that of the Geneva Convention on Refugees (Borjas 1990: 33). As distinct from other immigrants whose access to welfare benefits has entailed showing demonstrable need and meeting other eligibility requirements, the 1980 act extended aid to all persons in the refugee category (Tienda and Liang 1994: 337–8). What has not been noted in the welfare state and social policy literature is that a new category has almost imperceptibly been added to the categories deserving public assistance. Refugees have been the only major immigrant group eligible for welfare benefits immediately upon entry into the United States. In conclusion, US policy has been characterized by a sharply differential treatment of political and other immigrants specifically with regard to welfare benefits, and this differentiation continued even after Congress put severe restrictions on immigrants' social entitlements in the mid-1990s.

A further differentiation in access to benefits by entry categories occurred after reports that newly arrived immigrants were utilizing welfare benefits. A 1980 law strengthened the financial obligations of sponsors, which generally amounted to a three-year residency requirement before sponsored immigrants were eligible for welfare benefits (Parrott et al. 1998: 5–6). Finally, the 1986 legalization program barred legalizing immigrants from means-tested benefits for a period of five years, and those who had received welfare benefits of any kind could not become legal immigrants (Tienda and Liang 1994: 339). The increased stratification of immigrants' social rights foreshadowed a major trend of the 1990s.

Welfare state retrenchment

Major retrenchment efforts have occurred during two periods, in the early 1980s and again in the mid-1990s. In both instances, the government cut benefits in the welfare tier more deeply than social security benefits. In the 1990s the focus of reform was one of the major programs in the welfare tier—Aid to Families with Dependent Children (AFDC). The 1996 welfare act ended the federal entitlement program for single mothers, transferred responsibility for aid to families to the states, and limited durations for family aid. The social rights of immigrants became inextricably bound up with efforts to change welfare, and the welfare act of 1996 cut the rolls of recipients—both citizens and non-citizens.

"WELFARE REFORM" AND IMMIGRANTS' SOCIAL RIGHTS

In 1996 Congress passed the Personal Responsibility and Work Opportunity Reconciliation Act (PRWORA). The act altered the social entitlements of immigrants in several significant ways. It introduced citizenship as a condition of eligibility, thus distinguishing between the social rights of citizens and non-citizens. It also created new eligibility requirements for legal permanent residents for federal means-tested benefits, by differentiating between qualified aliens and unqualified aliens. Qualified aliens included refugees during their first five and in some cases seven years of residency, non-citizens who had served in the US military, and immigrants paying ten years of social security taxes. Unqualified aliens consisted of legal permanent residents who did not meet the new requirements and undocumented immigrants.[2]

---

[2] More specifically, two programs—SSI and Food Stamps—were reserved for citizens, although Congress restored eligibility to all non-citizens already receiving SSI benefits. Later Congress

A third major dividing line consisted of legal qualified immigrants who had to meet the tighter eligibility rules and naturalized citizens who had full access to means-tested federal benefits. A further division was between pre-enactment and post-enactment immigrants so that immigrants recently entering the country have been barred from many entitlements during their first five years (Fix and Passel 2002).

An additional feature of PRWORA was to shift responsibility to the states. The act granted states the authority to determine the eligibility of legal immigrants in federal-state and state benefit programs. In effect, Congress reversed the Supreme Court ruling of 1971 prohibiting the states from discriminating against legal permanent residents. Second, the act gave states the possibility to establish their own programs to replace federal benefits (Fix and Passel 2002). The overall result has been a fragmentation of non-citizens' social rights because some states decided to grant immigrants eligibility and implement their own programs, while other states did not. Different decisions by the states also created gaps in the social rights of pre-enactment and post-enactment immigrants. Several states extended eligibility to pre-enactment immigrants but they were more hesitant about post-enactment immigrants' entitlements. The patchwork quality of immigrants' social rights was further magnified as states introduced their own residency requirements and laws requiring immigrants to apply for citizenship in order to qualify for benefits (Pavetti 2001).

A final aspect of the 1996 welfare act was to intensify verification procedures and reporting requirements in establishing citizenship or legal immigration status as well as date of entry when claiming benefits. This feature built on the precedent set in the mid 1980s, and it has continued in legislation adopted in the 2000s. The Social Security Protection Act of 2004 eliminated the possibility of receiving social security benefits without a valid social security number, even when a non-citizen fulfilled the insurance requirements, such as payment of social security taxes. Similarly, the rules for documenting citizenship and legal immigration status in order to receive Medicaid were tightened in 2005 (SSB 2007).

Besides the restrictions introduced by PRWORA, the Illegal Immigration Reform and Immigrant Responsibility Act of 1996 stiffened the obligations of sponsors. It introduced an income requirement; sponsors had to have an income exceeding 125 per cent of the federal poverty threshold. Through deeming, the income of the sponsor is considered in determining the

amended eligibility requirements for Food Stamps by making them available to immigrants after five years in the country (2002). The act barred unqualified aliens from Medicaid, Temporary Assistance for Needy Families (TANF), social services block grants, and later from the 1997 State Child Health Insurance Program (SCHIP). Undocumented immigrants were entitled only to emergency medical aid and certain nutrition programs.

eligibility of the immigrant for benefits, which almost always ensures disqual-ification. The sponsor must also sign an affidavit pledging to support the immigrant until s/he becomes a citizen or has worked 40 quarters—a commit-ment of five to ten years. During this period the sponsor remains liable for reimbursing any public agencies that provide benefits to the immigrant, and the affidavits of support were made legally enforceable (Fix and Passel 2002). Together, the welfare and immigration acts expanded sponsorship and deem-ing in terms of duration, the range of programs, and the number of immi-grants (GB 2004: J-18).

THE IMPACT OF THE 1996 ACTS

The 1996 acts have had an impact on immigrants' social entitlements in the short and long run. In the short term, one of the most serious consequences was the loss of Food Stamps. PRWORA cut the number of recipient non-citizen households in half, affecting roughly 1 million participants, and the 1998 amendment improving non-citizen eligibility restored benefits to only a quar-ter of the previous beneficiaries. Even with the 2002 change in eligibility and the subsequent return of rolls to their previous levels, the number of non-citizen households receiving Food Stamps in the mid-2000s was still below the pre-PRWORA level (USDA 1999, 2003, 2007; Fix and Passel 2002: 182). Equally serious was the negative impact on immigrants' medical benefits. Despite the recent expansion of Medicaid as a result of giving priority to increasing the coverage of children, the proportion of insured non-citizen children fell between 1996 and 2004, while citizen children's coverage grew. More generally, low income immigrants have been less likely to have Medic-aid than low income citizens (CPR 2003: 6; Ku and Papademetriou 2007: 85–7). In a long-term perspective, non-citizen enrollment in SSI also slipped, falling from 12 to 9 per cent of the beneficiaries in the late 2000s (SSI 2008: 59, 64; Parrott et al. 1998: 21).

Of consequence to non-citizens and citizens alike, the 1996 welfare act led to an overall decline in the proportion of persons below the poverty line receiving benefits in the welfare tier. This trend can be observed for Food Stamps, Medicaid, housing assistance, AFDC and its successor TANF, and cash assistance payments.[3] Simultaneously, as we have seen, there was a sharper decline in the participation of non-citizens than citizens in these means-tested programs as well as SSI (Fix and Passel 2002: 185–7; GB 2004: J-30; Ku and Papademetriou 2007). In other words, through greater targeting

---

[3] This observation is based on an analysis of data in the Current Population Reports, *Dynamics of Economic Well-Being, Program Participation: Who Gets Assistance?* for the period stretching from 1993 to 2003 (the most recent report available) (CPR 1999b, 2004, 2006). Other sources confirm the trend (e.g. GB 2004: 15–48, L-7).

and lower benefits PRWORA deepened the stratification of the poor and non-poor, but among the poor, native born citizens were more likely to receive benefits than non-citizens.

In summary, "welfare reform" entailed a massive disentitlement, removing nearly one million non-citizens from the rolls of means-tested programs (Fix and Passel 2002: 182). The welfare act introduced tighter eligibility rules for non-citizens compared to citizens for several programs. The most dramatic change in eligibility rules was the introduction of a lengthy work test for SSI. Immigrants had to have a work history of ten years in covered employment. The welfare act created a new type of stratification by distinguishing between the rights of citizens and legal permanent residents. It also widened the gap between refugees and other immigrants. Refugees fared much better because they retained immediate eligibility for welfare benefits but now for a limited period.[4] These restrictions, of course, must be seen against the backdrop of the new lifetime limits of five years on citizens' eligibility.

The welfare and immigration acts of the mid-1990s illustrate both the reinforcing and competing logics of the welfare and incorporation regimes. The rationale behind both reforms reflected the liberal ideological preoccupation of economic incentives and the concern about free-riders. The reinforcing logic can also be seen in the traditional stance of excluding immigrants who were potentially public charges, and the emphasis on self-sufficiency via the market. Of additional importance was the rise of contractual liberalism which stresses that rights depend on the fulfillment of obligations. The unusual solution was to make immigrants' access to means-tested benefits dependent upon ten years of contributions. This solution was also in line with the liberal regime's preference for market solutions. The inclusive logic of the incorporation regime, however, provided a lower threshold to benefits through the possibility of becoming a citizen after five years of residence. The greatest tension has been between conferring citizenship on all children born in the US irrespective of their parents' immigration status (including undocumented immigrants), and efforts to bar illegal immigrants from all benefits (except emergency aid), and to deny them access to the benefits of their citizen children. The more rigorous conditions for sponsorship, especially the income requirement, strengthened the class dimension in family reunifications by limiting the ability of citizens and legal immigrants with low incomes to bring family members into the country. In effect, both the incorporation and welfare regimes stratify the rights of the non-poor and poor, offering lesser rights to the poor.

---

[4] Although the treatment of refugees' social rights appears very generous compared to those of legal aliens, the new rules disentitled many refugees since 60 per cent had been in the US over five years and 40 per cent over seven years (Fix and Zimmermann 2004: 340).

The United Kingdom: Liberal welfare regime—restrictive incorporation regime

At first glance, the British welfare state with its comprehensive social provision stands in sharp contrast to the "incomplete" welfare state of the United States. A guiding principle of the reforms that laid the foundations of the British postwar welfare state in the 1940s was universalism. The principle was manifested in uniform national programs covering the entire population. All major social benefits—retirement pensions, sickness compensation and disability benefits, maternity allowances, and unemployment benefits—were consolidated into a single national insurance scheme. A national assistance program ensured a safety net for all persons without adequate resources or insurance benefits; entitlement was not limited to the US definition of the deserving poor—the aged, disabled, and children. Non-contributory family allowances, covering all children except the first-born child, were introduced, and the National Health Service was set up to provide medical and dental care to the entire population. In sum the British welfare state, as distinct from that of the United States, has entailed a broader range of public provision, encompassing medical care, family and maternity benefits, housing and personal services; and the principle of universalism promoted coverage of the whole population.

In view of these differences, is it warranted to classify the United Kingdom and the United States as representatives of the same welfare regime? Despite Britain's comprehensive social programs, the two countries share the defining attributes of the liberal welfare regime: modest social insurance benefits, the prominence of means-tested benefits based on a bare minimum, and the importance of private welfare benefits and market solutions.

British social insurance benefits have been very modest, indeed often even lower than insurance benefits in the United States (Palme 1990: 60, 64). A distinctive feature of the national insurance scheme has been flat-rate benefits in return originally for flat-rate contributions. The architects of the postwar welfare state designed the insurance scheme to provide minimum benefits, but they believed that insurance benefits would marginalize the importance of assistance. The flat-rate benefit construction in combination with low benefit levels, however, was the Achilles' heel of the national insurance scheme. This combination paved the way for, first, an increasing reliance on means-tested benefits and, second, supplementary protection through the market.

In terms of the prominence of means-tested benefits Britain and the United States cluster together with Australia, Canada, Ireland, and New Zealand according to several measures. Compared to other countries, their total social assistance expenditures have formed a larger percentage of the gross domestic product (GDP), as well as a larger share of social security spending (for Britain 33 per cent compared to 40 per cent for the US in 1992). Likewise a larger proportion of their populations has received public assistance benefits (Eardley et al. 1996a: 35, 38, 41). In the British case the proportion of the population utilizing means-tested benefits has risen considerably since 1980. Despite the fairly large proportion utilizing means-tested benefits, the resources test used in both the US and the UK has involved a poverty test to restrict access to the needy, and benefit levels have been low. In the two countries, "less eligibility," the historical principle that public assistance benefits must be below the wages of the working poor, has justified low benefit levels. The UK, like the US, has been plagued by relatively high poverty rates, including children's poverty (Hills 2004: 57).

The private welfare component has been far less prominent compared to the United States, but by the mid-1990s Britain ranked second to the United States in the proportion of the GDP making up private welfare spending (Hacker 2002: 15). In the United Kingdom occupational pensions and fringe benefits long existed for only a small group of employees; they became more widespread in the first decades of the postwar period, but since the early 1970s the percentage of employees with an occupational pension has stabilized around 50 per cent. From the 1970s onwards private and occupational pensions have accounted for an increasing share of retirement income, rising from around 55 to 70 per cent of total pension income in the mid-1990s (Evans 1998: 283, 285). Parallel to this development, the value of public pension benefits declined, widening income inequalities among pensioners. For those with only public pensions, provision is minimal, while the middle class with access to private pensions has received more generous benefits. The rise of private pensions has also entailed a growth of tax relief on private contributions, and in the mid-2000s tax relief corresponded to one-third of current direct spending on pensions. As in the case of retirement income, these tax expenditures disproportionately benefit upper income groups (Taylor-Gooby and Mitton 2008: 160; McKay 2009: 173).

Since the 1990s another pro-market solution—tax benefits—has assumed growing importance in the UK (Hills 2004: 135). Tax credits for low income families date back to the early 1970s, and the scope of tax credits increased from the mid-1980s. Since 1997 the government has moved to supplant means-tested allowances with income-tested tax benefits to top up earnings for groups with low pay or what it has described as "in-work benefits" to supplement wages. In other words, the tax credit system focuses on wage supplementation in contrast to insurance benefits that aim at wage replacement. Besides more generous tax credits for low income families, the government introduced a pension tax credit, as part of the minimum income guarantee for seniors, and a tax credit for the disabled. Tax credits have become a vital part of the UK income transfer system (Millar 2003b: 135, 2009: 247). The design of these tax benefits has also meant the extension of means testing to a larger proportion of the population.

A restrictive incorporation regime

The British incorporation regime has differed from that of the United States in several significant ways. First, a series of immigration and nationality laws have delimited a previously encompassing citizenship based on British subjecthood—a legacy of the British Empire. The 1948 British Nationality Act established a sort of imperial citizenship by creating two categories of citizens: (1) citizens of the UK and the colonies and (2) Commonwealth citizens. Both categories had nearly identical rights: unrestricted rights of entry, employment, and residence; voting rights and the right to stand for election; and those from abroad could register as citizens of the UK after one year of residence. Immigration laws of the 1960s and the 1970s removed the privileges of overseas citizens from the colonies and Commonwealth with respect to entry, residence, and employment. The 1981 Nationality Act defined British citizenship without reference to the colonies for the first time, and it abandoned a pure application of *ius soli* that automatically accorded citizenship to all children born in the country (Hansen 2000). In sum, the postwar trajectory of United Kingdom citizenship has been one of rights contraction as British subjecthood, which had previously encompassed all colonials, has been supplanted by British citizenship limited primarily to the UK.

The formal requirements for naturalization were quite liberal but they became stiffer during the 2000s. Even before, the annual British naturalization rates were at the lower end of the scale (OECD 2004: 309). Nor has naturalization been considered a right. Naturalization decisions have been discretionary with generally no right of appeal against a refusal (Dummett and Nicol 1990: 247; Seddon et al. 2002: 26; Dummett 2006: 579). British naturalization policy has approximated a discretionary model, whereas US policy has represented an as-a-right model (Brubaker 1989: 109). The new requirements for naturalization further contribute to setting UK citizenship acquistion policy apart from that of the US. The British have introduced probationary citizenship ranging from one to five years so that the residence requirement for naturalization is six to ten years (HO 2008; BCIA 2009).

Settlement status also illustrates the more restrictive thrust of the British incorporation regime compared to the US. While the status of permanent resident is granted upon authorized entry into the US, settlement status has been delayed in the UK. It generally required four, then five years of residence, with a shorter period for family members joining an immigrant. Requirements for a permanent residence permit have become more rigorous. Since 2006 a language requirement has been introduced (Somerville 2007: 52), and the Borders, Citizenship and Immigration Act of 2009 extended the period between entry and permanent residence to a minimum of eight years and established additional conditions for permanent residence (BCIA 2009).

A final dissimilarity has been the government's goal of "zero immigration" and stringent immigration controls. Frequently immigration controls have rested on discretion or "concessions" (decisions outside the rules), precluding full and equal rights (Morris 1998). Immigration controls during the 1960s and 1970s were primarily constructed to limit the entry of New Commonwealth immigrants who were people of color. This contrasts with the expansive policy of the United States where net immigration between 1950 and 2000 amounted to over 30 million immigrants (calculated from MPI 2004). Moreover in 1965 the US scrapped the national origins quota system limiting non-European immigration. Since then the United States policy has been expansive not only in terms of numbers but also in admitting immigrants of ever greater racial and ethnic diversity.

Postwar immigration to the UK has consisted of three waves, dominated by different entry categories. From the mid-1950s until the early 1970s, the major source of immigration was labor migrants from the New Commonwealth countries (former colonies that, as independent countries, joined the Commonwealth in the 1950s and 1960s). Once New Commonwealth labor immigration was halted, family reunification was the main entry form, and asylum seeking dominated the 1990s. In the early 2000s skilled immigration was officially welcomed, and in 2008 the government introduced a points scheme, modeled after the Australian system (Wilkinson and Craig 2011: 179).

The evolution of immigrants' social rights

During the postwar period an alien who had been granted settlement status (a permanent residence permit) had the same social rights as citizens. The universalism of the early postwar welfare state further enhanced immigrants' social rights. Neither the National Health Service Act nor the National Assistance Act distinguished between aliens, subjects, and citizens. Immigrants from the former British Empire were accorded citizenship rights through the 1948 British Nationality Act, and as British subjects they had immediate access to all non-contributory benefits and services. A major exception was public housing since the local authorities imposed a residence requirement, usually five years, which barred newcomers—both aliens and British subjects (Layton-Henry 1985: 100). However, the responsibility of the local authorities to rehouse persons displaced by slum clearance or to house the homeless could result in faster access.

Employed immigrants have been entitled to national insurance benefits on the same conditions as employed citizens. Insurance benefits have been contingent upon contributions paid on earnings above a specified minimum. Immigrants with shorter working careers and interrupted earnings patterns because of greater vulnerability to unemployment or absences abroad have found it more difficult to meet contributions requirements—especially for entitlement to full pensions. Furthermore flat-rate contributions were a regressive construction. High income employees paid a smaller share of their income for the same benefits received by all contributors. When earnings-related contributions replaced flat-rate contributions in 1975, high income earners were compensated. By introducing a ceiling above which no contributions have been paid, earners in the high brackets have continued to pay a smaller share of their income in contributions than those below the ceiling.

For the most part, the expansion of the postwar British welfare state strengthened the formal social rights of immigrants. The major reforms of the 1960s were the introduction of earnings-related supplements in the national insurance scheme and the strengthening of entitlement to assistance, which established the claim to the supplementary benefit as a legal right. The 1970s were also a decade of reforms: the introduction of the family income supplement to aid low income families with children, the replacement of family allowances with child benefit covering all children, a supplementary earnings-related pension scheme (State Earnings Related Pension Scheme, SERPS), and the first non-contributory benefits for the disabled without means testing. One aspect of the 1975 child benefit reform was unfavorable to immigrants whose children were not in the United Kingdom. The reform abolished tax allowances for children irrespective of their place of residence.

Of additional significance to the social rights of immigrants and minorities has been a series of anti-discrimination laws. The first, the 1965 Race Relations Act, was modest in scope and enforcement powers. The 1968 Race Relations Act was much more important; it prohibited discrimination in the labor market, housing, education, banking and credit facilities, and the public sector. It aimed directly at equal treatment of immigrants and minorities in the provision of services, including those in the public sector. Indirectly, outlawing discrimination in the labor market potentially strengthened social rights based on work participation, that is, national insurance benefits and especially the newly introduced earnings-related benefits. The most recent legislation—the 2000 Race Relations Amendment Act—also has major implications for immigrants' and ethnic minorities' social rights through its ban on discrimination by public authorities (with the notable exception of immigration and nationality officials).

The changing importance of entry forms

The major fault line in immigrants' rights during the early postwar period was between (1) aliens and (2) Commonwealth immigrants and those from the colonies. As British subjects their rights were nearly identical with UK citizens, whereas aliens were subject to immigration controls and refused entry if they could not show that they had the means of decently supporting themselves and their dependents. An alien who became a public charge was liable to deportation (Cohen 2001: 36). The introduction of new immigration controls and changes in the nationality law recast the rights of New Commonwealth immigrants, reducing the sharp division between aliens and immigrants from the former British Empire. The 1971 Immigration Act brought most immigrants under one system of immigration controls, and the 1981 British Nationality Law eliminated the category British subjects, defined British citizens primarily as those born in the UK, and limited the right to enter and abode to British citizens.

Simultaneously the United Kingdom's joining the EEC (now the EU) in 1972 altered the definition of who was an alien among non-Commonwealth immigrants and transformed their rights. Gradually the rights of EU nationals have been harmonized with those of UK citizens. For non-EU nationals, including those from Commonwealth countries formerly privileged as British subjects, entry categories have increasingly determined and differentiated their social rights. This shift has entailed a deterioration in the rights of immigrants of color, while the rights of European newcomers have largely expanded. In addition, welfare state restructuring and retrenchment have further complicated the changing pattern of immigrant rights.

Welfare state restructuring, retrenchment, and immigrants' social rights

A series of reforms beginning in the early 1980s aimed at welfare state restructuring and retrenchment. The restructuring entailed two major shifts: (1) several transfers and benefits in kind were "privatized" and (2) means-tested benefits became more prevalent at the expense of insurance benefits. The expansion of tax credits has further extended means testing. Thus, two defining properties of the liberal welfare regime—the prominence of market solutions and means-tested benefits—have steadily strengthened since 1980. Retrenchment aimed at cuts in both insurance and means-tested benefits as well as increased targeting of means-tested benefits to the very poor. Welfare state restructuring, retrenchment measures, and benefit restrictions targeted specifically at immigrants have influenced the entitlements of newcomers and ethnic minorities.

PRIVATIZATION

The first shift—privatization—affected several national insurance benefits and the pension system. Sickness and maternity benefits, which had been provided by the national insurance scheme, were transferred to employers, and benefit levels were cut. The second tier of public pensions providing earnings-related benefits (SERPS) was reduced by about half (McKay and Rowlingson 1999: 68), at the same time as the government created substantial incentives to switch from the public scheme to personal or occupational pensions. The emphasis on private pensions continued into the 2000s as the government declared that its goal was to alter the private–public ratio in pension provision from 40:60 to 60:40 (Evandrou and Falkingham 2005: 183). SERPS was replaced by a new second tier pension that provides flat-rate benefits with favorable features for low income earners. A third tier of provision in the form of a private personal pension—the Stakeholder Pension—was introduced for moderate earners without an occupational pension (McKay 2009: 184).

The privatization of benefits has often weakened the entitlements of immigrants with poor earnings and other low income groups because they experienced cuts in benefits without always being able to take advantage of the private alternatives. For example, when Statutory Sick Pay and Maternity Pay were introduced, benefits were cut, hitting workers in low paid jobs hardest. As a result of lower benefits, employer sponsored maternity leave has become increasingly important, but it has been primarily available to employees in middle and upper echelon jobs. Changes in the pension system undermined immigrants and minorities' social rights in two ways. First, the benefit formula of SERPS was changed to lifetime earnings from pensions calculated on the basis of earnings during the "best" 20 years. The 20 year formula benefited immigrants whose working years were likely to be fewer than the native born population. Second, the growing private component in pensions has worked to the disadvantage of immigrants and members of ethnic minorities who have been much less likely to be covered by occupational or personal pensions than the white working age population (Ginn and Arber 2001). However, the 2008 pension reform made occupational pensions mandatory for nearly all employees.

INCREASED MEANS TESTING

The second shift involved greater means testing, and between the late 1970s and the mid-1990s the proportion of the population utilizing means-tested benefits climbed from 8 to 25 per cent (Sainsbury 1996: 209). The 1990s also witnessed legislation and extensive campaigns against benefit fraud and the rise of workfare—tying receipt of means-tested benefits to the requirement of actively seeking work and/or participation in work schemes.

The increased prominence of means-tested benefits has had negative consequences for immigrants and minorities. Most importantly, while ethnic minorities have been prone to higher poverty rates than the rest of the population (Modood et al. 1997: 160; Phillips 2005: 200), studies have documented that they have lower take-up rates for various means-tested benefits (Gordon and Newnham 1985: 57–9; Craig 1999: 209). Their lower take-up rates are related to several factors. Means testing involves more complex administrative procedures than insurance benefits. Interviews are part of the claiming process, and immigrants with language difficulties have reported reluctance about claiming benefits or the inability to do so. Newcomers with little knowledge of the system are often unaware of their eligibility; they often need help in claiming benefits and cite the enabling role of ethnic based advice agencies. Furthermore, many immigrants are either uncertain or mistaken about how their immigration status affects their eligibility; and, as we shall see below, the immigration status of claimants has increasingly been checked (Law 1996: 75). Although assistance benefits have been a right since the mid-1960s, discretionary judgments are still involved, offering opportunities for discrimination. Campaigns against fraud that indirectly cast suspicions on claimants and arguments that foreigners and bogus asylum seekers overuse benefits have hardly made it easier to claim benefits. The shift to tax credits may reduce problems of stigma but many of the other difficulties remain because the benefits must be claimed. Complex rules have weakened transparency, particularly in the case of low income families eligible for several tax credits (Millar 2003b: 138).

Welfare state restructuring has also affected EU immigrants' social rights. Insurance benefits have been accessible across the member states of the EU, while means-tested assistance has been much more of a gray zone. The weakening of the national insurance scheme has meant fewer contributory benefits and more means-tested benefits. By the end of the 1990s the two surviving short-term insurance benefits were the contributions part of the jobseeker's allowance (unemployment benefit until 1996) and the incapacity benefit, while the eligibility requirement was two years of contributions (McKay and Rowlingson 1999: 73, 75). In sum, EU nationals have confronted stiff contribution requirements in exchange for a couple of benefits with low replacement rates and short duration.

Benefit restrictions targeted at immigrants

While retrenchment and restructuring measures have been chronicled in detail (e.g. Pierson 1994; Sainsbury 1996; Powell 1999; Millar 2003a; Hills 2004; Hills and Stewart 2005; Driver 2008), social policy analysts have devoted little attention to efforts to restrict immigrants' access to social benefits. The efforts have involved: (1) stricter stipulations and controls concerning no recourse to public funds and (2) residence requirements that lengthen the period before newcomers have full and equal access to social benefits. In addition, severe restrictions have been placed on entry categories that have constituted the main forms of immigration to the UK.

FROM "NO RECOURSE TO PUBLIC FUNDS" TO "PERSONS SUBJECT TO IMMIGRATION CONTROLS FOR BENEFIT PURPOSES"
With the 1971 Immigration Act the public charge and self-sufficiency provisions of the earlier alien acts reappeared as no recourse to public funds in the administrative rules of the Act. Initially the rule served as a requirement for visitors to enter the country; they had to satisfy the immigration officer that they had sufficient means to support themselves without recourse to public funds. Eventually, however, it became a major vehicle for restricting immigrants' access to social benefits. From the early 1980s onwards, greater emphasis has been put on immigrants' ability to support themselves and their families without relying on social benefits. Already the 1980 benefit regulations stated that supplementary benefits, then the main assistance benefit, should be denied to persons from abroad. By the turn of the century the list had been extended to the allocation of social housing and the housing benefit, the means-tested portion of the jobseeker's allowance, income support, child benefit, a social fund payment, council tax benefit, family credit, and several benefits for the disabled and care allowances. The new tax credits, introduced during the 2000s, have also been defined as public funds (Morris 1998; Seddon et al. 2002: 94; Platt 2003: 259; Macdonald and Webber 2005: 836).

Immigration controls have become tighter, as the list of benefits has lengthened, and the penalties for breaking the no recourse to public funds rule have become more severe, including administrative removal (Seddon et al. 2002: 93, 81). Since 1996 immigration officers have been authorized to stamp the condition of no recourse to public funds in one's passport, making control easier. Eventually, in 2000, many immigrants—persons "subject to immigration control"—were denied benefits by statute (Macdonald and Webber 2005: 836, 838). In summary, a gradual process of disentitlement has transpired initially outside the public eye through administrative regulations; it has involved restricting access to an ever broader range of benefits and services through linking immigration status and benefit entitlement, and utilization of benefits can jeopardize both current and future residence in the United Kingdom.

CHANGES IN RESIDENCE REQUIREMENTS
The second type of restriction has involved changes in the residence period before newcomers gain entitlement to benefits. In 1994 the government

introduced the habitual residence rule that denied income support, housing benefit, and council tax benefit to newcomers who had not yet established residence, immigrants with temporary permits, and persons with breaks in their residence. The rule was prompted by alarm over the social rights of EU citizens; but in order to comply with the equal treatment regulations of the EU, the rule has also applied to British citizens. Especially British citizens of color who have ties to other countries have been among its victims (Morris 1998: 960). Even more important than the habitual residence test, newcomers have been denied access to benefits until they gain settlement status, and the residence requirement ranged from less than a year to four or five years according to entry category.

A new development with wider implications has been the emphasis on earned citizenship and tightening the relationship between citizenship and benefits. The changes included lengthening the period required for settlement status from four to five years. During this period newcomers have no access to non-contributory benefits or means-tested benefits. The introduction of a new stage in the naturalization process—probationary citizenship—further extends the period without recourse to benefits to between six and eight years. Finally the residence requirement for a permanent permit for immigrants who do not become citizens would be lengthened to a minimum of eight years and a maximum of ten years (HO 2005, 2008; Wilkinson and Craig 2011: 180). In other words, the period without access to benefits other than insurance benefits has generally increased from four years to a minimum of six years and in some cases as long as ten years.

RESTRICTIONS AND ENTRY CATEGORIES

Immigrants singled out for restrictive measures have been family members, EU citizens, refugees, and asylum seekers. Family reunification became a focus of restrictions once it was clear that family reunions would be a major flow of immigration. Besides stringent entry procedures for family members, especially spouses, a maintenance and adequate housing test have applied to both permanent residents and British citizens in granting family reunification. In addition, family reunification immigrants have been admitted under the no recourse to public funds rule. The 1996 Asylum and Immigration Act further increased the obstacles to family reunification by barring sponsored immigrants from a wide array of benefits. Rules on sponsorship and sponsored immigrants have also been tightened. Since 1980 social security officials have had the power to recover social assistance (Supplementary Benefit then Income Support) paid to a sponsored immigrant from the sponsor. Sponsored immigrants, even with permanent residence permits, have been barred from most means-tested benefits for a period of five years. In 1996 the rules were further tightened; even if their sponsor fails to support them, sponsored immigrants were not entitled to benefits (Seddon et al. 2002: 105).

As we have seen, not even the social rights of EU citizens have escaped attack. In addition to the habitual residence rule, the British have continued to impose restrictions on EU citizens' access to benefits. The 2002 Nationality, Immigration and Asylum Act barred persons who have rights of residence and support from other EU member states from support and housing by the local authorities (IND 2004: 3). When the UK granted labor market access to citizens of the new member countries after the 2004 EU enlargement, it barred them from most means-tested benefits, child benefit, tax credits, and public housing until they had worked 12 months or more (Macdonald and Webber 2005: 837; Morris 2007: 47).

Asylum seekers' social rights have experienced the most dramatic deterioration. First, in the early 1990s asylum seekers' benefits were set at a lower level; they received income support and housing benefit at 90 per cent of the standard rate. Then legislation withdrew the possibility of asylum seekers' claiming benefits after they had entered the country. Only asylum seekers who claimed benefits upon arrival were eligible, and the new rules disqualified the vast majority of asylum seekers. The 1999 Immigration and Asylum Act created a separate system of support, using vouchers providing a maintenance level at 70 per cent of standard minimum benefits (Morris 2002). The voucher system was short-lived and replaced with reception centers with provision in kind and a small amount of pocket money. Increasingly the benefits of asylum seekers have been partitioned off from those of the rest of the population through the separate scheme, and the lower benefit rates have been below the poverty line.

In summation, welfare state restructuring and retrenchment combined with benefit restrictions targeted at immigrants have seriously eroded the social rights of newcomers. Welfare state restructuring has diminished the role of insurance benefits and increased the importance of employer sponsored and means-tested benefits in British social provision. Retrenchment reduced the generosity of insurance benefits; and since newcomers only have access to insurance benefits they have borne the brunt of lower benefit levels and longer contribution periods. The growing role of private benefits at the expense of public benefits has impaired the entitlements of second and third generation immigrants; ethnic minorities have poorer coverage in private schemes. Despite the increased importance of means-tested benefits, restrictions have made them and non-contributory benefits off limits to immigrants and gradually lengthened the period during which benefits are unavailable. In effect, many newcomers have no safety net during their first years in the country. The trend of poorer benefits has been accompanied by unequal access to benefits, resulting in greater welfare state stratification between citizens and non-citizens as well as among different entry categories.

The logics of the British welfare regime and incorporation regime are both contradictory and complementary. A major tension has existed between the longstanding restriction on the entry of aliens not able to support themselves and their families and the universalism of the British welfare state. The principle of universal entitlement strengthened immigrants' access to services and benefits, but the doctrine of no recourse to public funds has gradually gained ground since 1980. At least initially, the effectiveness of these restrictive measures was limited because they amounted to a gatekeeper strategy. Once admitted to the country, immigrants' social rights were generally on a par with the rest of the population because most social legislation does not distinguish between aliens and citizens (Morris 2002). However, by specifying the benefits that qualified as public funds, newcomers have been effectively barred from benefits, contrary to the tenets of universalism. The creation of a separate support system for asylum seekers has represented a further break with universalism. The administrative responsibility for the system has been located within the Home Office not departments in charge of social policy.

On the other hand, there has been a strengthening of the nexus between the incorporation regime and the welfare regime in several respects. The first is the increased coordination between immigration rules and benefit regulations. The growing prominence of means testing has afforded opportunities to check claimants' immigration status, as does the conversion of means-tested benefits into tax credits. A second common denominator is the importance of discretion in the two regimes, and discretion undermines rights. Although discretion has declined in relation to assistance benefits (Silburn and Becker 2009: 60), discretionary decisions concerning benefit eligibility have not been eliminated. Discretion has been an integral component of the incorporation policy regime, as exemplified by naturalization, exceptional leave to remain, and the habitual residence rule. A third link is the underlying assumption that the individual is motivated generally by economic gain and specifically is out to get something for nothing. This is evident in government rhetoric about welfare abuse by those who could be working and bogus asylum seekers who are economic migrants in disguise. Likewise both welfare cuts and immigration controls have been justified out of consideration to the taxpayer.

The US and UK regimes compared

In concluding this chapter let us compare the importance of welfare and incorporation regimes for immigrants' social rights in the US and the UK. Initially I focus on the American and British welfare state regimes, comparing the implications of similarities and differences for immigrants' social rights. Then I move on to a comparison of their incorporation regimes and entry categories.

Welfare regimes

In the liberal welfare regime, the market has retained a central position through private welfare provision and tax benefits, which often require employment to qualify for these benefits. This defining property has under-pinned the view of the United States as the archetype of the liberal welfare regime. Private solutions have gained ground in the UK during recent decades, especially in the area of pensions. For programs that are employer sponsored schemes and not compulsory, we have found similar drawbacks for immigrants and ethnic minorities in both countries. Non-citizens and members of minorities have been less likely to have these sorts of benefits; and if they had them, benefit levels were generally low.

In a larger perspective, the overall distributional impact of private benefits is less progressive than public benefits (Hacker 2002: 35–7), which operates to the disadvantage of low income groups, including many immigrants and members of ethnic minorities. Accordingly, the different ratios of private to public provision in the two countries have major implications for immigrants' and ethnic minorities' social rights. Immigrants in Britain have had access to a variety of public benefits and services, which have no public counterparts in the US. British public benefits have included family benefits, a wider array of disability benefits, and medical care through the National Health Service. Furthermore, because benefits are public they are mandatory and thus avail-able to all claimants who fulfill the eligibility requirements. British legislation has also curbed the voluntary element and often made employer sponsored schemes mandatory, such as statutory sick pay, statutory parental benefits, and recent changes in private pensions that introduced automatic enrollment for nearly all employees unless they contract out. Conversely, corresponding private benefits in the US are only available to employees whose employer provides the benefits. Perhaps the most striking contrast between Britain's public provision and the US's private provision concerns medical benefits. In Britain immigrants have had access to the health service, whereas in the US roughly 40 per cent of non-citizens lacked medical coverage and 60 per cent of low income non-citizens were uninsured in the early 2000s (CPR 2003: 6).

In the case of retirement benefits provided by public insurance schemes, however, immigrants might have been better off in the US until 2010. To qualify for full benefits beneficiaries must meet a work test. In the US the work test has been less severe—35 years for social security benefits compared to 44 years for men and 39 years for women for the basic pension in the

UK. Furthermore, average social security benefits have been higher than average public pension benefits in Britain (Morissens and Sainsbury 2005: 651; MISSOC 2007: 53, 55; SSB 2007). However, the 2007 pension reform reduced the British work test to 30 years for persons retiring during or after 2010. Moreover, an increasingly elaborate system of credits for caring responsibilities, education and job training, unemployment, disability, and minimal earnings also strengthened the likelihood of meeting the work test (PS 2008). In effect, the reform seeks to improve coverage so all persons have a state pension that provides minimum flat-rate benefits, thus approximating Beveridge's goal of universality. Official explanations of the reforms have emphasized improvements for carers, the disabled, and low income groups, but the reforms also have the potential to enhance the pension entitlements of immigrants and ethnic minorities.

How has the prominence of means-tested benefits directed to the poor or near poor, typical of the liberal welfare regime, affected immigrants' social rights? Since the poverty rates of immigrants and ethnic minorities have been higher compared to the rate of the native born, they frequently benefited from means-tested benefits, having higher participation rates than citizens or the white population (Morissens and Sainsbury 2005: 644, 650). Differences in the safety nets of the two countries have affected immigrants' entitlements, however. With the exception of Food Stamps, the federal safety net has consisted of categorical assistance benefits directed to specific groups. Thus the US safety net has been less inclusive than the British safety net, which has provided benefits to the entire British population whose income has fallen below a set minimum standard. Moreover, a system of national administration and uniform rules has operated to provide the same assistance benefits irrespective of place of residence in Britain (Hill 1990: 84–92; Eardley et al. 1996b: 392, 400). By contrast, place of residence has been a determining factor in the availability of benefits and benefit levels in the US because of the federal system; and there have been huge geographical variations. The 1996 welfare act strengthened variations—and especially for immigrants. A final crucial difference concerns benefit levels. Although in an international context British assistance benefits have been at the lower end, they have been higher than those in the US (Nelson 2008: 114). Assistance benefits in the US have usually been below the official poverty line, whereas in Britain benefits have been at or slightly above the poverty line; and the poverty line has been more generous in the UK. The importance of these differences for immigrants in Britain has diminished as a result of restrictions on newcomers' access to means-tested benefits but remain important for denizens, ethnic minorities, and newcomers once they become eligible. On the other hand, benefits are unavailable during the period when immigrants are generally most vulnerable to poverty.

Means-tested benefits also assumed special importance in the retrenchment strategies of the two liberal regime countries. A common feature of their strategies was to tighten eligibility requirements for means-tested benefits, thus targeting the poor. In the process, the share of the poor receiving benefits has decreased. As a result of their higher poverty rates, immigrants, especially non-citizens and ethnic minorities, ran a greater risk of being among the losers when benefits reached fewer of the poor. Welfare state restructuring and retrenchment in Britain coincided with a dramatic rise in income inequality. By the mid-1990s income inequality in the UK outstripped many West European countries, approaching the income inequality of the US (Hills 2004: 29).

Incorporation regimes

How has the incorporation regime influenced immigrants' social rights in the two countries? A major difference has concerned their approaches to settlement status where the British have adopted a more restrictive stance. In the US immigrants by definition have been settlers and thus accorded permanent residence status upon legal entry. In many cases immigrants in the UK have had to wait four years before being granted settlement status. Recent changes have raised the requirements for settlement status so that they resemble naturalization requirements, and the government has stressed that immigrants must earn the right to stay. Among the requirements for earning the right to stay is economic self-sufficiency without recourse to public funds. As we have seen, the expanding definition of public funds has excluded immigrants from a growing number of benefits, which have included means-tested benefits, non-contributory benefits, such as the child benefit and various benefits for the disabled, and tax credits.

The British incorporation regime became more restrictive through the intertwining of immigration and nationality legislation. Immigration acts (Commonwealth Immigrants Acts of 1962 and 1968 and the 1971 Immigration Act) redefined the rights of British citizens, and the 1981 British Nationality Act introduced a modified version of *ius soli* as the basis of citizenship acquisition. Thus children born in the UK of non-citizens or immigrants without permanent status were not granted citizenship until their parents gained settlement status or became citizens. By contrast, the United States has adhered to the pure version of *ius soli*, which is more inclusive than the other countries in this book. Accordingly, all children born in the US are citizens irrespective of the citizenship or immigration status of their parents. The difference between a pure or modified application of *ius soli* may seem trivial, but as citizenship has become a basis of entitlement, it can have important implications for social rights. Of major consequence after the 1996 welfare act, citizen children of non-citizen parents qualified for benefits; whereas modified *ius soli* opens the possibility to deny social rights of native born on the basis of alienage.

The link between citizenship and access to social benefits has been strengthened. The British government's 2008 Green Paper, *The Path to Citizenship: Next Steps in Reforming the Immigration System*, envisioned several stages in acquiring citizenship with controls and requirements in moving to the next stage, and ultimately departure for those not meeting the requirements. During the "probationary citizenship" stage immigrants cannot claim non-contributory benefits. The requirements for naturalization included a residence requirement of eight years, with the possibility of six years in return for "active citizenship" in the form of voluntary service to the community, economic self-sufficency, payment of taxes, and good conduct (HO 2008: 31). The 2009 Borders, Citizenship and Immigration Act represented the first step in implementing these proposals (Wilkinson and Craig 2011:180). In effect, newcomers gain full social rights only after becoming citizens.

The restrictiveness of the British regime has also been reflected in the policy toward refugees and asylum seekers. Neither the UK nor the US is a paragon of virtue with respect to the rights of asylum seekers (Gibney 2004), but the countries have differed markedly in terms of their social and employment rights. In the US the 1996 welfare act included refugees and asylees as qualified aliens who were eligible for federal means-tested benefits during their first five and later seven years after entry. By contrast, the social rights of asylum seekers in the UK have seriously eroded since the early 1990s, and they no longer have the right to work. Curtailing asylum seekers' access to benefits and employment has been based on the conviction that removal of social rights is an effective deterrent in controlling the flow of asylum seekers.

Despite the restrictive bent of the British incorporation regime and the inclusive nature of the American regime, they share several features. The commonalities include the weight attached to economic self-sufficiency as an admission requirement and the deportation of public charges; tightening the economic requirements of sponsorship so it is more difficult for low income residents and citizens to bring family members into the country; a laissez-faire approach to immigrant settlement policy that has relied on the market and voluntary organizations; a pronounced reluctance to introduce effective sanctions on employers who hire undocumented immigrants; and strong anti-discrimination legislation to protect the rights and opportunities of ethnic minorities and immigrants. In both countries there has been an alignment between the welfare and immigration systems through verification of immigration status, and immigrants have become increasingly confused about their eligibility and the repercussions of claiming benefits (Morris 1998; Fix and Zimmermann 2004).

The rise of neoliberalism has also brought a new emphasis on the costs of immigration and its excessive burden to taxpayers in both countries, accompanied by exaggerated claims of immigrants' utilization of benefits and services. The British government went so far as to float the idea that immigrants should contribute to a transitional fund to finance the extra social costs of newcomers. This line of argument overlooks the fact that most immigrants pay taxes but they are ineligible for several of the benefits they help finance. It also ignores the evidence, which the British Green Paper acknowledges and research in the US has documented, that immigrants already are net fiscal contributors to the social protection system (Fix and Passel 1994; Büchel and Frick 2005: 25; Ku and Papademetriou 2007; HO 2008: 6–7, 25, 33).

A crucial nexus between the welfare regimes and incorporation regimes of the two liberal countries has been a contractual view of rights that has increasingly stressed the conditionality of rights. In this view, rights are earned through fulfillment of obligations; and obligations have been stiffened. In the US the deservingness of a "qualified alien" who is eligible for welfare benefits has stemmed from either military service or payment of social security taxes for ten years. In the UK obligations have multiplied; they include learning English, employment or employing others, payment of taxes, obeying the law and "joining in with the British way of life," including voluntary civic activities. The individual's responsibility of self-support and support of family members has also figured prominently as a justification for restricting immigrants' access to benefits. The very names of the US statutes— the Personal Responsibility and Work Opportunities Reconciliation Act and the Illegal Immigration Reform and Immigrant Responsibility Act—underscored responsibility; and the public debate highlighted restoring personal responsibility and the responsibility of sponsors to support newly arrived family members. The British government has fashioned its modernization of social policy as "opportunity to all; responsibility from all." More precisely, as expressed in a policy statement on a new contract for welfare, "The responsibilities of the individual who can provide for themselves and their families to do so must always be matched by the responsibility on the part of the government to provide opportunities for self-advancement" (Morris 2007: 42–3). Similarly the Green Paper on citizenship and reforming the immigration system emphasized "the rights and benefits are matched by responsibilities and contributions to Britain" (HO 2008: 5, 6).

In conclusion, the tension created by the public charge provisions in immigration laws and social legislation granting equal access to means-tested benefits in both countries has produced remarkably similar policy responses resulting in the contraction of immigrants' social rights. The US and the UK have introduced bans on newly arrived immigrants' utilization of means-tested benefits, emphasizing a dividing line between the social entitlements of citizens and non-citizens. However, a major difference was that immigrants' social rights were regulated largely through welfare legislation in the US, but through immigration regulations and laws in Britain. Thus a major lesson of the US–UK comparison is the importance of not confining the analysis of immigrants' social rights to social policy but including immigration legislation and even regulations. Limiting the analysis to social policy would have led to the conclusion of massive change in the social rights of immigrants in the US because of the 1996 welfare act, but only minor changes through social security regulations or indirect change in their rights through welfare state retrenchment and restructuring in the UK.

4

Conservative Corporatist Welfare States and Immigrants' Social Rights

The conservative corporatist regime is characterized by work-related social insurance schemes that offer generous benefits and are administered by corporatist structures representing employers and workers. Corporatism has also fostered occupationally segregated social insurance programs based on status identity and mutualism, leading to fragmentation and differences in entitlements. Rigorous work tests have determined benefits and preserved earning differentials. Policies have reaffirmed traditional societal values, celebrating the family and church. Traditional family roles are reinforced through the tax system and the derived social rights of family members, enhancing the authority of the head of the family. The principle of subsidiarity, a centerpiece of Catholic social thought, has operated to preserve the caring responsibilities of the family and thus women in the family. This principle holds that the state should only intervene when the family or civil society have exhausted their possibilities to provide welfare (Esping-Anderson 1990).

Taking Germany and France as representatives of the conservative corporatist welfare regime, this chapter addresses three major issues. The first question is how this type of welfare state influences the social rights of immigrants. More specifically, how do the defining attributes of the conservative corporatist regime affect immigrants' social rights? Second, what are the dynamics between the welfare regime and the incorporation regime in shaping immigrants' social rights in the two countries? Germany and France have been held up as exemplars of contrasting models of citizenship and incorporation. The final section of this chapter offers a reassessment of this proposition in the light of policy developments during the past two decades. Third, what impact has welfare state change had on immigrants' social rights?

Germany: Conservative welfare regime—restrictive incorporation regime

Germany is often pointed to as the prototype of the conservative corporatist welfare regime. Central to this regime are Bismarckian social insurance schemes, covering employees, financed by contributions, and administered by corporatist bodies. The overarching objective of the schemes has been to safeguard the standard of living of the insured workers and their families. Work performance has been deeply inscribed in the insurance schemes through stiff work tests and the principle of equivalence prescribing that benefits should correspond to contributions. Until 2005, work performance was even rewarded in public assistance where the benefit levels of unemployment assistance were higher than those of regular assistance, and benefits reflected earnings differentials. Nor was there a limit on duration of unemployment assistance if paid to persons who had exhausted their unemployment insurance benefits. The premium placed on work was also reflected in the lack of minimum insurance benefits.

Several features have tended to perpetuate class and status differentials. Class differences have been maintained through separate insurance funds for workers, white-collar employees, and civil servants, while status differentials within classes were preserved by the notion of suitable employment guaranteeing insured persons the right to refuse a job with lower pay or below their qualifications. Earnings-related benefits, combined with no or marginal taxation of benefits, resulted in higher benefit income for salaried employees compared to wage workers. German social benefits have been among the most generous but simultaneously the least redistributive (Manow 2005: 256–7). The weak redistributive capacity of the German system has not only been related to the construction of benefits but also to how the system has been financed. Civil servants and the self-employed have been outside the system and have not contributed to its funding. Nor have other types of income, such as capital returns, been a source of funding. For those paying contributions, an income ceiling has advantaged the higher income brackets. Contributions have functioned as a proportional tax but have started at a relatively low income level, lower than income tax (Alber 2003: 31). At the same time, the contribution rate levied on the earnings of German employees has been one of the highest in Western Europe, rising from 15 per cent in the mid-1970s to 20 per cent in the late 2000s (Alber 2003: 18; SSPTW 2010: 23).

The prominence of the principle of subsidiarity has also strengthened Germany's claim as the prototype of the conservative corporatist welfare state. The principle is inscribed in the constitution and major social legislation, and the Federal Constitutional Court has reaffirmed its importance for the provision of social services. Subsidiarity assigns main responsibility for provision of services to the family, local communities, and voluntary associations, while the state serves as the guarantor that these providers fulfill their tasks. As a result, six welfare associations—mainly denominational and working-class based—have long been the major providers of services; and between 65 and 70 per cent of the services directed to children and the elderly have been provided by private non-profit organizations (Freeman and Clasen 1994: 11). The provision of social services has been overshadowed by cash transfers of the social insurances schemes, and both transfers and services have been skewed toward the older generation. The consolidation of the pension system and changes in eligibility conditions for unemployment and disability benefits tilted transfers toward persons aged 50 +, while the introduction of long-term care insurance in the 1990s has stimulated more services for the elderly.

A restrictive incorporation regime

During most of the period of postwar immigration Germany was a prime example of an exclusionary incorporation regime. Policy makers insisted that Germany was not a country of immigration, despite the growing number of foreigners living in the country. The exclusionary nature of the regime was rooted in the notion of German citizenship based on ethnicity that denied incorporation to immigrants of different national origins but welcomed immigrants of German descent. Ethnic German immigrants (*Aussiedler*) could claim citizenship upon arrival in Germany. By contrast, other immigrants confronted the doctrine that naturalization was an exception and very demanding requirements for permanent residence and citizenship. Gradually requirements have become less arduous for non-German immigrants, and the privileges of co-ethnic newcomers have been reduced. Germany has moved from an ethnic toward a civic model of citizenship, and the 2004 Immigration Law acknowledged that Germany was a country of immigration. Despite major improvements, remnants of the exclusionary legacy have survived so that the German incorporation regime is currently best described as a restrictive regime. Many restrictions have been watered down but not eliminated, and new thresholds to inclusion have been added.

Postwar immigration has proceeded in three waves. The constitutional protection of the right of political asylum and forced expulsion led to the resettlement of ethnic Germans in the aftermath of the war, as the political boundaries of Europe were redrawn. This first wave was followed by nearly a decade and a half of labor immigration in the form of a guest worker system, based on the premise of the temporary presence of imported laborers. With the termination of labor migration in 1973, the major forms of immigration became family reunification and refugees. The early 1990s witnessed an unprecedented surge in the arrival of both asylum seekers and ethnic German immigrants following the collapse of the Soviet Union. Now, however, the Germanness of co-ethnic immigrants was questioned more than before, and they were viewed by many as foreigners rather than Germans.

The evolution of immigrants' social rights

In several respects, the strong work orientation of the German welfare state appears to enhance the social rights of foreign laborers. The main principle of entitlement to social benefits has been labor market participation. To avoid wage and job competition, the unions sought to incorporate foreign workers into the corporatist welfare state. As early as 1972 foreign workers were granted the right to participate in elections for works councils, and in the 1990s they gained voting rights in the election of representatives to social insurance administrative bodies (Guiraudon 2002: 137). More generally, unions assumed some responsibility for foreign workers' integration and safeguarding their rights (Heinelt 1993: 92; Ginsburg 1994). The social rights of migrant laborers were further strengthened by European conventions and bilateral agreements. Foreign workers were covered by health insurance providing medical benefits and sickness compensation, old age pensions and disability benefits, unemployment insurance, and child allowances. Moreover, these entitlements were not limited to German territory; pensions and child allowances, for example, have been exportable, although child allowances have been paid at a reduced rate if the child was living in a country with lower costs of living than Germany (Guiraudon 2000a).

The incorporation of foreign workers into these generous schemes has been marred on three counts because of the type of welfare regime. First, stringent work tests and contribution requirements have undermined immigrants' ability to receive full benefits. The requirement of 45 years of employment for a full pension has reduced the retirement benefits of newcomers arriving after the age of 20. Likewise the requirement of 35 years of work for an early retirement pension and stiff contribution requirements for extended unemployment insurance benefits have created substantial barriers to entitlement. Second, since benefits are earnings-related, Germans generally claim higher benefits than foreigners. Third, from the heyday of the guest worker system into the 2000s, non-German immigrants' insurance contributions have usually exceeded the benefits they received. Immigrants who had entered Germany as foreign workers and their offspring have remained net contributors (Ginsburg 1994; Büchel and Frick 2005), even though their utilization of benefits has increased. The increases in benefit use have been primarily in the areas of social assistance, housing allowances, and child allowances—and not the more lucrative insurance benefits. German citizens continued to benefit more because of their higher pensions and unemployment benefits (Kurthen 1998: 203–4).

The principle of subsidiarity fragmented the delivery of services to foreign workers and long blocked the development of a comprehensive public program to aid immigrants' settlement. The welfare organizations of the churches and the labor movement provided social services to foreign workers largely along ethno-religious lines, with the Roman Catholic Caritas responsible for Italians, Spaniards, Portuguese, and Catholic Yugoslavs; the Lutheran Diakonie seeing to the needs of Protestant immigrants and orthodox Christians (Greeks and Serbs); and the union affiliated AWO providing services to non-Christians (Turks, Tunisians, and Moroccans) as well as many Yugoslavian immigrants (Ireland 2004: 34–6). The subsidiarity principle, however, has encouraged the development of immigrant associations to deal with matters of welfare for their own ethnic communities.

Features of the incorporation regime have impinged upon foreign workers' social rights. Underlying foreign workers' admission and the employment opportunities of non-citizens has been the preferential treatment of German workers in filling jobs—or the priority principle (*Vorrangprinzip*). A foreign worker with a restricted work permit could be employed only if no German or EU workers or foreigners with an unrestricted permit were available for the job. In addition, non-German newcomers were barred from public sector jobs, which were reserved for citizens. This blocked them from high paid positions with generous social benefits. Just as work has conferred social entitlements, employment has been a central condition for a residence permit and the right of abode, and unemployment has put immigrants at risk. Immigrants with a restricted work permit were especially vulnerable because it was limited to a specific type of job or employer. If the employment office could not find work for an immigrant within a year, it concluded that the labor market was closed to him or her and revoked any claim to unemployment benefits (Faist 1995b: 183). Although foreign workers have been formally eligible for social assistance, its utilization could endanger renewal of their residence permit or prospects of obtaining a permanent permit. Long-term utilization led to expulsion and has also disqualified immigrants from acquiring citizenship (Diehl and Blohm 2003: 142–3). Any reliance on welfare was especially detrimental before an immigrant acquired an unlimited residence permit. In addition to employment, self-maintenance—as demonstrated by not relying on assistance and since 1990 having a contribution record of five years—has been decisive for an unlimited residence permit. In other words, the contribution requirement has amounted to a work test for permanent residence and thus citizenship for first generation immigrants. Furthermore, until the mid-2000s periods of education and care, which were usually accredited to one's contribution record, could not be used to meet the requirement for an unrestricted residence permit (Hansen et al. 2002). In short, work has been a crucial nexus between the welfare and incorporation regimes in Germany.

Forms of entry and immigrants' social rights

Features of the German insurance schemes have led to a differentiation between the benefits of immigrants and Germans. The incorporation regime has drawn a sharp line between Germans and foreigners, and entry categories have further stratified immigrants' social rights. At the bottom of the rights hierarchy are asylum seekers, while recognized refugees, German ethnic immigrants until recently, and immigrants from EU member states have occupied the upper rungs. What has been distinctive in the German case has been that they have made distinctions even within entry categories, and the distinctions affected social rights and the right to work.

Asylum seekers have had limited access to insurance benefits because their right to work has vacillated. Instead they have been entitled to assistance, often in kind, housing, emergency medical and dental care, and at times they could receive a restricted work permit. Before the passage of the 2004 Immigration Law, unsuccessful applicants, unable to return to their home country, had a tolerated presence (*Duldung*) or were granted humanitarian status (*Befugnis*), both with limited social rights. The rights of the few who received refugee status either based on the constitution or the UN Convention underwent a major transformation but even here there was a differentiation, with stronger rights for constitutional refugees.

Ethnic German immigrants have been in a more advantageous position than refugees. Because they were regarded as permanent settlers, or more precisely resettlers, they possessed special social rights unavailable to other newcomers. To assure parity in the social rights of *Aussiedler* and Germans, insurance contributions were waived, providing access to pensions, unemployment and disability benefits, and health care (Münz and Ohliger 1998). In addition, as citizens, they were accorded political rights; and as Germans, they enjoyed rights reserved for Germans by the constitution, such as rights of geographical mobility, freedom of occupation, and equal access to public employment (Neuman 1998: 269–70). A differentiation among co-ethnic immigrants occurred in the 1990s when new arrivals were re-categorized as late resettlers (*Spätaussiedler*), and the social rights of recent resettlers have been weaker than those of *Aussiedler*.

A final privileged entry category has been comprised of citizens of the member states of the European Union. With the deepening of European integration, the rights of these immigrants steadily increased. As workers, their rights of entry and residence as well as equal access to social benefits were strengthened in the late 1960s, and in 1990 economically non-active citizens with adequate resources gained the right of entry and residence. In the labor market, EU citizens enjoy the same status as Germans with regard to job openings, and they obtained access to employment in the public sector. This rights extension process has also been characterized by differentiation: (1) between citizens and non-citizen residents of the EU member countries and (2) between EU citizens before and after the 2004 and 2007 enlargements. Non-citizen residents of the EU, except for recognized refugees, have been excluded from several rights accorded to citizens. In connection with the 2004 enlargement, Germany, along with most EU members, decided to deny new members full access to the labor market, creating a provisional fault line between the rights of citizens of the EU. German policy makers utilized transitional rules for citizens of the countries in the 2004 enlargement for the maximum allowable duration—until early 2011.

In conclusion, let us consider the interplay of the welfare regime, entry categories, and the incorporation regime. In the conservative corporatist regime, lengthy work tests and contribution requirements of the German insurance schemes have posed a challenge for immigrants to qualify for standard benefits. Labor market participation is the primary basis of entitlement, but the right to work has varied by entry category. Newcomers without the right to work have had no access to social insurance benefits, the foundation of social provision. Furthermore, if immigrants utilized social assistance they endangered their prospects of gaining permanent residence and citizenship. In short, the welfare regime has led to class differentiation, and the incorporation regime to an ethnic differentiation. Simultaneously the differing rights attached to entry categories, combined with a complex system of work and residence permits prior to the 2004 Immigration Law, intensified the stratification of immigrants' rights. As we shall see later, the 2004 law streamlined the permit system but without ending the differentiation of rights by forms of entry.

Retrenchment and immigrants' social rights

Welfare state retrenchment has affected immigrants' social rights both indirectly and directly. Many changes were introduced with no consideration of their possible impact on foreigners; yet several changes have made serious inroads on their social rights. In other cases, immigrants, or more precisely specific entry categories, were direct targets of welfare cuts in the 1990s. First, I examine retrenchment during the past three decades focusing on the period since 1990 and the indirect impact on immigrants' entitlements. I then turn to the efforts to roll back the social rights of specific entry categories.

INDIRECT EFFECTS

Cutbacks in Germany from the mid-1970s to the 2000s can best be characterized as continuous cost containment or incremental retrenchment, and cuts affected all types of benefits. Thus, unlike the liberal regime countries, German retrenchment did not single out means-tested benefits for harsher treatment (Alber 2003: 34). Nor did the German welfare state move toward residualization—substituting means-tested benefits for insurance benefits—as in the UK. Utilization of means-tested benefits grew, but the growth was primarily due to persons without adequate insurance benefits. Since 2000 the government has strengthened the safety net through means-tested measures. Still insurance benefits continued to dwarf means-tested benefits in the late 2000s (Hinrichs 2010: 45).

Furthermore, contrary to the very notion of retrenchment, cuts were often combined with new benefits. Overall, the social benefits of wage earners were slated for cuts, whereas care-related benefits expanded (Bleses and Seeleib-Kaiser 2004). Among the most important new benefits and programs were a child care allowance (*Erziehungsgeld*) and leave (1986), the introduction and expansion of care credits in the pension system (1986, 1989, 1997, and 2002), long-term care insurance for the elderly (1993), and parental benefits (*Elterngeld*) and leave (2006). Besides these innovations, spending on traditional family benefits held its own.

Distinctive characteristics of the conservative corporatist regime have shaped retrenchment. Since insurance benefits have been the foundation of social provision and employer and employee contributions the primary source of funding, a main concern has been to limit the contribution rate to reduce the labor costs of production. Thus a major thrust of retrenchment efforts has been to curb spending on insurance benefits—unemployment compensation, retirement pensions, and disability benefits. The principle of equivalence stipulating that benefits should be equivalent to contributions—typical of the conservative corporatist regime—has underpinned the retrenchment of social insurance benefits. Changes have reinforced the importance of contributions and work tests. As a result, stratification of entitlements grew, privileging insider workers and disadvantaging outsiders—workers with weak or no attachment to the labor market, many of whom were immigrants.

The influence of the principle of equivalence has been very pronounced in the retrenchment of unemployment compensation. At the same time unemployment benefits have special relevance for immigrants because they have been more vulnerable to unemployment than Germans since the early 1980s (Ginsburg 1994: 200; BAMF 2007: 27). In accordance with the principle of equivalence, the government extended the maximum period of insurance benefits from 12 months to eventually 32 months for older workers with long contribution records in the mid-1980s. Although the maximum benefit period was scaled back to 18 months in the mid-2000s (Clasen 2005: 55, 65, 195), this still represented an improvement compared to the early 1980s. Moreover, the maximum benefit period was raised to 24 months in 2008 (Hinrichs 2010: 72). In effect these measures preserved or even enhanced the social rights of core workers, especially older workers. By contrast, as younger workers and newcomers, non-German immigrants had modest or poor contribution records, and they failed to qualify for extended insurance benefits. Simultaneously the contribution rate for unemployment insurance increased more sharply than other insurance schemes, tripling between 1975 and 2000 (Alber 2003: 18).

Retrenchment measures produced a shift toward reliance on unemployment assistance benefits among the jobless (Bleses and Seeleib-Kaiser 2004: 54; Clasen 2005: 59), and immigrants were more likely to utilize unemployment assistance than Germans (Nielsen 2004: 260). The controversial 2005 reform of unemployment assistance (Hartz IV) also adversely affected immigrants. The reform lowered benefits for a majority receiving unemployment assistance by converting an earnings-related allowance into a flat-rate benefit adjusted for family size—the unemployment allowance II (ALG II) (Clasen 2005: 75, 196-7). After the reform foreigners' utilization rate of ALG II was double the rate of Germans (BAMF 2007: 29).

Nor have the pension reforms of the early 2000s done much to improve immigrants' prospects of a better pension in the future. Pension reforms have not altered the link between lifetime earnings and entitlements, which is the chief feature of the pension system that has disadvantaged newcomers. In fact, reforms have lengthened the number of years of employment required to receive a pension providing more than minimum benefits (Hinrichs 2010: 391). In addition, the 2001 pension reform established a new tier of state subsidized private pensions to compensate for the lower replacement rate of pensions. Since the private pension tier is voluntary, there is a strong likelihood of uneven coverage, especially among low income groups, including low income immigrants. In 2008, coverage in the private tier amounted to only around 40 per cent of the workers paying contributions to the public insurance schemes (BMAS 2008). Finally, a 2003 social assistance reform created a de facto means-tested minimum pension for the elderly and the disabled by eliminating the intergenerational family responsibilities that included the children of the elderly in means testing (Bleses and Seeleib-Kaiser 2004: 77-8). If the minimum pension had been a benefit floor in the insurance scheme it would have represented a major gain for immigrants. However, as part of social assistance, its utilization may impinge on residence status or citizenship acquisition.

Several aspects of the retrenchment of wage earners' benefits have disadvantaged immigrants, but how have they fared with regard to reforms related to the care dimension of the German welfare state and the strengthening of family measures? These measures would appear to benefit immigrants and foreigners since they tend to have larger families than the native born German population. However, large families ran a higher risk of poverty than small families in Germany during the 1990s (Sainsbury and Morissens 2002: 317), and the poverty rate of children had risen compared to a decade earlier (Frick and Wagner 2001: 287).

The discrepancy between the expansion of family benefits and the higher poverty rate of children is related to the redistributive nature of German family benefits. In the early 1980s the government assigned priority to horizontal redistribution (from persons without children to parents) rather than a guaranteed social minimum for all children. Tax benefits for families, favoring high income parents, were regularly increased. Cash benefits were cut, as a retrenchment measure, and not upgraded until the mid-1990s (Bleses and Seeleib-Kaiser 2004: 80–2). Despite an overhaul of the system, family benefits continued to provide more generous benefits to high income parents (Clasen 2005: 155, 163, 207–10). In other words, family measures have provided poor support to low income families with several children, and immigrant families and children have a much higher poverty rate than those of native born Germans, with "foreigners" having higher poverty rates than German immigrants (Frick and Wagner 2001: 287; BBMFI 2010: 223).

In conclusion, German retrenchment of insurance benefits has involved strengthening work performance and contribution requirements—two key attributes of the conservative corporatist regime. This strategy has not only resulted in inferior and frequently inadequate insurance benefits for immigrants but also helps explain why foreigners have remained net contributors to the social protection system. They have often failed to meet new more rigorous qualifications for generous benefits, but have paid contributions that have steadily risen. Equally serious, immigrants' position on the labor market eroded so that they increasingly lacked entitlement to social insurance benefits. With inadequate or no insurance benefits, immigrants have had to rely more heavily on unemployment and social assistance. The expansion of care-related benefits may have aided immigrants, particularly families with a traditional division of labor. However, the horizontal principle of distribution underpinning state support for families through the expansion of tax benefits offered few gains to low income immigrant families.

RETRENCHMENT MEASURES AIMED AT IMMIGRANTS
The two main targets of retrenchment in the 1990s were newcomers of German origin and asylum seekers. Upon closer inspection, a similar strategy toward the two groups is discernible. It involved a substantial reduction of their social entitlements, imposing entry restrictions and redefining the entry

categories themselves. *Aussiedler* were reclassified as *Spätaussiedler* (late resettlers) in 1993, and termination of the special status was scheduled for 2011 (Münz and Ohliger 1998: 188; Joppke 2005: 212–13). The definition of asylum seekers was altered by a 1993 constitutional amendment; the right of political asylum no longer applied to asylum seekers entering Germany via safe third countries.

The privileges of the *Aussiedler* have eroded across the board. Their unique rights to insurance benefits were curtailed during the decade, and the generosity and duration of integration benefits steadily declined. After integration benefits, however, German immigrants were entitled to unemployment assistance and welfare benefits (Münz and Ohliger 1998: 171–2; Heinrich 2002: 82; Klekowski von Koppenfels 2002: 100, 112–14). The cost saving measures produced a huge drop in annual expenditures on the integration of German immigrants. Still the sum was roughly ten times the amount spent on non-German immigrants, and it did not include expenses for unemployment, social security, and welfare (Münz and Ohliger 1998: 194; Green 2004: 119). Thus despite a weakening of the social rights of co-ethnic immigrants, German newcomers continued to have better access to benefits than non-German immigrants.

The social rights of asylum seekers were seriously weakened in the early 1980s and they further deteriorated during the 1990s. Until 1993 asylum seekers' entitlements to welfare benefits, like those of Germans, were governed by the Federal Assistance Law (*Bundessozialhilfegesetz*), but subsequently their social rights have been regulated on a separate basis. Under the 1993 Asylum Seekers Benefits Law, they were only entitled to assistance in kind during the first year of their stay. Cash allowances paid to asylum seekers were set at a rate 20 per cent below the standard minimum. These regulations were extended to civil war refugees and to all foreigners with temporary status in 1997, and the duration of assistance in kind lengthened from one to three years (Minderhoud 1999: 141; Marshall 2000: 58).

Both the general retrenchment strategy and measures targeting specific entry categories resulted in a growing utilization of social assistance among immigrants. From being less likely to claim assistance, immigrants' utilization skyrocketed in the early 1990s. The introduction of the law on assistance for asylum seekers reduced utilization, but during the decade roughly 25 per cent of those receiving assistance benefits were immigrants. Inadequate pension income, unemployment compensation, and family benefits were major reasons for immigrants' increased reliance on assistance (Voges et al. 1998: 268–70; Alber 2003: 22–4; Maschke 2003: 231, 236).

Change and persistence in the incorporation regime

Immigrants' growing reliance on assistance benefits has underscored a problematic aspect of the German incorporation regime—the rules on utilization
of assistance that influence permanent residence and citizenship. Changes
have both diluted and strengthened the rules. The 2004 Immigration Law
made a secure livelihood a requirement for both a temporary and permanent
residence permit, specifying: "A foreigner's livelihood is secure when he or she
is able to earn their living, including adequate health insurance coverage,
without recourse to public funds." Importantly, and distinct from the UK,
public funds did not include child benefits, parental benefits, or benefits
"granted in order to enable residence in the Federal territory" (BMI 2004: 12,
14, 17). The 2000 Nationality Law did not alter the assistance rules: depen-
dence on assistance precludes naturalization except when the applicant cannot be held personally responsible (Neuman 1998: 290; BMI 2005: 6). In 2007
requirements for the naturalization of second generation immigrants were
stiffened. They must now provide evidence of a secure livelihood, and a secure
livelihood is calculated without utilization of the new unemployment assistance benefits (ALG II) or social assistance (BBMFI 2007a). In the mid-2000s
large numbers of second generation "foreigners" lacked educational creden-
tials, and they had high unemployment rates (BBMFI 2007b: Table 22).

The 2004 Immigration Law, officially recognizing that Germany was a
country of immigration, brought several important changes. It streamlined
the permit system by eliminating work permits and reducing residence permits to two types: a limited residence permit and a settlement permit. However, the limited residence permit is not a standard permit with uniform rights
and obligations. Instead the permit has been differentiated according to purpose of immigration, that is, entry categories: workers, students, family members, and asylum seekers. Although the law abolished work permits and
generally extended the right to work, the limited resident permit has specified
the conditions of employment. Like the former restricted work permit, work
authorization can limit the duration of employment, the type of occupational
activity, the workplace, and the region. Equally important, the priority principle excluding non-German and non-EU newcomers from equal access to the
labor market survived (BMI 2004). Restrictive features regulating the employment of foreigners have thus remained in place. The new permit system has
improved the situation of many immigrants, but over 40 per cent of the non-
EU immigrants had a limited residence permit in the late 2000s. The number
of foreigners lacking immigration status (having no permit) approached half a
million (SBD 2009), and those without a permit are barred from employment
and social benefits. Despite the simplification of the permit system, differentiation remains a cornerstone of the German incorporation regime, and

discrepancies persist in the rights and social entitlements of immigrants belonging to different entry categories.

The 2004 law also introduced an occupational stratification of immigrants' rights, privileging highly qualified employees, while retaining the official ban on labor immigration for unqualified and qualified employees. Qualified employees have been limited to specific vocations determined by federal administrative regulations. Self-employed persons who invest in Germany and create jobs also belong to this category. In contrast to other newcomers, highly qualified employees—scientists, prominent academics, and persons in senior management positions with a minimum monthly salary of €4000— have had immediate access to a settlement permit. They have been eligible if there are justifiable grounds to assume their integration into the German way of life and that their livelihood would require no state assistance. Otherwise the requirements for a settlement permit are: possession of a residence permit for five years, employment or adequate income, payment of insurance contributions for five years, no criminal record or record of anti-constitutional activities, German language skills, knowledge of the legal and social system and way of life, and adequate accommodation (BMI 2004: 17). Highly qualified employees can bypass these requirements, leading to a two-track system for the elite and the non-elite.

The exclusionary nature of the incorporation regime has been modified by improving naturalization opportunities for first and second generation non-German immigrants. The 2000 Nationality Law lowered the residency requirement for naturalization from 15 to eight years, and it has strengthened the right to naturalization upon fulfillment of the requirements. The law has offered new possibilities of acquiring German citizenship to children born in Germany of non-German immigrants; at least one parent has had to reside in Germany for eight years and have an unlimited residence permit or a settlement permit. The permit requirement has posed a serious barrier to citizenship acquisition since many foreigners have had a limited permit, but the change has meant German citizenship at birth for roughly half of the children of non-German parents born since 2000 (BBMFI 2007b: Table 8). A further barrier is that the law did not remove the requirement to forfeit one's previous citizenship, but this requirement can be waived in some cases (Green 2004).

Together, the 2004 Immigration Law and the 2000 Nationality Law have erected a double threshold to inclusion via stiff requirements for a settlement permit and naturalization. The requirements for a permanent residence permit have multiplied over time, and they resemble naturalization requirements. A settlement permit is not only a prerequisite for naturalization of first generation immigrants. It has also been a requirement for their children born in Germany to acquire citizenship, and recent changes have extended proof of a secure livelihood to second generation immigrants. Despite the dilution of the most exclusionary attributes of the German incorporation regime, requirements for permanent residence and naturalization have remained among the most rigorous of our cases.

France: Conservative welfare regime—inclusive incorporation regime

If Germany has been viewed as the archetype of the conservative corporatist welfare regime, the nature of the French welfare state regime has been in dispute. On a fundamental level, critics argue that the uneasy classification of France cast doubts on the robustness of Esping-Andersen's regime typology (e.g. Bonoli 1997; Levy 2000; Barbier and Théret 2003). Scholars have also called attention to dissimilarities between the French and German welfare states, such as France's affinities with the Southern European model of social provision (Bonoli and Palier 1996) and France's tradition of a strong state (van Kersbergen 1995).

Despite important differences between French and German social policies, both countries manifest the defining characteristics of the conservative corporatist regime. In France the Bismarckian social insurance model has been central in providing pensions, unemployment compensation, sickness and health benefits, and originally family allowances. Social benefits have been mainly based on contributions derived from employment and paid by employees and employers, with the social partners administering the schemes. Percentage wise, contributions have played an even larger role in funding French social policies than in Germany (Palier 2002: 134, 321), and the total contribution rate was higher in France in the late 2000s (SSPTW 2010: 23). As in Germany, separate schemes exist for different occupations and sectors, and benefits have reflected the occupational reward structure. Coverage is highly fragmented, resulting in a complex pattern of stratifying effects that has perpetuated occupational differences in benefits. Generous public sector pensions have occupied a privileged position in terms of retirement age, replacement rates, and years of contributions. Since benefits were not taxed until 1998, inequalities in benefit income remained. The safety net has also been characterized by fragmentation, with several social minimums to meet a wide range of needs (Palier 2002: 434). In sum, French social benefits and taxes have had little impact on income inequality (Cameron 1991: 89–90; Levy 2000: 311); rather benefits tend to reinforce the earnings status of beneficiaries—a hallmark of the conservative corporatist regime.

Services, in accord with the conservative corporatist regime, have been dwarfed by transfers, and the principle of subsidiarity has influenced provision of social services. With the exceptions of education and child care (*écoles maternelles*), the state has not been a provider of services. Instead social services have been delivered by associations and semi-public bodies, although funded by contributions and the state.

An additional shared trait is a low level of employment that creates a common challenge for the conservative corporatist countries. Their policies have promoted insider/outsider labor markets, which have contributed to unfavorable dependency ratios—a declining proportion of the population in the workforce combined with a rising number of welfare state beneficiaries. France pursued a policy of shedding of older male workers through early retirement and other schemes, which has been typical of the conservative corporatist regime. In the late 2000s the employment rate of older male workers was among the lowest of the West European countries, and lower than Germany (OECD 2011: 241, 245–7). Women's labor market participation rate has also been relatively low and similar to those of the other countries representing this regime type.

Inclusive incorporation regime

The incorporation regimes of the two countries have historically displayed fundamental differences, and they have often been viewed as representing opposite approaches. The most striking contrast has been rooted in their conceptions of nationality that have influenced the acquisition of citizenship. French regulations, as early as 1889, granted citizenship to persons born in the country of foreign parents either at birth (if one parent had been born in France) or upon adulthood (Weil 2001b: 58). Permanent settlement and family immigration have long been encouraged, and naturalization and assimilation considered the norm. Foreign nationals married to French citizens could apply for citizenship immediately or after a relatively short residence. Otherwise the residence requirement of five years for naturalization has not presented a barrier to citizenship, nor has dual citizenship. Conversely, non-German longtime residents had only a claim but not a right to naturalization until the early 1990s, and Germany continues to have rigorous naturalization requirements.

The pattern of French immigration distinguishes itself from the other European countries in this study. France has been a country of immigration, receiving substantial numbers of immigrants since the middle of the nineteenth century. During the interwar period the foreign population at its peak was 6.6 per cent (Kennedy-Brenner 1979: 10)—slightly above the percentage in the early 1970s. Unlike other European countries whose postwar immigration policies were mainly based on economic concerns, French policies were also influenced by demographic considerations, in particular the low birthrate. De-colonization further contributed to the flow of immigration, and the racial composition of immigrants, as in Britain, changed much earlier than in Sweden, Germany, and Denmark. Between 1962 and 1975 the share of Africans in the foreign population rose from roughly one-fifth to over one-third (Kennedy-Brenner 1979: 47). In 1974 France suspended labor immigration and for a brief period also family immigration. Subsequently labor migration declined but immigration continued in the form of undocumented immigrants, family reunions, and asylum seekers.

The evolution of immigrants' social rights

As in Germany, the Bismarckian system of social insurance based on work and contributions has meant that foreign workers have formally had access to many benefits shortly after their arrival. Immigrants were overwhelmingly employees, and eligibility requirements have been minimal in both France and Germany. Foreign workers also gained rights to participate in elections for employee representatives in management and eventually in the administration of social insurance in the two countries.

The construction of benefits and contribution requirements, typical of the conservative corporatist regime, has entailed disadvantages for immigrant workers similar to those in the German case. Earnings-related benefits mirror the occupational reward system, and foreign workers have been located in low paid jobs (Castles and Kosack 1985: 79–80). Moreover, foreign workers in the same job and with the same qualifications were paid between 10 and 20 per cent less than French workers (Freeman 1979: 190). Workers with low wages have also paid a larger portion of their income in contributions due to a ceiling on contributions that has benefited high income earners.

ACCESS TO NON-CONTRIBUTORY BENEFITS
Foreign nationals' access to non-contributory benefits followed a more tortuous course, resulting in delayed eligibility—especially in the case of assistance benefits. Non-citizens' access to family benefits was formally introduced when family allowances were revamped in the wake of the Second World War. The major modifications were the extension of family benefits to the non-working population, a change in payment of benefits from the head of the household to the person caring for the child/ren, and the removal of parents' nationality as a condition of eligibility for the single income family allowance (Lenoir 1991: 157–8). However, the reform differentiated between citizens and aliens by retaining a work test for foreigners to qualify for the single income family allowance. In 1978 this restriction was lifted if the children were in France (Steck et al. 1990: 65). However, family allowances ceased to be paid for children abroad if a non-citizen became long-term unemployed or suffered an occupation injury so she or he could no longer work (Vourc'h et al. 1999: 83).

Foreign workers have been much more prone to experience occupational injuries and diseases than French workers (Miller and Martin 1982: 70–1; HCI 2006: 129–30) and more recently to long-term unemployment.

Eligibility for national assistance benefits was delayed until the end of the1990s. Allowances paid to the elderly, disabled, and mothers from the National Solidarity Fund were reserved for citizens until 1990. Then the Constitutional Court ruled that eligibility should be extended to all regular residents; however, it was not until 1998 that legislation was amended in accord with the Court's decision (Guiraudon 2000b: 48). However, entitlement to the most important national assistance benefit (RMI since 2009 RSA) has been related to permit and work requirements. A non-EU immigrant must either have a permanent residence permit or meet a work test—originally three years but lengthened to five years in the late 2000s (Guendelsberger 1992–3: 694; S-P 2010). Finally, non-citizens' eligibility for local assistance benefits (*aide sociale*) has involved residence requirements, which have been reduced but not completely removed, but requirements related to nationality have been eliminated.

Contrary to the French celebration of universalism and equality, a separate organization or "regime" was created to meet the special needs of immigrants at an early date. In 1958 the Social Action Fund (FAS) was established to aid with reception, education—especially language training—and housing. Its establishment reflected the organization of welfare services typical of the corporatist conservative welfare regime and one facet of the French concept of social solidarity, namely intra-group solidarity, reflected in the tradition of mutual societies organized around occupational or other attachments. Originally the programs were directed to Algerian immigrants who then were French citizens, and a source of funding was via the immigrants themselves. Part of the difference between family allowances paid to children abroad, which were lower than allowances paid to children in France, was used to finance FAS programs. This sort of funding lessened the redistributive potential of programs, also along the lines of the conservative corporative regime. The agency's administrative council contained representatives of several ministries, but services and housing have been provided through private firms, voluntary agencies, and semi-public organizations (Freeman 1979: 79, 168–72; Lieberman 2005: 110–11)—much in the conservative corporatist mode. The voluntary organizations providing services have included immigrant associations, and in the early 1980s immigrants gained representation in the administrative council. Thus the solution of providing immigrants with services differed from German arrangements where immigrants on the basis of their nationality and religion became the responsibility of the major welfare associations run by the churches and unions.

Forms of entry

Immigrants' social rights have also been shaped by their form of entry, and two entry categories—asylum seekers and undocumented immigrants—have experienced a contraction of their rights, which is discussed below in connection with retrenchment. The national independence of Algeria and former French African colonies also altered the rights of newcomers from these countries. A series of bilateral agreements whittled away their former privileges, largely reducing their status to that of other non-EU nationals, with the exception of easier citizenship acquisition (Feldblum 1999: 26; Money 1999: 109–11).

Except for undocumented migrants and asylum seekers, the social rights of non-citizens have generally improved during the past decades. Despite the overall improvement, the ranks of disentitled immigrants have expanded, because the low success rate of asylum seekers (around 20 per cent of all applications during 1995–2005, calculated from UNHCR 2007: 334) has contributed to the growing numbers of undocumented immigrants who lack social rights. The weakening of the rights of undocumented migrants and asylum seekers has often been regulated through changes in immigration legislation. The changes have been justified as measures to control immigration. Similarly, legalization procedures have become central to the social rights of a growing number of immigrants.

The stratification of immigrants' social rights is patterned by entry categories, the incorporation regime, and the welfare state regime. The distinctive sets of rights associated with different entry categories have produced three major cleavages in the rights of non-citizens: (1) refugees vs. non-refugees, (2) illegal immigrants vs. legal immigrants, and (3) EU nationals vs. third country nationals. Previously a fourth fault line of differential treatment went between colonials and other immigrants. Lastly, the various bilateral accords that stipulate the specific requirements for benefits and benefit levels for different nationalities constitute a source of inequalities in the social rights of legal immigrants (Freeman 1979; Steck et al. 1990: 67–9).

The high fragmentation of the French welfare regime along occupational fault lines has stratified benefit levels. Most immigrants have received modest insurance benefits because they have been concentrated in low skilled jobs. The status reinforcing nature of benefits in this regime type has tended to limit redistributional outcomes. Finally, social minimums have been incorporated and administered by social insurance schemes, but most of these benefits based on the principle of national solidarity only became fully available to non-citizens through legislation in the late 1990s, removing a major source of differentiation in the social rights of citizens and non-citizens.

Welfare state retrenchment, restructuring, and immigrants' social rights

As a result of the rapid expansion of the French welfare state during the postwar period, social spending has steadily risen, and in recent decades France has ranked as the heaviest spender outside the Scandinavian countries (Levy 2000: 309; Adema 2006:10). Growing expenditures and continued slow economic growth produced a severe fiscal crisis, with huge deficits during the 1990s (Palier 2002: 171) and little improvement in the 2000s.

In coping with the deficits, French governments bolstered funding by increasing contributions as well as enlarging the tax base, and they cut spending. Contributions as a percentage of the pay roll were nearly 45 per cent in the late 2000s (SSPTW 2010: 23), and ceilings on contributions were gradually raised except in the case of old-age, disability, and survivors insurance. In 1991 the government expanded the tax base of social policies through a new tax, *contribution sociale généralisée* (CSG). As distinct from insurance contributions, this tax has been levied on all forms of income, including capital returns and property. From the introduction of the CSG, when it amounted to 1.1 per cent of all incomes, the rate had increased to 7.5 per cent in the mid-2000s (Palier 2006: 122).

The major targets for cutbacks during the 1990s and 2000s have been unemployment benefits, medical insurance, family benefits, and pensions. Work tests differentiated by age for unemployment insurance benefits were tightened; the tests determined the benefit period and privileged older workers. Replacement rates were successively reduced as the period without a job lengthened. The longer the duration of unemployment, the lower the replacement rate. Furthermore, unemployment assistance benefits, which were nearly the same amount as insurance benefits in the mid-1980s, have been substantially reduced, and the percentage of jobless persons receiving unemployment insurance benefits has declined (Barbier and Théret 2003: 139; Dollé 2004: 73). Among the many attempts to rein in medical expenditures, the amount of reimbursement to patients has been lowered to approximately 60 per cent of medical costs (Palier 2010: 93). In putting a brake on family benefits spending, income testing was introduced. The share of family benefits subject to means testing had climbed from 12 per cent in 1970 to 60 per cent in the late 1990s (Palier 2002; Barbier and Théret 2003: 137; Levy 2005:116).

By far the most important legislation in cutting spending has been a series of pension reforms. The 1993 pension reform reduced pension benefits in the private sector by (1) changing the formula for calculating benefits from the average earnings of the best ten years to the best 25 years, (2) increasing the number of qualifying years to 40 years, and (3) indexing pensions to prices instead of wages. Efforts to introduce similar cuts in the public sector pension system did not succeed until a decade later when the public and private sectors pensions were more closely aligned. In addition, the 2003 reform extended the number of years of contributions for a full pension to 42 years (coming into effect by 2020) and strengthened voluntary private retirement plans, shifting part of the responsibility for future pensions to the market (Mandin and Palier 2005). The 2007 and 2010 reforms further diminished differences between pensions in the public and private sector and raised the pension age.

Several of these cost-saving measures have adversely influenced immigrants' entitlements and have a parallel to the German case. As newcomers or second generation immigrants trying to enter the labor market, they have been unlikely to have the necessary work record to qualify for the more generous unemployment insurance benefits. Insider/outsider policies favoring older workers indirectly advantaged French workers because of differences in the age composition of the French and foreign labor force. The maximum period for unemployment benefits for older workers was much longer in France compared to Germany (60 versus 34 months). The population with immigrant backgrounds has also had higher rates of long-term unemployment and thus they were more likely to experience lower benefits determined by the duration of unemployment. The 1993 reform, which lowered private sector pensions, one-sidedly affected non-citizens since they have been barred from public sector employment. Raising the number of contribution years as well as the number of years in calculating benefits negatively affect the pension income of immigrants who have entered the country in midlife. Private pensions have had limited coverage, available primarily to state employees and the liberal professions (Mandin and Palier 2005), sectors with no or few immigrants. The reduction of reimbursement rates for medical costs hit low income groups very hard. To maintain high reimbursement, around 85 per cent of the population has had supplementary insurance (Levy 2000: 338). Those without such insurance suffered the full impact of the reform. However, as we shall see, the growth in income testing of family benefits may have worked to the advantage of legal immigrants whose families were in France.

CUTS TARGETING IMMIGRANTS

As retrenchment efforts gained momentum in the 1990s the benefits of asylum seekers and undocumented immigrants were targeted for cuts. Asylum seekers in 1991 lost access to the labor market, eliminating their claim to unemployment benefits and other insurance benefits. Instead asylum seekers became dependent upon one of the assistance allowances, without supplements for children. A new series of cuts aimed at reducing the flow of asylum seekers occurred in the early 2000s (ECRE 2004; Freedman 2004: 57, 63). The most serious deterioration in social rights of undocumented immigrants occurred in 1993 when they were barred from insurance benefits, including medical benefits, irrespective of their having paid contributions and taxes.

The legislation also denied them most social assistance benefits (HCI 1998: chapter 1).

DEPARTURES FROM THE BISMARCKIAN MODEL

At the same time as French policy makers have wrestled with fiscal constraints, they, like their German counterparts, have introduced new social programs and entitlements. Thus the two conservative corporatist countries introduced reforms, which ran counter to the emphasis on retrenchment and rollback underpinning the analysis of welfare states since the early 1980s. A major difference between the two countries' new programs, however, has been that French reforms often broke with the Bismarckian model and promoted non-contributory benefits, while several German reforms have strengthened the insurance component of social protection.

Historically family policy has occupied a unique position in the French welfare state, and family benefits represented an early departure from the Bismarckian model both in terms of their basis of entitlement and funding. Measures to promote different family types multiplied the allowances, tax benefits, and benefits in kind available to families (Lenoir 1991). Two features in the development of family policy have been of major significance to immigrants. The construction of benefits has tended to reward larger families, and family benefits underwent a shift from horizontal to vertical redistribution (Levy 2000: 131). Previously French policies primarily redistributed resources from the rest of the population to families irrespective of their income. Increasingly measures were targeted to low income families through income testing, although the tax system has continued to favor all families except the very wealthy (Barbier and Théret 2003: 136–8). Immigrants whose families live in France have tended to benefit from these trends because they generally have more children and lower incomes than French families. Indeed, immigrant families have been more likely to receive family benefits than native born families (Morissens and Sainsbury 2005: 650). The larger families of immigrants have also enhanced their claims to special supplements for beneficiaries who have raised at least three children in the case of retirement, survivor, and sickness benefits. The number of children has also affected the duration of maternity benefits (SSPTW 2010).

The development of non-contributory benefits was also spurred by a fundamental weakness of the Bismarckian model. High levels of unemployment since the mid-1970s have increased the number of people without social insurance, and retrenchment measures that have focused on insurance benefits contributed to shrinking coverage. To aid persons not covered by social insurance, the French have introduced new allowances targeted to those outside the social protection system. The most important was the 1988 introduction of the Minimum Insertion Income (*Revenu minimum d'insertion*, RMI), which has been hailed as the creation of a national safety net (Levy 2000; Palier 2002). As distinct from other minimum benefits targeted to categories, such as single parents, widows, the elderly, or disabled, the RMI has provided a general minimum income for those without social protection. Finally, to improve the coverage of medical insurance and eliminate inequalities in access to medical care, a special insurance became available on the basis of residence rather than work for people with no or low incomes in 2000 (Palier 2006: 120).

The Minimum Insertion Income was the most important innovation. By the mid-2000s, the number of recipients had climbed to 1.3 million, and with family members recipients comprised 3.5 per cent of the population (Palier 2006: 120). Utilization rates of the RMI also indicate that immigrants gained from the break with insurance principles (Lieberman 2005: 115). In 2009 the *Revenu de solidarité active* (RSA), with a stronger obligation to seek employment, replaced the RMI. The purpose of the RSA has been not only to provide a social minimum to persons without employment but also to supplement the earnings of workers with pay below the minimum wage. It was estimated that the RSA affected 10 million people or 16 per cent of the population in the late 2000s (Martin 2010: 84).

The balance sheet of immigrants' social rights in light of welfare state retrenchment and restructuring has been mixed. On the one hand, tightening the eligibility conditions for insurance benefits and the worsening employment situation for foreigners have eroded their entitlements. On the other hand, two facets of welfare state restructuring—the shift in family benefits from horizontal to vertical redistribution and the growth of non-contributory benefits—enhanced the social rights of many immigrants with legal status. Many immigrant families could claim both regular and means-tested benefits. The removal of the barrier to allowances financed by the National Solidarity Fund was a prerequisite for non-citizens to benefit from the expansion of non-contributory benefits. To some extent, the growth of non-contributory benefits may compensate immigrants who fail to qualify for insurance benefits. However, the benefit levels are much lower than those of insurance benefits, ushering in a new source of welfare state stratification or what has been labeled the dualization of the French social protection system (Palier 2006, 2010).

The German and French regimes reconsidered

To tie together the analyses of Germany and France, let us reconsider the basic similarities and differences between their welfare state regimes and then their incorporation regimes. As we have seen, work has figured prominently in the

German and French welfare regimes, and its prominence enhanced migrant workers' social rights in two important ways. Eligibility requirements for insurance benefits, the backbone of social provision in the two countries, were minimal with immediate access to health and sickness benefits as well as occupational injury benefits and modest requirements for unemployment insurance. Second, as workers, foreigners gained rights of election and representation on corporatist bodies involving industrial relations and administering social insurance, which can affect their social rights. The centrality of work as a basis of entitlement also led to the possibility to export benefits to immigrants' countries of origin, especially in the German case.

Conversely, work tests, the strong reliance on contributions, and the principle of equivalence have tended to weaken the social rights of newcomers. Stringent work tests have penalized newcomers who have been less likely to fulfill the requirements and thus not qualify for benefits. In Germany stiff contribution requirements and failure to qualify for more generous benefits have meant that immigrants, with the exception of *Ausseidler*, have been net payers into the social protection system. The disentitlement of undocumented immigrants in France has yielded a similar result for this entry category; even when they pay social insurance contributions they are ineligible for benefits. Finally, the earnings maintaining function of the conservative corporatist regime has been to the detriment of most immigrants, since they have largely been located at the lower rungs of the occupational and income hierarchies.

The French welfare regime has differed from the German regime on four scores with implications for newcomers. The principle of work performance has been less entrenched in French social provision, which has both disadvantaged and promoted immigrants' social rights. Negatively, France was slower to pay insurance benefits based on work performance—pensions, disability, and death benefits—to non-citizens living outside the country. Positively, work tests have been less arduous, especially before recent pension reforms, and they benefited immigrants with shorter employment careers in France. Second, the earnings differentials reflected in insurance benefits have been weaker in France; the replacement rates of benefits for low income earners have been higher in France than in Germany (Scharpf and Schmidt 2000: 372). Third, the contribution rate of employees has been much lower in France than in Germany (SSPTW 2010: 23). Fourth, minimum benefits not related to work performance have gradually become an important feature in the French social protection system. They have been almost entirely separate from social assistance, and fairly generous, especially the minimum pension (Korpi 1995: 25, 36). Non-citizens now are eligible for these benefits. This development contrasted with Germany where there were no minimum insurance benefits, and the social minimum is provided by public assistance whose utilization can impair renewal of a residence permit and acquisition of citizenship. The growing prominence of minimum benefits, together with the longstanding importance of family benefits, which are non-contributory, undermined the principle of equivalence—the major basis of rights in the Bismarckian model. Although this trend was set in motion during the 1950s, it has been a main facet of recent welfare state restructuring.

In both countries immigrants have had relatively easy access to family benefits because in this type of welfare regime they were historically an entitlement for workers, and in France a work test was retained for immigrants but not for citizens. By contrast, non-citizens' access to means-tested assistance benefits has been especially problematic in the two conservative corporatist countries. The 1961 Federal Social Assistance Act granted all German citizens a right to a statutory minimum, and the right has been extended to all residents but special conditions have applied to "foreigners" (Maschke 2003: 231). Non-citizens' rights to French national minimum benefits have been equally troublesome; France was the last country in this book to make most means-tested benefits available to immigrants on the same basis as the rest of the population. However, residence tests for local assistance have survived, and in the late 2000s newcomers from outside the EU did not have access to the main safety net benefit until they had worked five years or had a permanent permit.

Welfare state retrenchment has strengthened regime features but also produced innovations and departures from the Bismarckian social insurance model. In both countries, and as distinct from the countries representing other welfare regime types, retrenchment of insurance benefits highlighted the principle of equivalence and contributions, which safeguarded and even improved the rights of core workers at the expense of newcomers—both immigrants and labor market entrants. Work tests also became more strenuous for pensions and unemployment insurance benefits, something which has disadvantaged immigrants. In France the changes in eligibility requirements for a full pension have been more dramatic, but the requirements continued to be more lenient than in Germany. Eventually (in 2020) 42 years of contributions instead of 37 years will be necessary for a full pension in France compared to 45 years in Germany. The French also changed the benefits calculation from the best ten years of earnings to the best 25 years (from 2008), which was still more beneficial than the German formula of lifetime earnings. Nor did the French make as deep cuts in the maximum benefit period for unemployment insurance benefits for workers meeting work tests, and this was the case even for younger workers. However, in both countries the retrenchment of unemployment compensation has decreased the proportion of jobless persons receiving insurance benefits since the 1980s and reduced benefit levels of unemployment assistance in relation to insurance benefits. Retrenchment has resulted in dual welfare: core workers as insiders receive generous benefits, whereas outsiders are entitled to minimum benefits.

Among the innovations, a common response has been to assign more weight to voluntary private pensions and, in accord with corporatist arrangements, to propose greater involvement of the unions in the voluntary tier. The patchy coverage of voluntary private pensions, with lower income groups more poorly covered, affects immigrants' enrollment in both countries. Without private pensions, immigrants will experience the full effect of the deterioration in public pensions. France and Germany have also introduced new taxes to finance social provision, with France having gone further in this direction (Manow 2010: 292), but contributions overwhelmingly remain the source of funding in both countries. Generally contributions have been more disadvantageous to immigrants in Germany because the contribution rate for employees has been twice as high as the French rate.

In terms of other innovations, the paths of Germany and France have diverged. Although the Germans have introduced measures departing from the Bismarckian model since 2000, several innovations have more closely conformed to the conservative corporatist regime. Major reforms have consisted of a new insurance scheme to cover the costs of long-term care for the elderly; care credits in the pension system, which have reinforced the role of the married woman as caregiver and the traditional division of labor in the family; and a minimum pension that is not a part of the insurance system but provided through social assistance. In other words, the Germans opted for a solution to minimum pension benefits that did not compromise strong work tests as the basis of pension entitlement. Nor was the German answer to the problem of persons not covered by health insurance to establish a new public scheme based on residence but instead to introduce a legal obligation to join an existing scheme or take out private insurance. German policy makers also expanded tax benefits for families; tax benefits have underlined the centrality of work, and they have been aimed at the head of the family as the major earner. The recent improvement of parental benefits introduced an insurance component. With the exception of care benefits targeted at women, the repercussions of these innovations have tended to be negative for immigrants. Although coverage has become more universal (Hinrichs 2010: 66), the proportion of uninsured in the foreign population has grown during the past two decades. In addition, incorporating minimum benefits for the elderly and disabled into social assistance is problematic for immigrants as long as claiming assistance benefits influences permanent residence status and access to citizenship.

French innovations broke with the Bismarckian welfare system and insurance principles. The French strengthened the non-contributory benefit component in their social security system by introducing programs for persons with no or inadequate insurance benefits. Second generation immigrants have automatically qualified for these benefits, while newcomers must be legal residents, and until 1998 not being a citizen influenced eligibility.

In sum, German and French decision makers initially responded differently to the fundamental weakness of the Bismarckian model when full employment no longer existed and a growing proportion of the population was without adequate social protection. The French introduced non-contributory benefits for people without social insurance, while the Germans tended to rely on insurance solutions and improved coverage. They established new insurance schemes or modified existing schemes to grant carers and persons in marginal employment rights to a retirement pension. However, the risk of poverty remains for persons who lack insurance. In light of the continued decline of the foreign population as contributors to social insurance schemes, the German response to the fundamental defect of the Bismarckian model provides cause for worry. Still newcomers' access to non-contributory benefits has been better compared to the US and the UK where immigrants confront a ban on such benefits for five years or longer.

Incorporation regimes

Turning to incorporation regimes, it needs to be stressed that the attention given to different national models of citizenship has obscured the affinities of the French and German regimes. The resemblances have included a discretionary approach to naturalization, the view that citizenship is the badge of integration, and similar anti-discrimination legislation. Convergence during recent decades has further heightened commonalities. Both earlier affinities and convergence raise the issue of the inclusive nature of the French incorporation regime.

Despite contrasts in their citizenship models, France and Germany have represented a discretionary rather than an as-a-right approach to naturalization (Brubaker 1989: 110–11). The French and German naturalization processes have allowed considerable bureaucratic discretion in interpreting fulfillment of requirements. In France discretion has occurred at both the prefect and ministerial levels, but since 1993 all rejections have required written justifications (Weil and Spire 2006: 203–6). In Germany the discretionary tradition in the naturalization of foreigners has been much stronger, but since 1990 legislation has limited discretion. Still because the German *Länder* (or states) are responsible for implementing the nationality law, discretion has led to dissimilar outcomes (Hailbronner 2006: 239–43).

Moreover France and Germany have shared a preoccupation with citizenship reform. The dominant view has been that citizenship represents the culmination of the integration process rather than an instrument to achieve integration through political participation. Viewing citizenship as the main path of incorporation also delayed the development of comprehensive integration programs for newly arrived immigrants until the 2000s.

Germany and France have pursued similar anti-discrimination or, perhaps more aptly, anti-racist policies. Racist public statements and incitement to racial hatred are criminal offenses, and penalties have been very stiff. A feature of the German and French policies has been the centrality of criminal law rather than civil law, and the strong burden of proof for conviction in criminal cases has meant relatively few discrimination court cases. Their policies have tackled expressive racism vigorously, influenced by a fear of the resurrection of the racist legacy of the Nazi regime and the Vichy government, but policies have been less effective in combating acts of discrimination involving unequal treatment on the basis of race or ethnicity (Lochak 1992; Fennema 2000; Bleich 2003).

With regard to family reunification the French have become increasingly restrictive, and in a few instances they have adopted more rigorous requirements than the Germans who have eased their regulations. France has made the support obligations stiffer for family reunification, by gradually excluding all benefits in the calculation of income, and the French income test became more stringent than the German one formulated in the 2004 Immigration Law. French reforms in the 2000s raised the requirements for permanent residence permits and citizenship acquisition for spouses of citizens, who in many countries have privileged access to the right of abode and naturalization (Weil 2001a: Table 1–3). The residence requirement of spouses of French citizens for the ten year permit was raised from two to three years. In 2006 the French marriage test for naturalization was lengthened to four years, which was longer than the German requirement.

Convergence has also characterized the French and German permit systems in two respects. First, work requirements for a permit have grown in importance in France. Initially the French permit system was much more liberal than the German system. All residence permits were renewable, and the residence requirement was three years for a privileged permit valid for ten years. An ordinary permit could not be withdrawn unless the immigrant had committed an act that made him or her liable to deportation (Minces 1973). From the early 1970s onwards, work requirements have assumed greater significance in the French permit system. The reinstatement of labor migration during the 2000s in both countries has also created new stratifying effects based on class and occupation, with seasonal and contract workers having few rights compared to professionals, executives, and wealthy entrepreneurs.

The second source of convergence has been requirements of successful integration in granting a permanent residence permit. The German incorporation regime has long stressed Germanness, previously privileging co-ethnic immigrants and excluding other immigrants. Proficiency in German has been a requirement to obtain a permanent residence permit, and it became an admission requirement for ethnic German immigrants in the 1990s. A new requirement of Germanness for a settlement permit, introduced in the 2000s, was successful completion of a test of cultural knowledge and better language skills. Belatedly in France, the requirement of integration has been strengthened for obtaining a permanent residence permit. According to the 2003 Law on Immigration and Nationality, "republican integration of the foreigner into French society, and in particular adequate knowledge of the French language and of the principles governing the French republic" became conditions for issuing the first permanent residence permit and permit renewals (Legifrance 2003: 4). In other words, the imperative to become French is no longer confined to naturalized citizens but has been extended to foreign permanent residents. The introduction of integration contracts for all new arrivals in 2007 has underlined the foreigner's obligation to adopt French values, and the new ministry of immigration, integration and national identity also pointed to the importance of Frenchness, blurring the distinction between a civil and ethnic model of citizenship (HCI 2009). In short, both countries in the 2000s have introduced new requirements for a permanent residence permit, and the requirements resemble previous conditions for naturalization. In effect the new requirements represent the first hurdle of a double threshold to inclusion.

Given the convergence in several dimensions of the two countries' incorporation regimes, is it still justifiable to classify the French regime as inclusive? It is primarily the dissimilarities in the citizenship acquisition dimension of the incorporation regime that form the major basis for France's claim of representing an inclusive regime. French naturalization requirements have long been more lenient than those in Germany, and the French naturalization rate of first generation immigrants has been roughly double the German rate (Minkenberg 2003: 230). Tellingly, the improvements in the 2000 German Nationality Law resulted in a peak in the number of naturalizations in 2000 but since then the number has fallen (BBMFI 2010: 443). Acquisition of French citizenship among second generation immigrants was also higher—slightly over 60 per cent (calculated from INSEE 2005: 35). In a broader comparative perspective, France's claim is weak. It is not based on *ius soli*, as in the US and the UK, but on double *ius soli* that first accords citizenship at birth automatically to third generation immigrants (Weil 2001b). Instead inclusiveness has derived from semi-automatic attribution of citizenship to second generation immigrants upon adulthood.

The nexus between the welfare state regimes and the incorporation regimes has been work. An underlying requirement for naturalization in Germany and France has been economic self-sufficiency, that is, employment with an adequate income, without recourse to assistance benefits (Weil 2001a: Table 1–2). Thus in both countries utilization of social assistance can jeopardize an immigrant's prospects of citizenship, and work has assumed growing importance for legalization and residence permits in France. Unlike French citizens, immigrants have confronted a work test for family allowances and the most important assistance benefit. Still the nexus is much stronger in Germany than in France. The centrality of work has been much more pronounced in the German welfare state regime. This is also true of the German incorporation regime with its work tests for permanent residence and naturalization, and since 2007 even for citizenship acquisition of second generation immigrants.

Lastly, the German–French comparison provides two major lessons. First, it calls attention to the importance of intra-welfare regime variations for immigrants' social rights. Second, the comparison illuminates the difficulties of focusing on the differences in a single policy dimension of the incorporation regime. Although citizenship policy is crucial to inclusion, the German and French citizenship models are not historically fixed and impermeable to change. Instead they have converged during the past two decades, and their permit systems have assumed greater significance as requirements for settlement status have multiplied, creating new obstacles to inclusion.

5

Social Democratic Welfare States and Immigrants' Social Rights

A hallmark of the social democratic welfare state regime has been comprehensive social provision where a major basis of entitlement has been citizenship. During the postwar period citizen benefits have been increasingly complemented by work-related benefits. As a result, the social democratic regime features a combination of universal schemes with entitlement based on citizenship or residence and programs with income replacement rates. This combination, Esping-Andersen (1990, 1999) argues, diminishes the importance of the market, and it minimizes the stratifying effects of social policies. Funding has reflected the idea of social citizenship rather than the insurance principle. Contributions paid by the insured in social insurance schemes have played a small role, and there has been a heavy reliance on taxation. Comprehensive social provision has also included a wide range of public services; and the costs of care have been subsidized through state involvement in programs for children, the elderly, and the disabled. A further distinctive aspect has been the importance assigned to full employment, where "the right to work has equal status to the right of income protection" (Esping-Andersen 1990: 28). A final characteristic has been a commitment to equality as policy goal, and this commitment has not been limited to equal opportunities but has extended to equality of results or outcomes. The central questions of this chapter are: How have the distinguishing features of the social democratic welfare regime influenced the social rights of immigrants? And what have been the effects of contrasting incorporation regimes on their rights?

Sweden: Social democratic welfare regime—inclusive incorporation regime

Just as the US has been viewed as the epitome of the liberal welfare regime and Germany as the prototype of the conservative corporatist regime, Sweden has exemplified the social democratic welfare regime. The prominence of univer-salism in Swedish social provision, which has promoted coverage of the entire population, has manifested itself in several ways. Sweden's first major social insurance scheme—the 1913 old age and disability insurance—differed from both the means test approach in Britain's and Denmark's early pension pro-grams and the Bismarckian model in Germany. Instead the Swedish scheme established the principle of individual entitlement to a pension regardless of income, labor market participation, sex, or marital status. However, the prin-ciple was not achieved until the 1946 reform that introduced a flat-rate pension available to all citizens without the requirement of labor market participation or means testing. Similarly, and distinct from the other countries here, the introduction of universal child allowances in the mid-1940s imme-diately extended benefits to all children. In the 1950s health insurance provided maternity grants to all mothers; and all adults were eligible for a modest sickness allowance, while employed persons also received an earnings-related supplement. Since maternity benefits were converted into parental benefits in the 1970s, benefits have covered all parents—both those in and outside the labor market.

Universalism has also underpinned the expansion of public services avail-able to the entire population, especially health care, education, employment services, and child care. Conversely, the private sector played a marginal role in providing these services until the 1990s. The prominence of public services is revealed in social policy expenditure patterns. Since the late 1960s Sweden has spent between 20 and 25 per cent of its GDP on public provision of services and roughly the same percentage of its GDP on cash transfers. In health care, however, British universalism surpassed Sweden until the 1970s. Although the Swedish parliament adopted the goal of universal health care in the immediate postwar years, it was not until 1955 that a national health insurance replaced state subsidized voluntary schemes, and in 1970 modest fees at the point of delivery supplanted the system of reimbursement of hospital and physician costs.

A major trend since the 1950s has been the introduction of work-related benefits to protect against the loss of earnings. Among the most important reforms were earnings-related pensions covering retirement and disability (ATP), improved sickness compensation, and parental benefits. This develop-ment has caused some observers to emphasize the diminished role of universal benefits and a convergence with the conservative corporatist regime. It needs to be stressed, however, that earnings-related benefits did not replace flat-rate benefits. Instead they were superimposed on citizen benefits, resulting in two tiers of benefits. Importantly, as a result, benefits have been available to those in the workforce as well as those outside the labor market. The combi-nation of citizen benefits and earnings-related benefits has also quite different redistributive effects compared to the mixes of means-tested benefits and the work-related insurance benefits prevalent in the countries representing the liberal and conservative corporatist regimes. Citizen benefits have provided basic security to all, and earnings-related benefits have provided income security to employees whose numbers increased in part because of active labor market measures. Earnings-related benefits have decreased the income gap between the working population and persons whose main source of income was benefits. A further dissimilarity is that until recently work tests have been less arduous and contributions of the insured have had much less significance in determining entitlements.

An additional characteristic has been the goal of full employment and the right to work for everyone. Sweden embarked on an active labor market policy in the 1950s; measures were directed to persons who had lost their jobs, labor market entrants, and the hard to employ. The Swedish unemployment rate was low (generally around 2 per cent) until the 1990s, and active labor market measures helped to keep the unemployment rate low during the economic slumps in the 1970s and 1980s (Sainsbury 1996: 20). These measures also helped boost the proportion of the economically active in the working age population, and the increase meant that more people qualified for work-related benefits. Although performance has not always matched the goal of full employment since the economic recession in the early 1990s, active labor market measures have remained an important policy component. The labor market participation rate has been higher than in the liberal and conservative corporatist regime countries in the 2000s (EUROSTAT 2009; OECD 2011: 239).

An emphasis on egalitarian outcomes and the redistributive impact of welfare state policies has also been a distinctive feature. Although income inequality has increased in Sweden since the 1980s, it has still been less pronounced compared to the liberal and conservative corporatist regime countries (Hills 2004: 29; NOSOSKO 2010: 30). In the early 2000s Swedish policies reduced income inequality substantially, and no major decline in the redistributive capacity of policies has been evident during the last three decades (Sainsbury and Morissens 2010).

Inclusive incorporation regime

The Swedish incorporation regime has become inclusive during the postwar period, and its underlying principle has been rights based on residence or domicile (*ius domicilis*) (Hammar 2003). As stated in a commission report, arguing for voting rights for immigrants, "the principle of domicile or residence is the basic precondition regulating public rights" (SOU 1975:15, p. 100). Initially the rights of Nordic citizens who were Swedish residents came to approximate those of the Swedes.[1] Subsequently denizen status and rights based on residence were extended to other immigrants. The 1954 Aliens Law represented the cautious beginnings of denizen status for other immigrants. Distinguishing between temporary visitors and permanent settlers, the Law introduced a special permanent residence permit for the latter group, strengthening their right of abode. By the mid-1950s denizen status had been accorded to three groups of non-citizens: citizens of the other Nordic countries, political refugees, and immigrants with a permanent residence permit (Borevi 2002: 80–1).

The inclusive nature of the incorporation regime has also been reflected in the trend to simplify the permit system that eventually led to permanent residence permits being granted shortly after arrival, an encompassing definition of refugees and equal treatment of convention refugees and persons granted asylum for humanitarian reasons, generous rules for family reunification, and the introduction of culture and political rights for immigrants. Through a school reform to add immigrant languages to the curriculum and subsidies to ethnic associations, immigrants were encouraged to preserve their cultural heritage, and a constitutional amendment strengthened the rights of minorities and immigrants. In 1975 immigrants received the right to vote and stand for office in local and regional elections. Nor has citizenship been a barrier to public employment, as in the conservative corporatist regime countries.

An anomaly of this successively inclusive incorporation regime is that the principle of descent (*ius sanguinis*) has continued to determine citizenship. However, conditions of naturalization have been quite liberal, and the naturalization rate has been high, even exceeding the US rate of naturalization in the 2000s. The residence requirement was reduced from seven to five years and the requirement of economic self-support to become a citizen was removed in the mid-1970s; there has been no language or civics test and no oath of allegiance. The 2001 Nationality Law introduced dual citizenship, removing the requirement that naturalized Swedish citizens renounce their previous citizenship and further improving the prospects of naturalization.

The broad contours of postwar immigration resemble the German pattern in several respects. Immediately after the war the first foreign workers were recruited, and labor migration was the predominant form of immigration until its termination in 1972. Family members and refugees then became the main sources of immigration, with each entry category accounting for

---

[1] Nordic citizens have been privileged in terms of entry rights and citizenship acquisition. During the Second World War work permits were eliminated for Nordic citizens, and the 1954 Nordic Convention removed passport requirements and residence permits for citizens of the other Nordic countries. Nordic citizens have also had shorter residence requirements for Swedish citizenship.

roughly half of the immigrants entering Sweden since the mid-1970s (Lundh and Ohlsson 1999; MV 2009). Like Germany, Sweden experienced a massive influx of asylum seekers in the early 1990s.

The evolution of immigrants' social rights

At first glance, citizenship as a principle of entitlement appears antithetical to the social rights of immigrants of a different nationality. Increasingly, however, residence has supplanted citizenship as a criterion of eligibility. In addition, the growing importance of work-related benefits helped to strengthen immigrants' claims to retirement and disability benefits based on citizenship.

At the outset foreign workers were incorporated as equals in terms of pay and working conditions. As in Germany, but not in France or the UK and the US, the trade unions were involved in approving work permits, and they made sure that foreigners were hired under the same conditions as Swedish workers. Foreigners also had equal access to unemployment and occupational injury benefits at an early date. When other benefits based on labor market participation were enacted, foreign workers were of course entitled to them. Immigrants' high labor market participation rate, along with modest work tests and earnings requirements promoted their access to these social benefits. National health insurance has been available to immigrants upon registration after a short period of residence. All children under the age of 16 were covered without registration. Child allowances could be claimed by immigrants after six months' residence. All residents irrespective of citizenship could claim educational aid, housing allowances, and social assistance.

Immigrants' access to social benefits was further improved during the 1970s when the Swedes addressed the remaining differences in entitlements. The differences concerned benefits for single parents, long-term utilization of social assistance, and the basic pension. The thorniest issue was the basic pension based on citizenship, which provided old age, disability, and survivor benefits. Many but not all immigrants were entitled to the basic pension through bilateral agreements and the 1955 Nordic Convention on Social Security. To eliminate inequalities, an inquiry commission recommended that "all permanent residents should be guaranteed a statutory minimum in the form of entitlement to the basic pension after a specific period of residence" (SOU 1974:69, p. 148). The issue was finally resolved in 1979 by linking entitlement to the basic pension to the state earnings-related pension scheme, ATP, whose minimum qualifying condition was three years of earnings. Residence requirements, varying between ten years for the old age pension and five years for disability and survivor benefits, were introduced for non-citizens without ATP (Elmér 1994). This solution substantially

lowered the barriers to basic pension benefits compared to pension requirements in the liberal and conservative regime countries.

In summary, immigrants were formally incorporated into the welfare system on relatively equal terms with citizens by the early 1980s—and *with little
differentiation in social rights among entry categories*. Residence as the basis of
social entitlement—a welfare regime attribute—combined with a simplified
residence permit system which granted settlement status almost immediately
or within a couple of years—a feature of the inclusive incorporation regime—
minimized a stratification of social rights based on entry categories during the
1970s and 1980s. Once family members or asylum seekers, the two major
entry forms after 1972, were granted a residence permit, they acquired equal
access to social benefits and the labor market. In contrast to the Germans and
French, the Swedes did not ban family members from the labor market. Nor
did they distinguish between the social rights of various categories of refugees.
Nonetheless, as we shall see, permanent residence versus temporary residence
became a fault line in determining immigrants' social rights during the
1990s; a trend toward greater differentiation in immigrant rights also gained
momentum.

Immigrants' social rights in the 1990s and 2000s

The 1990s was a decade of welfare state downsizing in Sweden, and immigrants together with other vulnerable groups bore the brunt of the contraction
of the welfare state. The decade was also marked by economic turbulence, as
Sweden in the early 1990s experienced a severe economic downturn, with
negative economic growth during three consecutive years (1991–3) and a
massive loss of jobs. Sweden went from full employment to an unemployment rate of 8 per cent in 1993, and unemployment remained at that level
until 1998. A government budget surplus was transformed into a deficit,
amounting to 12 per cent of the GDP in 1993 (Kautto 2000: chapter 2). The
economic recession of the 1990s hit immigrants very hard, and mass asylum
seeking coincided with the height of the economic downturn, worsening
the employment prospects of newcomers. Overall immigrants experienced a
sharp decline in their employment rate, which reduced their earnings and
limited their access to work-related benefits, and many did not benefit from
the return of prosperity at the end of the decade (Sainsbury and Morissens
2010).

WELFARE STATE DOWNSIZING IN THE 1990s
Confronted by an enormous budget deficit and soaring social expenditures, an
initial phase of the government's strategy was to tighten eligibility requirements, raise user fees, and cut benefit levels. Contrary to the liberal regime

countries whose retrenchment strategies focused on means-tested benefits and the conservative corporatist regime countries whose strategies emphasized the principle of equivalence, a key facet of the Swedish government's strategy was across-the-board cuts encompassing virtually all benefits. Nearly everyone was affected. In this respect, the retrenchment strategy reflected a universalist logic typical of the social democratic welfare regime. A downside of the strategy was its impact on low income groups. Another universalist feature of the strategy was to avoid cuts in public services—especially education, health, and child care—as much as possible. In a second phase, benefit cuts were accompanied by tax increases to consolidate public finances, and by 1998 the budget had been balanced (Kautto 2000).

The benefits that were critical to many immigrants during the 1990s were social assistance, family benefits, and housing allowances. Social assistance benefits have become increasingly important as the composition of immigrants has changed from labor migrants to asylum seekers and refugees. The high rates of unemployment among refugees have prolonged their utilization of assistance and deprived them of work-related benefits, such as sickness and unemployment benefits (SOU 1996:55, p. 93; Bergmark 2000: 147–8; SS 2007: 21). The foreign born were also heavily involved in several active labor market programs, such as labor market training and job creation schemes, in the mid-1990s (SOU 1996:55, p. 91).

Family benefits and housing allowances were cut. In 1995 the government decided to lower the child allowance and retain entitlement for all children rather than to introduce means-tested family benefits. The cuts in family benefits were short-lived, and in 1998 benefits were restored, although the supplement for families with three or more children was not as generous as previously. As distinct from social assistance and child allowances, changes in the housing allowance drastically reduced the number of recipients during the 1990s and the 2000s. Among the losers were two-parent families with children.

Of the decade's retrenchment measures, the revamping of the pension system has major long-term consequences, and two features of the scheme entailed a serious weakening in immigrants' future pension rights. First, the new system, which will be fully implemented in 2018, has strengthened Bismarckian elements—work performance and contributions—in the state earnings-related pension. The new qualifying conditions of 40 years of employment and the calculation of benefits on the basis of lifetime earnings present a serious handicap for immigrants. Contributions were reintroduced, and they determine pension benefits. However, an elaborate set of credits for periods of post-secondary education and other studies, military service, unemployment, sickness, and parental care mitigate breaks in contributions and the effects of lifetime earnings. Second, a guaranteed pension has replaced the basic pension in providing basic security, but the residence requirement for a full pension was lengthened to 40 years for citizens and non-citizens. An additional innovation is the introduction of a mandatory private pension, which is supposed to compensate for reduced public retirement benefits. The mandatory nature of the pension contrasts with most of the other countries in this book. Their schemes have been voluntary or offered the possibility to contract out, whereas all employees, including immigrants, are covered in the Swedish scheme.

Neither the benefit cuts in the 1990s nor the pension reform took into account the implications for immigrants' social rights and the possibility of disproportionate harm to their economic well-being. Nonetheless, the combined effect of retrenchment and the recession was a drop in the disposable income of the foreign born during the decade, while that of the Swedish born increased slightly (SOU 2000:41, p. 70).

ASYLUM SEEKERS' BENEFITS
As the economic downturn deepened, the government introduced measures that affected the benefits of asylum seekers. Already in the late 1980s, special allowances for asylum seekers replaced social assistance. The law introducing the allowances stipulated that asylum seekers had a right to benefits that guaranteed an acceptable standard of living, which was the same as the minimum laid down in the Social Assistance Law (Prop. 1987/88: 80). In 1992 the government lowered asylum seekers' daily allowances by 10 per cent, arguing that since the benefits of everyone else were being reduced, asylum seekers' allowances should be cut as part of the general austerity package. Again in 1994 the government lowered the allowances but now it severed the link between the allowances and the social minimum. The bill declared that during the application process it was justified that asylum seekers had a lower economic standard than permanent residents, and that the government should determine the allowance independently of the social minimum (Prop. 1993/94: 94). The 1994 changes were part of a reform of the reception system for asylum seekers, and a consequence was to shift asylum seekers' benefits from the realm of social legislation to that of immigration legislation. This shift shunted asylum seekers' benefits into the background and separated them from the general debate on social policy. As distinct from most other social benefits, the daily allowances for asylum seekers were not raised once the economy recovered. Nor had they been adjusted to changes in the cost of living since their reduction in 1994 (SOU 2009:19, p. 167), and the allowances were extremely low in the late 2000s. In sum, asylum seekers' benefits have not been in the spotlight as in the UK, Germany, and France. Instead they have been off the agenda and largely in limbo, but with similar results.

SOCIAL REFORMS SINCE THE LATE 1990s

Several expansive reforms enacted after economic recovery at the end of the 1990s have benefited newcomers, and a new elder allowance (*äldreförsörjnings-stödet*) has counteracted one of the major negative features of the new pension system—the stringent residence requirements for the guaranteed pension. In 2003 the government introduced the allowance to insure minimum benefits for all residents who failed to meet the requirements for the guaranteed pension. Other important reforms were the introduction of a ceiling on child care fees paid by parents and the right to a place in child care for unemployed parents (2000), increases in child allowances (2000 and 2001), free preschool for all four- and five-year-old children (2003), improved access to survivor benefits for children irrespective of their parents' pension rights (2003), and more generous parental benefits for parents outside the labor market. A common feature of these reforms is that they have bolstered universalism, and many have been child-centered. The child care reforms increased both availability and affordability; in the mid-2000s immigrant parents had the same utilization rate as Swedish born parents (SV 2007). The reform of survivor benefits also clearly improved the situation of children of immigrant parents who were likely to have weak pension rights.

Despite measures that have improved immigrants' social rights, a serious enduring problem has been newcomers' low employment rate. Even before the 2008–9 global recession, during the years of strong economic performance, the employment rate of the foreign born did not display a continuous upward trend, but dropped again in the mid-2000s. The slump in their employment rate may be related to the arrival of over 150,000 newcomers between 2004 and 2007, and many were refugees (MV 2009). At the same time official statistics revealed that those who were most vulnerable to poverty were persons with neither earnings nor work-related social benefits, and immigrants have disproportionately fallen within this category (Sainsbury and Morissens 2010).

Changes in the incorporation regime

The years around 1980 represented a high point in the inclusiveness of the Swedish incorporation regime. Since then inclusive reforms have been introduced, but so have restrictive measures. Pressures for change have included increasing economic inequalities between newcomers and the rest of the population, the rise in asylum seeking, and EU membership leading to a harmonization of immigration policy among member states.

FROM "IMMIGRANT POLICIES" TO "INTEGRATION POLICIES":
INTRODUCTORY AND ANTI-DISCRIMINATION MEASURES

The 1990s recession led to growing differences in the economic well-being of non-citizens and citizens, and decision makers began to reconsider immigrant policies, concluding that policy changes were necessary to meet the challenge of rising inequality. In the mid-1990s immigrant policies were redefined as integration policies, and the focus shifted to introductory and anti-discrimination measures. Introductory measures were aimed at newly arrived immigrants during their first five years to improve their prospects of employment and participation in society. In addition to Swedish language instruction, the introduction program included individual plans, complementary education, vocational training, and other active labor market measures. The scope of participants was expanded from refugees and their family members to include other newcomers who would benefit from the program. One of the innovative proposals—a taxable introductory allowance set at a higher rate than social assistance—was rejected because of budget restraints. Instead local governments retained the option of providing an introductory allowance, which had been established in 1992 and was conceived as a means of differentiating financial support from social assistance and creating an incentive for newcomers to participate in introduction programs (Ds 1991: 79; SOU 1996:55; Prop. 1997/98: 16).

Although hailed as a major policy reorientation, the government settled for a policy that largely consolidated existing introductory measures, and subsequent reforms have mainly consisted of similar types of measures. The main change was the institutionalization of a proactive stance and positive measures to combat unequal treatment based on ethnicity and race through the establishment of a new national integration agency. The tasks of the agency were to promote equal rights and opportunities irrespective of ethnic and cultural background; to prevent and combat discrimination, xenophobia, and racism; and to monitor immigrants' integration. Already in the mid-1980s an anti-discrimination commissioner had been established to deal with ethnic discrimination in the labor market. In 1994 parliament adopted a law against ethnic discrimination in the labor market, which was strengthened in 1999. The focus on labor market discrimination has had significance for immigrants' social rights that are work-related, but did little to address unequal treatment in housing, education, health care, or other public services.

The continuing difficulties of newly arrived refugees in joining the labor force prompted major changes in the introductory benefits system in the late 2000s. Introductory benefits became a state rather than a local government responsibility with the public employment service (*arbetsförmedlingen*) assigned the task of coordinating introductory measures. Benefits have been standardized so that they are the same for the entire country. To create work incentives, additional income from paid employment does not reduce introductory benefits, and the introductory benefits will be more generous than assistance, but the maximum benefit duration was shortened to two years. The introductory program is largely the same: Swedish language instruction, a course in Swedish society, and labor market training measures (Prop. 2009/10: 60).

A negative development affecting both refugees' and asylum seekers' social rights was the introduction of sanctions in the early 1990s; introductory benefits and asylum seekers' benefits can be withdrawn or reduced. Failure to follow one's introduction plan can affect introductory benefits. Asylum seekers' benefits can be reduced or withdrawn for failing to cooperate with the authorities in processing their application or not participating in the activities of the reception centers without a reasonable excuse.

THE PERMIT SYSTEM

Mass asylum seeking, EU membership, and the resumption of labor immigration have brought changes to the permit system. In coping with the large number of asylum seekers—nearly 180,000 persons—between 1991 and 1994, the government reintroduced the practice of issuing temporary rather than permanent residence permits. The permits were issued for six-month periods, which meant that these immigrants could not register as permanent residents and thus were not entitled to the universal health insurance (Prop. 1993/94: 94). In this instance the principle of domicile was converted from a mechanism of inclusion to one of exclusion.

Gradually the resident permit system has become increasingly complex, resulting in a differentiation in rights by entry category. Asylum seekers granted temporary asylum in the mid-1990s had lesser rights compared to the full rights of refugees. Similarly, the worsening of asylum seekers' rights during the height of the economic crisis was justified on the grounds that they were not permanent residents. After the spike in asylum seeking, routines returned to granting successful applicants regular residence permits again.

EU membership has entailed changes in the permit system to accommodate the rights of citizens of the member states and to incorporate EU directives. EU citizens were granted local voting rights after one year of residence, thus differentiating between the political rights of other newcomers who have a three-year residence requirement. The 2006 revision of the Aliens Law formally incorporated the residence rights of EU citizens, more or less putting them on a par with Nordic citizens who have not needed a residence or work permit. The rights of EU citizens stem from being a registered resident, not a permanent resident. The 2006 amendments privileged the mobility of workers and adopted the principle of priority in hiring EU citizens. Simultaneously the requirement of sufficient means was introduced for EU immigrants who were not workers.

In late 2008 Sweden reopened its doors to labor migration beyond the EU. As distinct from Germany, France, Britain, and Denmark, Sweden has put less emphasis on limiting labor immigration to professionals or wealthy entrepreneurs. The return of labor immigration has affected permit requirements and social rights. The new rules specified that only temporary permits were available to migrant workers. Foreign laborers can acquire a permanent residence permit after four years of employment, but the temporary permits are conditional upon employment and the ability to support oneself. The law also altered the recruitment system by assigning responsibility to individual employers, and corporatist arrangements involving the consultation and veto of the labor market partners were abandoned. A condition for granting a permit was that the pay, insurance benefits, and other working conditions of foreign workers were not inferior to those in collective agreements (Prop. 2007/08: 147; SFS 2008: 884).

Thus the new labor permit system differed sharply from the German and British systems. As distinct from Germany, it did not differentiate between the rights and requirements of entrepreneurs, skilled, and unskilled labor. In the Swedish system there were no counterparts to the German wealth or income requirements or the social insurance requirements. Nor have the wealthy or highly paid had the possibility of immediate access to a permanent permit, as they have in Germany. The Swedish permit system also contrasts with developments in Britain, where the government has introduced a point system as the basis of acquiring settlement status and earning the right to stay.

In short, both mass asylum seeking and labor immigration expanded the role of temporary permits, weakening the practice of granting a permanent resident permit immediately or within two years. However, accommodating the rights of EU citizens and even those of foreign workers has entailed an enlargement of the rights of those with temporary permits compared to the 1990s. On the other hand, the incorporation of EU directives into Swedish legislation and the return of labor immigration have been accompanied by a greater emphasis on employment and economic self-sufficiency as conditions of entry and stay. The 2010 introduction of maintenance obligations for family reunification produced a new differentiation in rights based on entry category. A major justification for their introduction was that all the other EU member states had support obligations.

Despite restrictive moves since 1980, several distinctive inclusive elements have survived and even expanded. Although the 1996 asylum bill eliminated specific categories to be considered for asylum, it argued for broad protection and that the Geneva Convention's definition of refugees was too restrictive. The Swedes continued to make no differentiation in the rights of persons granted protection irrespective of the type of refugee. When self-maintenance and accommodation requirements for family reunification were introduced, they applied to very few applicants (Prop. 2009/10: 77). The Swedish 2001 Nationality Law strengthened the principle of domicile (*ius domicili*) in citizenship acquisition (Bernitz and Bernitz 2006: 524–5, 27–8) and permitted dual citizenship. Neither language proficiency nor integration tests have been a requirement for a Swedish permanent residence permit or citizenship. The inclusiveness of Swedish policy was also evident in Sweden being the only member state of the EU that did not impose transitional rules on citizens of the new member states after the 2004 and 2007 enlargements (Lundborg 2009: 69; Borevi 2010: 114); nor did Sweden bar them from social benefits.

To sum up, in a longitudinal perspective, inclusive aspects of the Swedish incorporation regime have become frayed. In a cross-national perspective, the inclusiveness of the Swedish incorporation regime in the late 2000s continued to stand out, since several countries have multiplied or stiffened the requirements for permanent residence status and becoming a citizen. Nor has Sweden restricted access to social benefits as a strategy to curb immigration. Lastly, although challenged by the growing weight attached to employment and economic self-sufficiency, residence remains a key nexus between the welfare and incorporation regimes; it potentially provides a more inclusive foundation for rights than either need or work.

Denmark: Social democratic welfare regime—restrictive incorporation regime

A problematic aspect in theorizing the social democratic welfare regime has been that Esping-Andersen has taken Sweden as his prime frame of reference, and he has designated Sweden as the model example of this regime type (1990, 1999). This focus has tended to make any differences between Sweden and the other Nordic countries regime deviations and cast doubts over the status of the other countries, especially Denmark, as representatives of the social democratic regime.[2] To identify the nature of Denmark's welfare regime, let us examine the basic contours of Danish social provision and in the process consider first the similarities between the two countries and then the differences.

As in Sweden, universalism in the form of unified programs covering the entire population and citizenship based benefits—both transfers and services—

---

[2] Occasionally Esping-Andersen has expressed doubts about Denmark's classification, concluding in one instance that the Danish welfare regime was liberal (Esping-Andersen 1992: 111–13), but on the whole he has argued that Denmark belongs to the social democratic regime (1990). His more recent analysis (1999) has further underlined the basic similarities between the two countries since he has paid attention to defamilialization—the degree to which individual adults can uphold a socially acceptable standard of living independently of family relations, either through paid work or social security provision.

has figured prominently in Danish social provision. Accordingly, citizenship or residence has been a major principle of entitlement, which is a defining property of the social democratic regime. As distinct from the other regime types, the state has been a main provider of services, either through regional or local government. Danish expenditures on social services have also equaled, and recently exceeded, spending on transfers (Adema 2006; Goul Andersen 2008: 47). Public services have been a vital component in socializing the costs of familyhood, especially through the widespread provision of affordable day care.

Taxation has played a major role in funding benefits and services. This form of funding facilitates universal coverage because contribution requirements have often excluded persons without adequate contributions from benefits. Since the 1970s Denmark and Sweden have ranked as top spenders in terms of social expenditures as a percentage of the GDP, and income taxes provided a substantial share of funding. Income and corporate taxes amounted to roughly one-third of the Danish GDP, a much higher share than any other OECD country in the late 1990s. Sweden, at slightly above 20 per cent, had the next largest share (Scharpf and Schmidt 2000: 364, 361; Adema 2006: 8, 10).

The principle of work—emphasizing the right to work and promoting access to paid employment—has led to high activity rates among the working age population of both sexes and smaller employment gaps between women and men compared to most other countries. Both countries also adopted the Ghent model of unemployment insurance. Membership is voluntary; the insurance is administered by the trade unions and has been heavily subsidized by the state. Despite voluntary membership, coverage has been high. Benefit levels have been adequate, and the duration of benefits has been long, especially in Denmark.

A final common feature is the egalitarian thrust of policies. Social policies have promoted a high employment rate so that the vast majority of the working age population has earnings. Wage setting policies have contributed to flattening earnings differentials, resulting in a wage structure characterized by low dispersion (Scharpf and Schmidt 2000: 358). Together with taxation, these policies have decreased differences in net market income. Social benefits have been very effective in alleviating poverty by lifting large proportions of the pre-transfer poor above the poverty line. As a result, poverty rates have been consistently low. Furthermore, generous benefits and affordable public services have crowded out market alternatives that tend to produce more inegalitarian distributional outcomes. This matrix of policies has worked to reduce income inequalities, and in a comparative perspective, the income distribution of the Danish and Swedish populations has been less unequal than in countries representing the liberal and conservative corporatist regime types (Korpi 2002: 102; NOSOSKO 2010: 30).

These commonalities of Danish and Swedish social provision squarely place the two countries within the social democratic regime, but important differences exist. Denmark has a stronger legacy of means testing, and proposals for means testing have intermittently surfaced during hard times. On the other hand, the Danes have introduced innovative reforms, such as taxation of means-tested benefits, which lessens the employment trap of assistance benefits. They have also partially individualized social assistance by paying benefits to the individual irrespective of family relationships, but household income has determined eligibility so that disincentives for a partner to get a job have not been eliminated. Instead both partners have had to meet a work test to qualify for assistance since 2007. Second, the combination of basic security (provided by flat-rate citizen benefits) and income security (via earnings-related benefits) has been less developed in Danish social insurance programs than in Swedish schemes. In the area of pensions, citizen benefits have contributed a larger share of retirement income than they did in Sweden. Danish citizen or basic pensions have provided generous benefits and earnings-related pensions very low benefits.[3] Danish benefit levels are also low in sickness, maternity and parental, and unemployment insurance schemes. Third, Denmark failed to maintain full employment from the mid-1970s onwards, while Sweden succeeded in doing so until the early 1990s. Initially, the Danish response to high levels of unemployment was to introduce passive measures that improved benefits for jobless workers. In the early 1990s, however, there was a major policy reorientation toward active labor market measures, resulting in convergence in the policies of the two countries (Eitrheim and Kuhnle 2000: 55–6). Fourth, Danish social provision has been largely financed by general revenues. In contrast, Swedish cash transfers were increasingly financed by employer payroll taxes; at the same time employee contributions were largely eliminated. Fifth, in an international context, Denmark has stood out as having the highest coverage of services for both children and the elderly (Anttonen and Sipilä 1996: 94; NOSOSKO 2010: 60, 154).

In conclusion, some of these differences have represented departures from the ideal type of the social democratic regime, especially means testing. In at least four respects, however, Denmark has approximated the social democratic regime more than Sweden. Entitlements based on citizenship have been more prominent, especially for pensions; to a greater extent, general revenues have been a major source of funding; child care and other family services have traditionally had higher coverage; and in the 2000s the Danish labor

---

[3] In 2005 the standard benefit of the Danish basic or citizen pension was €7,586 plus a supplement of nearly the same amount for a single pensioner, whereas the maximum benefit of the work-related pension for a person who had worked full time for 40 years was a mere €2,990 (Green-Pedersen 2007: 469–70).

participation rate was higher than the Swedish rate, and Denmark had come closer to the goal of full employment. Finally, whatever the existing policy differences, they have not altered the fact that Denmark clusters together with the other Nordic countries when it comes to low poverty rates and less unequal income distribution.

An increasingly restrictive incorporation regime

At first glance, features of the two countries' incorporation regimes also seem similar, in part because of earlier efforts to harmonize nationality legislation and the rights of Nordic citizens. Denmark, like Sweden, has granted Nordic citizens special privileges, including the waiver of residence and work permits, along with easier rules to become a citizen. Both countries have also had liberal asylum policies, defining refugees in broader terms than the Geneva Convention, recognizing a larger proportion of asylum seekers as either Convention or de facto refugees than other countries, and granting both types of refugee similar rights. Denmark also introduced several innovative policies initiated by Swedish reformers, such as instruction in immigrant languages in schools, along with other special measures to aid immigrants, and the right of non-citizens to vote and run for office in local and regional elections. Nevertheless, the Danish and Swedish incorporation regimes have increasingly diverged on the ease or difficulty in acquiring citizenship and permanent residence status. They have also grown apart concerning family reunification and treatment of refugees.

Even prior to the recent restrictions, Danish requirements for naturalization were stiffer than those in Sweden. The residence requirement and requirement of no criminal record have been more demanding in Denmark compared to Sweden. The Danes have also required proficiency in the Danish language, together with knowledge of Danish society and culture, an oath of allegiance, economic self-sufficiency, and renunciation of previous citizenship to become a citizen, while the Swedes have not. During the 2000s the Danes lengthened the residence requirement to nine years, stiffened the requirement of no criminal record, raised the language proficiency requirement, and eliminated the possibility for second generation immigrants and immigrants who came to Denmark as children to become citizens through declaration. Since 2005 all nationals, with the exception of citizens of the Nordic countries, can only become Danish citizens through naturalization (MFII 2003–4: 3). In short, the principle of *ius sanguinis* remains intact, buttressed by barriers to naturalization that have increased in number and have become higher.

The sharpening of requirements to become a citizen has been accompanied by a parallel trend with regard to settlement status. Since 2002 Danish requirements for a permanent residence permit have become among the most rigorous of our cases. The residence requirement was raised to seven years, and other requirements were no criminal record, completion of the introduction program, a work test of two and half years of full time employment, knowledge of Danish and Danish society, and no public debts. The permit system also became increasingly restrictive for family members and refugees—the two main entry categories in the 1980s and 1990s.

The restrictive stance on citizenship, permanent residence, family reunion, and asylum seekers seems paradoxical since Denmark has the lowest proportion of foreign born in its population of the countries examined here. Postwar immigration first gained momentum in the early 1960s when large numbers of labor migrants started to arrive in Denmark. The first steps to halt spontaneous immigration were taken in the late 1960s, and the government introduced a total ban on labor immigration in 1973. As in the other countries, the number of asylum seekers coming to Denmark skyrocketed during the 1980s. Around 2000 the foreign born accounted for between 5 and 6 per cent of the Danish population (Hansen et al. 2002: 12), compared to 12 per cent of the Swedish population. If the scale of immigration does not explain the growing restrictiveness of the Danish incorporation regime, perhaps the acceleration of immigration and its ethnic and racial composition does. Compared to Sweden, a larger share of immigrants in Denmark has come from the developing countries (Blume et al. 2005: 325), increasing ethnic and racial diversity in Danish society. On the other hand, since the volume of Swedish immigration has been much greater, immigrants from the developing countries have actually constituted a larger proportion of the population in Sweden.

The evolution of immigrants' social rights

For the first wave of postwar immigration, consisting of migrant laborers, there were no differences in the formal social rights of immigrants and Danes in the area of working conditions and work-related benefits. Immigrants had equal access to employment services, holiday pay, and eventually vocational training. Furthermore, to ensure equal coverage, it became mandatory for foreigners who had a work permit to join the voluntary unemployment insurance scheme in the early 1970s.

Instead the major challenge of immigration to the social democratic regime countries has been the importance of entitlements based on citizenship and their extension to non-citizens. In coping with this challenge, Danish policy makers have been slow to grant immigrants social rights based on citizenship and entitlement to long-term assistance, which originally was enjoyed only by Danish citizens.

Initially child allowances and other family benefits were not available to non-citizens during their first three years of residence. Only citizens of countries that had bilateral agreement with Denmark were eligible usually after six months (Betænkning 589: 310), but in 1972 roughly half of the foreign workers were not covered by any agreement (calculated from Hjarnø et al. 1973: 132, 134). The residence requirement for general child allowances was shortened to one year in the early 1970s and to six months in the mid-1980s (Betænkning 761: 10; Hammer 1995: 324). There has been a one-year requirement for special child benefits, along with a three-year requirement for extra benefits for single-parent families (Hansen et al. 2002). Compared to Sweden, Denmark has been more reluctant to extend family benefits to immigrants. The process has been slower, and for special family benefits, restrictions were still in place during the 2000s.

Likewise access to pensions for the elderly and disabled whose entitlement was based on citizenship has been a problem. The modest retirement income provided by the state work-related pension scheme (ATP) and the lack of work-related disability benefits, except for occupational injuries, exacerbated the problem. In the early 1970s a foreigner who was not covered by an international agreement had no right to a pension, and for those covered by an agreement the residence requirement was 15 years for an old-age pension with five years immediately before reaching retirement age (Hjarnø et al. 1973: 154). In the mid-1980s the requirement was reduced to ten years for both old-age and disability pensions, with more lenient conditions for those covered by bilateral agreements (Hansen et al. 2002: 41).

Even more problematic, residence has determined pension benefits. The requirement for a full old-age pension has been 40 years of residence in Denmark. The 40-year requirement was introduced when Denmark joined the EEC (now the EU) in 1973; its purpose was to limit the access of citizens of the member states who otherwise would be eligible for the Danish pension on the same conditions as Danish citizens, which was three years of residence (Goul Andersen 2007: 258). The amount of the old-age pension is set as a proportion of the number of years of residence. For example, in the case of ten years of residence, benefits would be one-fourth of the full amount. Favorable treatment of refugees has often meant higher benefit levels compared to other entry categories (Pedersen 2000: 166–7). In short, both access to and benefit levels of citizen pensions were still marked by differentiation in the early 2000s. However, differentiation was counteracted by social assistance benefits or a special supplement (Hammer 1995: 29–32, 231–2).

A final stumbling block has been entitlement to social assistance. Although all legal residents have the right to assistance, not all of them are entitled to permanent support (longer than one year). Originally this social right was reserved for Danish citizens, but it has been extended to Nordic citizens, EU nationals, citizens covered by bilateral agreements, and refugees. Other nationals have not been eligible and subject to expulsion; however, they could not be expelled if they intended to settle permanently and had lived in Denmark for three years or longer (previously two years). There has been little discussion about eliminating this provision of the Social Assistance Law. In fact, it was modified in a restrictive way during the 1990s, discussed below. To sum up, not only has the acquisition of citizenship been difficult, Danish policy makers have been hesitant to grant immigrants citizen-based social benefits and full entitlement to social assistance. Nevertheless, immigrants' access to several citizen-based benefits has substantially improved since the late 1960s.

Two distinctive features of the Danish social provision have been of special significance to immigrants. The first is the prominence of flat-rate benefits in schemes whose entitlements are based on citizenship/residence. In these schemes everyone receives equal benefits irrespective of former work and income, and these benefits as well as assistance have been pegged at a relatively high level that safeguards against poverty. The second feature is the construction of the main work-related schemes, which include unemployment compensation, sickness, and maternity/parental benefits. In contrast to the conservative corporatist regime, where insurance benefits have preserved income differentials, the benefit ceiling in the Danish work-related schemes has been low so that most beneficiaries have received maximum benefits. This construction has been to the advantage of average and low income earners who have high net replacement rates, whereas replacement rates diminish as earnings increase (Hansen et al. 2002: 49–50). Immigrants receiving these benefits are favored because many of them have lower earnings than Danes (Büchel and Frick 2005). The construction of Danish unemployment benefits has also been important for immigrants because of their higher unemployment rates compared to the native born. Roughly two-thirds of unemployed immigrants got insurance benefits, and differences were very small in the benefit levels of immigrants and Danes (Morissens 2006a: 224–7).

Benefit cuts, welfare state reforms, and immigrants' social rights

The decade from the mid-1970s to the mid-1980s was a period of cutbacks as the unemployment rate climbed from roughly 1 per cent at the beginning of the 1970s, peaking at 10 per cent in 1983 (Scharpf and Schmidt 2000: 341). Unemployment was accompanied by rising social expenditures. Denmark confronted a serious imbalance in its economy with a huge deficit in the government budget of 8 per cent of the GDP in the early 1980s. The array of immediate cuts included means testing family benefits, tightening qualifications for unemployment benefits, suspending indexation of benefits, increasing fees for services, and making cuts in assistance (Johansen 1986: 361–3).

The long-term effect was a decline in replacement rates of several work-related benefits—sickness compensation, unemployment benefits, and occupational injuries (Korpi 2002: 75).

Some observers view the retrenchment of the 1980s as a prerequisite of the economic recovery in the 1990s and the further consolidation of the universal welfare state. Even during the years of welfare state roll-back, expansion occurred through the continuous growth of social services and the introduction of new unemployment benefits, such as severance pay (*efterløn*) and an allowance for the unemployed 50 years or older. When the economy improved, universal child benefits were reinstated; universal student allowances were introduced; and maternity leave extended. Benefits based on citizenship emerged relatively unscathed. Basic pension benefit levels remained fairly stable, and the purchasing power of family benefits increased (Benner and Vad 2000: 449). Although unemployment was high until the mid-1990s, the unemployed enjoyed a substantial measure of economic security. New allowances protected the income of the elderly unemployed, while younger workers had virtually an unlimited right to unemployment benefits because of lenient eligibility requirements and work tests. This more or less amounted to a citizen wage—or the ultimate universalism. In short, reforms reinforced the universal nature of the Danish welfare state (Goul Andersen 2000: 72–5).

A main feature of welfare state change has been a reorientation in labor market policies. The reorientation was the major change in the 1990s, but opinions have been divided about whether it is in accord or at variance with the social democratic regime. In accordance with the ideal type, the reorientation has involved more emphasis on active measures, promoting the right to work and a high employment rate. On the other hand, sanctions, such as cuts in the duration and levels of unemployment benefits, along with cuts in social assistance for refusal to take part in activation schemes or an employment offer, have increased the conditionality of social rights. Sanctions have applied to both younger and older workers. Stricter rules have applied to persons under 25 and persons on assistance. Young people could only receive benefits for six months, after which they had to accept 18 months of education and their benefits were reduced by 50 per cent. At the same time allowances for the elderly unemployed have been phased out, and requirements for severance pay have been tightened. These restrictions were accompanied by strong incentives for older workers to stay in the labor market (Benner and Vad 2000; Goul Andersen 2000). In the 2000s the stringency of sanctions increased (Goul Andersen 2008), and, as discussed below, sanctions directly affected immigrants.

Pension reform has not been as comprehensive in Denmark as it has been in Sweden. The most dramatic changes in public pensions introduced by the 2006 reform were an upward revision of the retirement age, whose implementation has been pushed into the distant future (2019–2040), and tougher contribution requirements (30 years of contributions) for early retirement benefits. Access to disability pensions has also been limited. Work-related pensions have continued to be underdeveloped and very fragmented. The major improvements have been the expansion of pensions provided by collective agreements between the unions and employers, and financed by contributions. Private pensions remain basically unregulated. Means testing has been strengthened in the public pension system so that the expansion of work-related pensions could easily disqualify seniors from means-tested supplements in the public system in the future. In the late 2000s the major means-tested supplement amounted roughly half of the basic pension, while a supplement topped up benefits of the poorest (Goul Andersen 2008: 41–5).

As in the other countries, neither cutbacks nor expansive welfare reforms were generally considered in terms of their impact on immigrants. The initial passive approach of the Danes, easing the hardship of unemployment by introducing new benefits for the unemployed, especially older workers, resembled the continental strategy. In effect, it disadvantaged both immigrants by requiring 20 years of contributions for the new benefits. In the late 1990s the contribution requirement was raised to 25 years, and then to 30 years in 2006 (Goul Andersen 2008: 46), making benefits even more out of reach for many immigrants. Moreover, one group poorly covered in work-related pension schemes has been the self-employed, and among immigrants from non-Western countries a larger share has been self-employed compared to Danes (Schultz-Nielsen 2000: 108–13). On the other hand, high minimum benefits in the public pension system and means testing may aid immigrants disqualified from benefits in work-related schemes and without private pensions. Still the lengthy residence requirement means that immigrants are less likely to receive full benefits.

THE INTEGRATION PROGRAM AND CUTS
IN IMMIGRANTS' BENEFITS

In the late 1990s the Danes legislated a comprehensive three-year integration program. The program has consisted of Danish instruction, a course in Danish civics, and active labor market measures, such as vocational guidance, job training, or other educational programs, including higher education, on the job experience, and internships. The target groups have been refugees, the family members of refugees, and other foreigners who are from the developing countries and cannot support themselves. Recent proposals extended participation to foreign workers, students, and newcomers from the EU member states (MFII 2010).

The reorientation in labor market policy, especially its punitive aspects, has left an imprint on the new program. The introductory allowance received by persons in the integration program was set at a substantially lower rate than standard social assistance benefits. After much protest the allowance was raised to the same rate as assistance. In 2002 the introductory allowance was lowered again, and the residence requirement for receiving full social assistance was changed to seven years. Otherwise the applicant received the lower introductory allowance (*starthjælp*), which has ranged from 50–70 per cent of the standard assistance benefit (calculated from MFII 2004: 37; Goul Andersen 2007: 263). In effect, this change established a two-tier system of public assistance—full benefits for Danes and second-class benefits for newcomers during their first seven years in Denmark—and the gap in benefit levels has been quite sizable. The Danes recently stiffened the requirements for newcomers to receive regular assistance benefits by adding a work test of two and half years of full time employment (MFII 2010).

The disciplinary streak is also evident in the reduction of benefits for failure to comply with rules. As in Sweden, benefits can be withdrawn or reduced for failing to cooperate with the authorities in processing asylum seekers' applications or not participating in the integration program. In addition, moving to a new municipality without its consent during the introductory period, not registering and maintaining regular contacts with the employment service, and refusing a job offer have also affected benefits.

A final penalizing feature in the treatment of non-citizens is the emergence of non-reliance on assistance as a condition for receiving a residence permit. Family reunification or formation can also be denied because of utilizing assistance. To create an incentive not to rely on assistance, it became possible to obtain a permanent residence permit more quickly in 2002. Well-integrated foreigners could receive a permit after five years, later reduced to four years. Besides proficiency in Danish and knowledge of Danish society, the criteria of being well integrated include having employment and not having received assistance benefits during the last three years (MFII 2010).

The social rights of refugees have also been weakened by the 1998 Integration Law and subsequent changes. Previously refugees had the same entitlements as Danish citizens once they were officially recognized and received their permanent residence permit. By placing refugees under the Law, they initially were not entitled to assistance until completion of the introductory program. With the change in the residence requirement for full assistance benefits, they too have had to wait at least seven years to become eligible for regular assistance benefits.

In conclusion, social policy has become a facet of immigration policy in that benefit cuts have been viewed as an instrument to deter asylum seeking and family reunions. In the process restrictive measures have whittled away the social rights of immigrants since the 1990s. The most questionable development has been the inroads on refugees' rights that are protected by the

Geneva Convention. Furthermore, social rights, especially the utilization of assistance benefits, have been linked to central dimensions of the incorporation regime—permanent residence status and acquisition of citizenship. The social rights of family members have been increasingly compromised, especially those of married spouses because of support obligations and the introduction of work tests for assistance benefits. On the other hand, immigrants' formal access to other social benefits has not been curtailed, and these benefits have not been coupled to the restrictive features of the incorporation regime. Transfers, especially housing benefits and family benefits, have often boosted the income of newcomers.

Swedish and Danish regimes in comparative perspective

Compared to the liberal and conservative corporatist regime countries, the countries representing the social democratic welfare state regime have confronted a distinctive challenge posed by immigration because citizenship has been a major basis of entitlement. Although Denmark and Sweden approached this challenge in dissimilar ways, and the timing in extending social rights to newcomers has differed, most social entitlements based on citizenship have been converted into rights based on residence in the two countries. Already in the 1950s the Swedes accorded citizen-based benefits— child allowances and maternity grants—to immigrants, whereas the Danes were slower in extending child allowances and other family benefits to newcomers. By the mid-1980s, however, the main family benefits were available on roughly the same condition—a simple residence test of six months—in the two countries. Nor have there been any moves to terminate eligibility as in the UK.

Denmark and Sweden initially adopted different solutions in extending immigrants' rights to citizen pensions, but they have moved closer to each other since 1990. Initially the primary method of improving immigrants' rights in Denmark was to enter bilateral agreements with an increasing number of countries, while retaining the ten-year residence requirement. This approach stratified the social rights of immigrants both with respect to newcomers without any agreement and those with differing agreements. The Swedes opted for a general solution for immigrants not covered by bilateral accords, and the new provisions were often more generous than the rules of the accords. More importantly, the Danes introduced a hefty residence requirement to safeguard their universal pension when Denmark became a member of the EEC in the 1970s. Sweden's affiliation to the European Economic Area and EU membership brought about an alignment in the pension residence requirements of the two countries. Sweden adopted the Danish solution when joining the EU seemed imminent. The 40-year requirement for a full pension is the most extreme residence requirement for benefits in this book, and it approximates the work tests for a full pension in several of the other countries but is less severe than the German work test. In return, however, both Sweden and Denmark have introduced measures to ensure that all residents, including immigrants, who fail to meet the residence requirements for a full pension, receive adequate minimum benefits.

The universalism characterizing Danish and Swedish social provision has promoted inclusion and equal outcomes. A shared feature has been services aimed at all residents, and Sweden and Denmark stood out compared to the other countries in this book through their provision of social services other than health care in the early 2000s (Adema 2006). Privatization has eroded universal services, but the pattern of privatization has varied across services, making generalizations about the consequences for immigrants difficult. However, services for children, especially child care, have expanded in both countries, reducing differences in the utilization rates of foreign and native born parents in the 2000s (Goul Andersen 2007: 262; SV 2007).

Taxation of benefits and the type of funding have also furthered equal outcomes. Sweden has primarily taxed earnings-related benefits but not most non-contributory benefits, such as child allowances and basic pensions (although old-age pensions became taxable in the early 2000s) or means-tested benefits. Taxation of benefits has reduced income inequalities produced by earnings-related benefits. Denmark has adopted a more comprehensive approach to taxing benefits; the 1994 tax reform added social assistance and basic pensions to the list of taxable benefits. Funding through taxes rather than contributions enhances redistribution since the entire adult population with an income finances universal benefits, whereas contributions finance the benefits of members belonging to a particular scheme. Taxes as a basis of funding have also promoted the inclusion of immigrants. On both scores—taxation of benefits and funding—Denmark and Sweden have differed from the conservative corporatist regime countries. The non-taxation of earnings-related benefits and fragmentation of social insurance schemes typical of the conservation corporatist regime has limited the potential of the welfare state to reduce inequalities.

The Swedish and Danish unemployment insurance schemes, because of their voluntary nature, hardly seem to be candidates for promoting equal outcomes. Still both countries did a better job in delivering unemployment insurance benefits to the jobless in the 1990s than did most other European countries, and the low ceiling of maximum benefits in the Danish and Swedish schemes has tended to produce less differentiation in benefits. Until recently the state heavily subsidized the insurance scheme, which reduced the contributions paid by workers. The subsidies encouraged widespread coverage, lowered the barriers to access caused by contribution requirements, and minimized the problem of wasted contributions—paying contributions but failing to qualify for benefits.

An additional commonality has been adequate minimum benefits—or the provision of basic security. Danish minimum benefits in the form of assistance have been more generous than in many other countries. Until the late 1990s Swedish minimum benefits were roughly 60 per cent of the median income. The generosity of minimum benefits in Sweden and Denmark, with the exception of introductory benefits for immigrants, contrasts with those in the liberal regime countries, while their higher utilization rates contrasts with the conservative corporatist countries. Compared to both the liberal and conservative regime countries, means-tested benefits in Sweden and Denmark have been more effective in lifting beneficiaries over the poverty line (Sainsbury and Morissens 2002).

Finally, the retrenchment strategies of Sweden and Denmark differed from those of the conservative and liberal regime countries. In the two social democratic countries, services—especially for children—expanded during periods of welfare state downsizing; both were reluctant to make cuts in services. In contrast to the liberal countries Sweden and Denmark adopted across the board cuts in transfers. Although Sweden and Denmark have increased contribution requirements for benefits as a retrenchment strategy, they have generally not engaged in the elaborate differentiation of insurance requirements pursued by the conservative corporatist countries.

Turning to the major dissimilarities between Denmark and Sweden, what impact have differences had on immigrants' social rights? As noted earlier, one of Sweden's claims to a stronger universal policy stance than other countries involved the introduction of child allowances, available to all children, in 1948. Simultaneously tax deductions for children were eliminated. The allowance was viewed as the child's benefit and promoting the well-being of all children, thus making it more difficult to deny the benefit to immigrants. By contrast, Denmark did not introduce universal child allowances until 1967; its first postwar scheme of family support, introduced in 1952, and subsequent schemes involved means testing. Child allowances have generally been more contentious in Denmark, and popular support has been lukewarm (Goul Andersen 2007, 2008).

A second difference has been the development of a combination of flat-rate benefits providing basic security and earnings-related benefits providing income security in Sweden. This construction survived when maternity benefits were converted into parental benefits. Thus parental benefits have been available to both working parents and parents who are not in the workforce, although benefits have been much more generous for working parents. As a result, nearly all mothers, including immigrants, have received parental benefits in Sweden. On average, however, foreign born mothers, especially those from Africa and Asia, have received lower benefits (Duvander and Eklund 2006: 45, 54). Foreign born mothers were more likely to receive flat-rate benefits because they were not employed, and when they received earnings-related benefits their benefits were lower than Swedish born mothers because of poorer pay. In sum, the universalism of the Swedish welfare state has promoted widespread coverage that has encompassed immigrants. Its downside has been a differentiation in benefit levels with immigrants from certain countries receiving lower benefits. Danish maternity and parental benefits have required an attachment to the labor market (NOSOSKO 2010: 38–9), and immigrant women's lower labor market participation rate has affected their access to these benefits. Although immigrant women of color have a higher birthrate than Danish women, they were less likely to receive maternity benefits (Pedersen 2000: 171).

By contrast, Danish policies' special claim to universality has been the prominence of flat-rate or equal benefits. Even earnings-related schemes that compensate for loss of earnings have tended to provide de facto flat-rate benefits, such as the Danish ATP pension, unemployment, sickness, and parental benefits. As a result, when immigrants have received benefits, there has been little differentiation in benefit levels of non-citizens and citizens.

An additional divergence has concerned the role of contributions in determining eligibility to benefits. Paradoxically, since general revenues have constituted a larger share in the funding of Danish social provision, contributions appear to be a greater barrier to entitlement in Denmark. Particularly worrisome for immigrants are requirements stipulating payment of contributions for a specific number of years, which are likely to exclude them, such as the 30-year requirement for an early retirement allowance or the 40-year requirement for full ATP benefits. Conversely, work tests, minimum earnings requirements, and contribution requirements were generally modest in the Swedish work-related insurance schemes, and most contributions were eliminated in the mid-1970s. Then there were no contributions for public pensions, health insurance, sickness compensation, and parental benefits. Thus immigrants in Sweden did not confront the problem of wasted contributions or paying a disproportionate share of their earnings as contributions typical of the insurance schemes in both the liberal and conservative corporatist regime countries.

A final difference has been a much stronger legacy of means testing in Denmark and its linkage with citizen benefits. The Danish trajectory of means testing entailed eliminating stigma through an expansive approach that made the benefits available to all citizens. The coupling of means testing to citizen benefits seems to have been a source of the reluctance to extend family benefits, pension benefits, and long-term assistance to non-citizens. By contrast, the strategy of the Swedes in reducing the stigma associated with assistance has been to introduce new benefits, such as unemployment support (KAS), asylum seekers benefits, introduction allowances, and most recently elder allowances. Swedish policy makers have been generally unwilling to assign more weight to means testing, viewing it as a departure from universalism. Still once immigrants have gained entitlement to benefits, means testing and its greater prominence in Denmark have often promoted their claim to benefits.

Lastly, residence as a basis of social entitlement, in theory, is inclusive because eligibility encompasses all residents. Nonetheless, as we have seen, residence can also serve as a basis of exclusion by distinguishing between permanent and temporary residents or by imposing residence requirements for eligibility to benefits. Although the residence requirement for the basic pension was regulated by social legislation, curtailment of social rights via residence requirements has frequently occurred through immigration legislation and changes in the incorporation regime.

Incorporation regimes

A major development in the incorporation regimes of the two countries has been increasing divergence with respect to citizenship acquisition and permanent residence status, and the trend accelerated in the 2000s. Sweden has modest naturalization requirements; over time the Swedes have relaxed requirements through eliminating economic self-sufficiency as a condition and allowing dual citizenship. Eligibility to register to become a citizen has also expanded. By contrast, Denmark has multiplied naturalization requirements and increased their stringency. The Danes had the most rigorous requirement of non-utilization of assistance benefits to become a citizen— six months during the past five years. They have also limited registration to become a citizen, first to persons with no criminal record and then to Nordic citizens. Changes in the nationality law so that naturalization is the main route to Danish citizenship have also entailed an economic self-sufficiency requirement for second generation immigrants similar to the one in Germany.

These differences have reflected deliberate policy goals: to make citizenship an available option for newcomers in Sweden, and to reduce the number of naturalizations in Denmark. These policy goals have been reflected in the two countries' naturalization rates: the Danish naturalization rate was only 33 per cent in the mid-2000s—or roughly half the Swedish rate (Sainsbury 2005). In short, the Swedish rules for becoming a citizen were the most generous among the countries in this book, while the Danish requirements had become the most stringent at the close of the 2000s.

Acquiring permanent residence status has also become increasingly difficult as Denmark moved from a modest to an extremely stiff residence requirement for a permanent permit and added several new requirements. Likewise when the Danes reintroduced labor immigration, they adopted a selective approach closer to Germany than to Sweden. Favorable entry and permit conditions have existed for occupations with labor shortages, corporation employees with special skills or qualifications, and persons with high incomes, initially an annual income of 450,000 Danish crowns (approximately €60,000) later lowered to 375,000 Danish crowns (nearly €50,000). Denmark also adopted strict transitional rules for citizens of the new EU member states after the 2004 enlargement, limiting their access to benefits (Vad Jønsson and Petersen 2010: 199). Although settlement status in Sweden was less likely to be granted immediately in the 2000s compared to earlier, its attainment has not been encumbered by multiple requirements that resemble those to become a citizen, such as integration and language tests as well as specific requirements of economic self-sufficiency, which France, Germany, the UK, and Denmark have introduced.

On other policy dimensions of the incorporation regime, such as the introduction of participatory rights, anti-discrimination policies, and settlement policies or integration measures, there are several similarities between Denmark and Sweden. These similarities often contrast with the policies in the liberal and conservative corporatist regime countries. Both Sweden and Denmark granted local political rights to *all* immigrants, although this has remained a contested issue in Denmark, and the Danes raised the residence requirement in 2010. Germany and France have resisted the introduction of such rights, and it was in the face of much opposition that these rights were introduced to citizens of the member countries of the EU, in accordance with the Maastricht Treaty. In the UK, Commonwealth immigrants as British subjects were granted equal political rights as were the Irish and then EU citizens but there has been no discussion of political rights for immigrants generally, and in the US it has been a dead issue. Despite a number of local campaigns for immigrant voting rights, the entrenched view in the US has been that citizenship confers the right to vote (Hayduk 2006).

In the case of anti-discrimination policies, the initial response of Sweden and Denmark was closer to the conservative corporatist countries. Sweden and Denmark incorporated anti-discrimination provisions into the criminal code; but they, and especially Sweden, were quicker to realize the weaknesses of relying on the criminal code as the main legal instrument to combat discrimination than Germany and France. Both Sweden and Denmark introduced anti-discrimination legislation in the early 1990s. Important Swedish–Danish contrasts have been a much stronger emphasis on positive measures in Sweden and the creation of the anti-discrimination commissioner in the mid-1980s, whereas Denmark was slower to create state agencies to handle complaints of discrimination and into the late 1980s it pursued a criminal code approach in combating discrimination (Vad Jønsson and Petersen 2010: 185).

Looking more closely at the integration policies and introductory programs that developed during the 1990s, the main similarities between Denmark and Sweden are: the types of measures in the introductory programs, the encompassing scope of participants, the mode of delivery through the strong involvement of the municipalities, and state financial aid to program participants. In several instances these similarities also stand out in comparison with the liberal and conservative corporatist regime countries. For example, the Danish and Swedish programs have had a strong component of labor market training, participants have been encouraged to develop individual plans, the programs have been free of charge, and they have been available for family members and have provided welfare benefits.

Nevertheless, several differences between Denmark and Sweden are noteworthy, and they impinge on immigrants' social rights and prospects of inclusion. From the outset, Danish introductory benefits were deliberately set at a lower rate than regular assistance, thus differentiating between the social rights of non-citizens and citizens. Further strengthening this differentiation, immigrants were denied access to regular assistance for seven years, and now they must also fulfill a work test of two and half years of full-time employment. In Sweden local governments have had the option to provide an introductory allowance and determine its amount, which led to variations for immigrants living in different municipalities, but non-citizens and citizens have equal entitlement to social assistance. To eliminate the local variations in introductory benefits, the government in 2010 proposed a standard introductory benefit more generous than the social minimum provided by assistance. A second major difference is that completion of the introductory program is a requirement for a Danish permanent residence permit—but not in Sweden. Finally, and extremely important, the utilization of introductory, rehabilitation, and assistance benefits has blocked or delayed becoming a Danish citizen. The naturalization requirements concerning the use of assistance have become so stringent that in the late 2000s, *six months* of assistance during the last five years disqualified a newcomer from citizenship (MFII 2008). In other words, participation in the *three-year* introductory program with the explicit purpose of integrating immigrants simultaneously worsens their possibility of inclusion by becoming citizens and thus attaining equal status and equal benefits conferred by citizenship.

A further contrast concerns the vision of the society into which immigrants are incorporated. Although the goals of Danish and Swedish integration policies have a strong participatory thrust, the Danes have emphasized that the introductory program should convey Danish values that immigrants are expected to embrace. As part of the integration process, immigrants must sign a declaration, pledging to work for the integration of oneself and family members and active citizenship in Danish society. The declaration resembles a loyalty oath, and it involves a commitment to fundamental Danish values. It also includes the obligation to learn Danish, to support oneself and family members as soon as possible, to see that one's children learn Danish and to cooperate with day care centers and the school, and to combat terrorism (EI 2010). The Swedish goals of integration policies stress "a social community based on diversity and the development of a society characterized by mutual respect and tolerance, in which everyone irrespective of background takes part and is jointly responsible" (SOU 1996:55; Prop. 1997/98: 16, quotation p. 1). Although democratic values and liberties are mentioned, they have not been exclusively identified as Swedish values. Introductory courses on Swedish society have been seen as a vehicle to enhance participation by strengthening immigrants' knowledge and thus their participatory resources (SOU 2010:16, p. 23). Nor have newcomers been required to sign an integration pledge or contract.

In the late 2000s Denmark had one of the lengthiest bans on regular assistance benefits—seven years—of our countries. Still the Danes have not banned newcomers from all means-tested and non-contributory benefits as the Britons did—or all major federal means-tested benefits as the Americans did. Furthermore, during the ban of assistance benefits, newcomers receive introductory benefits. Admittedly introductory allowances have been pegged at a much lower level than assistance, but newcomers are not entirely deprived of social benefits during their first years in the country. Regular assistance benefits are off-limits, and introductory and rehabilitation benefits can affect permanent residence status and citizenship acquisition but all other benefits have been available to immigrants.

In conclusion, the comparison of Sweden and Denmark underlines the importance of distinguishing between the impact of the welfare regime and the incorporation regime on immigrants' social rights, and not simply assuming that restrictions on immigrants' social rights stem from the defining properties of the welfare regime. Likewise the Swedish–Danish comparison reveals that an inclusive welfare state regime does not necessarily lead to an inclusive incorporation regime. The comparison further warns against generalizing the experiences of a country representing a specific welfare regime type to other countries with the same regime. Welfare and incorporation regimes can vary independently of each other and changes in their policy dimensions can move in an inclusive or an exclusionary direction. Finally, the comparison points up the significance of the interface between social policies and immigration policies. In Denmark cuts in immigrants' social benefits have been inextricably bound to the immigration policy goal of reducing the flow of "non-Western" immigrants, whereas so far no such linkage has existed in Sweden.

6

Immigrants' Social Rights across Welfare States

Diane Sainsbury and Ann Morissens

After having mapped out the formal social rights of immigrants in our six countries, a series of crucial issues focusing on substantive or effective rights must be addressed. Most central are two questions. The first is: to what extent have immigrants' formal rights been translated into substantive rights in terms of receiving benefits? The second is: how do the substantive rights of newcomers compare with those of citizens? The preceding chapters have pointed to a deterioration in immigrants' social rights and many examples of newcomers and ethnic minorities having poorer access to social benefits and lower benefits than others. This chapter offers a systematic cross-country comparison of the quality of the social rights of immigrants and citizens. We use three gauges to assess the quality of social rights: decommodification, the utilization of rights in relation to needs, and the stratification of rights.

The chapter is structured in the following way. We first discuss our three gauges of the quality of social rights. The second section deals with the data, methods, and operationalizations used in our study. Subsequently we analyze the outcomes for immigrants and citizens. To capture the impact of the ethnic/racial dimension produced by immigration, we also deal with the outcomes for visible ethnic minorities who have come as immigrants.

Quality of social rights

In assessing the quality of social rights in his three types of welfare state regimes, Esping-Andersen has utilized decommodification as a major yardstick. He defines decommodification as the ability to enjoy a socially acceptable standard of living independently of market participation (1990: 37). The concept of decommodification, however, is marred by a fundamental difficulty—its dual meaning. In a narrow sense, decommodification presupposes commodification, that is, one's labor power has become a commodity by virtue of being sold on the labor market. In Esping-Andersen's words, "the concept of decommodification has relevance only for individuals already fully and irreversibly inserted in the wage relationship" (1999: 45). Decommodification conceptualized in this manner may be of less relevance to some immigrants and ethnic minorities. Many immigrants have a hard time finding employment or they have a weak attachment to the labor market. Furthermore, just as in the case of women, policies that "commodify" immigrants— that is, policies that improve their access to paid work—can be a useful strategy. However, a narrowly conceived notion of decommodification diverts attention from this course of action. An additional problem is that Esping-Andersen's operationalization of decommodification may be misleading in the case of immigrants and ethnic minorities. His decommodification scores for different countries are based on data for the average production worker in a highly paid manufacturing sector (1990). The scores might indicate the quality of the social rights of this type of worker but the question remains whether they sum up the quality of immigrants' or ethnic minorities' social rights.

In a broad sense, Esping-Andersen notes that decommodification occurs when a service is rendered as a right, when rights are not granted strictly on the basis of performance, and when a person can maintain a livelihood without reliance on the market (1990: 21–2). It is in this sense that we use decommodification, and we define an acceptable standard of living in minimal terms—a standard above the poverty line. This sort of conceptualization offers a useful lens in analyzing the situation of immigrants. It allows us to examine to what degree welfare states provide immigrants, and especially those outside the labor market, the possibility of a socially acceptable life.

Our second gauge is the utilization of benefits in relation to a variety of needs. The purpose of social provision has been to protect individuals and families from a range of contingencies, such as old age, sickness, disability, unemployment, extra costs of bringing up children, and poverty or low income. We assess the quality of social rights in terms of the availability of benefits when individuals and families find themselves in such situations of need. To measure use of benefits in relation to needs we can compare the utilization rates of pensions with the number of elderly, the receipt of unemployment benefits among the unemployed, etc. Our procedure differs from studies that have focused on the composition of beneficiaries of specific social programs (Pedersen 2000; Nielsen 2004; Goul Andersen 2007). These studies report the share of immigrants among beneficiaries compared to the native population but do not consider utilization in relation to need.

The third gauge is stratification. Esping-Andersen argues that although the welfare state affects structures of inequality, it also constitutes a system of stratification. He maintains that a particular pattern of stratification is associated with each regime (1990). In the liberal regime social policies lead to a series of dualisms that stratify the population into the poor and non-poor. The stratifying effects of the conservative corporatist regime have been to reinforce traditional status relations. The emphasis on universalism in the social democratic regime minimizes the stratifying effects of social policy. Our approach is more open-ended and focuses on the stratifying effects of conditions of eligibility and benefit levels. Conditions of eligibility stratify persons in terms of whether or not they are entitled to particular benefits, and different benefit levels result in a stratification of beneficiaries.

In summary, on the basis of these gauges we pose the following major questions regarding immigrants' substantive social rights. First, how decommodifying are social policies for immigrants and ethnic minorities in different types of welfare states? Or put differently, what role do social policies play in aiding immigrants and ethnic minorities to maintain an acceptable standard of living? Do benefits have different decommodification levels for immigrants and citizens? Second, are immigrants more or less likely than citizens to receive benefits when they experience various types of need? Third, what are the stratifying effects of social policies for immigrants and ethnic minorities? And are they the same for immigrants and citizens?

Data, definitions, and methods

Our analysis is based on the *Luxembourg Income Study Database* (LIS), utilizing the most recent available wave for 2004–5.[1] LIS is a cross-national database with detailed information about the sources of household income in approximately 35 countries. Because the main income variables—disposable income, gross income, and market income—are harmonized, LIS is a very useful data bank for analyzing poverty, distribution of income, and income inequality across countries. By providing information about who receives social transfers and how much they receive, LIS also furnishes possibilities to go beyond formal rights and assess substantive or effective social rights.

However, the possibilities for identifying immigrants in the LIS data are limited, and comparability among the countries and over time is far from ideal. The LIS data sets contain three variables that can be used to identify the immigrant and ethnic population. The first variable is the ethnicity/

---

[1] For more information about the *Luxembourg Income Study Database*, consult <http://www.lisdatacenter.org>.

nationality of the head of the household, and the second is the immigration status of the head of the household. Unfortunately there is no uniformity in the country data sets regarding the inclusion or content of these variables.

In the US data set the immigration status of household head variable contains the following categories: native born, foreign born naturalized citizens, and non-citizens. The ethnicity variable mixes race and ethnicity. It distinguishes between Black, Hispanic, Native American/Eskimo, Asian/Pacific Islander, and White. The 2004 data set also includes the year of arrival, but no information about the country of origin of the immigrant is available. For three of our European countries—Germany, France, and Sweden—the data sets contain more information on nationality and immigration status, making it possible to establish the country of origin. This information has been used to select the main ethnic minority groups in these countries when the analysis deals with ethnicity and race.

The Danish and British data are the most problematic. Changes in the 2004 Danish data set have eliminated the possibility of analyzing the ethnic dimension. The nationality variable, which previously contained country of birth, has been reduced to three categories: Danish nationals (limited to native born citizens), first generation immigrants, and second generation immigrants. An additional consequence is that it is no longer possible to identify naturalized citizens.

For the UK there is only an ethnicity variable and no variable for immigration status. As in the US case, the British ethnicity variable conflates race and ethnicity. It consists of the following categories: White, Black-Caribbean, Black African, Black-other, Pakistani, Bangladeshi, Indian, Chinese, Asian-other, Other, and Mixed. We use ethnicity as a proxy for immigration. This use is justified not only because the ethnic groups are the result of immigration but primarily because members of the ethnic groups are much more likely to be born overseas. The 2001 census revealed that the white population is overwhelmingly born in Britain (95.2 per cent), while a large share of the other ethnic groups is foreign born (Morissens 2006a: 54). Accordingly, the white category serves as the non-immigrant group in our analysis, even though EU citizens and other "white" immigrants are likely to be represented. Similarly, the other ethnic categories represent the immigrants despite a number of British born who are likely to be included in the sample. Given all these difficulties, the results of our analysis must be treated with caution.

The analysis here examines the outcomes for five types of households:

- citizen households, defined as households comprised of native born citizens,
- immigrant households, consisting of all foreign born households,
- naturalized immigrant households,

- non-citizen immigrant households, and
- ethnic minority immigrant households, comprised of visible minorities.

In the case of ethnic minority immigrant households we have data for only four of the countries. The Danish data contain no information on ethnicity. For the UK the immigration status of ethnic minority households is unknown, and we report the findings for all ethnic minority households rather than ethnic minority immigrant households.

The measurement of poverty constitutes a central aspect in our operationalization of decommodification—the ability to enjoy a socially acceptable standard of living independently of the market. We define an acceptable standard of living as a standard above the poverty line, and adopt a relative approach in measuring income poverty amongst immigrants and citizens. This means that poor households are defined as those households that have a disposable income below a certain threshold representing the level of well-being of the population in a specific country. As in many comparative studies, we use 50 per cent of the median income adjusted to family size as the poverty line. To adjust for family size, we employ the OECD equivalence scale.[2]

All households have been included in the analysis in order to illuminate the full decommodification capabilities of the welfare states. The decision to include the entire population and not to limit selection to working age households has important implications for our results regarding the incidence of poverty and poverty reduction effectiveness. Our analysis encompasses pensioners, and their incomes differ from those of working age persons because of the importance of social benefits.[3] In addition, the age structure of the immigrant populations differs from that of the citizen populations. Generally the immigrant population has been younger with fewer pensioners. However, this is changing as the immigrants who entered the countries in the 1960s and 1970s reach retirement age. In fact, elderly immigrants appear to be much more vulnerable to poverty than elderly citizens in most countries.

To measure the decommodifying effects of social policies (transfers and taxes), we use the relative poverty reduction effectiveness scores. Compared to the decommodification scores used by Esping-Andersen, relative poverty reduction effectiveness scores have two major advantages. First, his scores are based on model recipients—the standard production worker in several OECD countries. Accordingly, his scores reflect a major weakness of the model

[2] The OECD equivalence scale, used in the analysis, assigns a value of 1 to the first adult in the household, a value of 0.7 to any additional adults, and a value of 0.5 to each child. Different equivalence scales can produce substantial differences in poverty rates, and this appears to be particularly the case for immigrants when household size differs from the average. For an example, see Berthoud (1998: 39–42).

[3] For analyses of immigrant and citizen households limited to the working age population, see Morissens (2006a, 2006b).

recipient approach; they are based on hypothetical recipients, whereas we examine the economic outcomes of actual beneficiaries. Second, his scores assume commodification and underestimate or ignore the decommodifying effects of means-tested schemes.

The relative poverty reduction effectiveness scores measure the extent of poverty reduction through the percentage of pre-transfer poor lifted above the poverty line by transfers and taxes. To compute the scores we compared the economic situation of households before transfers and taxes and after transfers and taxes, using the following formula:

Pre taxes and transfers poverty rate – post taxes and transfers poverty rate/Pre taxes and transfers poverty rate * 100 (Mitchell, 1991: 65).

The poverty rate based on market income is used as a measure for the pre taxes and transfers situation. Market income is comprised of earnings and salaries, income from self-employment, and returns on capital. The poverty rate based on disposable income adjusted for family size serves as a measure for the situation after transfers and taxes. The difference between the two provides a measure of the effectiveness of transfers in lifting people above the poverty line, and the decommodifying effects of social policies. By comparing immigrant and citizen households we can shed light on the question whether transfers and taxes have a different impact on their economic situation—and accordingly whether the decommodifying effects are different.

Social rights and decommodification

Formal social rights do not guarantee decommodification, that is, an acceptable standard of living independent of the market. In this section, we examine decommodification in relation to immigrant and native citizen households across the six welfare states. As a first step, we determine the incidence of households having a socially acceptable standard of living, that is, the proportion of households above the poverty line. Obviously this outcome is the combined result of market income and social benefits. To disaggregate the effects of the two, we analyze the impact of social policies on household income using relative poverty reduction effectiveness scores. In this way we can establish the role of these policies in reducing poverty or, conversely, in maintaining a socially acceptable standard of living. Next we examine the poverty rates of households by major source of income—market income and social transfers. This provides another measure of decommodification by indicating the likelihood of being at risk of poverty when social transfers are the main source of livelihood compared to earnings.

The proportions of households with a socially acceptable standard of living are reported in the upper section (A) of Table 6.1. Looking at the first two columns that present the percentages of all households and native born citizen households, the overall picture corresponds fairly well with the expected performance of the three welfare regime types. The highest proportion of households enjoying an acceptable standard is found in the countries representing the social democratic welfare regime, followed by the conservative corporatist regime countries, with lower proportions in the liberal regime countries. Turning to the various types of immigrant households, we find that they are less likely to be above the poverty line than native born citizen households across welfare regimes. The disparities increase for non-citizen immigrant households and for visible ethnic minority households. It is also worth noting that in none of the countries do naturalized citizen households achieve parity with native born citizen households, although in the US they nearly do.

As can be observed in the lower section (B) of Table 6.1, significant proportions of immigrant households are below the poverty line, and this is more pronounced for non-citizen and ethnic minority immigrant households. These results suggest that both immigrant status and ethnicity/race are associated with a higher risk of poverty. In the US case the data allow us to separate ethnicity and immigration status. They show that ethnic and racial minorities have higher poverty rates than whites, but households in most ethnic/racial categories, including whites, headed by a non-citizen immigrant have higher poverty rates than households headed by a citizen in the same category. The main exception is native born African Americans who together with Indians have the highest poverty rates among native born ethnic minorities. By contrast, foreign born blacks, both naturalized and non-citizens, have lower poverty rates.

Across the countries there is substantial variation in the poverty rates—ranging from roughly 15 per cent to over 30 per cent for non-citizen immigrant households and ethnic minority immigrant households. The pattern of variations largely conforms to expectations based on levels of decommodification by welfare regime type, although there are considerable differences between the two liberal regime countries.

Decommodification and poverty reduction

So far we have established that significant differences exist between citizen and immigrant households in maintaining a socially acceptable standard of living. Now we turn to the decommodifying effects of social policies based on relative poverty reduction effectiveness scores. To what extent have social

Table 6.1. Households above and below the poverty line. Percentages

Country	All households	Native citizen households	Naturalized immigrant households	All immigrant households	Non-citizen immigrant households	Ethnic minority immigrant households
A. Households above the poverty line. Percentages						
United States	83.2	84.9	83.0	74.4	67.8	73.2*
United Kingdom	89.7	90.7	—	—	—	79.2**
Germany	92.3	93.2	87.1	85.6	84.0	75.3
France	91.3	92.8	83.3	80.2	78.8	80.0
Sweden	95.2	96.4	90.5	88.4	83.8	81.0
Denmark	95.4	96.2	—	85.6	—	(81.4)***
B. Households below the poverty line. Percentages						
United States	16.8	15.1	17.0	25.6	32.2	26.8*
United Kingdom	10.3	9.3	—	—	—	20.8**
Germany	7.7	6.8	12.9	14.4	16.0	24.7
France	8.7	7.2	16.7	19.8	21.2	20.0
Sweden	4.8	3.6	9.5	11.6	16.2	19.0
Denmark	4.6	3.8	—	14.4	—	(18.6)***

Notes:
— Data unavailable.
* Taking the ethnic minority population without reference to immigration status, that is, operationalizing ethnic minority households in the same way as the UK, the respective percentages are 72.3 and 27.7.
** Refers to ethnic minority households with unknown immigration status.
*** The percentages are calculated using Danish Register data for 2002. The ethnicity variable also differs from the other countries by including East Europeans whose poverty rate was lower than those of visible minorities (Morissens 2006a: 127, 134). For Sweden, using this operationalization, the percentages were 82.4 and 17.6.

Source: Luxembourg Income Study; own calculations.

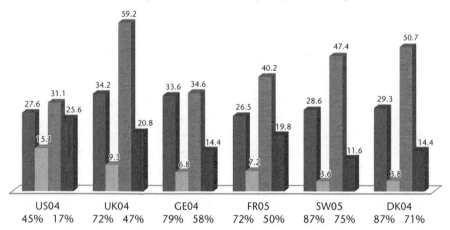

Figure 6.1. Pre- and post-transfers and tax poverty rates for native citizen and immigrant households.

benefits pulled pre-transfer poor households out of poverty across welfare regimes?

Figure 6.1 presents the pre- and post-transfers and taxes poverty rates of native born citizen households and immigrant households and the relative poverty reduction effectiveness scores for each type of household. The percentages at the bottom of the figure are the poverty reduction scores, and they tell us the proportion of the pre-transfer poor that was lifted above the poverty line via transfers after taxes.

A comparison of the poverty reduction scores indicates that transfers had greater decommodifying effects for citizens than for immigrants in all the countries. Across the welfare states the decommodifying effects ranged from 45 per cent to 87 per cent for citizen households and from a mere 17 per cent to 75 per cent for immigrant households. In other words, social policies lifted between 45 per cent and 87 per cent of the pre-transfer poor citizen households and between 17 per cent and 75 per cent of the immigrant households above the poverty line. An inspection of Figure 6.1 also discloses appreciable differences in the scores for immigrants and citizens in each of the countries. Although they are not included in Figure 6.1, we have also calculated the poverty reduction scores for non-citizen immigrant households and naturalized immigrant households. Their scores reveal a split pattern in decommodifying effects that exists across welfare states. The scores of non-citizen immigrant households are lower than those for all immigrant households; the lowest score was 10 per cent and the highest score 68 per cent. By contrast, the scores of naturalized immigrant households were higher than all immigrant households, ranging from roughly 30 per cent to nearly 80 per cent. However, in no case do the decommodifying effects for naturalized immigrants match those for native born citizens—and the gap was widest in Germany, followed by France. In short, not only are citizens more likely to be above the poverty line, if citizens are poor before transfers they are more likely to be lifted above the poverty line compared to immigrants irrespective of whether they are citizens or non-citizens.

However, the decommodifying effects of social policies, as measured by the relative poverty reduction effectiveness scores in Figure 6.1, broadly cluster according to welfare regime type.[4] In the two liberal regime countries the scores are generally lower than those of the other countries, but the United States is an outlier because of its poorer performance in lifting both citizen and immigrant households over the poverty line. Transfers did very little to alter the poverty status of immigrant households, while benefits aided 45 per cent of citizen households. By comparison, in the United Kingdom the poverty reduction score for immigrants (48 per cent) was higher than the US score for citizens, while the British score for citizens was slightly over 70 per cent. Although the British score for citizens was the same as the French score, it was lower than the score for citizens of our other conservative corporatist regime country (roughly 80 per cent) and the scores of the social democratic regime countries (over 85 per cent).

The gap in poverty reduction for citizens and all immigrants, as expressed in the percentage differences in decommodifying effects of transfers and taxes, also corresponds to the regime type. The gap was widest in the liberal regime countries (28 per cent for the US and 25 per cent for the UK), followed by the conservative corporatist countries (22 per cent for France and 21 per cent for Germany), and it was narrowest in the social democratic countries (16 per cent for Denmark and 12 per cent for Sweden).

---

[4] In Morissens and Sainsbury (2005), the results for Denmark deviated sharply from the expectations based on the type of welfare state regime, and they contrasted with the Swedish results. Data idiosyncrasies appear to account for the differences. The 1997 Danish data set, which we used, was later recalled by the Danes, and subsequent waves have eliminated the ethnic variable so it is impossible to replicate that part of the analysis. Other analyses (FM 2004: 17; Morissens 2006a) present results that are closer to those reported in this chapter, but, using Danish register data for 2002, Morissens also found higher poverty rates among non-Western immigrants, with Somalis having the highest poverty rate (37 per cent) (see also Blume et al. 2005). Although data problems no doubt have influenced the results in our article, two important changes in Danish policy may also have contributed to the different results. First in 1995 the Danes admitted approximately 20,400 asylum seekers but in the mid-2000s the number had fallen to around 1000 annually. Second, the unemployment rate among immigrants peaked at roughly 40 per cent in the mid-1990s (Nannestad 2004: 761), and it had declined to roughly 15 per cent in the early 2000s.

On the other hand, the gap in poverty reduction for the white population and ethnic minority immigrants does not conform to regime type. The
differences in decommodifying effects were widest in Germany (40 per cent),
followed by the US (30 per cent), the UK (25 per cent), France (20 per
cent), and Sweden (14 per cent). Moreover, the gap in the effects of policies
reducing poverty was wider in relation to visible minorities and the white
population than in the case of native citizens and immigrants.

Decommodification without market participation

Our final measure of decommodifying effects rests on the broad conceptualization of decommodification—the ability to enjoy a socially acceptable standard of living independent of market participation. In effect, it offers a litmus
test of decommodification by establishing whether welfare states provide
persons outside the labor market the possibility of a decent standard of living.
This type of comparison also controls for the importance of the disadvantageous position of many immigrants on the labor market, which may account
for the higher poverty rates of immigrant households. Furthermore, a
comparison of the poverty rates of households reliant upon transfers with
those dependent upon earnings can elucidate another aspect of decommodification—the lack of a penalty for exiting the market.

Figure 6.2 sets out the poverty rates of native citizen households and immigrant households by main source of income. The upper graph presents the
rates for households whose main income is earnings, and the lower graph the
rates for households whose main income is transfers.

Unsurprisingly in all countries households whose main source of income is
earnings are much more likely to enjoy an acceptable standard of living
compared to those where benefits make up the bulk of their income. However,
immigrant households with earnings consistently have higher poverty rates
than citizen households, and non-citizen immigrant households have the
highest poverty rates. Especially in the US and the UK, a large portion of
immigrant households is below the poverty line in spite of earnings, suggesting poorer pay or a weaker attachment to the labor market, even though in the
US immigrants have a higher labor market participation rate than natives.

Turning to households whose main source of income is social transfers,
citizen households have lower poverty rates than immigrant households in
all countries. In other words, there are considerable gaps between citizen and
immigrant households in enjoying an acceptable living when their main
source of income is transfers. However, in the social democratic regime
countries the poverty rates for citizen and immigrant households are much
lower than in the other countries, and here there is a smaller penalty for
exiting the market for both citizen and immigrant households compared to

Poverty rates native and immigrant households with earnings as main source of income

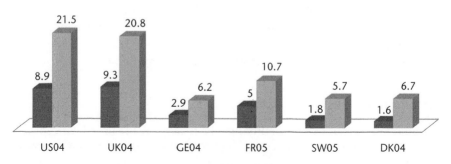

Poverty rates native citizen and immigrant households with transfers as main source of income

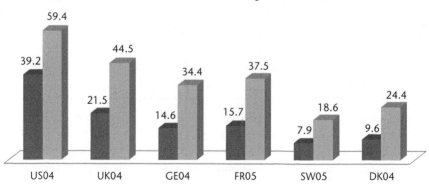

Figure 6.2. Poverty rates of native citizen and immigrant households by main source of income.

the other types of welfare states. Households in Sweden and Denmark irrespective of their main source of income stand a better chance of being above the poverty line. At the other extreme, households in the United States regardless of their type of main income run a higher risk of being poor, and despite this they also face a very stiff penalty if they leave the market. In the remaining countries there is a high penalty for exiting the market, and it is considerably higher for immigrant households (Figure 6.2).

With respect to regime types the decommodification of native citizen and immigrant households largely conforms to expectations, as does the performance of the United States as an outlier. The two liberal countries exhibit the highest poverty rates and the least decommodification. Furthermore, the poverty rates of both citizen and immigrant households in the US ranked highest, followed by the UK. Although Germany approximates the social democratic countries when the main source of income is earnings, Germany and France cluster together with regard to households whose main source of income is benefits. The poverty rates of citizen households were 15–16 per cent and those of immigrant households ranged from 34 to 38 per cent. The lowest poverty rates were in the two social democratic regime countries where citizen households' rates were 8–10 per cent and immigrant households' rates were 19–24 per cent.

To sum up, the decommodifying effects of social policies are different for native citizens and immigrants across welfare states. Overall citizens are more likely to enjoy a socially acceptable standard of living than immigrants. If citizens fall below the poverty line prior to transfers, they are more likely to be lifted out of poverty by social benefits than immigrants. Finally citizens confront a lower penalty if they are outside the labor market; citizen households whose main source of income is transfers are much less likely to be at risk of poverty compared to immigrant households.

Social rights and needs

The quality of social rights can also be assessed in terms of receiving benefits in relation to one's needs. Since the LIS data focus on income formation, we must limit the analysis to participation in the core programs of income maintenance. How do immigrants' social rights compare those of citizens in terms of receiving benefits in relation to their needs?

Table 6.2 shows the participation of citizen and immigrant households in several major transfer programs, as reflected in their utilization rates. It needs to be underlined that the important comparisons are among households in the same country and not across countries. Inequivalencies make cross-country comparisons hazardous.

An inspection of family benefits discloses that immigrant and citizen households with minor children have very similar rates, except for France and the UK. The lower participation of French citizen households is due to the particular construction of family benefits: to be eligible, a family must generally have two children, and several benefits are income tested. In the UK, immigrant families have a lower utilization rate than citizen families. Newcomers have been barred from non-contributory benefits, and the major family benefit is of this type. Still immigrants and citizens have high utilization rates, and nearly all families receive benefits.

Pensions display a pattern of lower immigrant participation rates compared to citizens in all the countries. Immigrant households are even more disadvantaged in the case of unemployment benefits. The utilization rates show

Table 6.2. Participation in social transfer programs by type of household (utilization rates)

	Family benefits % households with children	Pensions % elderly households	Unemployment benefits* % unemployed households	Social assistance** % households
United States				
Citizens	n/a	86.6	27.6	2.2
Immigrants	n/a	72.3	21.4	2.2
Non-citizens	n/a	57.4	17.5	2.6
Ethnic Immigrants	n/a	68.1	22.5	2.4
United Kingdom				
Citizens	96.6	98.9	68.9	7.4
Immigrants	88.5	92.7	63.6	13.2
Germany				
Citizens	98.4	94.7	28.0	1.5
Immigrants	98.2	94.6	24.2	2.9
Non-citizens	97.7	92.8	14.9	2.9
Ethnic Immigrants	98.3	—	—	5.0
France				
Citizens	60.4	94.5	23.9	2.4
Immigrants	64.4	89.6	16.7	7.4
Non-citizens	61.6	93.0	14.8	8.3
Ethnic Immigrants	62.0	—	—	6.5
Sweden				
Citizens	94.9	99.5	41.4	2.4
Immigrants	95.5	97.4	25.0	13.4
Noncitizens	95.9	92.7	24.0	18.7
Ethnic Immigrants	96.2	—	—	43.7
Denmark				
Citizens	94.4	92.0	78.1	5.9
Immigrants	92.7	82.3	60.7	25.9

Notes: — Data unavailable or numbers too small for reliable estimates.
n/a Not applicable.
* Refers to unemployment insurance benefits except for the UK which includes both the insurance and means-tested components of the job seeker allowance.
** Refers to the major safety net benefit.
Source: Luxembourg Income Study; own calculations.

that a larger proportion of citizens consistently receive unemployment benefits than immigrants, despite the higher unemployment rates of immigrants. Conversely, social assistance is utilized less by citizen households than immigrant households. Where we have data for ethnic minority immigrant households, they tend to exhibit a higher utilization rate than immigrant households in general. The utilization rates reported in Table 6.2 are for the major safety net benefit. Utilization rates for means-tested benefits reveal a similar pattern but with much higher utilization rates for all households. The rates of citizen households ranged from 14 to 32 per cent and those of ethnic minority immigrant households from 35 to 80 per cent (Morissens and Sainsbury 2005: 650).

The pattern of utilization that emerges in Table 6.2 underscores two points. Immigrant households are less likely to receive standard benefits than citizen households in relation to their needs in the case of old age and unemployment. Even though immigrants might receive a larger share of unemployment benefits than citizens, a smaller proportion of unemployed immigrants enjoy benefits compared to unemployed citizens. Second, immigrants' higher utilization of assistance benefits is related to their lower recipient rates of other standard benefits.

Social rights and stratification

Stratification focuses on differentiation or inequalities in social rights. In our approach, welfare state stratification results from, first, inequalities in access or participation in social programs and, second, inequalities in benefits. In this section we examine differences in the access and participation patterns of citizens and immigrants in social transfer programs and in benefit levels.

Table 6.2 reveals that there are stratifying effects in immigrants' access to pensions and unemployment benefits, but not to family benefits. In the case of pensions, citizens' participation is nearly universal, followed by less participation of immigrant households, and even lower participation by non-citizen and ethnic minority immigrant households across countries. The reverse was true in the case of assistance. Citizens participate least, while immigrants generally have higher participation rates, with a further increase for non-citizen and ethnic minority immigrants.

To what extent do benefit inequalities between citizen and immigrant households exist? To explore this issue we examine the benefits paid to citizen and immigrant recipients. Table 6.3 reports the average payments in the currency of the country. Immigrants' benefits tend to be lower for pensions. Although unemployed immigrant households are less likely to receive unemployment benefits, those households that did receive benefits had higher benefit levels than citizen households in the US, Germany, France, and Denmark. It is also worth noting that even though benefit levels are similar for family benefits or slightly higher for immigrant families, benefit inequalities may exist because immigrant families on average have more children.

In our earlier study (Morissens and Sainsbury 2005) we found that means-tested benefits played a larger role in the income packages of non-citizen immigrants compared to those of citizens. However, in all countries, with the exception of the US and the UK, the share contributed by other social transfers equalled or exceeded that of means-tested benefits.

Looking specifically at the importance of means-tested benefits for ethnic minority immigrant households' income packages for countries where we had

Table 6.3. Benefits levels in social transfer programs by type of recipient household. Average (mean) amount of payment

	Family benefits	Pensions	Unemployment benefits	Social assistance*
United States				
Citizens	n/a	16,840	4273	3519
Immigrants	n/a	14,691	4956	4278
Non-citizens	n/a	12,724	5258	4424
Ethnic Immigrants	n/a	13,936	5151	4158
United Kingdom				
Citizens	1344	6385	2504	4726
Immigrants	1457	5528	2421	5582
Germany				
Citizens	3218	17,623	5729	4068
Immigrants	3614	14,359	8270	5197
Non-citizens	3621	13,652	7913	6407
Ethnic Immigrants	4025	—	—	5690
France				
Citizens	2722	16,446	6319	3942
Immigrants	3658	13,864	6408	4528
Non-citizens	3728	13,490	4248	4762
Ethnic Immigrants	3625	—	—	4171
Sweden				
Citizens	20,147	174,941	66,731	29,458
Immigrants	22,598	159,141	52,644	58,445
Non-citizens	21,151	138,651	47,167	64,895
Ethnic Immigrants	22,760	—	—	71,147
Denmark				
Citizens	20,608	116,255	95,383	58,203
Immigrants	24,311	97,948	98,893	89,944

Notes: — Data unavailable or numbers too small for reliable estimates.
n/a Not applicable.
* Social assistance refers to the major safety net benefit.
Source: Luxembourg Income Study; own calculations.

data (Denmark, France, and Sweden), we found that means-tested benefits comprised a larger portion of their income packages than these benefits did in the income packages of all immigrants. In the most extreme cases in Sweden and Denmark means-tested benefits comprised between 40 and 50 per cent of their income packages. Nonetheless, other social transfers also made an important contribution to these households in the three countries. For the US our data revealed discrepancies between citizens and immigrants with regard to the contribution of regular social transfers to household income. For immigrant blacks, Hispanics, and Asians, other social transfers were a much smaller share of their income package than for citizens in the same ethnic group (Morissens and Sainsbury 2005: 651–3).

In conclusion, an important dimension of stratification has to do with the differential capacities of social programs in maintaining a socially acceptable standard of living—or preventing a dualism between the poor and the non-poor. Our analysis discloses such a dualism. There is a higher incidence of immigrant households below the poverty line compared to citizen households, and non-citizen and ethnic minority immigrant households are usually even more vulnerable to poverty.

Examining participation in a variety of transfer programs, we have found a differentiated pattern for citizens and immigrants with the exception of family benefits. Immigrant households have less access to unemployment benefits and pensions. Conversely there is greater utilization of social assistance by immigrants, and means-tested benefits form a larger component in their income packages compared to citizens. The pattern was more pronounced for visible minority immigrants. To the extent that social assistance is associated with stigma and inadequate benefits, the quality of immigrants' social rights suffers and there is no parity with citizens' social rights. Furthermore, the larger role of means-tested benefits in immigrants' income packages, together with higher utilization rates, across welfare regimes does not fully square with Keith Banting's line of argument (2000) about the prominence of means-tested benefits and heavier reliance of immigrants on these benefits in the liberal regime countries. Major differences exist between the income packages of citizen and immigrant households along with their utilization of means-tested benefits in the two social democratic regime countries. For many immigrants the stratifying effects of social policies run counter to the minimal stratification that supposedly typifies the social democratic welfare regime.

Immigrant households across welfare states have less access to major insurance benefits, and their pension benefits are also lower, reflecting poorer earnings. Larger social assistance payments and family benefits to immigrant households offset inadequate insurance benefits, but not completely as evidenced in their higher poverty rates.

Conclusions

In contrast to the widespread assumption in the international migration literature that there is little difference in the social rights of citizens and immigrants who are legal residents, the preceding analysis has found major disparities in the substantive social rights of immigrant and citizen households across welfare states. Furthermore, discrepancies widened with respect to non-citizens and immigrants of color. Compared to citizens, immigrants are less likely to enjoy a socially acceptable standard of living even when the market is the main source of their income. They are less likely to be pulled out of poverty by transfers, and when benefits are their main source of income they run a greater risk of being poor than citizens. Immigrant households are less likely to receive benefits in relation to their needs compared to citizens;

when they belong to groups that are vulnerable to poverty, immigrant households have higher poverty rates than the citizen households in these groups.

Equally important, the analysis underlines that immigration is a source of differentiation in social rights. Table 6.1 revealed that, irrespective of welfare state regime, immigration status influences the likelihood of being poor. The foreign born are at higher risk of being poor than native born citizens, and even naturalized citizens failed to close the gap between native born citizens. Most vulnerable are immigrants who are non-citizens. Not only is the likelihood of poverty differentiated along these lines, so are the decommodification levels of social policies. In short, a new pattern of stratification related to immigration and citizenship status emerges, and it largely cuts across welfare states.

Another aspect of stratification related to immigration is the differentiation in formal rights associated with different entry categories. These rights are hierarchically structured. Recognized refugees, co-ethnic citizens, and EU citizens are privileged, while family members, asylum seekers, and undocumented immigrants are often disadvantaged. Unfortunately the LIS data offer few possibilities to explore this sort of stratification, but the earlier chapters point to its potential impact on immigrants' substantive social rights.

A final type of stratification is the ethnicization and racialization of social exclusion defined in terms of poor employment opportunities (reflected in poverty rates based on market income) and poverty status (reflected in post-transfer and taxes poverty rates). This phenomenon occurs across welfare regimes in the five countries for which we have LIS data on ethnicity and race, and Ann Morissens (2006a) found a similar pattern for Denmark. In many instances, immigration status and being a member of a visible minority interact: ethnic minorities have higher poverty rates than the white population and the foreign born have higher poverty rates than the native born. Furthermore, the decommodifying effects for visible minorities were smaller than those for the white population, that is, social transfers were less effective in lifting them out of poverty. Failure to reverse this pattern is likely to entrench and strengthen socio-economic divisions along ethnic and racial lines.

Despite these commonalities, important variations exist between the countries representing different welfare regimes. Although weaker for immigrants, the decommodifying effects of social policies for citizens and immigrants correspond to expectations based on welfare regimes. The US is an extreme case with its poor overall performance in poverty reduction, and it has the highest poverty rate for non-citizens. Nevertheless, the US and the UK cluster together in significant ways with regard to immigrants' social rights. Both liberal regime countries distinguished themselves from the other regime countries by their higher poverty rates among immigrants having earnings as their major source of income and the very high poverty rates among immigrants whose main source of income is transfers. By contrast, the decommodifying effects of policies in the social democratic regime countries are greater for immigrants and non-citizens, and as a result they have substantially lower poverty rates, especially compared to immigrants and non-citizens in the liberal regime countries but also in the conservative corporatist countries. The differences between the poverty reduction scores of citizens and immigrants were narrowest in the social democratic regime countries and widest in the liberal regime countries. Perhaps most striking, and indicative of the decommodifying capacity of welfare state policies in Sweden and Denmark, is the lower poverty rates of citizens and immigrants when transfers are their main source of income compared to the other regime types. Still the poverty gap between native born citizens and immigrants in Sweden and Denmark is notable (4 per cent versus 12 per cent in Sweden and 4 per cent versus 14 per cent in Denmark). Swedish and Danish policies do an excellent job in keeping native citizens out of poverty, but only a good job when it comes to immigrants.

In conclusion, the analysis in this chapter demonstrates that the type of welfare state regime has major consequences for immigrants' social rights and economic well-being. Although the stratifying effects of welfare regimes tend to fall apart when immigrants are included in the analysis, the dissimilar decommodifying effects of welfare state regimes remain robust. These differences are of utmost importance to the quality of immigrants' social rights, newcomers' ability to enjoy a socially acceptable standard of living, and their social inclusion.

Part II
The Politics of Inclusion and Exclusion

7

Introduction to Part II

As distinct from Part I where the analysis dealt with policy outcomes in terms of immigrants' formal and substantive social rights, the focus now shifts to politics in order to understand policy variations. It examines the politics of inclusion and exclusion, analyzing the hows and whys of policy outputs in the six countries. It looks at the interface of the politics of social and immigration policies. As documented in Part I, immigrants' social rights are shaped by welfare state regimes through specific social policies, entry categories regulated by international agreements and national legislation, and immigration policies. In other words, changes in immigrants' social rights require that we analyze the politics of social and immigration reforms. If we were only to consider how changes in social policies affect immigrants' entitlements, we would miss a major source of the deterioration of their social rights in many of the countries. Accordingly, analyzing the politics of inclusion and exclusion requires a dual focus on (1) the politics of social rights extension and contraction and (2) changes in the policy dimensions of the incorporation regime that impinge on immigrants' social rights and their prospects of inclusion or exclusion.

Theoretical perspectives

Again the literature on welfare regimes and immigration regimes and their explanations of regime variations provides a useful starting point. A common denominator in the two bodies of scholarship is an emphasis on historical legacies as a source of differences. The welfare regime literature stresses the ideological legacy and its importance in shaping contemporary policy decisions (Esping-Andersen 1990), whereas the immigration literature has attached weight to the legacy of distinctive conceptions of nationhood (e.g. Brubaker 1992; Hansen 2000).

The two research traditions diverge markedly, however, in their view of politics as a determinant of regime variations and the extension of rights. They differ not only about the importance of politics but also about the type of politics, and *it is in this area that the two can fruitfully complement each other*. The discussion of welfare regime variations has assigned much more significance to politics. Central to the discussion has been the power resources approach, which highlights social classes as collective actors and major agents of social change. The approach views the balance of class power as decisive to redistributional outcomes (Korpi 1980). In this view, class mobilization, class alliances, and the relative strength of parties of the left, center, and right largely determine welfare regime variations. The welfare regime literature and power resources approach have paid little attention to state actors and bureaucratic politics. Essentially, the dynamics behind the expansion of rights is "politics from below."

The international migration literature has tended to stress that expansive policies result from limiting the scope of conflict and the roster of participants. In an influential article, "Modes of Immigration Politics in Liberal Democratic States," Gary P. Freeman (1995) proposes a general model based on actors' calculations of the costs and benefits of immigration. He hypothesizes that public opinion is rationally ignorant because of the high costs of securing information. The costs are increased by serious barriers to acquiring information about immigration and the constrained boundaries of legitimate discussion of immigration policy. Consequently, opinion is slow to mobilize, even if preferences are for a more restrictive policy. Political parties promote consensus on immigration policy and attempt to keep the issue off the public agenda. Freeman further argues that the calculus of interest group politics and group mobilization is characterized by diffuse costs and concentrated benefits, resulting in client politics. The calculus provides greater incentives to those who benefit from immigration—employers, businesses, and ethnic groups making up the flow of immigrants—to organize than to persons who bear the costs. The immediate costs fall upon the minority of the population who compete with immigrants, but they are poorly organized and lack political resources. Otherwise the costs fall upon the population as a whole. In this model state actors are elected officials who make the policy. Following their self-interest to be re-elected, they respond to the better organized interest groups, and the politicians act in accordance with a strong "anti-populist norm" that they should not use racial, ethnic, or anti-immigration related arguments to win votes. In summary, the typical mode of immigration politics is client politics where politicians and a narrow circle of well-organized and intensely interested groups craft policies, largely insulated from outside interference.

Subsequent theorizing emphasized that the courts and bureaucracy are the major political agents operating in the direction of inclusion, and that the politics of rights expansion are relatively closed and an elite affair. Christian Joppke (1999, 2001) underlines the importance of constitutional politics and the legal process in understanding the expansive and inclusive nature of immigration politics in liberal democratic states, and he argues that independent and activist courts are critical to the expansion of immigrant rights. Virginie Guiraudon (1998, 2002) concludes that the courts and administrative agencies in charge of immigrant affairs have promoted the extension of rights, emphasizing that the decisions were made behind closed doors. She further argues that the electoral arena is characterized by "a self-reinforcing negative dynamic between the press, public opinion and electioneering politicians" (1998: 292). As distinct from the welfare regime scholars, the perception that "politics from above" is the driving force behind expansive policies pervades much of the international migration literature. The most extreme version claims that democratic politics in the form of parties and elections are not the friend but the foe of inclusion.

Thus the two research traditions differ radically in the importance they assign to political parties. In the power resources approach the partisan composition of government is a crucial determinant, if not the decisive factor, shaping policies. By contrast, the international migration literature and national case studies frequently note partisan agreement and left–right alliances on the immigration issue (Tichenor 2002: 35). Policies extending immigrants' rights have been introduced by left and right governments—or conversely both have introduced restrictive legislation (Hammar 1985; Guiraudon 1998, 2000b, 2002; Joppke 1999; Hansen 2000). Since mainstream parties are perceived as having similar stances on immigration and immigrant policies, they are not conceived as a variable determining policy outputs. On the other hand, the international migration literature has increasingly come to focus on extreme right-wing and anti-immigration parties and their political consequences (Schain et al. 2002; Koopmans et al. 2005; Schain 2007; Messina 2007). In sum, the role of political parties, with the exception of far right parties, has been largely missing in the international migration literature.

Furthermore, in Freeman's model, parties are individual elected officials primarily interested in re-election. Indeed, initial criticisms of the model centered on the treatment of parties and the strength of the anti-populist norm that keeps immigration policies out of electoral politics. One line of argument complained that the anti-populist norm was not conceptually derived from the model, that restrictive appeals were not confined to fringe parties but were voiced by major European parties, and that it was a crucial empirical question to investigate the extent of the norm's presence across countries (Brubaker 1995: 907–8). The second line of criticism underlined the centrality of parties in European politics and party incentives for politicizing or depoliticizing the immigration issue. Ted Perlmutter (1996) proposed to amend the discussion of parties by interjecting the importance of the left–right ideological dimension in shaping policies and the relationship between the parties and the political system in determining their preferences for a closed or open arena of policy debate. A difficulty of his typology, however, is its assumption that pro-system parties prefer a closed arena, which precludes politicization of immigration and immigrant policies by mainstream parties. More recent theorizing has focused on party strategies and the structure of party competition in influencing whether or not a party politicizes the issue (Bale 2003, 2009; Meguid 2005, 2008; Green-Pedersen and Krogstrup 2008).

Finally, comparing theorizations on both sides of the Atlantic reveals different emphasis. A major difference concerns who are identified as the critical actors. American theorists, as exemplified by Freeman and his model, have often included ethnic mobilization and immigrant organizations among the key actors, whereas immigrants are either missing or viewed as uninfluential in many European discussions (e.g. Guiraudon 1998: 276–8; Statham and Geddes 2006: 56). Instead recent European theorizing has focused on the courts and bureaucracies, while the bureaucracy and administrative politics have been undertheorized in the American literature. Europeanists also argue for bringing parties back into the analysis of immigration and immigrant policies. Second, there is an imbalance in focusing on the politics of either exclusion or inclusion, with more attention to the politics of exclusion in the European context at the expense of the politics of inclusion. Again, as in the case of the major theoretical perspectives of the welfare state and international migration literature, a well-rounded approach requires a synthesis of the insights of both sets of theorists.

Studying the politics of inclusion and exclusion

The past two decades have witnessed conscious efforts of theory-driven comparisons, and this theorizing has identified a number of crucial factors that serve as markers in my analysis of the politics of inclusion and exclusion. I deal with the politics behind the policies affecting immigrant rights, and the focus is the policy process. Building on previous research, my account of the politics of rights extension and contraction in the six countries highlights (1) issue framing, (2) institutional arrangements, policy venues, and policy coalitions, (3) the territorial dimension, (4) political parties, and (5) the nature of immigrant organizing and penetration of the policy process. For each analytical component I develop a set of research questions to explore the importance of these factors in formulation of policies shaping immigrant rights in the six countries.

Framing

Framing is a crucial element in the policy process; it involves both problem construction and justification. Problem construction often determines the policy venue and the relevant policy network. Thus framing establishes who should have jurisdiction over an issue and formulate solutions. Shifts in framing and problem construction can also dictate a change in the policy venue and the roster of participants. Framing and the politics of justification can influence the scope of support for policies, mobilizing both backers and opponents, and thus have an impact on alliance building and policy coalitions. To illustrate, framing of immigrant policies in terms of social or economic integration instead of cultural integration makes a difference. In the case of social or economic integration, the main policy venue is the ministry of social affairs or the ministry of labor, whereas cultural integration entails a different policy venue. My research questions here are: *What have been the major frames of immigrants' social rights and immigrant policies more generally? What impact have they had on immigrant rights? How has framing influenced the policy venues?*

Policy venues

In analyzing the rights extension process, policy venues and institutional arrangements have been assigned major importance. Using the notion of "policy venues" or alternatively, "institutional venues," Guiraudon (1998, 2002) underlines the critical nature of the locus of policy decisions. She defines policy venues as the "institutional locations where authoritative decisions are made concerning a given issue." A particular venue has its own rules of the game, priorities, and privileged set of actors. For example, in legislative settings, negotiation, compromise, and reciprocity are prized, while the principal norms in bureaucratic venues are expertise, rational procedures, and impartiality (1998: 293–5, quotation p. 293; Baumgartner and Jones 1993: 32). This theorizing alerts us to the importance of examining institutional arrangements as sources of variation in outcomes within and across countries.

More specifically, Guiraudon presents what might be called the policy venue thesis. She argues that bureaucratic and judicial venues have been especially favorable in granting rights to immigrants primarily because these sites are insulated from public view and pressure. This claim represents a substantial expansion on Tomas Hammar's observation of the prominence of administrative politics in the areas of immigration and immigrant policies and the tendency of legal and administrative decisions to supplant political decisions (1985: 279, 289). The conclusion that bureaucratic and legal "venues are systematically biased toward extending rights to aliens" (Guiraudon 2002: 139) is based on the experiences of three nations—France, Germany, and the Netherlands—and the claim needs to be re-examined and evaluated using a wider range of countries. Furthermore, Guiraudon's aim is to explain the extension of social rights with no attention to their contraction. In testing the policy venue thesis I examine the politics of both successful and failed cases of social rights extension. *What policy venues have been in charge and what impact do policy venues have on immigrant rights?*

The territorial dimension

The territorial dimension involves two components and the interplay between them. The first is the distribution of powers and responsibilities between the levels of government and its relationship to social and immigrant policies. What level/s is/are responsible for formulating these policies, and for implementing and financing them? The territorial dimension exists in both unitary and federal states but, as we shall see, they can offer different opportunity structures for the proponents and opponents of immigrant rights. The second element is the pattern of immigrant settlement and the degree of immigrant concentration, which varies across countries, with the United States and the United Kingdom exhibiting high levels of concentration (OECD 2004: 95). Equally important is how immigrant settlement is mapped on to local and regional political jurisdictions, the political clout of subnational institutions in relation to national institutions, and the linkages between local politics and national politics. More generally, it has been hypothesized that decisional powers at the local level and decentralization work against the social rights of immigrants and minorities (Wilensky 1975; Lieberman 2005: 59–60).

The territorial dimension requires us to rethink the cost–benefit calculus. Because immigrants are often concentrated in specific areas, the costs may not be as diffuse as Freeman's client politics model assumes (Brubaker 1995). In fact, Jeannette Money (1999: 60) argues that competition over resources in localities with high concentrations of immigrants can alter the calculus of immigration policy leading to a restrictive rather than an expansive policy. In revisiting his model, Freeman (2002) acknowledges the spatial component. If immigration results in concentrated cost and diffuse benefits, the mode of politics would involve a higher level of political conflict and restrictive outcomes.

In theorizing the importance of the territorial dimension and the cost–benefit calculus I apply them to an analysis of immigrant rights, not to immigration policies. The cost–benefit calculus of social policies and the policy dimensions of the incorporation regime is not necessarily the same as that of immigration policies. In the calculus of settlement policies, as in the case of social policies (Freeman 2001: 83, 2006: 30), costs and benefits can be concentrated. However, because of the territorial dimension, the cost–benefit calculus of immigrants' social rights cannot be assumed to be the same as the calculus for the population as a whole. Finally, in the case of anti-discrimination policies, both the costs and benefits can be diffuse. The key research questions here are: *When and how does the territorial dimension promote the extension or contraction of immigrants' social rights in our six cases? Does decentralization adversely affect their social rights?*

Political parties

In accord with the welfare regime theorists who assign a major role to political parties, the analysis here brings parties back into focus and makes their importance a major empirical concern. Parties matter in three significant ways. First, they are a major actor in the framing of issues and policies. In other words, political parties through framing can influence public opinion and voters' perceptions. The relationship between public opinion and parties is interactive and not unidirectional; it is not limited to public opinion influencing the actions and preferences of parties. Second, winning elections and vote maximization are crucial to parties, and one strand of the literature on parties and immigration emphasizes the electoral politics as a source of policy change (Money 1999; Tichenor 2002; Schain 2008: 21–8). Third, and most important in my analysis, political parties are crucial in formulating policies and are key actors in the policy process. Of prime significance are the partisan composition of government, the degree of fragmentation of the party system, and the structure of party competition.

Furthermore, recent research has moved beyond an exclusive focus on far right anti-immigration parties, arguing that the role of mainstream parties is generally underestimated and that their strategies determine the success of anti-immigration parties (Bale 2003, 2009; Meguid 2005, 2008, Green-Pedersen and Krogstrup 2008). One line of argument has stressed that center-right parties require examination because they are often in government and these parties have had restrictive stances of immigration and integration, in line with their traditional positions on law and order, low taxes, and national security (Bale 2009: 5). Parallel with this development, a number of scholars have documented the importance of the left–right dimension among parties in determining positions on immigrant policies especially with regard to immigrant rights and citizenship policy (Gimpel and Edwards 1999; Joppke 2003; Lahav 2004: 134; Givens and Luedtke 2005; Hix and Noury 2007;

Howard 2009). In examining immigrants' social rights and the interface between social and immigration policies, the left–right dimension is likely to assume fundamental significance. My key research questions concerning political parties are: *What evidence do we find for Freeman's anti-populist norm thesis that mainstream parties do not politicize immigration and immigrant issues in election campaigns? How important are left–right differences in politicizing these issues in elections and in shaping policies affecting immigrant rights?*

Immigrant organizing and penetration

Much research on immigration in the European countries has played down the political influence of immigrants (e.g. Guiraudon 1998: 276–8; Money 1999: 55; Södergran 2000; Songur 2002). The main arguments have been that immigrants lack political rights, they are minorities, and they have fewer political resources compared to the majority population. The European literature that has analyzed immigrant politics in a comparative perspective has tended to concentrate on ethnic mobilization, immigrant organizing, claim-making, and protests (e.g. Ireland 1994; Koopmans and Statham 2000; Koopmans et al. 2005). I propose a broader conceptualization of immigrant politics. Rather than confining immigrant politics to ethnic mobilization and claims, we should consider the policy process and the "politics of presence," which redirects attention from the "what" to the "who" in representative politics (Phillips 1995). Consideration should not be confined to elected positions but include appointed posts, such as members and experts of government inquiry commissions and positions in government and the state administration. We should also investigate the extent of ethnic penetration of the political parties. In short, the analysis needs to examine immigrants' penetration of the policy process and the potential policy impact of immigrant participation. *To what extent and how have immigrants penetrated the policy process and to what effect?*

In summary, drawing on comparative welfare state research and the international migration literature I identify several crucial determinants of variations in policy responses. I examine the policy making process with reference to these determinants, and the analysis illuminates the degree of their importance across the six countries. This allows me to address two problems in the existing literature. First, the existing theoretical propositions have been influenced by the national contexts specifically studied. A major question is the extent to which they are artifacts of the cases selected for study or whether they have broader relevance. The coming chapters offer the possibility of assessing the theoretical assumptions and conclusions across the six countries. Second, the focus of several international migration and ethnic relations studies has been on policies with much less attention to politics behind the policies (Aleinikoff and Klusmeyer 2002; Boeri et al. 2002; Tranæs and

Zimmermann 2004; Guild et al. 2009; Carmel et al. 2011). My analysis seeks to rectify this shortcoming.

The policy decisions examined constitute the most important legislation affecting immigrants' rights identified in Part I. My examination utilizes process tracing in the formulation of policies. Process tracing has several advantages. It can detect possible variations in seemingly similar phenomena and identify combinations of political factors that produce specific policy outputs. Process tracing has the potential to unearth significant factors that are not immediately apparent. It also highlights sequencing and thus aids the analyst in ruling out factors that come into play after the event. Finally process tracing makes specific cases more comprehensible.

My methodology combines a case study approach with a comparative strategy. For each country I trace the rights extension and contraction processes, and I compare the politics of the two countries representing the same welfare regime. Each pair of countries presents a distinctive puzzle. In the liberal regime countries, the policy outputs worsening immigrants' social rights have been quite similar, but process tracing reveals quite different politics behind the policies. Furthermore, in terms of several components of my analytical framework, the United States and the United Kingdom differ hugely. The comparison of the liberal regime countries provides an instructive example that cautions against assuming that similar policies emerge from approximately the same politics, but it also helps us to pinpoint a major explanation. The conservative corporatist countries adopted several similar policies but they also diverged in their policies affecting immigrants' social rights. The comparison of France and Germany focuses on their differing policy responses and explains why they differed. The policies of the two social democratic countries, whose institutions and social policies have many commonalities, have moved in opposite directions during the past two decades. Several policy dimensions of the Danish incorporation regime have become increasingly exclusionary and have impinged on immigrants' social rights, whereas the Swedish incorporation regime remained quite encompassing and citizenship policy became more inclusive. Here the comparison seeks to understand the different policy trajectories affecting immigrant rights in Sweden and Denmark. The final step of my analysis is a comparison across all six countries.

Overview of Part II

The chapters in Part II are again structured by welfare regime type, comparing the policy processes of the countries in each regime pair. Chapter 8 examines the politics of inclusion and exclusion in the liberal regime countries (USA and the UK), Chapter 9 the conservative corporatist countries (Germany and France), and Chapter 10 the social democratic regime countries (Sweden and Denmark). The chapters provide an in-depth analysis for each of the six countries. I analyze the political forces of inclusion contra exclusion in the six countries, concentrating on key actors in the policy process, including the bureaucracy and the courts.

Chapter 11 compares the importance of the components of my analytical framework in shaping immigrant rights across the six countries. I return to my major research questions and synthesize the evidence from the analysis of the individual countries. I also discuss the extent to which the analysis here confirms or differs from earlier research and its theoretical claims.

8

Liberal Welfare States and the Politics of Inclusion and Exclusion

In examining the politics of inclusion and exclusion in the two liberal regime countries this chapter focuses on the changes in immigrants' social rights in the United States and the United Kingdom. In the US the politics of inclusion and exclusion have centered on the extension and contraction of immigrants' welfare rights. In Britain the universalism of the early postwar welfare state encompassed all residents so that immigrants were eligible for most benefits. Thus the politics of inclusion have been less concerned with the extension of social rights to immigrants but rather with strengthening their social rights through anti-discrimination legislation.

A common denominator of the rights contraction process in the liberal welfare states has been a focus on means-tested benefits. The retrenchment strategies of both countries aimed at cutting means-tested benefits for citizens and non-citizens alike. In the 2000s newcomers in the US and the UK confronted a four-to-five-year ban on utilizing means-tested benefits and in many cases even longer. Because of the prominence of means-tested benefits in the social provision of the liberal regime countries, the bans have been particularly damaging, and in the UK the ban has been extended to non-contributory benefits and tax credits.

Despite similar policy outputs, the politics of exclusion have been quite different in the two liberal welfare states, as revealed by process tracing and the components of my analytical framework. I initially deal with the politics of inclusion and exclusion in the United States and then in the United Kingdom. The concluding discussion summarizes the contrasts and similarities in the politics of exclusion in the two liberal welfare states.

The United States: The swift rise and fall of immigrants' welfare rights

In an international context, two aspects of the development of immigrants' social rights in the US stand out. The first is the fragile nature of their welfare rights, which is most apparent in their swift rise and fall and the disentitlement of immigrants with legal residence status. The second is the peculiar connection between means-tested and social insurance benefits. All six countries have either barred non-citizens or continue to bar them from means-tested assistance, but US law makers took the unprecedented step of making social insurance contributions an eligibility requirement for means-tested benefits for legal alien residents.

The standard description of the US political system as highly fragmented with abundant veto sites, prone to gridlock and the status quo, suggests a puzzle in understanding the swift rise and fall of immigrants' welfare rights. In unraveling this puzzle the first step is tracing the extension of immigrant rights, paying special attention to framing, policy venues and coalitions, the territorial dimension, the political parties, and ethnic mobilization and penetration of the policy process. I then move on to the politics of rights contraction and partial restoration. Finally I sum up the insights provided by my analytical framework that help us to understand the trajectory of immigrants' social rights in the United States.

The politics of extending welfare rights to immigrants

The politics of rights extension provide several clues to understanding the fragility of immigrants' social rights. An important feature is the lack of a single trajectory; the politics varied according to entry category. Bureaucratic politics in the executive branch were initially decisive to refugees' rights, whereas judicial and congressional politics shaped the welfare rights of other immigrants. Framing, policy networks, the involvement of activist coalitions, and the degree of partisan conflict also differed. These differences require that we examine refugees, legal alien residents, and undocumented immigrants separately.

REFUGEES' RIGHTS AND THE 1980 REFUGEE ACT
The first newcomers to receive federal welfare assistance were refugees, fleeing from communist regimes during the Cold War. Policy makers framed this aid as part of America's tradition as a humanitarian sanctuary, particularly for those who sought refuge because of their political and religious beliefs. That the refugees were opponents of communism heightened their deservingness.

Cold War rhetoric emphasized that the successful re-establishment of refugees demonstrated the superiority of the political and economic systems of the West compared to those of the Soviet bloc countries (Pedraza-Bailey 1985: 154–5).

The executive branch, in particular the President and the State Department, exercised direct influence over refugee policy through an obscure clause in the 1952 Immigration and Nationality Act. The clause established the power to parole (conditionally admit) any alien to the United States in an emergency or in cases "deemed strictly in the public interest." Repeatedly presidents used the parole power to admit refugees *en masse* to the United States (Freeman and Betts 1992: 82). With each wave of admissions, the President promised settlement aid, which was later formally authorized by Congress. Eventually Congress through the 1980 Refugee Act codified and extended the welfare rights of refugees.

A major catalyst of the 1980 Refugee Act was the desire to eliminate the ad hoc nature of refugee policy and the problems associated with the power of parole. The power created friction between Congress and the executive, which was exacerbated by its frequent use to authorize the admission of Indochinese refugees in the 1970s. Congress also began to confront the Nixon and Ford administrations on human rights issues and their double standard in treating refugees from communist countries positively and rebuffing refugees from other oppressive regimes (Reimers 1985; Loescher and Scanlan 1986).

The stage for reform was set when Jimmy Carter, a Democrat and strong advocate of human rights, was elected President and Senator Edward Kennedy (Democrat-Massachusetts) was appointed chair of the Judiciary Committee and its subcommittee on immigration (Loescher and Scanlan 1986). Kennedy, a liberal activist supporting open immigration policies, succeeded a conservative southern Democrat. The House subcommittee on immigration was also chaired by a liberal, Elizabeth Holtzman (Democrat-New York). This political constellation provided a window of opportunity that existed only during the 96th Congress (1979–80).

With the endorsement of President Carter, Kennedy introduced a bill, which contained the main features of the 1980 Refugee Act (CQA 1979: 329). It called for an increase in the admission of refugees, the termination of the parole power, and the expansion of resettlement aid. The Senate voted overwhelmingly for the bill, but it met stiff opposition in the House of Representatives and was only narrowly approved. The 1980 Refugee Act produced sharp partisan divisions in the House, especially on redistributive issues and the creation of a new welfare agency, the Office of Refugee Resettlement. Voting on the final bill largely followed party lines; around three-quarters of the Democrats in favor and three-quarters of the Republicans against the bill (Gimpel and Edwards 1999: 124–31).

Ethnic minority members of Congress supported the 1980 Refugee Act to a greater extent than white members (Gimpel and Edwards 1999: 132). Both African Americans and Hispanics voted on the basis of promoting equal rights. The Act sought to end the special treatment given to refugees fleeing communism and extended equal rights to all political refugees. Especially important were the differences in the treatment of Cuban and Haitian asylum seekers. The Congressional Black Caucus, which championed the cause of the Haitians, was a key player in the struggle for the equal rights of refugees, seeing it as an extension of the fight for equal rights for blacks (Fuchs 1990: 297–300). The 1980 Refugee Act codified refugees' welfare rights, making them less susceptible to future legislative corrosion, but it did not safeguard their rights from administrative erosion and defunding.

LEGAL PERMANENT RESIDENTS AND THE ENTITLEMENTS
REVOLUTION
Immigrants' gaining access to federal welfare benefits was part of the entitlements revolution from the mid-1960s to the mid-1970s. Entitlements grew through the establishment of new programs and the expansion of eligibility. The social entitlements of legal permanent residents were framed in terms of equal rights and equal treatment, and the deservingness of settlers stemmed from their contributions to society.

Expanding immigrants' entitlements involved both judicial and legislative politics. A 1971 Supreme Court decision improved immigrants' welfare rights at the state level, while an act of Congress set in motion the extension of immigrants' entitlement to federal welfare benefits. The 1971 court decision argued that the states could not bar immigrants from assistance programs because they as persons enjoyed equal protection and due process rights under the Fourteenth Amendment of the Constitution (Joppke 1999: 46). Non-citizens gained access to federal benefits in 1972 when Congress replaced federal-state assistance schemes with a new federal program for the needy elderly and disabled—Supplementary Security Income (SSI)—and legal resident aliens and refugees became eligible for benefits.

The passage of the SSI program and immigrants' entitlements went largely unnoticed. Instead the center of political controversy was President Richard Nixon's proposed Family Assistance Plan, which would have made Aid to Families with Dependent Children (AFDC) a federal program guaranteeing a minimum income in the form of a negative income tax. During congressional deliberations, the bills of both chambers federalized other assistance programs, but they were divided on family assistance. The differences were ironed out by jettisoning the Family Assistance Plan and retaining SSI. Other reforms deflected attention away from SSI (Bowler 1974: 147; Derthick 1990) since it was only one of several major changes contained in the 1972 Social Security Amendments.

Refugees gained entitlement to regular welfare programs largely on the coat tails of legal alien residents. Senator Lawton Chiles (Democrat) from Florida—then the state with the highest concentration of refugees—introduced amendments that extended the SSI eligibility to refugees and parolees (Parrott et al. 1998: 4). The amendments were introduced during the final vote on the bill, and his amendments were approved by a voice vote (CQA 1972: 911–13). Without the amendments the states would have had to pick up the whole tab for assistance to elderly, disabled, and blind refugees. The politics of rights extension in this instance deviates from the logic of the concentration of benefits and diffusion of costs in Freeman's client politics model. Instead the concentration of costs and an attempt to spread the costs to the entire nation prompted the amendments.

UNDOCUMENTED IMMIGRANTS, THE COURTS, AND HISPANIC MOBILIZATION

The social rights of undocumented immigrants are extremely tenuous and controversial since their deservingness is tarnished by illegal entry. As law-breakers, opponents dismiss any claim of undocumented immigrants to rights. Defenders argue that, first, they have rights as persons; second, because of their vulnerability, undocumented immigrants require protection; and, third—a variant of the contribution argument—as a hardworking but exploited underclass they should be eligible for benefits. Minimal provisions, such as emergency medical care, have also been justified on humanitarian grounds. An additional justification has stemmed from the broad interpretation of *ius soli* in US nationality law. As parents of US citizens, undocumented immigrants were entitled to benefits for their children.

The courts played a major role in establishing the fledging rights of undocumented immigrants, and Congress made education and health services available to legalizing aliens and emergency medical treatment and nutrition programs available to illegal aliens. Immigrant and ethnic mobilization also promoted the social rights of undocumented newcomers and legalizing immigrants. Focusing on both judicial and legislative politics, Hispanic organizations have pursued a twin strategy of litigation and lobbying.

The first milestone was the 1982 Supreme Court decision in *Plyler* v. *Doe*, and it represented a victory for the Mexican-American Legal Defense and Education Fund (MALDEF) (O'Connor and Epstein 1988). The Court declared a Texas statute denying public education to the children of illegal aliens unconstitutional. In a closely divided decision, the majority argued that the children were innocent and should not be punished for their parents' illegal acts. Although the Court noted that education was not a fundamental right, it distinguished education from other public benefits. Education was essential to the maintenance of democratic institutions and for individuals to "lead economically productive lives to the benefit of us all." The Court also pointed to contributions as a basis of deservingness, observing that undocumented aliens worked, paid taxes, and underused social services (HLR 1983: 1304–30, quotation 1305). Court decisions also made prenatal care and nutrition programs available to pregnant undocumented women on the grounds that their unborn child was a US citizen (Fix and Zimmermann 1994: 279).

The Immigration Reform and Control Act (IRCA) of 1986 had important repercussions for the social rights of undocumented immigrants, and its adoption was a source of protracted controversy. The Act introduced limited amnesty for undocumented immigrants, and it simultaneously extended and restricted their social rights. Disagreement over the amnesty program revolved around eligibility requirements, the costs and funding of the program, and the social rights of legalizing immigrants. The Reagan administration voiced deep concerns about the costs of the amnesty program, and opponents to amnesty stressed that legalizing immigrants would be an enormous burden on the welfare system. The ultimate result was a five-year period of ineligibility for benefits. As in the case of refugees, the amnesty program divided Congress, especially the House, along partisan lines, and non-white members, almost without exception, voted for the amnesty program (Gimpel and Edwards 1999: 137–9, 155–9, 163–7, 169, 175–6).

The Hispanic lobby together with its allies in Congress managed to expand eligibility for the amnesty program and prohibit discrimination on the basis of immigration status. Immigrant groups also monitored the implementation of the legalization program. Faced with a far more liberal amnesty program than he desired, President Reagan turned to administrative politics to achieve what Congress had failed to do. The Immigration and Naturalization Service drew up rigorous eligibility rules to limit legalizations, but immigrant rights groups successfully challenged the rules in the courts (Tichenor 2002: 263–6).

SUMMING UP RIGHTS EXTENSION

Congressional scholars maintain that immigration is a Congress driven policy area (Gimpel and Edwards 1999), and correctly identify the legislature as the major policy venue. Still this view overlooks the importance of both bureaucratic and judicial politics in extending immigrant rights.

The executive branch and bureaucratic politics influenced refugee policy and the most extensive settlement policy measures available to newcomers in the US. Even after the 1980 Refugee Act, the executive branch retained a strong role in admissions and funding refugee resettlement aid. Bureaucratic influence also contributed to newcomers' eligibility for federal welfare benefits. Although Congress granted immigrants' access to these benefits, it seems that Social Security Administration officials were responsible for the inclusion of immigrants in the draft legislation of the SSI program (Bowler 1974; Derthick 1990).

Judicial politics were significant to rights extension in three ways. First, the Supreme Court struck down barriers to legal permanent aliens' welfare rights at the state level. Its ruling against resident and citizenship requirements also facilitated the inclusion of immigrants in SSI. Second, the courts extended access to benefits to immigrants in the twilight zone, such as mothers and children without legal status and aliens with a tolerated status. Third, the judiciary undermined the possibilities of deportation of "public charges" as laid down in immigration law. The courts ruled that non-citizens were liable for deportation *only* if they refused to repay assistance that they were legally obliged to pay (Parrott et al. 1998: 28). Since most assistance programs did not contain such provisions, the court decisions made deportation an empty threat.

The eligibility of immigrants admitted for permanent settlement was a non-issue, while refugees' and legalizing immigrants' entitlements produced serious conflicts between the White House and Capitol Hill. Welfare aid to refugees and legalizing immigrants also fuelled partisan dissension. House votes divided along party lines over assistance benefits for refugees and for legalizing immigrants and their funding. The territorial dimension assumed importance because of the costs of refugees in the immigration states. Legislators from these states attempted to offload the costs through proposals for refugees' access to federal welfare benefits.

There were no advocacy groups outside Congress promoting legal permanent residents' access to welfare benefits, while interest and advocacy groups mobilized around extending rights to refugees and undocumented immigrants. In the 1970s a broad coalition of church and religious groups, immigration lawyers, human rights and civil rights activists, and immigrant and ethnic organizations emerged. Of special importance, Hispanic groups began to try to influence immigration policy and immigrant rights. Rallying around pan-ethnic labels, such as Hispanic or Latino, Spanish speaking minorities joined together in an encompassing coalition. The Congressional Hispanic Caucus, founded in 1976, also provided a focus for lobbying efforts.

The fragmented nature of the politics of rights extension contributed to the fragility of immigrants' social rights. There were relatively few points of convergence and no policy coalition for immigrant rights across entry categories. As a non-issue, the social rights of legal permanent residents generated little opposition but also little enthusiasm. Being a non-issue was an advantage in the extension of rights, but a liability when immigrants' rights came under attack. There were few defenders of the rights of legal permanent residents, and their defenders were divided.

The politics of rights contraction and disentitlement

Almost immediately after the legislation granting non-citizens with permanent residence status access to welfare benefits came into effect in 1974, newcomers' participation in welfare programs was called into question (GAO 1975). Congress introduced the first restrictions in 1980, ushering in a trend of excluding immigrants from federal welfare benefits, which culminated in the 1990s. In 1996 Congress passed welfare and immigration acts that had an enormous impact on immigrants' social rights.

IMMIGRANTS AND "ENDING WELFARE AS WE KNOW IT"
Welfare reform, famously spelled out as "ending welfare as we know it," was a campaign pledge of Bill Clinton during the 1992 presidential election. The main target of reform was the family welfare program (AFDC), but immigrants' benefits were cut as part of the reform. Originally the Personal Responsibility and Work Opportunity Reconciliation Act (PRWORA) of 1996 disentitled most non-citizen beneficiaries, who were legal permanent residents, from major federal means-tested programs—one of the largest disentitlements in welfare history.

The spotlight was not on immigrants but on single mothers and getting them off welfare (Weaver 2000). Immigrants' benefits entered the picture initially as a means of funding the reform. The Clinton administration's 1994 welfare bill proposed to increase sponsors' responsibilities through deeming (attributing the economic resources and income of the sponsor of the entering immigrant, which disqualified the newcomer from means-tested benefits). The bill extended deeming so that newcomers would not have access to the major federal assistance programs (SSI, AFCD, and Food Stamps) for five years, but it retained immigrants' eligibility for federal welfare benefits (Parrott et al. 1998: 6).

The politics of welfare reform and immigrants' benefits changed dramatically with the Republican party's sweeping victory in the 1994 congressional elections, resulting in a majority in both the House of Representatives and the Senate for the first time in 40 years. The House Republicans' bill to overhaul welfare barred aliens from approximately 50 programs, with the exception of refugees and legal immigrants over the age of 75. All other current alien beneficiaries were to be removed from the program rolls one year after enactment (HR 4, January 1995). For the House Republicans, cutting immigrants' benefits was not merely a matter of funding reform but a policy goal.

With their bill, the House Republicans seized the lead, putting the Democrats on the defensive. A major facet of the battle for immigrants' social rights revolved around who were eligible or qualified aliens defined by various criteria of worthiness, such as military service, economic contributions, a severe handicap, and refugee status (Parrott et al. 1998: 7–9). Democrats in both the House and the Senate sought to gain eligibility for legal immigrants who worked and paid taxes. Influential Republicans in the Senate did not share the zeal of the House Republicans in denying legal immigrants welfare benefits. The Senate bill included immigrants who had paid social security taxes for ten years among the aliens who would not lose eligibility to welfare benefits, while the House bill did not (CQA 1995).

Negotiations reconciling the differences between the House and the Senate bills were a Republican affair, shutting out the Democrats (CQA 1995: 7-50-1). The gap between the two bills on legal immigrants' entitlements was wide. Republicans in the House and Senate entertained very different visions of how to limit the entitlements of legal immigrants. House Republicans sought to curtail their access to benefits through changes in eligibility requirements, differentiating between the entitlements of non-citizens and citizens. Moderate Republican Senators proposed an indirect route, strengthening the financial responsibilities of sponsors.

The bill sent to the President for his approval combined the two approaches. It made all non-qualified aliens ineligible for SSI and Food Stamps until they became citizens, and it created a five-year ban for newly arriving immigrants for all other federal means-tested programs but gave the states the option to grant legal aliens eligibility to the new family assistance program (TANF), Medicaid, and federally funded social services. The bill also contained stiffer requirements for sponsors and deeming for future immigrants. After the five-year ban the sponsor's resources could be deemed for most means-tested benefits, and the sponsor's financial responsibility was extended until the immigrant had worked ten years or became a citizen.

In January 1996 President Clinton vetoed the 1995 welfare bill, condemning its cuts in Food Stamps and school lunches and its effects on children and legal immigrants. When in August the President reluctantly signed the 1996 welfare bill, whose non-citizen provisions were nearly the same as the bill he had vetoed earlier, he vowed to change "cuts in programs for legal immigrants that are far too deep" (Parrott et al. 1998: 9, 12).

IMMIGRATION REFORM
Immigration reform came onto the Republican agenda largely because of the belief that it was a vote-winning issue and committee changes in Congress. First, Californian voters in 1994 overwhelmingly supported Proposition 187 to bar illegal aliens from most benefits and services, including school attendance. Its passage brought immigration and immigrant welfare rights to the attention of the nation and demonstrated that restrictions were popular with the electorate. The new Speaker of the House, Newt Gingrich (Republican-Georgia), and other Republicans thought that immigration restrictions could

be used as a "wedge issue" to wean away the support of blue-collar workers from the Democrats in critical states, such as California and Texas. Second, the 1994 Republican election victory brought a change in the leadership of the immigration subcommittees of both chambers. The new chairpersons were restrictionists, who wanted to reduce legal immigration (Gimpel and Edwards 1999: 212–16, 238; Tichenor 2002: 277–8).

The chair of the Senate Judiciary Subcommittee on Immigration, Alan Simpson (Republican-Wyoming), got the ball rolling. His strategy was to combine illegal immigration, immigrants' benefits, and a proposal to reduce legal immigration in a single bill. Simpson's bill defined legal permanent residents as eligible aliens and was thus much less restrictive than the welfare act. On the other hand, the immigration bill put teeth into the existing public charge provisions. The bill also highlighted deeming, which applied to all means-tested benefits until the immigrant became a citizen (S 269).

House Republicans wanted to incorporate a tougher stance on illegal immigrants and sponsors. The most contentious proposal, introduced by Elton Gallegly (Republican-California), permitted states to deny public education to unauthorized alien children. In effect, the measure would have reversed the Supreme Court's decision in *Plyler* v. *Doe*, requiring the states to educate all children irrespective of their legal status. He also presented a controversial amendment requiring that public assistance payments be made to only those personally eligible for benefits, thus foreclosing the possibility of illegal alien parents receiving welfare benefits for their citizen children. The House bill also extended the public charge provisions from five to seven years, and it raised the income needed to sponsor immigrants to 200 per cent of the poverty level compared to the Senate's proposal of 125 per cent. These measures were opposed by the Senate and the White House. President Clinton promised to veto the act if it denied education to unauthorized alien children (Freeman 2001: 72).

With the end of the session rapidly approaching in an election year, the difficulties of the Republicans in reaching agreement gave the President leverage. The White House insisted that the immigration bill be wrapped into the omnibus appropriations bill and stripped of several provisions. Its inclusion in the fiscal 1997 omnibus spending resolution minimized opportunities for obstruction. In a deal between the White House and the House Speaker, Gingrich agreed to lower the sponsor income requirement to 125 per cent of the poverty line, eliminate the stiffer public charge provisions, drop denial of education to unauthorized alien children, and remove a clause that would have denied citizenship to immigrants who utilized assistance benefits for 12 months. The Speaker stood his ground on tougher measures affecting refugees and asylum seekers—provisions on removal, detention, and limited appeals (CQA 1996: 5-16-7; Gimpel and Edwards 1999: 282–3).

In conclusion, there was a clamor to limit immigration in the wake of California's Proposition 187, but the Illegal Immigration Reform and Immigrant Responsibility Act (IIRIRA) of 1996 mainly aimed at preventing illegal immigration and restricting legal and illegal immigrants' access to public benefits. Simpson's proposal to reduce legal immigration went down to a resounding defeat, as did similar provisions in the House immigration bill (Gimpel and Edwards 1999; Tichenor 2002: 283). Observers have likened the passage of Proposition 187 to a political earthquake that sent shockwaves all the way to Capitol Hill, but they have concluded that in the end it did little to inhibit the expansive impulse of immigration policy (Joppke 1999: 55). Looking at immigrant rights rather than immigration policy, the conclusion is quite different. The earthquake was the Big One; welfare and immigration reform transformed the welfare rights of legal immigrants.

The politics of rights restoration

The 1996 welfare act rolled back the social rights of immigrants and represented the nadir in their entitlements. Almost immediately forces were at work to reverse this, and Clinton tied his promise to change cuts in the programs for legal immigrants to his re-election (Freeman 2001: 74). The Democratic party platform condemned cutting off aid to legal immigrants (CQA 1996: D-64), and Clinton renewed his pledge to change non-citizen eligibility provisions in the new welfare act during the campaign.

The Republicans attacked Clinton's immigration record, pointing to his opposition to Proposition 187 and "Republican efforts to ensure that noncitizens do not take advantage of expensive welfare reforms." Their platform lambasted sponsors for failing to provide for the immigrants they bring into the country. It proposed to disqualify undocumented immigrants from benefits for their offspring born in the US, and advocated sharpening the nationality law to deny automatic citizenship to children born in the US of illegal aliens (CQA 1996: D-29). In a bid to win California and the voters of Proposition 187, the Republican presidential candidate, Senator Bob Dole of Kansas, rejected education to unauthorized alien children, and he accused Clinton of weakening the immigration reform.

The Republican strategy did not pay off. Dole failed to win California or the other immigration states—with the exception of Texas. Reprimanding immigrants and excluding them from benefits galvanized the ethnic vote. Exit polls revealed that nationwide over 70 per cent of Hispanics supported Clinton, which was a substantial increase compared to their vote for Clinton in 1992 (Freeman 2001: 75). Exclusion from benefits hit Latinos very hard. Immigrants from Latin American countries comprised over 40 per cent of the non-citizen beneficiaries of SSI scheduled to lose entitlement because of the welfare act (calculated from Parrott et al. 1998: 25).

After his re-election, President Clinton worked to restore welfare benefits, but the Republicans still controlled Congress. He skillfully used omnibus legislation, the veto threat, and measures desired by Republicans, such as a balanced budget and farm subsidies. The restoration of SSI and Medicaid eligibility for all *disabled* legal immigrants who had entered the US prior to the 1996 act was folded into an omnibus spending bill, the Balanced Budget Act of 1997. When the House bill limited eligibility to aliens on the SSI rolls prior to the welfare reform, the President threatened a veto, and the House eventually conceded (CQA 1997: 2-18, 2-50-51). The following year Congress agreed to reinstate eligibility to SSI and Medicaid to *all* persons who had been beneficiaries of SSI (CQA 1998: 20-16).

Clinton also sought to restore Food Stamps to the elderly, disabled, and children who had been dropped from the rolls through the welfare act. He included the proposal in a bill on mandatory spending programs benefiting farmers. The bill was an intricate compromise between the Senate that wanted to promote agricultural research, the White House, the Hispanic caucus wishing to restore Food Stamps to immigrants, and law makers from the farm states seeking aid for crop insurance. Many House Republicans were against any further rollback of the 1996 welfare act. When the Republican leadership called for a vote on the bill without the immigrant provisions, President Clinton promised to veto the bill, and nearly 100 Republicans backed the bill restoring Food Stamps to these groups of previous beneficiaries (CQA 1998: 4-3-9).

Again in 2002 farm legislation altered the welfare act's restrictions on legal immigrants' access to Food Stamps. A Senate floor amendment, sponsored by Senator Dick Durbin (Democrat-Illinois), to restore food stamps to legal immigrants after five years of residency and to immigrant children without a residency requirement passed with little opposition. Despite the support of the Bush administration, three-quarters of the House Republicans voted against restoration. In urging the House to approve the Senate amendment, Joe Baca (Democrat-California) emphasized the discrepancy between all residents paying taxes and benefits being reserved for citizens. Enough Republicans joined the Democrats to form a majority for restoration (CQA + 2002: 4-5, 4-8).

In summary, the politics of benefits restoration remedied a number of the most excessive restrictions introduced by the 1996 welfare act, but the improvements hardly amounted to a return to pre-enactment entitlements. The major achievements were reinstating disqualified immigrants who had been SSI beneficiaries to the rolls, restoring Food Stamps to a quarter of those disentitled, and later easing restrictions on Food Stamps. SSI benefits continued to remain off limits for newly arriving legal immigrants until they become citizens or work ten years. For other core welfare programs, five-year bans have been put in place. Deeming and financial responsibilities of sponsors have extended the ban until naturalization or ten years of employment. Although the residence requirement for citizenship is only five years, immigrants often wait much longer before becoming citizens. For many newcomers, the period before gaining access to federal welfare benefits has increased to between five and ten years or possibly longer.

The puzzle of immigrants' fragile welfare rights

In unlocking the puzzle of the fragility of immigrants' welfare rights and especially their disentitlement in the mid-1990s, let us return to the components of my analytical framework. How have they contributed to the tenuous nature of immigrant welfare rights?

FRAMING
In granting immigrants' access to welfare benefits, equal rights and equal treatment were an important frame—but not social rights. In fact, social rights are not part of the US political vocabulary. Instead Americans emphasize civil and political rights. Even the favored term "entitlements" fell into disrepute because of its association with welfare, which has long had a pejorative clang and little popular support. Immigrants' contributions to the nation have been the master frame of deservingness, but contributions as a basis of entitlement are a double-edged sword. They entail a hurdle to inclusion, and the removal of benefits can be achieved through reframing the nature of contributions.

Three facets of the framing of welfare and immigration reform worked against immigrants' entitlements. First, participation in welfare programs was framed as the problem. Reform proponents equated utilization of benefits with dependency, and the goal of welfare reform was to restore personal responsibility and economic self-sufficiency. The frame of restoring self-sufficiency and individual responsibility was given a special spin in relation to immigrants. Advocates of disentitlement resurrected the principle of self-sufficiency in US immigration policy and stressed the responsibility of sponsors of newcomers.

Second, self-sufficiency and responsibility were accompanied by stressing the contractual nature of rights—fulfillment of obligations as a prerequisite of rights. In the 1990s immigrants' entitlements were no longer framed in terms of equal rights or equal treatment. Instead both adherents and opponents underlined contributions and the fulfillment of obligations. This shift increased the vulnerability of immigrants' entitlements and eventually led the unusual arrangement of requiring contributions for eligibility for means-tested benefits to insure that legal immigrants who were taxpayers were exempted from disentitlement. The contribution argument also weighed heavily in the restoration of benefits.

Third, together with contributions, citizenship became a major frame of deservingness. Emphasis was on the entitlements of citizens versus non-citizens. The category "non-citizen" bracketed together legal and illegal aliens, blurring the distinction between them. The dichotomy also highlighted the significance of citizenship. By naturalizing, immigrants could acquire social rights that otherwise were beyond their reach (SSI and until 2002 Food Stamps). Critics who viewed the equal entitlements of citizens and legal permanent residents as devaluating American citizenship, along with other observers, interpreted the welfare act as a re-evaluation of citizenship (Schuck 1998b: chapter 8; Joppke and Morawska 2003: 2).

POLICY VENUES AND INSTITUTIONAL ARRANGEMENTS

Several policy venues have influenced immigrant rights, and this has been a source of inconsistencies. Just as important, the policy venues themselves have produced contradictory policies that have advanced and restricted immigrant rights. The Supreme Court improved immigrants' social rights by overturning state statutes, but the Court in 1976, in *Mathews* v. *Diaz*, ruled unanimously that Congress had unrestricted power to set conditions based on immigration status for federal benefits (Fix and Zimmermann 1994: 272), officially sanctioning congressional limitations on immigrants' social rights. Likewise bureaucratic venues both aided and undermined the social rights of newcomers.

The contradictory trends in entitlements have been further aggravated by the separation of powers at the federal level, as policy venues in the executive, legislative, and judiciary branches of government have pursued their own agendas. In the area of immigrants' rights and social entitlements, the judiciary has taken decisions that weakened, ran counter to, or reversed legislation at the national and state levels (Melnick 1994; Schuck 1998a, 1998b). In the mid-1990s Congress redressed earlier court decisions by making sponsors' affidavits legally enforceable. Additional policy inconsistencies arose from conflicts between the executive and legislative branches over the social rights of refugees and legalizing immigrants. Republican administrations cut reimbursement to states for refugee resettlement aid and attempted to limit the number of legalizing immigrants.

One of the deepest inconsistencies of relevance here resulted from the compartmentalization of policy networks within the legislative branch and the different policies of the congressional committees dealing with immigration and social policies—not inter-branch conflict. The 1952 immigration law called for immigrants who utilized public assistance within five years of entry to be deported (Hutchinson 1981: 449–50). The set of legislators dealing with social policy, as part of the entitlements revolution, granted legal alien residents eligibility to SSI benefits after 30 days of entry. Shortly after, the General Accounting Office reported the high use of benefits by newly arriving immigrants, stressing the public charge provisions. In 1980 the social policy legislators took the first step that eased the policy conflict, but they do not seem to have been aware of the contradiction in policies. The law makers introduced deeming for the SSI program for three, not five years, and the main justification for deeming was to prevent a decline in public confidence in the welfare system (Parrott et al. 1998)—not that immigrants had violated the public charge provisions of the immigration law. Only with the 1996 legislation were the inconsistencies eliminated.

POLITICAL PARTIES

Party positions on immigration have been notoriously fluid, and cross-party coalitions have often determined the fate of immigration reforms. By contrast, support for immigrants' access to welfare benefits has tended to follow the left–right dimension. Party differences on immigrants' social rights were quite pronounced in the 1990s, with the deepest divisions between the House Republicans and President Clinton. The House Republicans sponsored a broadside of restrictive measures, ranging from massive disentitlement to stiffer penalties for utilizing assistance, including deportation and ineligibility for naturalization. The Republicans also sought to capitalize on anti-immigration sentiments in California gubernatorial contests and the 1996 presidential election. Partisan differences on immigrants' entitlements had already emerged during the votes on the 1980 Refugee Act and again during the enactment of the 1986 immigration law.

THE TERRITORIAL DIMENSION

The territorial dimension assumed growing importance through changing federal–state relations. A facet of welfare state retrenchment has been to shift responsibilities to the states. Over the years federal funding for welfare purposes generally and reimbursement for immigrants' welfare declined, forcing states to come up with the necessary revenues. The financial squeeze on the immigration states was especially tight. Increasingly state and local governments financed immigrants' services, while a large part of the taxes paid by immigrants went to the central government through federal income taxes and social security taxes (Joppke 1999: 56).

The disproportionate concentration of immigrants to six states has created its own cost–benefits calculus, encouraging members of Congress from states with large immigrant populations—especially Florida and California and more recently Texas and Illinois—to be especially active in both the politics of inclusion and exclusion. Generally these law makers expanded immigrants' social rights when benefits were federally funded, and they sought to curtail them when the states paid the bill.

Finally, the concentration of immigrants has also enhanced the electability of ethnic candidates. Most minority members of Congress have come from constituencies with a large ethnic vote, and in Congress they have been among the most supportive of immigrant rights. Furthermore, immigrants have settled in several of the most populous states whose votes are crucial in winning presidential elections, which has strengthened their political clout.

ETHNIC MOBILIZATION AND COALITION BUILDING

The simultaneous consideration of welfare and immigration reform made effective mobilization and coalition building difficult. Most immigrant and Latino organizations concentrated on influencing the immigration legislation, while African American groups focused on the welfare act. Ethnic organizations have had less access and leverage with Republicans than Democrats. Immigrant groups have been marginal in the welfare lobby, and the lobby's main concern was changes in the family assistance program and its impact on single mothers and their children—not cuts in immigrants' benefits. Latino groups assigned priority to combating efforts to reduce legal immigration through ceilings on family immigration and to stiffen deeming and sponsorship requirements. In seeking to influence immigration reform they joined forces with libertarians, business and growers, church organizations, groups promoting family values, immigration lawyers, and civil rights activists. The common goal of this coalition was to prevent restrictions on legal immigration—not to safeguard immigrants' access to benefits, and considering legal immigrants' benefits in a bill primarily dealing with illegal immigration made it a hard case to argue.

The highly fragmented US political system with abundant veto sites would seem to work against swings in immigrants' rights. However, as emphasized by Daniel Tichenor (2002: 31–4), the fragmentation of power also creates openings—or opportunity sites—in the policy process. This has heightened the importance of mobilization and policy coalitions inside and outside Congress, once issues come onto the agenda. The importance of coalitions is revealed through a comparison of the politics of disentitlement and benefits restoration. During the passage of the 1996 welfare act, ethnic minorities were divided and isolated, and they faced a formidable welfare reform coalition. By contrast, when immigration reform moved off the agenda, immigrant and ethnic groups, and especially the Hispanic lobby, redirected their attention to social benefits. They succeeded in forging a broad alliance to ease restrictions on Food Stamps in 1998 and 2002. It consisted of nutrition groups, social policy experts, farmers' organizations, state officials, and a supportive Senate and President.

In summary, the framework elucidates the reinforcing interplay of several factors that contributed to the fragility of immigrants' welfare rights in the US. The contested nature of welfare programs and the absence of social rights as a frame of deservingness weakened the entitlements of citizens and immigrants alike, while other frames of deservingness—contributions and citizenship—were marshaled against newcomers' access to welfare benefits. Multiple policy venues have often pulled policies affecting immigrant rights in opposite directions. The courts, the bureaucracy, and Congress have improved *and* restricted immigrants' welfare rights. Likewise the cost–benefit calculus of the territorial dimension provided incentives both to extend and contract entitlements. Multiple venues, the policy venues themselves, the territorial dimension, and the fluidity of the policy process have all operated to produce uncoordinated policies, making immigrant welfare rights susceptible to change.

The United Kingdom: From "universal" welfare and declaratory race legislation to selectivity and racial monitoring

The politics of inclusion in the British case differed from the US in that the universal welfare state extended social rights to immigrants. Early postwar social legislation made no distinctions between aliens and citizens. Furthermore, immigrants arriving from the former British Empire were not classified as aliens but as British subjects with citizenship rights. Instead the politics of inclusion centered on settlement or integration policy. The flagship of British integration policy has been anti-discrimination and race relations legislation. The original purpose of anti-discrimination legislation was to enhance New Commonwealth immigrants' rights, including their social rights. The first act was quite innocuous, and many of its supporters believed that the main force of the act stemmed from declaring a ban on discrimination. Despite its modest nature, the 1965 Race Relations Act triggered a process of increasingly stronger anti-discrimination measures, and ultimately a duty of public agencies to develop ethnic and racial monitoring to assess the impact of social policies and services on different ethnic groups.

As distinct from the US, British anti-discrimination legislation from its inception was fused with immigration controls. This nexus produced a huge contradiction because several restrictions were specifically aimed at curtailing the entry of immigrants of color, while the goal of anti-discrimination legislation was to ensure that they had equal rights. Restrictive immigration policy has had a major impact on immigrants' social rights, and immigration legislation and regulations have been crucial in effecting the contraction of their rights. Thus the politics of exclusion requires an examination of both immigration policy and welfare state restructuring, especially the increasing prominence of means-tested benefits or growing selectivity.

Integration policy and the politics of inclusion

Initially the British adopted a laissez-faire approach toward Commonwealth newcomers assuming that the recently erected universal welfare state would accommodate their needs. The laissez-faire approach was reinforced by the tradition of voluntarism in the delivery of social services. Local voluntary organizations or welfare committees were established, often with church or charity involvement, to aid immigrants in the settlement process (Hill and Issacharoff 1971: chapter 1). The concentration of immigrants in a limited number of localities, however, created strains at the points of welfare delivery. Since there was no official central government policy, it fell upon the local authorities to deal with the pressures. The perception that the universal welfare state made an integration policy unnecessary began to change in the late 1950s. By the mid-1960s an integration policy had emerged, and two of its key components were (1) anti-discrimination legislation and (2) social measures targeted at immigrants.

ANTI-DISCRIMINATION LEGISLATION

Anti-discrimination legislation came onto the agenda in the wake of racial disturbances in 1958. The unrest, instigated by white youths, brought a new sense of urgency to the issues of race relations and immigration. Following the disorders, two policy alternatives crystallized. The Conservatives and a few Labour MPs advocated restricting the entry of immigrants of color from the New Commonwealth countries, while Labour proposed attacking racial prejudices (Bleich 2003: 44–5).

The contours of the Labour party's fledging integration policy were presented in its 1964 election manifesto. An important change was that integration policy was linked to the acceptance of immigration controls. The manifesto declared, " ... a Labour Government will legislate against racial discrimination and incitement in public places and give special help to local authorities in areas where immigrants have settled. Labour accepts that the number of immigrants entering the United Kingdom be limited" (Craig 1990: 56). The manifesto promised to introduce anti-discrimination legislation if elected, and Labour won a very narrow majority of four seats—later reduced to two seats (Money 1999: 88).

A legacy of the 1958 anti-black riots was the framing of the race relations issue as a problem of public order, but it was also framed in terms of the full rights of citizenship because of the special status of New Commonwealth immigrants. The responsible minister for the 1965 Race Relations Act maintained that its task was "the settling of new arrivals into our community as in every sense first-class citizens" (Hansen 2000: 144). Similarly the purpose of the 1968 Race Relations Act was described as "to protect society as a whole against actions which will lead to social disruption, and prevent the emergence of a class of second-grade citizens" (Bleich 2003: 74).

The frame of public order and the emphasis on the immigrants made the Home Office the logical policy venue, and its head, the Home Secretary, was pivotal—first Frank Soskice (1964–5) and then Roy Jenkins (1965–7). The tasks of the Home Office included border control, immigration, citizenship acquisition, internal security, the police, and prisons. The dual frames, however, broadened the policy network formulating the legislation of the 1960s so that it included professionals with expertise on race relations and social policy (Hansen 2000: 139; Bleich 2003: 50–1, 65).

Labour's slim majority contributed to Parliament substantially influencing the 1965 Race Relations Act. Criminal sanctions in the original bill were replaced by conciliation and an administrative approach. The opposition and Labour backbenchers wanted the change for different reasons. The Conservatives apparently viewed conciliation as a way to weaken the legislation, whereas the Labour critics, inspired by the US anti-discrimination legislation, regarded an administrative approach as superior. Confronted with this coalition, the government modified the bill, which was then adopted with broad support (Bleich 2003: 52–7). Thus the act differed from continental legislation to prevent discrimination by making it a criminal offense.

The 1965 Race Relations Act was quite limited, and it was extended already in 1968. The act prohibited discrimination on the basis of color, race, ethnic, or national origins in public places, such as restaurants, pubs, and theaters. It also banned incitement of racial and ethnic hatred. Roy Jenkins, who became Home Secretary in 1965, regarded the new legislation as inadequate, and he set out to strengthen it. He proposed to prohibit discrimination in the labor market, housing, education, banking and credit facilities, and goods and services. His strategy was to expose the weaknesses of the new administrative agency and demonstrate the existence of widespread discrimination in the areas of employment and housing (Bleich 2003: 75). Jenkins emphasized that the law was necessary to guarantee the rights of the second generation immigrants, that is, the full citizenship of the children born in Britain of immigrant parents (Rose 1969: 521, 539–40). He believed that the success of the integration policy hinged upon the elimination of discrimination in employment (Bleich 2003: 72). The next important legislation, the 1976 Race Relations Act, also adopted under Jenkins as Home Secretary (1974–6), strengthened the employment and education provisions.

SPECIAL IMMIGRANT MEASURES

The idea of special welfare measures for immigrants gained acceptance only gradually. A prime source of resistance was official thinking, which held that the welfare needs of immigrants were "different in degree rather than kind" and the objective was "to treat them in the same way as other citizens" (Rose 1969: 346). There was also a desire to avoid any measures giving the impression of preferential treatment (Freeman 1979: 163–4). By the mid-1960s, however, it was commonly acknowledged that voluntary and municipal action backed by public funds was necessary to meet the special needs of immigrants and minority communities. On the eve of the 1966 election the Labour Prime Minister, Harold Wilson, announced the first special program to aid immigrants. In order to overcome the contradiction between separate programs for immigrants and universalism, Labour veered toward selectivity through targeted measures to underprivileged communities. This sort of selectivity has masked measures directed specifically to immigrants.

At the end of the 1960s the Labour party described its social policy strategy, echoing Richard Titmuss' definition of the real challenge in welfare (1968: 134–5):

> [O]ne of the lessons of the last decade is that providing universally available services and benefits is not enough. We must positively discriminate in favor of the poor and the handicapped, the deprived, the homeless, and the social casualties of our society. It is not a matter of choosing between universal and selective welfare services. It is a question of providing a basic structure of universal services on which various *additional* selective services can be added. (Freeman 1979: 167)

This strategy was embodied in the two policies developed during the decade to meet the needs of newcomers—measures to aid immigrants *qua* immigrants (Local Government Act 1966) and measures to help immigrants *qua* deprived (Local Government Grants (Social Need) Act 1969)—seeking to resolve the tensions between universalism and selectivity in a constructive fashion. Still measures directed to immigrants or ethnic minorities rather than to victims of deprivation remained controversial.

In summary, anti-discrimination and social policy measures were the main features of an emergent integration policy, supplanting the previous laissez-faire approach. With the 1968 Race Relations Act, race became an independent policy arena with its own policy machinery. In the next round of policy formulation during the mid-1970s, race relations were no longer framed in terms of social rights of immigrants or full citizenship, but in terms of equal opportunities and racial equality. Integration policy became synonymous with race policy and to a lesser extent with welfare measures aiding immigrants and ethnic minorities. Race policy was institutionalized in the duties of the Commission for Racial Equality and its local agencies, and welfare measures specifically targeted to immigrants but increasingly to ethnic minorities were among the Commission's tasks (Bleich 2003: 87, 99–100). Importantly, race policy machinery had the task of recommending policy improvements, which has contributed to the gradual strengthening of anti-discrimination legislation. The policy machinery also served as a platform for race activists, many of whom were immigrants and members of ethnic minority communities, and over time they consolidated their positions in race policy institutions at both the local and central levels.

THE INTEGRATION-IMMIGRATION NEXUS

In Britain the issue of integration was inextricably bound up with the issue of immigration controls. As famously expressed in 1965 by Roy Hattersley, later a member of the Labour government, " ... integration without limitation is impossible; equally ... limitation without integration is indefensible" (Hill and Issacharoff 1971: 16). On immigration controls, Labour confronted a major dilemma. The party became convinced that the immigration issue was an electoral liability after the defeat of prominent pro-immigration candidates in the 1964 election and subsequent by-elections. To neutralize the issue, the Labour government vied with the Conservatives in introducing restrictions (Layton-Henry 1992: 154–5; Money 1999: 86–9; Hansen 2000: 150–1). Internally, the party needed to appease its liberal wing that opposed immigration restrictions and unequal treatment of New Commonwealth immigrants, and anti-discrimination legislation was part of the solution.

Labour's strategy consisted of combining positive measures with restrictions. The 1965 Race Relations Bill preceded the presentation of the White Paper, *Immigration from the Commonwealth*, which proposed immigration restrictions. The contrast between positive measures and controls was even more pronounced in the 1968 legislation. The 1968 Race Relations Act substantially strengthened anti-discrimination and race relations measures, while the 1968 Commonwealth Immigrants Act created the controversial category of "qualifying connection," a forerunner of the notorious "patrial" (a person connected to the United Kingdom by parentage and exempted from immigration controls) that was a centerpiece of the 1971 Immigration Act. Both categories privileged immigrants from the Old Commonwealth countries (Australia, Canada, New Zealand, and white settlers in Africa) in relation to New Commonwealth immigrants from the Caribbean, Africa, and South Asia (Hansen 2000: 163).

The integration–immigration nexus also had administrative consequences. Integration measures, even those related to welfare, were located in the Home Office, whose major preoccupation was immigration controls. Already in the late 1960s race relations experts criticized the administrative linkage of integration and immigration policies (Rose 1969: 683–5), and in opposition

Labour recommended that integration policies be transferred to the Department of Health and Social Security (Layton-Henry 1992: 87–8). Once Labour returned to government (1974–9) no administrative change was made, probably because Roy Jenkins was once again Home Secretary and anti-discrimination legislation was high on the policy agenda. This pattern of administrative responsibilities facilitated the Home Office's eventual assumption of a larger role in social policy affecting immigrants.

The politics of exclusion and rights contraction

The politics of exclusion, which have seriously eroded the social rights of immigrants, consisted of two processes: (1) altering the citizen status of immigrants coming from the former British Empire so that they increasingly were subject to the same immigration controls as aliens and (2) barring aliens from means-tested benefits. At the same time welfare state retrenchment and restructuring elevated the importance of this type of benefit.

The 1971 Immigration Act, adopted by the Conservative government with Edward Heath as Prime Minister (1970–4), was watershed legislation in that it created a unified system of immigration controls for aliens and New Commonwealth immigrants regarding admission and residence. The Act replaced earlier legislation, but its provisions were quite broad, and the Home Secretary was empowered to fill in the details. It introduced the notion of "partial," which privileged citizens from the Old Commonwealth countries and defined away the rights of New Commonwealth immigrants. Among the regulations, which were to have major ramifications for immigrants' social rights, was the rule that visitors had to satisfy the immigration officer that they had the means to support themselves and family members without recourse to public funds (Layton-Henry 1985: 104–5; Macdonald 1987: 17–20; Hansen 2000: 194).

Under the Conservative governments headed by Margaret Thatcher (1979–90) and John Major (1990–7) the rights contraction process gained momentum. A major feature of their governments was to tighten the interface between immigration policy and social policy. The politics of rights contraction under Thatcher assumed two forms. First, her administrations used benefit regulations and immigration rules to deny immigrants' access to social benefits. Second, the Thatcher governments broadened the circumference of immigrants who were subject to immigration controls and whose immigration status affected their eligibility for social benefits. Through the 1981 British Nationality Act, her government brought nationality legislation in alignment with the 1971 Immigration Act, further underscoring that New Commonwealth citizens were aliens.

THE INCREMENTAL POLITICS OF RIGHTS CONTRACTION
AND WELFARE STATE RESTRUCTURING

The incremental nature of the contraction of immigrants' social rights was made possible by the Conservatives' long period in government—nearly two decades. Both Thatcher and Major scaled back immigrants' social rights through a series of changes, first in regulations and later in statutes.

The process of restricting immigrants' access to social benefits needs to be seen against the backdrop of the Conservative governments' efforts to roll back and restructure the British welfare state. Their efforts amounted to a twin shift in social provision toward increased "privatization" and means testing. In contrast to the architects of the postwar welfare state who viewed means-tested benefits as providing a final safety net, the Thatcher and Major governments envisioned this type of benefit as the foundation of public provision. The Conservatives claimed that means-tested benefits were more effective because they were targeted to the needy. Accordingly, Conservative governments reduced insurance benefits and streamlined means-tested programs during the 1980s, and targeting increased by tightening eligibility requirements. The 1980s also witnessed legislation and extensive campaigns against benefit fraud. At the end of the decade workfare—tying receipt of benefits to the requirement of actively seeking work and/or participation in work schemes—emerged as a strategy.

In the process social rights were recast. The logic of contractual liberalism, underlining rights in exchange for obligations, has emphasized the conditionality of social rights, whereas rights had formed the core of social citizenship. The case was candidly put by Thatcher's Social Security Minister, John Moore, in 1988. He argued for the need to correct "the balance of the citizenship equation," stating "the equation that has 'rights' on one side must have 'responsibilities' on the other. . . . For more than a quarter of a century, public focus has been on citizens' 'rights' and it is now past time to redress the balance" (Lister 1991: 103). Insinuations of fraud and depicting claimants as welfare scroungers further undermined the legitimacy of social rights.

RESTRICTING "FOREIGNERS'" ACCESS TO BENEFITS

Upon entering office, the Thatcher government lost no time in taking steps to curtail the access of persons from abroad to the welfare state. The major frame in introducing restrictions was welfare abuse and fraud. Newcomers were discredited in various ways—from claims of abuse, opportunism, and benefit tourism to fraudulent entry. This framing dovetailed with the government's proclaimed goal to crack down on welfare waste and fraud.

In 1980 changes in the benefit regulations made persons from abroad ineligible for supplementary benefit. In addition, the regulations made sponsors liable for the maintenance of an immigrant relative and authorized welfare authorities to seek reimbursement for a sponsored immigrant who had received supplementary benefit. The next year the Social Security Minister announced that all visitors would be charged for medical treatment by the National Health Service (NHS). His justification was the "fairly widespread abuse by foreigners of the NHS" (Gordon 1985: 80).

The second approach to restricting immigrants' access to benefits, which first occurred in 1985, was through clarifying "public funds" related to no recourse to public funds as a condition of entry. An amendment to the immigration rules defined "public funds" to mean supplementary benefit, housing benefit, family income supplement (a tax credit for low income working families), and housing for the homeless (Macdonald 1987: 208). This clarification removed the safety net for many newcomers.

The next target for restrictions, as signaled in the 1987 Conservative election manifesto, were asylum seekers, framed as "fraudulent refugees" (Layton-Henry 1992: 206–7), but this task was to be carried out by Major. The Major government restricted immigrants' access to benefits through legislation as well as social security and immigration regulations. Although the main focus was on asylum seekers, restrictions under Major included other entry categories.

In tackling asylum seeking, the government depicted asylum seekers as undeserving and without genuine reason for protection. As explained in 1992 by Michael Howard, future Home Secretary (1993–7), "By claiming asylum, those who have no basis to remain here can not only substantially prolong their stay, but gain access to benefit and housing at public expense . . . Of the 40,000 asylum applicants currently being supported on benefit, very few will be found to merit asylum" (Schuster 2003: 147).

His remarks anticipated the benefit restrictions introduced in 1993 and 1996. The 1993 Asylum and Immigration Appeals Act lowered the benefit level to 90 per cent of the major assistance benefit—income support—and restricted access to homeless assistance but retained eligibility to all other benefits (Burchardt 2005: 222). The government altered the 1996 social security regulations, denying asylum seekers income support and housing benefits unless they claimed them immediately upon arrival. When the courts ruled that the regulations were invalid, the government reversed the court decision through the 1996 Asylum and Immigration Act, which distinguished between persons applying for benefits upon arrival and applicants already in the UK (Griffith 1997: 202–3). The act limited the benefits of applicants on arrival to income support, housing benefit, and the council tax benefit, and it disentitled in-country applicants from all benefits.

The 1996 Asylum and Immigration Act also adopted a harsher approach in restricting immigrants' access to benefits via no recourse to public funds. The act authorized that the admission condition of no recourse to public funds be stamped in the passports of all persons entering the country. The 1996 immigration rules extended the list of benefits defined as "public funds" to all non-contributory benefits so that they now included child benefits, several disability benefits, and the means-tested portion of the jobseekers' allowance (Jackson 1999: 242, 272–4). Simultaneously the Home Office stepped up efforts to establish cooperation and exchange of information between the immigration service and the agencies in charge of benefits especially regarding eligibility to benefits and legal presence in the country (Morris 1998: 958–9, 964–6).

In summary, a basic feature of the rights contraction process under the Conservatives was framing the issue as foreigners' abuse of benefits irrespective of entry category, and that British benefits were a magnet attracting immigrants. The Conservative governments further justified cutbacks out of consideration for the British taxpayer. In curbing the availability of benefits to newcomers, Major outdid Thatcher. The Major premiership not only restricted access to benefits through expanding the number of benefits categorized as public funds, it also pegged minimum benefits at a lower level for asylum seekers and then withdrew all benefits for asylum seekers who claimed them after entering the country. Pegging benefits at a lower rate for asylum seekers set a precedent in differentiating the benefits of non-citizens and citizens.

New Labour's "third way"

After suffering four consecutive defeats at the polls, the Labour party, under Tony Blair's leadership (1994–2007), adopted the label New Labour and launched the "third way." New Labour depicted its course as a renewal of social democracy that differed from the old left and the conservative right (Powell 1999: 13). This was a major theme in presenting New Labour during the 1997 election, as the party sought to capture the middle ground in British politics. Together with Major's growing unpopularity, New Labour's strategy resulted in a landslide victory and a massive parliamentary majority.

IMMIGRATION POLICY AND IMMIGRANTS' SOCIAL RIGHTS
Among the jettisoned policies was the party's pro-immigrant stance during the 1990s when in opposition (Statham 2003: 171). In government New Labour largely reverted to old Labour's practice of balancing positive and harsh measures. The Labour government introduced the 1998 Human Rights Act that incorporated the European Convention on Human Rights into domestic law, and the act was praised by immigrant and minority rights activists. On its heels, however, came the 1999 Immigration and Asylum Act, which was as harsh as the preceding immigration act passed by the

Conservatives. The 1999 act created a separate system of support for asylum seekers (NASS); it replaced cash benefits with vouchers with benefits pegged at 70 per cent of regular assistance benefits; and it introduced mandatory dispersal for those requiring accommodation. The Race Relations Amendment Act of 2000 preceded the 2002 Nationality, Immigration and Asylum Act, introducing tighter immigration controls and naturalization requirements. The 2000 Race Relations Act prohibited discrimination by public authorities, such as the police and public officials, but with the exception of immigration and nationality officials. It also made ethnic monitoring and positive action by government agencies and local government authorities mandatory. Finally, the 2006 Racial and Religious Hatred Act, which made incitement of racial and religious hatred an offense, counterbalanced new restrictions in the 2006 Immigration, Asylum and Nationality Act and the 2007 Borders Act.

It is difficult to detect any major differences in the restrictive immigration policy of the Tories, described as "firm and fair," and New Labour's policy billed as "firmer, faster and fairer," and the policy effects on immigrants' social rights. New Labour continued to limit the availability of social benefits to newcomers and introduced new restrictions. The 2002 Nationality, Asylum and Immigration Act reinstated benefit restrictions for those applying for asylum after arrival. Those who did not apply "as soon as reasonably practicable" were ineligible for support through NASS. New Labour also strengthened the links between immigration status and benefit entitlement by adding benefits, mainly tax credits, to "public funds." The 1999 Immigration and Asylum Act excluded persons subject to immigration controls from most social security benefits by statute instead of immigration rules (Macdonald and Webber 2005: 836).

New Labour echoed the Tories' negative framing of asylum seekers as bogus claimants. Its first White Paper on immigration and asylum asserted, "There is no doubt that the asylum system is being abused by those seeking to migrate for purely economic reasons. Many claims are simply a tissue of lies" (Home Office 1998 in Burchardt 2005: 223). New Labour also embraced the Tories' emphasis on the costs of immigration, proposing that immigrants pay into a transitional fund to cover the "extra costs" of their using the health and education system. One of the government's main concerns in reforming the asylum support system was to cut its costs (HO-UKBA 2009).

In two respects, the Labour government's policies broke with the past. It favored a reorientation toward labor immigration and a system of selective admission related to skills, which was fashioned as managed immigration. Thus the government allowed EU citizens of new member states of the 2004 enlargement to enter as labor migrants, but on the condition that they did not utilize social benefits until they had worked a minimum of 12 months. A second departure was New Labour's proposals to expand the significance of citizenship, which has implications for non-citizens and their social rights. The 2009 Borders, Citizenship and Immigration Act introduced probationary citizenship and lengthened the residence requirements, thus extending the period that newcomers are ineligible for many social benefits.

Labour has confronted a credibility problem through the enduring contradiction between its restrictionist immigration measures and an integration policy with race and ethnic equality as its goal. Ethnic minorities and race equality activists have continued to call attention to the contradiction (e.g. CFMB 2000; Craig 2007). There has also been a growing disjuncture in the social rights of ethnic minorities and immigrants. Now ethnic minorities are comprised of British citizens and immigrants. British citizens have full formal rights, while the entitlements of immigrants subject to immigration controls have been severely restricted. Generally the measures directed to ethnic minorities at the local level, and especially "community cohesion" measures, have not included immigrants. Instead policy efforts have focused on support for asylum seekers through separate programs and barring newcomers from benefits for an ever longer duration.

THE THIRD WAY AND THE WELFARE OF IMMIGRANTS AND MINORITIES

What were the implications of the third way for the British welfare state and, in turn, its impact on the social rights of immigrants and ethnic minorities? In presenting its blueprint for modernizing the welfare state, New Labour emphasized five themes: (1) the importance of work in preventing poverty backed by measures that make work pay, (2) an active, preventative welfare state where investment in human capital has priority over direct provision of economic maintenance, (3) equal opportunities rather than equal distribution, (4) rights combined with responsibilities, and (5) social provision through public/private partnerships and civil society (Powell 1999: 14–20). The third way also elevated the importance of inclusion and exclusion by supplanting equality with inclusion and inequality with exclusion (Giddens 1998: 102).

Among the potentially positive facets of the third way's vision of the welfare state for immigrants and minorities was the weight attached to investing in human capital and services, such as education and training programs, medical services, and child care. Newcomers were barred from cash benefits and public housing but not services; however, by the mid-2000s their access to services was in question. Child-oriented measures also advantaged newcomers once they have permanent residence status since the immigrant population has been younger and more likely to have children (Law 2009: 82). The goal to end children's poverty also boded well for ethnic minorities because their children have high poverty rates. Likewise the introduction of the national minimum

171

wage and its successive upgrading has benefited immigrants and ethnic minorities. Newcomers often have low incomes especially during their first years in the country, and ethnic minorities have been more likely to have low pay. New Labour's pension reforms enhanced the social rights of immigrants and ethnic minorities, especially changes in the contribution requirements for the state basic pension and the automatic enrollment of most employees in private pension schemes. The priority assigned to work and the work-to-welfare programs at least initially benefited ethnic minorities, whose employment has lagged behind the majority population. A cross-departmental ethnic minority employment task force, created in 2003, set specific targets for reducing the ethnic minority employment gap (Platt 2007: 177).

Several negative features of the third way for ethnic minorities reflected continuities with the Tories' policies. The third way continued to increase selectivity, and New Labour failed to remedy a number of problems associated with means-tested benefits. Most seriously, the government retained the low benefit levels of the means-tested component of the jobseekers' allowance and the major safety net benefit. Neither was substantially upgraded for adults during New Labour's period in office (Ridge 2009: 163). Because ethnic minorities have higher unemployment rates and lower economic activity rates, these benefits have been crucial to their income. Ethnic minority children have also been more likely than white children to live in households with no full-time workers or no earners, and these households have been especially vulnerable to poverty (Platt 2007: 182; Stewart 2007: 415).

The third way's emphasis on social inclusion, which displaced social citizenship and equality, resulted in a new form of selectivity. Instead of social inclusion, the Labour government assigned priority to social exclusion and established the Social Exclusion Unit (SEU), originally located in the Cabinet Office. Social exclusion involved targeting; measures were aimed at the most excluded groups. As aptly put by Tania Burchardt (2005), it amounted to selective inclusion, and an inherent weakness of this approach was the omission of other vulnerable groups. Policy makers largely ignored that immigrants, both adults and children, have been vulnerable to social exclusion.

The 2000 Race Relations Act put ethnic minorities center stage, especially by assigning the government departments and units administering social services and benefits the duty to assess the possible differential impact of their services and policies on ethnic minorities and to monitor the extent of differentiation (Platt 2003: 270). Ten years on, fulfillment of the race equality duties by the public authorities appeared uneven. Ethnic and racial monitoring figured prominently in employment programs and some areas of education, but monitoring has been extremely spotty with regard to the administration and delivery of benefits (Aspinall and Mitton 2007; Platt 2007; DWP 2008: 11; Law 2009: 86–7). Substantial ethnic differences in benefit utilization and poverty rates exist, as shown in Chapter 6, but deficient monitoring of benefits has failed to provide the necessary information for tackling the problem of poorer poverty reduction effectiveness for ethnic minorities, that is, that benefits do a better job of lifting whites over the poverty line than they do for ethnic minorities.

In conclusion, the changes from social rights to conditional welfare and the conviction that life on benefits must be made less attractive have affected the economic well-being of immigrants and ethnic minorities. Means-tested benefits have contributed a larger share to the income packages of ethnic minorities than the rest of the population (Morissens and Sainsbury 2005: 652). New Labour carried on the Tories' social security legacy of selective measures in three respects. The Labour governments did not reverse Conservative reforms that led to a dramatic increase in the utilization of means-tested benefits. They did not improve the adequacy of means-tested benefits for working age adults, and they expanded means testing through tax credits. This contrasts with Labour's social policy strategy of the late 1960s, which entailed universal benefits supplemented with selective measures directed to those with special needs. New Labour's record in improving the incomes of the poor during its first two terms in office was better than Thatcher's and Major's, but its record in reducing income inequality and poverty pales in comparison to the Labour governments in the 1960s and 1970s (Hills and Stewart 2005: 340–2).

The paradox of the politics of exclusion and inclusion

The politics of exclusion and inclusion in the UK represent a paradox in terms of policy outputs. A restrictionist immigration policy that has been increasingly detrimental to immigrants' social rights has coexisted with an increasingly ambitious anti-discrimination policy, especially by European standards. To understand this paradox, let us examine the importance of the components of my analytical framework.

FRAMING
As distinct from the US case, framing was important in determining the policy venue and the roster of relevant participants in the policy process. The public order frame contributed to making the Home Office the chief policy venue and to relegating the role of the Department of Social Security in integration policy. The Home Office became responsible for both immigration and integration policies. The worsening of immigrants' social rights beginning in the 1980s was accompanied by a new frame—welfare abuse and deception. The new frame pertained to immigrants and citizens, and it also made the

Department of Social Security a policy venue during the Thatcher and Major governments.

An important effect of the initial framing was to broaden the policy network to persons outside the Home Office bureaucracy. The frame of social citizenship and full rights for New Commonwealth immigrants and anti-discrimination measures as the solution brought lawyers, academics, and research institutes dealing with race relations into the policy network. The policy coalition encompassed immigrant activists who tried to include the existing ethnic and immigrant organizations. This framing also promoted the inclusion of social policy experts and welfare organizations, such as the newly formed Child Poverty Action Group (CPAG) (1965) and Joint Council for the Welfare of Immigrants (JCWI) (1967). A major difference was that the establishment of special policy machinery made the race experts and lawyers insiders, while both CPAG and JCWI have been outsiders, functioning as advocacy organizations.

POLICY VENUES AND INSTITUTIONAL ARRANGEMENTS

The Home Office has been the single most important policy venue, and discretionary powers and institutional arrangements have strengthened its authority. The discretionary powers of the Home Secretary and delegation of powers to high ranking civil servants and immigration officers have removed decisions from the public eye. Although the Home Office appears to be the epitome of wide discretionary powers, other ministries, including those in charge of social benefits and services, have such powers. Frequently acts of Parliament confer broad discretionary powers on the ministries or departments to implement the policy of the statute (Jowell 2007: 18). The Department of Social Security, also through formulating regulations, complemented the Home Office in restricting immigrants' eligibility to benefits. Barring immigrants from social benefits has been administrative politics par excellence. Despite the more recent trend to regulate the social rights of immigrants through immigration legislation, the discretionary powers of the Home Office remained important in filling in the details of legislation through regulations. A patent example was the 2000 asylum support regulations that stipulated the conditions of eligibility (HO-UKBA 2009: 23).

Institutional arrangements, more precisely, modest legislative and judicial checks on the executive, have given the government and administration an upper hand. The fusion of executive and legislative power in the Westminster model of majority parliamentarianism has militated against effective checks by the legislature on executive power. In the case of the immigration rules, legislative control has been marginal. Although the immigration rules and rule changes must be presented to Parliament, they cannot be amended, only approved or rejected in their entirety (Sales 2007: 156). Even when Parliament has disapproved, disapproval did not result in much change in the rules (Hansen 2000: 201–2).

The role of the judiciary has been limited by the legal doctrine of legislative sovereignty. As authoritatively stated, "The principle of Parliamentary sovereignty means . . . that Parliament . . . has the right to make or unmake any law whatever; and, further, that no person or body is recognized by law as having a right to override or set aside the legislation of Parliament" (Dicey in Bradley 2007: 28). Accordingly, the courts cannot review the validity of acts of Parliament. The standard argument for legislative sovereignty has been that laws should be made by the elected legislature and not the unelected judiciary. Instead the courts have examined either the legality of administrative decisions or the compatibility of subordinate laws with acts of Parliament. The 1998 Human Rights Act opened the way for courts to examine the compatibility of statutes with the European Convention of Human Rights and to declare incompatibility, but the act did not empower the judiciary to strike down legislation (Lester and Beattie 2007: 68–74). Instead it has been the task of the government to eliminate the incompatibilities.

Despite the narrow scope of judicial review, the courts have acted to protect the social rights of immigrants. The High Court restored the right to a social minimum to asylum seekers disentitled by the 1996 social security regulations, declaring that "the regulations necessarily contemplated for some a life so destitute that no civilised nation could tolerate it" (Griffith 1997: 203). The 1996 immigration act stripped the majority of asylum seekers of all benefits, but the High Court ruled that the local authorities had the duty to support asylum seekers who were destitute. The law lords found that the 2002 immigration act, with a similar disentitlement clause, was in breach of the European Convention of Human Rights (Somerville 2007: 96). Both Conservative and Labour governments countered by introducing new legislation that overrode the court rulings.

Finally, as the policy venue of both immigration and immigrant policy, the Home Office has simultaneously taken the lead in rights contraction and rights extension, indicating that the "policy venue" per se is not decisive here. Instead the answer to this paradox is related to the political parties, electoral politics, and immigrants' and ethnic minorities' penetration of the political process.

POLITICAL PARTIES AND ELECTORAL POLITICS
Political parties are crucial to the Westminster model since the majority (or largest) party forms the government, but the importance of parties in shaping policy has been a matter of ongoing debate. In the case of immigration policy, the standard interpretation has emphasized bipartisan support of strict immigration controls. The explanation of the initial consensus that emerged during

the 1960s has focused on electoral politics (Messina 1989; Layton-Henry 1992; Money 1999; Hansen 2000). Labour in opposition condemned the imposition of controls in the 1962 Commonwealth Immigrants Act but by the late1960s the party outflanked the Conservatives when the Labour government introduced the 1968 Commonwealth Immigrants Act. In the interim, election setbacks convinced the Labour leadership that restrictions were necessary. The unexpected victory of the Conservatives in the 1970 election, when immigration was an issue, led to a widespread perception in both parties that immigration was a losing issue for Labour and a winning issue for the Tories (Studlar 1978; Layton-Henry 1992: 84).

At first glance electoral politics seems a remote explanation to the bipartisan consensus in the late 1990s to reduce asylum seeking by all means, including removal of the social benefits of asylum seekers. Immigration was not an issue in the 1997 election. However, a crucial feature of New Labour's long-term strategy was to capture and dominate the center ground in British politics to assure electoral success (Beech 2008). In the 1997 election, the party moved closer to the Conservatives on issues where the voters had given the Tories a high rating, such as management of the economy, taxation, and law and order (Fielding 2003: 100). The party's tough stance on asylum seekers in government can be seen as part of its strategy to increase its electability by eliminating the image that Labour was soft on immigration.

Political analysts have also argued that anti-discrimination legislation enjoys the same bipartisan support as immigration controls (Favell 1998a, 1998b; Hansen 2000: 228; Somerville 2007: 18). This interpretation requires sharper specification. It holds only if one assumes that bipartisanism entails failure to overturn the legislation. The Conservatives did not support the 1976 Race Relations Act; they mainly abstained, but if Thatcher had had her way, the party would have voted against it (Bleich 2003: 98). The Thatcher and Major governments did not introduce any major anti-discrimination legislation. Proposals for improvements by the Commission for Racial Equality fell on deaf ears. By contrast, the New Labour government substantially strengthened the Race Relations Act. As one policy expert, Erik Bleich, has concluded, "having a Labour government in power appears to be a necessary condition for the passage of race legislation" (2003: 112).

ETHNIC MOBILIZATION AND PENETRATION

The most important aspect of ethnic mobilization has been penetration of Labour party, which has influenced internal party politics. Already in the early 1960s the Labour party founded the British Overseas Socialist Fellowship; the party fielded immigrant candidates in the local government elections, and a New Commonwealth candidate for Parliament ran in the 1964 election. The Labour party as the initiator of race relations policy attracted minority activists, and the policy has also given them some leverage within the party. Minority activists and organizations were part of the policy coalition supporting the first two race relations acts (Rose 1969: 221, 507–10, 526–7; Bleich 2003: 85). Again in 1975 when anti-discrimination legislation was on the agenda, an internal pressure group for racial equality—the Labour Party Race Action Group—was formed. During the 1980s demands for greater minority representation accelerated, and the issue of black sections was raised. Separate sections, which were rejected by the party leadership, were eventually replaced by the demand for increased minority representation in party and elected positions (Solomos 2003: 199–201). Pressure generated by the campaign for black sections helped to secure the nomination of more ethnic minority candidates for local government and parliamentary seats (Layton-Henry 1992: 163–9). A breakthrough in parliamentary representation did not occur until the 1987 election when four minority Labour candidates were successful. The number of candidates and MPs has successively risen but with very lop-sided success rates for the candidates of different parties—nearly all racial minority MPs have come from the Labour party. Finally, two MPs with strong anti-racist records, Anthony Lester and Paul Boateng, played an important role in Labour's campaign for the 1998 Human Rights Act (Lester and Beattie 2007: 66–8). The positive policy moves in race and rights legislation have in part been influenced by informal ties with the racial organizations and human rights activists, ethnic minorities' penetration of the party, and the increasing strength of the ethnic vote for Labour (CFMB 2000: 341).

While anti-racist and immigrant activists can point to anti-discrimination legislation and the Human Rights Act as major accomplishments, similar successes concerning the social rights of immigrants are hard to find. Since 1980 immigrants' social rights have been subordinate to admission policies and immigration controls. With the passage of time, the social rights of ethnic minorities were no longer synonymous with those of immigrants. Finally, major political constraints have confronted immigrant and minority activists in influencing the policy agenda. The constraints have included the fragmentation of ethnic interests, unfavorable media, and a two-party system with majority single seat elections (Studlar 1993: 21).

Minority and ethnic groups' penetration of the policy process also included race policy machinery. The legislation creating a single Equality Act and the establishment of the Equality and Human Rights Commission in 2006 to deal with discrimination on the basis of race, ethnicity, religion, gender, sexual orientation, age, and disability may result in a broad coalition. However, the disbandment of the Commission for Racial Equality in the late 2000s entailed the removal of an important political platform for minority activists.

To sum up, the nucleus of the paradox of the politics of inclusion and exclusion is found in the initial dual frames of immigrant policy. This framing consolidated the position of the Home Office as policy venue, but at the same time it led to a wider roster of participants in the policy network that included both race relations experts and social policy advocates. The exclusionary bent of Home Office policies was reinforced by institutional arrangements and electoral politics, while internal politics in the Labour party, specifically its liberal members and the penetration of ethnic minorities who joined together as rights activists, promoted an inclusive approach through strengthening anti-discrimination legislation.

Conclusion

Tracing the politics of rights contraction in the US and the UK has revealed quite dissimilar political processes shaped by differing dynamics between policy venues, institutional arrangements, and political actors. The strong fragmentation of power in the US policy process contrasts with the fusion of executive and legislative powers in the UK. Fragmentation has led to multiple policy venues in the US, whereas a single policy venue has held almost a monopoly position for long periods in the UK. US political parties, accommodating a wide array of political positions, united primarily for election purposes, and the importance of candidate centered politics in securing office also contribute to the fluidity of the policy process, while British parties have remained more programmatic with stronger party discipline. Legislative politics, with the House of Representatives as a driving force to bar immigrants from federal welfare benefits, were crucial to disentitlement; whereas administrative politics in the Home Office and, to a lesser extent, in the Department of Social Security, were decisive in the UK. The social affairs ministry was an ally of the Home Office in restricting newcomers' benefits, whereas in the US, Social Security Administration officials promoted immigrants' access to welfare benefits.

In assessing the importance of the judiciary and the courts as a policy venue, it is necessary to distinguish between the potential impact of judiciary politics in the two countries and the courts' records in terms of rulings. As we have seen, the scope of the courts' impact in the UK has been limited by the doctrine of legislative sovereignty. Until recently judicial review largely involved overturning administrative decisions—and not, as in the US, striking down statutes that violate the constitution. In terms of judicial decisions, the US courts generally have a solid record in extending immigrants' social rights at the state level. The US Supreme Court has been less assertive in countering rights contraction at the federal level because of the legal doctrine of plenary power—the unqualified power of the federal government in matters concerning aliens. The UK courts adopted an activist stance against the total disentitlement of asylum seekers, delivering negative rulings on the 1996 social security regulations and the immigration acts of 1996 and 2002. In this respect the British High Court has been bolder than the US Supreme Court, but with little effect since new statutes negated the court rulings. In sum, legal doctrines in both the US and the UK have set limits on the scope of judiciary politics and the impact of the courts on immigrants' social rights.

Disentitlement in the US occurred as a big policy bang through the adoption of the 1996 welfare and immigration acts. Although the welfare act was preceded by a series of congressional acts and administrative decisions that eroded immigrants' social rights, the 1980s was a decade of contradictory trends involving both rights contraction and extension. The openness and fluidity of the political process has provided ample opportunities for both the opponents and proponents of immigrant social rights, and after the 1996 act, proponents began working to restore immigrants' social rights. Restoration was initially a protracted battle between a Democrat President and a Republican House. The battle ended in the President managing to restore the eligibility of many previous beneficiaries and pre-enactment immigrants; the House Republicans succeeded in retaining the bans on benefits for newly arriving immigrants.

Rights contraction in the UK has been a gradual process that was still unfolding in the late 2000s, as witnessed by the 2009 Borders, Citizenship and Immigration Act and proposals to reform the asylum support system so as to limit eligibility. The concentration of power in the executive and bipartisan consensus on curtailing newcomers' social rights have been prerequisites of the incremental politics of disentitlement that began in 1980, and both Conservative and Labour governments have been involved.

Ironically, given the less programmatic character of US parties, partisan disagreement on immigrants' social rights has tended to reflect a left–right dimension that periodically has been quite marked. Although the two major British parties have not differed on desirability of rights contraction, left–right differences on social policies have persisted, despite New Labour's embrace of greater selectivity. Indirectly these policy differences have been of importance to immigrants once they gain eligibility. Several of New Labour's social policy reforms have benefited immigrants and ethnic minorities, and they have strengthened their social rights.

The territorial dimension was quite similar with regard to the heavy concentration of immigrants and their offspring in relatively few locations. Both the US and the UK have ranked high with respect to the geographical concentration of immigrants, but institutional arrangements shaped the political outcomes in different ways. In the US the fragmentation of the legislative process, affording many "opportunity sites," ranging from congressional committee positions to the possibility of introducing floor amendments during votes on bills, has allowed law makers from immigration states to exert direct influence on legislation affecting immigrants' social rights. By contrast, in the UK political impact of the concentration of immigrants was funneled through the political parties and electoral politics. In both countries ethnic minorities and immigrants have been a constituency of the left parties, and they have had a stronger presence in these parties, which is reflected in the larger numbers of elected representatives from these parties in the legislature. The formation of caucuses by minority members of Congress has forged a link between them and their ethnic constituencies and lobbying organizations.

As distinct from the many contrasts in the politics of rights contraction in the two countries, framing and the politics of justification have had much in common and have been rooted in liberalism. In justifying restrictions, politicians and officials in both countries have appealed to economic self-interest, stressing the costs of immigrants using the welfare system and its burden to the taxpayers. They have also underscored a contractual view of rights, that rights are earned through fulfillment of obligations, and obligations and responsibilities have been stiffened for citizens and non-citizens alike. The individual's responsibility for self-support and support of family members has also been a justification for limiting the availability of benefits generally and restricting immigrants' access to benefits.

In the UK a positive framing of immigrants' entitlements on the basis of their contributions to society has been eclipsed by a negative framing of asylum seekers and other immigrants as fraudulent and abusing the welfare system. A free-rider mentality has been attributed to all newcomers. In the US the argument of immigrants' contributions to society has had more resonance in a country of immigrants, and proponents of immigrants' social rights have utilized the argument to counter disentitlement. The focus on contributions in the UK has not emphasized immigrants' contributions but rather that newcomers must earn the right to stay and the right to citizenship. Most importantly both countries have introduced a differentiation in the social rights of citizens and non-citizens where only citizens have full rights, and this differentiation supplanted equal social rights for all residents.

9

Conservative Corporatist Welfare States and the Politics of Inclusion and Exclusion

Although the conservative corporatist welfare regime accorded many social rights almost immediately to migrant workers, several regime attributes—such as benefits preserving earning status, rigorous work tests, and stiff contribution requirements—have adversely affected immigrants' entitlements. Newcomers have been further disadvantaged by a retrenchment strategy distinctive to the conservative regime countries that privileged insider workers at the expense of outsiders.

Regardless of regime commonalities, France and Germany initially differed in their responses to the most serious flaw of the Bismarckian model: the poor social protection of persons who are not in the labor market or who have inadequate insurance benefits. The French adopted a series of welfare reforms that departed from the Bismarckian model and improved the minimum benefits of persons outside the labor market, and eventually immigrants gained eligibility to these benefits. This was an integral component of the extension in immigrants' social rights in France. Despite overall improvements, the social rights of asylum seekers, undocumented immigrants, and even legal alien residents have suffered setbacks.

German decision makers, in dealing with the weaknesses of the Bismarckian system, often attempted to mend its defects through new insurance schemes and better insurance coverage. Simultaneously the share of the foreign population outside the insurance system has grown over the years, making recourse to assistance benefits their only option. However, foreign residents' utilization of assistance benefits can affect their possibilities to become a citizen, and it has jeopardized acquisition of a permanent residence permit. The failure to fully resolve this problematic relationship has stemmed from negotiated policies and the fusion of the politics of inclusion and exclusion. German policies stand out in another respect. Restricting immigrants' welfare benefits became a strategy of deterrence to combat unwanted immigration much earlier than the other countries in this book. Already in the early 1980s, the Germans sought to deter asylum seekers by introducing welfare benefits in kind and removing their right to work. Although the US and the UK limited newcomers' access to welfare benefits in the early 1980s, the main purpose in these countries was to eliminate alleged misuse of the welfare system—not to curb immigration.

Finally, in the two conservative corporatist countries, immigration legislation and policy dimensions of the incorporation regime have become increasingly important in regulating the social rights of newcomers. In France changes in immigrants' social rights have usually occurred through immigration legislation since 1990. In Germany their social rights have been coupled to requirements for becoming permanent residents and citizens, and the politics of incorporation regime change have affected newcomers' prospects of inclusion and their social entitlements.

In examining immigrants' social rights in the conservative corporatist countries, this chapter initially traces the politics of inclusion and exclusion in France and then in Germany. The concluding section compares the politics of rights extension and contraction in the two countries, highlighting contrasts. The first focus of comparison is the contrast between their policy responses to the defects of the Bismarckian system of social protection. The second contrast elucidates the importance of the territorial dimension in the rights contraction process.

France: The extension of social rights punctuated by reverses

The extension of immigrants' social rights in France has been marred on two counts. Formal parity in the social rights of citizens and newcomers with regard to the basic safety net has not yet been achieved, and since the mid-1980s immigrants' social rights have experienced reversals.

The politics of inclusion and exclusion have been influenced by the dynamics of left–right politics. Patterns of mobilization on the left and the right have influenced the parties' prospects of election. The victory of François Mitterrand in the 1981 presidential election and the left's subsequent victory in the legislative elections produced a massive mobilization of the right. Proposals by the extreme right and an increase in racist incidents led to a counter mobilization among immigrant and ethnic associations and to the formation of new anti-racist organizations—SOS Racisme (1984) and France Plus (1985)—along with huge protest marches in the mid-1980s (Silverman 1992: 63). The mobilization of the right helped to seal its gains in the 1983 municipal elections and the 1986 legislative elections, while immigrant and ethnic organizing strengthened the ethnic vote in the re-election of Mitterrand in 1988 (Wihtol de Wenden 1994: 104).

Even more important, alternations in power between the left and the right have produced constant immigration law revisions that have shaped not only admissions and settlement policies but also the social rights of newcomers. Changes in government also affected the nationality code. The growing electoral strength of Jean-Marie Le Pen and the National Front (*Front national*, FN), with their repeated demands to bar non-citizens from social benefits since the mid-1980s, makes the expansion of immigrants' social rights in France seem all the more remarkable.

The politics of inclusion: National solidarity and equality

The politics of inclusion have consisted of (1) legislating reforms that departed from the Bismarckian model and (2) granting immigrants eligibility to the benefits established by the reforms. National solidarity was an important frame during both phases of the process, while the constitutional principle of equality has been a major justification in expanding the rights of immigrants and persons of immigrant origins.

REFORMS BREAKING WITH THE BISMARCKIAN APPROACH

The adoption of policies deviating from the Bismarckian model was set in motion by the contradiction between the official aspiration of universal coverage and the highly fragmented and incomplete system of social protection actually established by early postwar legislation. The patchwork nature of the Bismarckian schemes spawned a series of piecemeal solutions to provide minimum benefits for those with inadequate or no benefits, and by the mid-1980s several minimum benefits existed (Ashford 1991; Palier 2002). The growing emphasis on the problem of social exclusion from the mid-1970s and onwards promoted a broader solution compared to earlier minimum benefits which were categorical, that is, designed to aid a specific category of need, such as old age, disability, or solo motherhood. Since the excluded (*les exclus*) comprised many diverse groups, a general safety net was required to combat exclusion. The Minimum Insertion Income , RMI, introduced in 1988, came to serve as a general safety net.

The resurrection of solidarity during François Mitterrand's presidency (1981–95) was also important to the enactment of measures breaking with the Bismarckian model. Mitterrand campaigned on the theme of solidarity in the 1981 and 1988 presidential elections. His 1981 election platform called for improvements in social security and welfare under the banner of "a solidaristic society." In 1988 Mitterrand stressed that solidarity meant vertical redistribution, and he promised to introduce a minimum benefit for the "new poor" (the RMI) to be funded from a tax on the wealthy (Macridis 1990: 118; Messu 1999: 113, 117; Stjernø 2005: 155).

Framing the issue of social security and welfare as solidarity was politically advantageous because it generated broad support. Since solidarity has been fused with republicanism, it has been embraced by the left and the right. In the 1988 election both the left and the right campaigned on proposals for the RMI (Silver 1994: 534), and the National Assembly unanimously adopted the new safety net. Its popularity stemmed not only from its justification as a measure to strengthen solidarity and social cohesion, and thus the French Republic, but also from ambiguities in the legislation. The socialists supported the RMI because of its rights enhancing capacity, aiding the disadvantaged, while the right favored its contractual construction (Palier 2006: 126).

IMPROVING IMMIGRANTS' RIGHTS AND ACCESS TO BENEFITS
Parallel with the reforms introducing non-contributory minimum benefits, immigrants' rights were strengthened in a variety of ways. The first advances concerned immigrants' rights as workers and occurred in part because of pressure from the unions and the left. The growing strength of the left was witnessed in the common program adopted by the socialist and communist parties in 1972 and Mitterrand's strong showing in the 1974 presidential election. Mitterrand won 49.2 per cent of the vote and Valéry Giscard d'Estaing 50.8 per cent (Macridis 1987: 118). Between 1972 and 1975 foreign workers gained the right to vote in union elections for work committees, to stand for election, and to be shop stewards. The expansion of rights was justified as the "confirmation of the government's dedication to assuring the equality of social rights between foreign and French workers" (Ireland 1994: 54). Their rights were extended again in 1979 when foreign workers were granted the right to vote in elections for industrial conciliation boards (*conseils des prud'-hommes*) (Guiraudon 2002: 137).

During the Mitterrand presidency the extension of immigrant rights continued. His 1981 election platform addressed immigrants' social and participatory rights. He pledged equal social rights for immigrant workers, ending discrimination, and introducing the right of association and the right to vote in local elections after five years of residence. In attempting to combat illegal employment practices the government granted illegal immigrant workers the same social rights as legal workers in 1981 (Verbunt 1985: 142). A year later, labor legislation (*lois Auroux*) further improved immigrants' participatory rights in the workplace. The government also removed the ban on newly arrived family members' access to the labor market in 1984, enhancing their social rights through the possibility of obtaining insurance benefits. Of special importance, the association law of 1981 introduced parity in the right of association between non-citizens and French citizens, which led to a spectacular growth in immigrant and ethnic organizing. Socialist governments included and later extended immigrant representation on the governing council of FAS, the agency for immigrant welfare. The government also established the National Council of Immigrant Populations, which was a consultative body attached to the ministry of social affairs. However, the campaign promise of local voting rights was quickly abandoned, although Mitterrand continued to express his support of the idea (Ireland 1994; Hayward and Wright 2002: 226–7, 239–41).

A marked shift in the official understanding of national solidarity during the Mitterrand presidency promoted immigrants' social rights. The shift involved the inclusion of resident aliens in the realm of national solidarity. Their inclusion was critical because non-contributory minimum benefits, synonymous with national solidarity, had been reserved for citizens. Already in the 1981 election campaign, Mitterrand declared his intention to welcome immigrants and their families to "national solidarity," and the Minister of National Solidarity (social affairs) in the new government also emphasized that solidarity pertained to "everyone, French and immigrants alike" (Ireland 1994: 61; Freedman 2004, quotation, p. 37). During Mitterrand's two terms in office, "a new solidarity" was enlisted in the fight against social exclusion. Immigrants were one of several excluded groups, but the broader focus on the excluded deflected attention away from immigrants. This framing made the population with immigrant backgrounds a target of the measures but avoided politicizing the issue of their social rights.

Court decisions also played a major role in extending immigrants' eligibility to non-contributory minimum benefits, and the rulings emphasized equality before the law and the rights of the individual. Importantly, in the early 1970s the *Conseil constitutionnel*, the Constitutional Court, broadened the body of constitutional principles (*bloc de constitutionnalité*) relevant to judicial review. Rather than limiting itself to the text of the 1958 constitution, the court included the constitutional preamble, which reaffirms the 1789 declaration of rights, and the preamble of the 1946 constitution. The inclusion of the 1946 preamble was crucial in two respects. First the preamble includes basic social and economic rights. Second, as distinct from the 1958 constitution that uses the term *citizens*, the 1946 preamble accords rights and equal protection to all *persons* (Guendelsberger 1992–3: 698) and thus to non-citizens.

Most decisive was the 1990 ruling of the Constitutional Court that established equal access of non-citizens, regularly residing in France, to minimum benefits provided by the National Solidarity Fund. The Court invoked the constitutional principle of equality upholding the liberties and fundamental rights of all persons residing in the French Republic. This decision was preceded by a similar ruling of the *Conseil d'État*, the High Administrative Court, which had invalidated a local family benefit whose eligibility requirements

The Politics of Inclusion and Exclusion

excluded many aliens. The grounds for annulment were that the municipal rule violated the constitutional principle of equality (Guendelsberger 1992–3).

The translation of the court decisions into law had to wait until the "plural left" government, comprised of the socialist, communist, and green parties, headed by Lionel Jospin (1997–2002). The 1998 immigration law removed the requirement of nationality for non-contributory benefits (HCI 1998: 17), and it made it illegal for local authorities to deny local social benefits to non-citizens (Freedman 2004: 99).

The Jospin government strengthened immigrants' social rights in other respects. Non-citizens gained the right to be elected to bodies administering social insurance benefits (DF 2003: 21). Indirectly the government also enhanced the social rights of undocumented immigrants through a large-scale legalization program, and it introduced the possibility of legal status after ten years of residence. This move was prompted by the difficult situation of undocumented immigrants who had lived in France for several years but could not acquire legal status because of restrictive immigration legislation introduced in 1993 and early 1997. The government raised minimum benefits paid to asylum seekers (Delouvin 2000: 66), an unusual step in a comparative perspective. Several of these measures exhibited continuity with the left governments during Mitterrand's first term in office. Finally, the Jospin government introduced legislation and executive orders that reversed or eased several restrictions introduced by right governments since 1993, including the exclusionary 1993 reform of the nationality code, discussed below.

The development of anti-discrimination policies since the late 1990s has also strengthened the social rights of immigrants, especially for the second generation and immigrants who have become citizens. Both domestic and EU politics put anti-discrimination policies on the agenda. Domestically, one of the most powerful arguments was that anti-discrimination measures were necessary to enforce the constitutional principle of equality and ensure equal treatment. Special emphasis was placed on insuring the equal treatment of French citizens with respect to social security, education, housing, and employment (HCI 1998). After much delay, the government created the High Authority for the Struggle against Discrimination and for Equality (HALDE) in late 2004. Its establishment offers an alternative avenue in improving the social rights of the population of immigrant origins by addressing discrimination in employment, housing, and education. Importantly, as Guiraudon has noted, anti-discrimination measures have altered the construction of the problem. The problem of integration is not solely the responsibility of immigrants; it includes addressing discrimination embedded in French institutions and exercised by the French themselves (2005: 163).

At times immigrant mobilization has influenced the rights extension process. A protest march of young second generation immigrants from North

Africa and an audience with Mitterrand represented a turning point in gaining the president's support of the single permit combining the residence and work permits, introduced in 1984 (Silverman 1992: 62; Weil 2004: 248, 253–6). Immigrants also lobbied for the creation of a ministry of integration. Instead the government established the High Council of Integration in 1990 (Silverman 1992: 139), but a few years later the Cresson government (1991–2) reshuffled ministerial duties, creating the Ministry of Social Affairs and Integration and appointed Kofi Yamgnane junior minister of integration (Weil 2004: 287). The formation of the *sans-papiers* (undocumented immigrants) movement, whose protests gained much sympathy among the left (Waters 2003: 82–92; Schain 2008: 54), helped bring about the Jospin government's legalization program and legislation improving the rights of undocumented immigrants in the late 1990s. Demonstrations by immigrant and pro-rights organizations have also blocked proposals to worsen immigrant rights, to which I now turn.

The politics of exclusion: Non-assimilation, illegal immigration, and the priority of the French

Crucial to the politics of exclusion and rights contraction has been a gradual change from a positive to negative framing of immigrants, which occurred before immigration became a national election issue. Rather than politicians or the media it was state administrators and technocrats who initially framed immigrants in negative terms. The negative framing had both indirect and direct repercussions for immigrants' social rights. The demands of Le Pen and the National Front further challenged immigrants' social rights. Still, as we shall see, the direct influence of Le Pen and the FN on non-citizens' social rights has been marginal. Instead the mainstream parties, especially the right-wing parties, have been responsible for the contraction in immigrants' social rights.

FROM POSITIVE TO NEGATIVE FRAMING
Initially immigration and immigrants were framed in terms of their contribution to France's economic recovery after the Second World War, and opinion surveys show that the French were generally positive to immigrants in the early 1970s (Money 1999: 134). The shift toward negative framing began in 1969 when an expert report claimed non-European immigrants were incapable of assimilation. The frame of non-assimilation was buttressed by the threshold of tolerance (*le seuil de tolérance*) thesis that emphasized social problems, including a rising crime rate, once local concentrations of ethnically and racially diverse immigrants reached a specific threshold (Freeman 1979: 87–8, 158–60; Schain 1985: 176–82).

With the introduction of measures to halt immigration in the mid-1970s, an additional negative frame—illegal immigration—emerged. Rather than illegal immigration, the French speak of clandestine immigration and "*les clandestins*," suggesting an insidious phenomenon beyond control (Weil 1991; Silverman 1992: 136–8). Finally, immigration has been framed in terms of danger to the public order, with immigrants representing subversive and criminal elements (Freedman 2004).

Drawing upon the frames of non-assimilation, clandestine immigration, and criminality, Le Pen and the FN began to campaign against immigration in elections during the early 1980s. They emphasized the priority of the French spelled out in the slogan "French First!" (*Français d'abord!*) (Taguieff 1996: 221).

To sum up, framing the problem as non-assimilation tied the issue to the French model of citizenship and eroded confidence in integrative capacity of the nation. It also contributed to bringing the issue of citizenship reform onto the political agenda. The notion that many newcomers could not be assimilated reinforced the emphasis on tight immigration controls and repatriation. The illegality of their presence further justified illiberal restrictions. Simultaneously the frames of the threshold of tolerance, illegality, and the priority of the French threatened immigrants' social rights. Emphasizing immigrants were a problem also led to a shift in the policy venue from a technocratic-administrative setting to the legislative and electoral arenas (Schain 1996: 174–6), heightening the role of the political parties.

POLITICAL PARTIES AND GOVERNMENT POLICIES

Government efforts to curb immigration took a restrictionist turn in the mid-1970s during Giscard d'Estaing's presidency. The illiberal and arbitrary nature of the executive orders that terminated labor and family immigration prompted the courts to invalidate them. Among the restrictive measures affecting immigrants' social rights in the early 1970s were those giving priority to French workers in the labor market.

With the electoral breakthrough of the FN in 1983–4, immigrants' social rights came under direct attack. The party rejected equal social rights for non-citizens, stressing the priority of the French. Initially, in 1984 the FN demanded the suspension of family benefits to persons of immigrant origins, but the priority of the French has appeared in a variety of guises over the years. The FN's fifty proposals on immigration, announced in Marseille in 1991, called for the immediate implementation of the priority of nationals in the areas of employment, public housing, family allowances, and social security. During the 1995 presidential election, the FN campaigned on employment, job training, and wage increases for French citizens only and separate social security programs for French citizens and foreigners (Safran 1998: 122–3;

Knapp 2004: 298). In the 2007 presidential campaign Le Pen proposed to end welfare abuse by reserving local social aid and family benefits for the French, introducing higher contributions on immigrants' health and unemployment insurance, and terminating non-citizens' eligibility for RMI and medical assistance (AME) (FN 2007).

The left's victory in 1981, and the inclusion of the communists in the government, unified the right and broadened the opposition so that it ranged from moderates to the extreme right. The right condemned the laxity of the government's immigration and immigrant policies, and it rallied around the issue of citizenship reform and campaigned on the issue in the 1986 legislative elections. The joint election platform of the two mainstream right parties—the RPR (Gaullists) and the UDF (centrists)—presented revision of the nationality code as a way to strengthen French national identity (Feldblum 1999: 60–4). The mainstream right led by Jacques Chirac won the elections, and France experienced its first round of co-habitation, with the presidency and the government representing different parties.

The Chirac government (1986–8), known for its passage of restrictive immigration legislation (Pasqua I) and its efforts to change the nationality code, also took the first step in worsening undocumented immigrants' social rights. The government tightened eligibility for family benefits by requiring that both the parents and children had legal immigration status (Massot 1990: 87–8). Prior to this, Chirac had been involved in curtailing immigrants' access to benefits at the local level. The Paris city council, with Chirac as mayor, modified the requirements for entitlement to a local non-contributory benefit for the third child so that many aliens became ineligible, and this was the benefit and its requirements that the High Administrative Court later invalidated (Guiraudon 2006: 138).

The right was unsuccessful in its bid to revise the nationality code. In the end the government withdrew its bill, which would have converted the right to citizenship acquisition of children born in France of foreign parents into a voluntary request to become a citizen. Widespread protests, growing public opinion against the reform, and Chirac's ambitions to win the 1988 presidential election contributed to the retreat (Feldblum 1999).

Mitterrand defeated Chirac in the 1988 presidential election and he appointed a socialist government with Michel Rocard as prime minister (1988–91), succeeded by Edith Cresson (1991–2). In 1991 the Cresson government eliminated asylum seekers' access to the labor market and unemployment benefits (Hayward and Wright 2002: 237–8). Asylum seekers became dependent upon a social minimum benefit (AI), which could also be claimed by expatriates, stateless persons, and ex-prisoners (Eardley et al.1996b: 149).

In 1993, after campaigning on immigration and citizenship reform, the mainstream right came into office with an overwhelming majority, 80 per cent of the seats in the National Assembly. Within roughly six months the Balladur government (1993–5) had introduced new immigration and nationality laws (Feldblum 1999: 148). The immigration legislation (Pasqua II) worsened immigrants' entitlements. Following in the steps of the Chirac administration, the government made legal residence a requirement for nearly all social insurance benefits and minimum benefits for the elderly and handicapped. At the same time, the law made it more difficult to obtain legal status. Although the government did not bar immigrants from family benefits, it excluded family benefits in the calculation of the minimum income required for family reunification. The revised nationality code tightened requirements for children born in France of parents of Algerian origin or from former colonies as well as for spouses of French citizens (Weil and Spire 2006: 199).

The 2002 legislative elections, following the re-election of Chirac as president, reaffirmed the right government, and during the rest of the decade both the president and the government came from the mainstream right. The two immigration laws introduced by Interior Minister, Nicolas Sarkozy (2002–4 and 2005–7), forged a link between integration and immigration controls and made family reunification more difficult even in the case of spouses of French citizens, and the laws also eroded immigrants' social rights.

The major innovation of the 2003 law (Sarkozy I) was to make assimilation a condition for being issued a permanent permit, and integration contracts were introduced on a trial basis. The law also tightened the requirements for a permanent resident permit. It raised the minimum residence requirement from three to five years (Legifrance 2003), affecting access to the major safety net benefit, the RMI.

New asylum legislation in 2003 cut the benefits of asylum seekers. It limited the duration of benefits to the application process, and benefits were completely eliminated for asylum seekers whose applications were decided by the accelerated procedure, which became more common. Asylum seekers' access to medical care was further restricted (ECRE 2004; Freedman 2004: 63).

The 2006 immigration law (Sarkozy II) made fulfillment of the integration contract a requirement for a permanent permit. This requirement was one facet of a major tightening of the conditions for family reunification. More generally, however, fulfillment of the contract strengthened the possibility of permanent permit after five years of residence if one had an income sufficient to support oneself. For others, the residence requirement for a permanent permit remained ten years. The law also repealed the provisions that granted legal status after ten years of residence in France, indirectly worsening undocumented immigrants' prospects of gaining access to social benefits. Instead of a general residence requirement, requests for legal status were to be determined on an individual basis. Finally, the 2006 law made family reunification more difficult by eliminating all social benefits from the calculation of an adequate income to support family members (JO 2006).

Under Sarkozy's presidency (2007–12), a major administrative reorganization occurred at the ministerial and agency levels, which was also a pledge in his election platform (NS 2007: 14). National identity, the watchword of the right during the mid-1980s, resurfaced, and the new ministry was named the Ministry of Immigration, Integration, National Identity and Co-development. At the agency level, a casualty of the reorganization was FAS, the immigrant welfare agency. The 2007 immigration law further tightened the resource test for family reunification, and it authorized withdrawal of family benefits for parents who did not fulfill their obligation to integrate their children into French society. It also required family members to take a course in order to evaluate their language skills and knowledge of French values, prior to entering France (Legifrance 2007).

In the area of social policy, the conservative governments attached more weight to the contractual nature of insertion measures, stiffening obligations and sanctions. The 2008 reform of the general safety net—introducing the *Revenu de solidarité active*, RSA—had both inclusive and exclusionary effects. The reform tightened work requirements, but it extended entitlement to encompass not only the excluded but also those in precarious employment (*le précariat*) and lowered the age requirement (formerly 25+) (Martin 2010: 84), which can benefit the population with immigrant origins. Importantly, the delay in eligibility for immigrants not from the European Economic Area (the EU, Switzerland, Norway, and Iceland) was increased from three to five years, widening the gap in its availability to citizens and legal aliens.

In short, overwhelmingly but not exclusively, it has been conservative governments that have restricted the social rights of immigrants, with marked continuities in the policies of mainstream right administrations. They also introduced legislation to make key policy dimensions of the incorporation regime—citizenship acquisition, the permit system, integration measures, and family reunification—more restrictive during the past two decades.

THE IMPACT OF LE PEN AND THE NATIONAL FRONT

In assessing the impact of the National Front and its leader, it is useful to distinguish between electoral and policy impact. Electorally, the party has definitely had an impact. Since 1984 the FN and Le Pen have received at least 10 per cent of the vote—and in some elections close to 20 per cent. The FN has made immigration a campaign issue since the early 1980s. Its continuous emphasis on the immigration issue has made it impossible for the mainstream parties to remove it from electoral politics. In other words, the FN rendered Freeman's anti-populist norm inoperative in French politics. By making immigration an election issue and a concern of the voters the party has influenced the political agenda.

While it is clear that the FN has altered the party landscape and kept immigration and immigrant issues on the political agenda, it is much trickier to gauge its influence on policy making. The party has lacked direct access to the policy process. Despite winning between 10 and 15 per cent of the vote in legislative elections, the FN has usually had only one member in the National Assembly or has been unrepresented (Knapp 2004: 36–7). Still a common view is that the existence of the FN and its popularity has forced the mainstream parties, especially the right, to adopt policy positions similar to those of FN. The major difficulty is disentangling the existing preferences of main-stream right officeholders from FN demands—and the question of whether restrictive measures would have been introduced without the existence of the FN (Schain 2008: 101).

Comparing the demands of the FN with policy outputs affecting immi-grants' social rights provides a handle in assessing its policy impact. A longstanding demand has been eliminating immigrants' access to family benefits. Restrictions on immigrants' eligibility to family benefits were intro-duced at the local level where the FN had elected officials. As we have seen, the Jospin government passed legislation to prevent local politicians from exclud-ing immigrants from local benefits. Conservative governments have neutra-lized family benefits so that they could not contribute to family immigration, but they have not barred immigrants from these benefits. Can the limits on immigrants' access to the safety net be attributed to the FN? A plausible alternative explanation has to do with the construction of the RMI; it was modeled upon a local minimum benefit (Levy 1999: 97–8), and local social aid has traditionally had a residence requirement. On the other hand, influence on the adoption of the five-year work requirement for the major safety net benefit cannot be ruled out. Le Pen campaigned on ending non-citizens' access to the RMI. The right government limited access to the safety net, but it did not disentitle immigrants as desired by the FN. Finally, long before the FN's electoral breakthrough, a mainstream right government introduced the first measures embodying the priority of the French on the labor market in 1972. In a similar vein, a conservative government abolished the immigrant welfare agency, FAS, but this was not a demand of the FN. Thus right govern-ments have introduced restrictive measures without being under the sway of the FN, but they have also shied away from the most extreme FN demands.

In summation, this analysis has documented the importance of alternations in power between left and right governments that have produced changes in legislation affecting immigrants' rights, including their social rights. Although conservative governments strengthened the rights of foreign workers during the 1970s, their subsequent record has been quite poor in terms of immigrant rights. The analysis has also revealed strong continuities in the policies of the right and left respectively since the early 1980s. Left governments have introduced measures improving immigrant rights. By contrast, reversals of the rights extension process have largely occurred when the right has controlled the executive. Since the French policy process is executive-led with few veto sites, the partisan composition of government has left its mark on immigrant rights.

Germany: Negotiated policies and the fusion of the politics of inclusion and exclusion

Negotiated policies based on party deliberations and compromise typify the German policy process. Institutional arrangements, especially the federal system but also multiparty governments, entail power sharing and a variety of veto/opportunity sites that have necessitated party negotiations. Negotiated policies have often meant a fusion of the politics of inclusion and exclusion. As compromises, laws have simultaneously incorporated inclusive and restrictive measures. Thus despite a general inclusive thrust, party negotiations on major legislation have perpetuated and at times even strengthened the restrictive features of the German incorporation regime that have affected immigrants' social rights.

German federalism has made the states, *Länder*, key players in the policy process in quite a different way from the US federal system. The influence of the *Länder* in the federal legislative process is institutionalized in the upper chamber of parliament, the Federal Council (*Bundesrat*). Its strongest legislative powers are in matters that affect *Länder* administration and finances. In these matters, which include immigrant policies and welfare, the Council has an absolute veto and the right to initiate legislation. Since the Federal Council reflects the political composition of the state governments, its political majority is not necessarily the same as that of the directly elected chamber—the *Bundestag*—and the majority of the upper chamber can be altered by state elections with immediate effect. The government has frequently confronted an upper house whose majority could stop its legislative proposals or extract major concessions (Manow 2005: 234–5, 254). This veto power has required cooperation with the opposition to pass legislation and has resulted in what has been called grand coalition policy making (Schmidt 2003: 204).

Coalition governments have also been the norm in German politics, which has led to party compromises and negotiated policies. Coalition agreements on the government's policy and the distribution of ministries are hammered out in party negotiations. The principle of ministerial responsibility has allowed ministers substantial autonomy in running their ministries and in drafting legislation proposals, but wider government approval by the coalition parties has set limits on the actions of individual ministers.

This section first examines the politics of inclusion characterized by nego-tiated policies that have fused inclusive and exclusionary measures. It also discusses the failure to eliminate the problematic relationship between assis-tance utilization and residence status and citizenship acquisition that has set limits on the social rights of newcomers and permanent residents who are non-citizens. Since the German case represents far-reaching incorporation regime change, I pay more attention to citizenship reform here compared to the French analysis. Then I consider the process of rights contraction affecting the entitlements of asylum seekers and co-ethnic immigrants, underlining the party-electoral and territorial dimensions of politics.

Inclusion with multiple requirements

Change in the German incorporation regime has revolved around three mod-ifications: the transition from an ethnic to a civic territorial model of citizen-ship, the replacement of discretionary naturalization by naturalization as a right upon fulfillment of specified requirements, and the move toward equal treatment of non-German and ethnic German immigrants. The changes have represented an expansive twin shift: inclusive changes in citizenship policy and the transition from a foreigner policy (*Ausländerpolitik*) to an immigration policy (Green 2004). These advances, however, have been offset by new requirements for inclusion, reflecting the fusion of inclusive and exclusionary measures and a tightening in the interface between social policy and the incorporation regime.

To shed light on the expansive twin shift, my discussion focuses on (1) the initial framing of immigrant and citizenship policies and the emergence of a counterframe, (2) political parties, and (3) negotiated policies and the coali-tions behind the policies. The politics of inclusion in Germany presents us with two interesting puzzles. The first is that Germany is an example of major policy change, but political analysts describe German politics as prone to incrementalism, decision traps, and non-decision (Katzenstein 1987; Scharpf 1988; Green 2004). How did major regime change occur in an institutional setting characterized by incremental decision making and non-decision? In a long-term perspective, regime change may simply appear as incrementalism, but the policy process in this area has been marked by long periods of non-decision interrupted by four major policy breakthroughs combining inclusive and restrictive measures: the 1990 Foreigner Law, the 1992 asylum compro-mise, the 2000 Nationality Law, and the 2004 Immigration Law.

The second puzzle is that the political parties have been the main motors in this process despite the absence of electoral incentives and substantial risks

(Murray 1994: 24). As non-citizens and non-voters, foreigners have not been a political constituency, and they have had little access to the federal policy process formulating measures that have directly affected them (Esser and Korte 1985: 202; Green 2004: 67). By contrast, the early co-ethnic immigrants, as citizens, were immediately a political constituency, and they became MPs and even held ministerial posts. Over the years German ethnic immigrants gravitated increasingly to the main conservative party, the Christian Democratic Union (*Christlich-Demokratische Union*, CDU). Ethnic immigrant voters have had substantial clout because of their strong support of the CDU (Münz and Ohliger 1998). In office and as voters, they have tended to favor the status quo on immigrant and immigration policies. Finally large sections of the electorate have been suspicious of immigration and immigrant rights (Karapin 2002: 195–6).

POLICY FRAMES
The overarching policy frame until the late 1990s was the official view that Germany was not a country of immigration. This view was reinforced by a model of citizenship that defined the citizenry as members of a community exclusively based on German descent. Accordingly defenders of the model viewed immigration as a threat to the unity of the political community, and they proposed extraordinary high thresholds for non-Germans' membership, resulting in the doctrine that naturalization was an exception and must be in the interests of Germany.

This framing had several consequences. First and foremost it produced a sharp differentiation in policies for co-ethnic and non-German immigrants. Ethnic German newcomers were not immigrants; they were settlers returning to their home country. As repatriates, they deserved assistance through generous programs for their integration in society. Non-German newcomers were defined as foreigners—not as potential settlers. Accordingly there was no settlement policy for them but instead a foreigner policy. Second this frame engendered a politics of denial that made consideration of an integration policy difficult. Eventually there was the recognition of the need for temporary integration measures in the mid-1970s, followed by policy guidelines assigning "future priority to the 'social integration of the second and the third generations.'" Third, the frame put a premium on naturalization as a policy instrument. Through naturalization, immigrants would no longer be foreigners or the subjects of the *Ausländerpolitik*. The original target of this policy was not foreigners but their children (Esser and Korte 1985: 180–4, quotation p. 183). Fourth, the emphasis on naturalization also privileged a specific policy network where the Interior Ministry has been pivotal policy venue. As long as integration was conceived as measures promoting the welfare of foreign workers, the main policy venue was the Ministry of Labor and Social Affairs, and the policy network included corporatist bodies.

A reorientation began in the mid-1970s, eventually offering a counterframe. The reorientation—most evident in the policy statements of federal government—emphasized social and humanitarian concerns and criticized an exclusively economic approach (Esser and Korte 1985: 174, 183; Katzenstein 1987: 241–2). The call for action was fed by a dual specter of social unrest: first, the problem of several million inhabitants living outside the national community and, second, nationalist rhetoric and rising anti-foreigner sentiments that created a breeding ground for neo-Nazism. Advocates of a reorientation also stressed the responsibility of the government to integrate foreigners because their presence was the result of deliberate recruitment policies, and that the Nazi legacy made it a collective responsibility to find a solution (Murray 1994). The thrust of the argument underlined that the current policy of exclusion was detrimental to the national interest. In effect, the argument challenged a cornerstone of the restrictive naturalization guidelines, which only allowed naturalization on the grounds that it served the interests of Germany.

POLITICAL PARTIES AND FRAMING

A counterframe on citizenship emerged from the left-center political parties during the 1980s, and it emphasized immigrant rights and the right of citizenship. The Social Democrats (*Sozialdemokratische Partei Deutschlands*, SPD) argued for inclusive reform of citizenship acquisition. The party advocated the right of citizenship for young foreigners, some form of *ius soli* for non-citizens born in Germany, and acceptance of dual citizenship. In justifying party proposals, the Social Democrats emphasized an alternative view of membership as the basis of citizenship—membership in the state rather than the nation. They spoke of foreigners as co-citizens (*Mitburger*) and recommended local voting rights after ten years of residence (Murray 1994: 32–8).

The Free Democrats (*Freie Demokratische Partei*, FDP), a liberal party which has defended civil rights and individual liberties, underlined the need for a more humane policy toward foreigners based on human dignity and the worth of the individual. The FDP also attached major weight to tolerance, asserting that foreigners had a right to tolerance. Liberal politicians argued that the foreigners' issue was a test for Germany's liberal democracy, and they were highly critical of the existing "law's relegation of foreigners to a 'position without rights.'" Party proposals favored a right to citizenship for young foreigners and dual citizenship, but the Free Democrats were skeptical toward *ius soli* during the 1980s (Murray 1994: 39–43, quotation p. 43).

The arrival of the Greens on the party landscape in the early 1980s brought a greater emphasis on equal rights, and initially they called for rights, including voting rights, based on residence. The party's concrete proposals were a right to citizenship after five years of residence without having to repudiate one's previous nationality, *ius soli* along the lines proposed by the SPD, and upon adulthood naturalization of children of persons with the right of abode. The Greens argued that equal rights were essential to democracy, and that they were a prerequisite for respect for foreigners. The party further underscored that "citizenship is a 'legal status,' which grants 'equal rights and obligations' without regard to ethnicity or cultural background, not an institution meant to unite people of common descent" (Murray 1994: 32–46, quotation p. 46). In effect, the three parties put forward an alternative vision of citizenship that challenged the ethnic model.

Despite its defense of the ethnic model of citizenship and many members' belief that foreigners could not and should not become Germans, the Christian Democratic Union eventually acknowledged the harmful potential of excluding a large segment of the population from the citizenry. This acknowledgement necessitated rethinking the requirements for citizenship. Although the party was adamant in its opposition to *ius soli* and dual nationality, the CDU could contemplate a right of citizenship for foreigners who had grown up in Germany, and especially if they had attended German schools (Murray 1994). The most die-hard resistance has come from the Christian Social Union (*Christlich-Soziale Union*, CSU), the Bavarian sister party of the CDU. However, prominent CDU politicians have also been ardent restrictionists (Boswell and Hough 2008).

NEGOTIATED POLICIES, PARTIES, AND POLICY COALITIONS
The 1990 Foreigner Law has been heralded as the first legislation signaling a more inclusive approach (Joppke 1999: 202; Thränhardt 1999: 54). Negotiations on the law were confined to the parties in the coalition government, and the law was not an example of grand coalition policy making. The other three major policy breakthroughs—the 1992 asylum compromise, the 2000 Nationality Law, and the 2004 Immigration Law—involved grand coalition policy making, and all four combined inclusive measures with restrictions. In the case of the 1992 asylum compromise, restrictions outweighed inclusive features, and the compromise is discussed under the politics of rights contraction.

The 1990 Foreigner Law
Years of gridlock preceded the enactment of the 1990 Foreigner Law. In 1982 the FDP entered a coalition with the CDU-CSU, with Helmut Kohl as chancellor. The government was deeply divided because FDP and the CSU had diametrically opposed positions on immigration and immigrant rights. Dissensions peaked in 1988 when the Interior Minister, Friedrich Zimmermann (CSU), unveiled the draft of a new highly restrictive foreigner law,

which led to his transfer to another ministry (Green 2004: 57–63; Boswell and Hough 2008: 23–4).

The appointment of Wolfgang Schäuble (CDU) as Interior Minister, together with growing pressure on the government, set the stage for a policy breakthrough. Policy inertia was an increasing embarrassment and liability to the government. The emergence of far right parties and their electoral successes in 1989 created additional anxiety, and the possibility that the governing parties would lose their majority in the Bundesrat spurred the government into action. As long as the opposition was not included in deliberations, the CDU-CSU had a position of strength vis-à-vis the FDP, whereas inclusion of the opposition would tip the balance toward in favor of parties advocating greater inclusiveness.

The compromise behind the 1990 law married stiffer requirements with relaxations, reflecting the differing views within the government. Adequate accommodations had been a requirement for family reunification, but the 1990 law made it a requirement for a permanent residence permit. The law also strengthened the link between social benefits and the acquisition of citizenship in two ways. First, the law made payment of insurance contributions for five years a requirement for a permanent residence permit. Second, economic self-sufficiency, a requirement of citizenship, was concretized as the ability to support oneself and family members without utilizing social assistance or unemployment assistance. Proponents of more generous measures—the opposition parties, the Commissioner of Foreigner Affairs, unions and church organizations—were largely shut out of the process of formulating the bill. The influence of the opposition parties was limited to the extension of the simplified naturalization procedure to first generation immigrants, but a very rigorous residence requirement of 15 years was necessary for its inclusion. The economic self-sufficiency requirement was also modified so that it did not apply if utilization of assistance were for reasons beyond one's control. The bill was rushed through parliament, and a few days after its passage the SPD and Greens gained a majority in the Bundesrat (Neuman 1998: 290; Green 2004: 65–77). The swift passage of the law also kept the immigration issue out of the 1990 federal election (Joppke 1999: 84).

On balance, the 1990 Foreigner Law strengthened non-citizens' residency rights but it also multiplied the requirements for a permanent residence permit and sharpened requirements related to a secure livelihood. Similarly, the law enlarged long-term alien residents' possibility of naturalization, while raising the residence requirement and making it one of the most stringent in Europe. It only opened the door provisionally; the more generous possibility to naturalize was to end in 1996. More positively, the law facilitated young immigrants' acquisition of German citizenship for those who had lived in

Germany eight years, attended German schools for six years, and renounced their previous citizenship.

The 2000 Nationality Law and amendments
Although the 2000 Nationality Law contained substantial advances, restrictive elements also found their way into the law and its implementation legislation. The major political battles dealt with the introduction of some form of *ius soli* for immigrant children born in Germany and dual citizenship. In the end, the *ius soli* requirements excluded many children with immigrant backgrounds, and the original bill's major innovation—dual citizenship—was deleted. The inclusive features of the law were lowering the residence requirement for naturalization from fifteen to eight years and strengthening the right to naturalization.

The red-green government headed by Gerhard Schröder (1998–2005) entered office with a strong mandate; the CDU-CSU experienced its poorest polling since the 1949 election. Citizenship reform had been a campaign pledge of the two parties, and the new government introduced a draft bill in early 1999. The Greens favored naturalization after five years of residence, introducing citizenship based on land of birth (*ius soli*) for foreigners born in Germany, and dual citizenship. The Social Democrats also supported dual citizenship, but their stand on *ius soli* was more cautious. The Social Democrat Interior Minister, Otto Schily, preferred a solution of *ius soli* for the third generation. The coalition parties eventually reached a compromise: *ius soli* would apply if one parent was born in Germany or had immigrated before the age of 14. Other restrictive aspects were the retention of existing requirements for naturalization, such as non-utilization of assistance benefits, codifying adequate knowledge of German as a requirement, and introducing a loyalty oath to the constitution (Green 2004: 95–7).

The deletion of dual citizenship from the nationality law was achieved by a campaign mounted by the CDU-CSU. Campaigning against dual citizenship, the CDU won the Hesse state election, which robbed the governing parties of their majority in the Bundesrat. The SPD's strategy was to seek the support of the FDP through modifying the bill, thus bypassing the CDU. Rather than endorsing dual citizenship, the final bill increased the number of exceptions allowing dual citizenship. The FDP also favored *ius soli* for second generation immigrants, which was written into the bill, with a residence requirement of eight years and that the parent had had a permanent residence permit for three years—which disqualified roughly half of the foreigners born in Germany. Still the requirements were more generous than the original bill, which had required that one parent was born in Germany or had immigrated before the age of 14 (Green 2004: 102–3, 97; Hailbronner 2006: 224).

The 2000 law was not the final word in citizenship policy. Two sets of amendments have tightened requirements. The first set incorporated changes required by the 2004 Immigration Law. The changes increased permit requirements: the level of language proficiency and completion of an integration course (Hailbronner 2006: 225–7). The nationality law was amended again in 2007 during the grand coalition government (CDU-CSU and SDP) headed by Angela Merkel (2005–9), and the amendments were mainly restrictions. In the Merkel government, the Interior Ministry went to the CDU, with Wolfgang Schäuble as minister. The 2007 amendments added new naturalization requirements: a civics test, increased language skills, and a stricter version of no criminal record. The most exclusionary measure was to extend the secure livelihood requirement to young foreigners, who had previously been exempt (BBMFI 2007a). Thus it created a new barrier to the inclusion of non-citizens born in Germany.

The 2004 Immigration Law

The law has generally been hailed as a major breakthrough in legislation—the culmination of a long process of coming to grips with the social reality that Germany was a land of immigration. Nonetheless it too combined improvements with restrictions, in part because of the difficulties in securing its passage. By the time the 2002 Immigration Law reached parliament, the position of the red-green government in the Bundesrat had further deteriorated. When the government tried heavy handed tactics during the Bundesrat's final vote, several CDU-led states challenged the constitutionality of the law due to the voting procedure, and the Federal Constitutional Court invalidated the 2002 law on these grounds (Green 2004: 126–7).

Now the government had no alternative but to renegotiate the law taking the views of the opposition into account. Disagreement over the scope of labor immigration led to the jettison of the point system in favor of a permit system with more controls—admissions based on a prior job offer and work authorization that can limit the duration of employment, occupation, workplace, and region. The final version also laid down high entry thresholds: for the self-employed, investment of €1 million in Germany creating a minimum of ten jobs or a minimum monthly salary of €4000 (MN 2002–4; BMI 2004).

The fuzzy definition of a secure livelihood in the 2004 law also smacks of grand coalition policy making. The law made a secure livelihood a requirement in issuing and renewing residence permits as well as granting settlement permits. A secure livelihood was defined as the ability to earn a living, including adequate health insurance coverage, without recourse to public funds (BMI 2004: 12). On the one hand, prohibition of recourse to public funds is a broader formulation than utilization of two assistance programs, satisfying restrictionists. New requirements were also added: adequate health insurance and in some cases adequate pension coverage. On the other hand, family benefits, social insurance benefits, and benefits for residence in Germany were excluded from public funds, and the formulation "benefits for residence" is extremely vague and open to interpretation. The ambiguities are important because implementation is at the *Länder* level. In justifying of both restrictive and lenient decisions, officials can invoke the letter of the law.

An innovation of the law was federally funded integration courses for both foreigners and ethnic German immigrants. Although framed as an entitlement for newcomers, failure to attend an integration course can affect the renewal of the residence permit and acquisition of a permanent permit. The law also laid down an obligation for foreigners relying on unemployment benefits and those "in special need of integration" to participate in the courses; it sanctioned reduced benefits for failure to do so. In the late 2000s the CDU Interior Minister stiffened obligations and sanctions. Those who received assistance benefits had to sign integration contracts, and a fine of up to €1000 and loss of benefits for non-attendance were introduced, along with the possible withdrawal of the residence permit (Klusmeyer and Papademetriou 2009: 281–2; Wiesbrock 2009: 307).

In conclusion the preceding analysis highlights the importance of the political parties in the politics of rights extension. Thus it differs from Christian Joppke's interpretation (1999: 75), which emphasizes the centrality of judiciary politics behind the extension of immigrant rights and a more inclusive policy. Joppke sees the political parties as either largely ratifying court rulings or adversely affecting immigrants' rights. Major court decisions did uphold the right to a permanent permit and family reunification, and blocked several arbitrary deportations. The rulings legally affirmed continued immigration and contributed to the second shift—the official recognition that Germany was a country of immigration. However, court decisions have frequently supported a restrictive approach to citizenship and rejected political rights for non-citizens. Instead the political parties and negotiated policies have been the linchpin in the rights extension process, even if this has involved the fusion of inclusive and restrictive measures as well as an ebb and flow in immigrant rights.

The politics of rights contraction: Party-electoral and territorial dimensions

The politics of rights contraction have been most evident in the erosion of the social rights of asylum seekers and ethnic German immigrants. The rights of asylum seekers came under attack in the late 1970s, while the rights of resettlers became the target a decade later. In an atmosphere of national crisis, the rights of these two entry categories became fatally intertwined in the 1992 asylum compromise. The SPD agreed to alter the constitutional right of asylum in exchange for CDU concessions to end co-ethnic immigration in the long term.

The party-electoral and the territorial dimensions of conflict have influenced the rights contraction process (Joppke 1999: 86). Party competition in elections and an anti-immigration majority opinion have spurred the rights contraction process and resulted in a recurring electoral cycle of disentitlement. The territorial dimension involved the responsibilities of the *Länder* and municipalities for social assistance and reception of asylum seekers. These responsibilities furnished incentives to curtail immigrant rights. The involvement of the *Länder* in the policy process via the Bundesrat provided a platform to press their demands.

THE PARTY-ELECTORAL DIMENSION
The initial response to the rising number of asylum seekers (over 100,000 in 1980) was a strategy of deterrence that sought to make asylum seeking less attractive by tightening legal procedures and restricting entitlements. Electoral politics were central in the adoption of the measures. Restriction-minded politicians from the CDU-CSU, especially the CSU, called for more stringent measures several months before an election. In justifying harsher measures, they portrayed asylum seekers as economic immigrants abusing the right of asylum and pointed to public opinion opposed to more foreigners. To eliminate the issue from the coming election, the government passed legislation before the election campaign got under way (Perlmutter 2002: 273–9, esp. pp. 276, 281; Schuster 2003: 200–3).

Initially the electoral cycle resulted in two federal laws passed in 1980 and 1982 to deter asylum seeking. The 1982 law included limiting entitlements to communal shelter and in-kind benefits and barring asylum seekers from work. The number of asylum seekers declined, but the strategy backfired. Eliminating the right to work caused the municipalities' costs for welfare to escalate. It forced asylum seekers into an idle and depressing existence, and reinforced Germans' impressions that asylum seekers were fake refugees living on welfare at the expense of the taxpayers, paving the way for further backlash against newcomers (Joppke 1999: 89).

When the number of asylum seekers started to rise again in the mid-1980s, attention turned to amending the constitutional right of asylum. The Social Democrats, who viewed the constitutional right of asylum as sacrosanct—as atonement for the deeds of Nazism—rejected the idea. The FDP, in the governing coalition, also opposed an amendment. The CSU leader, Franz-Josef Strauss, urged the government to introduce an amendment to expose the pro-immigration stances of the SPD and FDP to the electorate. Chancellor Kohl and other moderates insisted that the issue should remain outside the realm of electoral controversy. Instead a new round of party negotiations produced restrictive legislation (including a five-year work ban) prior to the 1987 election (Perlmutter 2002: 274–6; Schuster 2003: 202).

Ethnic immigration and the social rights of resettlers became a political issue with the collapse of communism and the elimination of travel restrictions in the late 1980s. The arrival of nearly two and a half million newcomers between 1988 and 1992 heightened the importance of immigration issues to the voters. A vast majority of the electorate favored restrictions on asylum seekers and co-ethnic immigrants but doubted the ability of the established parties to deal with these issues (Perlmutter 2002: 279–81). Mounting social tensions and racist attacks on immigrants added to the urgency of the situation. The CDU-CSU also exploited the crisis atmosphere to press the SPD to come to the negotiating table, which resulted in the 1992 asylum compromise (Green 2004: 85–6).

The adoption of the asylum policy package demonstrated that the parties could act decisively. The compromise package combined restrictions with inclusive measures, as the SPD succeeded in broadening the negotiations agenda. A first set of measures, dealing with *asylum seekers*, consisted of a constitutional amendment limiting the right of asylum and the reduction of welfare benefits of asylum seekers during the application process. A second set of measures established an informal annual ceiling for the admission of *co-ethnic immigrants*, the phasing out of *Aussiedler* status, and requiring proof of ethnic persecution for applicants from Central and Eastern Europe with the exception of the former Soviet Union. The third set, at the insistence of the Social Democrats, concerned *citizenship policy*. The most important concessions were: (1) the simplified naturalization process, scheduled to end in 1996, was made permanent, (2) the right to naturalization was strengthened, and (3) the government promised to assign priority to a comprehensive citizenship reform (Marshall 2000: 94–6; Green 2004: 86–7).

The compromise profoundly altered admission policies for asylum seekers and co-ethnic immigrants but it also had major consequences for their social rights. Emerging from the compromise was the 1993 Asylum Seekers Benefits Law, which eased the financial obligations of the municipalities and *Länder* in welfare provision and worsened the benefits of asylum seekers. The main blow to the social rights of co-ethnic immigrants consisted of measures to phase out *Aussiedler* status with its privileged access to social insurance benefits and continued cuts in the benefits available to late resettlers.

Neither the compromise nor the 1993 law removed the social rights of asylum seekers from the policy agenda. In 1995 the Kohl government announced that it planned to extend the law to all aliens who were temporarily in Germany. The CSU urged cuts in benefits, emphasizing the enormous burden to the economy. The SPD voted down the government's proposals in the Bundesrat but later gave in. The 1997 changes extended lower benefits to civil war refugees and tolerated failed asylum seekers, cut the level of benefits, and lengthened the period of lower benefits to three years (Minderhoud 1999: 141–2). On the eve of the 1998 election the parties supported a new round of cuts in welfare benefits for asylum seekers (Bosswick 2000), and again consensus emerged on extending cuts in the 2002 Immigration Law. In short, electoral cycles from the early 1980s to the 2000s successively weakened the social rights of asylum seekers.

THE TERRITORIAL DIMENSION

Rights contraction was not solely driven by party politics, electoral competition, and a strong anti-immigration opinion; it was also fed by a territorial dynamic related to the residence patterns of immigrants and the division of responsibilities between different levels of government. In the German case, both the dispersion and concentration of immigrants contributed to state and local government opposition to newcomers.

The residence patterns of immigrants have not been as concentrated in Germany compared to the two liberal regime countries. A quota system administered by the federal refugee agency has allocated asylum seekers more evenly across the states since the mid-1970s. Accordingly, asylum seekers as a percentage of the population in each *Land* has been roughly the same. The more even dispersion, in combination with the system of funding the costs of asylum seekers, created economic incentives shared by the states and municipalities. Since social assistance was exclusively financed by the state and municipal general revenues, it was in the interests of the state and local governments to reduce the number of asylum seekers, to cut their welfare entitlements and to offload benefit costs onto the social insurance funds. Thus the *Länder* and municipalities became a major pressure group favoring restrictions—contrary to Freeman's thesis that the dispersion of costs promotes an expansive thrust in immigration politics.

Nevertheless, a few states and localities have been more affected by the flow of asylum seekers than others; they have included the states along the southern border (Bavaria and Baden-Württemberg), and those with major airports (Berlin and Frankfurt). Bavaria and Baden-Württemberg, at times joined by Berlin, were in the forefront advocating restrictions, among them welfare in kind and the work ban. Welfare in kind was first introduced by Baden-Württemberg, a conservative stronghold, and the 1982 Asylum Procedures Law incorporated welfare in kind for asylum seekers. Baden-Württemberg and Bavaria kept up the pressure for more restrictions on asylum seekers' benefits. The 1993 Asylum Seekers Benefits Law strengthened the welfare in kind component, and the 1997 amendment further limited exceptions from the rule of welfare in kind. The conference of *Länder* interior ministers—a body for horizontal policy coordination across the states—reintroduced the work ban in the late 1990s (Bosswick 2000: 45, 52; Marshall 2000:16–17).

In contrast to asylum seekers, ethnic German immigrants were more unevenly distributed. They tended to locate in the southern *Länder* and Rhineland-Palatinate (Marshall 2000: 34), and the Bavarian CSU spearheaded the restrictions on resettlers' benefits (Joppke 2005: 210). The strategy of the two southern *Länder* seems to have been to spread the costs of the late resettlers. In response to repeated complaints about the unequal division of responsibility and economic burdens, the Kohl government introduced a system of distributing German resettlers, similar to the one for asylum seekers, and established sanctions—the loss of benefits—for moving away from the allocated locality. The equalization of burdens across the states has been a typical solution in German federalism, and it has been reinforced by the equalization of funding of the *Länder* (Katzenstein 1987: 51–2; Manow 2005: 235).

To sum up, on the issue of asylum seekers' and resettlers' benefits, the party-electoral and territorial dimensions of conflict intersected, putting the conservative faction of the CDU and the CSU in a pivotal position. Electorally, this faction and especially the CSU often attempted to inject the issues of immigration and asylum into federal election campaigns and exploit anti-foreigner sentiments, putting pressure on the government irrespective of its composition. Territorially, the two conservative states of Bavaria and Baden-Württemberg used the Bundesrat, federal-*Länder* commissions, and the standing conference of state interior ministers to pursue a restrictionist agenda. The intersection of the party-electoral and territorial dimensions also put pressure on the leadership of the two major parties, when local and *Länder* party officials complained of growing burdens as the number of newcomers increased. The shift in policy venue from a corporatist setting to the Ministry of the Interior meant there were fewer organized voices expressing immigrant interests. The Minister of Labor and Social Affairs, with roots in the unions, represented the social Catholic wing of the CDU; unions and church organizations often rallied to the support of inclusive measures. By contrast, the post of Interior Minister in the Kohl governments was held by a hardliner for long periods (1982–9 and 1993–8). The change in policy venues further strengthened the position of the *Länder* and the importance of state/federal executive bargaining rather than corporatist bargaining.

The politics of rights extension and contraction compared

In comparing the politics of rights extension and contraction in the two conservative corporatist regime countries, I discuss two major contrasts. The first is the initial differing policy responses to the defects of the Bismarckian model. To understand the policy responses, I explore dissimilarities in framing, the partisan composition of government, and corporatist politics. The second contrast concerns the role of the territorial dimension in shaping immigrants' social rights.

Responses to the Bismarckian model

FRAMING

Although the rise of new forms of poverty was a concern in both countries, there were basic differences in problem construction, framing, and the politics of justification. The French defined the crisis of the Bismarckian model as a problem of social exclusion and framed the issue in terms of rights and solidarity. As early as the mid-1970s René Lenoir, a high ranking social policy bureaucrat, coined the expression "social exclusion" explicitly referring to persons outside the social insurance system, and focus was on *les exclus*. The solution was insertion policies and a new type of entitlement, the right to insertion (*le droit à l'insertion*) encompassing re-integration into society (Silver 1994; Enjolras and Lødemel 1999: 484–5). Social exclusion was viewed as the breakdown of solidarity, a social fracture that required remedy if society was to function as it should.

The Germans highlighted the changing nature of work and new forms of employment without full social security status, and the emergence of new risks was part of a fundamental critique of society and the welfare state (Beck [1986], 1992; Offe 1991). Although critics attacked the link between work and social protection, their emphasis on risks inadvertently helped to sustain insurance schemes as the principal solution; insurance schemes had been devised precisely as a protection against risks. Furthermore, the German critics were academics, whereas influential French analysts were part of the political establishment. French officials were quicker to recognize that the new forms of poverty and exclusion stemmed from the Bismarckian welfare system itself, while the German decision makers from the mid-1970s to the mid-1980s viewed the task at hand as cost containment and readjustments of the existing social insurance system (Alber 2003; Clasen 2005: 26).

The French emphasis on rights created marked differences in the politics of justification. Rights have figured prominently in the French social policy debate, but had no parallel in the German debate because social rights have almost exclusively been determined by the principle of equivalence. Accordingly, when rights have been mentioned in the German case it has been as "earned rights" or "property rights" through deferred wages (Clasen 2005). By contrast, rights in the French discourse have also been connected to non-contributory and means-tested programs, such as the right to housing, the right to health care, and the right to insertion. Insertion measures have had as their objective "to ensure participation in the life of the community in the name of the right to citizenship" (Morel 2004: 97).

The principle of solidarity has been intrinsic to the conservative corporatist regime, but an important intra-regime variation among the conservative corporative countries is the scope of the principle of solidarity. The principle underlines the social interdependence of members of the community and their obligations to one another, and it holds that the community must share the costs of benefits for those without means or sufficient contributions. Accordingly, how the community is defined determines the parameters of solidaristic relationships.

In France, where the concept of solidarity has been integral to social reform, the concept has gradually gained wide applicability. The bases of solidarity have expanded from occupational or professional communities to the inter-professional and the national communities. Increasingly national solidarity has been related to the role of the state in social provision, whereas occupational or professional solidarity has the centerpiece of social insurance schemes (Ashford 1982: 251–5; Spicker 1991: 17; MIRE 1998: 192–3; Waters 2003: 121–2; Palier 2010: 96).

In Germany the principle of solidarity has had a limited scope covering only the contributors to social insurance schemes (Freeman and Clasen 1994: 10), that is, it has roughly corresponded to the French notion of occupational or professional solidarity. National solidarity, linked to the German idea of cooperative federalism, has mainly been invoked as an argument for fiscal equalization of resources and burdens across the *Länder*—and not as a reason for increased state involvement in social provision.

PARTIES AND THE COMPOSITION OF GOVERNMENT

The differences in framing were also related to the constellation of parties in political power and the partisan composition of the government. In the early 1980s France and Germany saw important alternations in power when Mitterrand was elected president and Kohl became chancellor. A main theme during Mitterrand's presidency was solidarity, which he linked to improvements in social security and welfare. Conversely, the rise of Helmut Kohl to executive power led to a new emphasis on subsidiarity and a shift away from solidarity. The CDU's brand of solidarity has been tempered by the principle of subsidiarity that has limited the role of the state. The Kohl coalition government, comprised of the CDU-CSU and the FDP, fashioned its policy as the Turn (*Die Wende*) whose aim was to roll back the state. The major components included deregulation of the economy; cuts in social spending; lower taxes; self-help, voluntary action, and for-profit providers in the social services sector; and more flexibility in the labor market (Mangen 1991: 100–1, 111–12; Stjernø 2005: 155, 215). One facet of the Turn of immediate importance to immigrants was the change from universal family allowances to tax benefits for families. Of long-term consequence were measures to promote labor market flexibility, leading to the growth of a-typical work and increased segmentation of the labor market.

CORPORATIST POLITICS

The conservative corporatist regime has privileged the social partners as key political actors by virtue of their joint administration of social insurance benefits. Corporatist arrangements and their impact on the politics of social policy have generally been viewed as an explanation of the specific policy trajectory of the conservative regime countries—sluggish retrenchment and cuts combined with expansion. The unions, as insider players, were able to dilute proposed cutbacks or negotiate new benefits in exchange for cuts. Despite commonalities, corporatist politics have diverged in France and Germany and the dissimilarities help to explain the differing policy responses to the Bismarckian model. The French–German comparison underscores the importance of unions' mode of access to the policy process and the nature of the social policy coalition.

Although the organizational strength of French unions has been marred by fragmentation and notoriously low membership rates (around 10 per cent of employees in the 1990s), the political importance of the unions should not be underestimated. A power resource of the French unions has been corporatist organizational structures that have furnished them with access to the social policy process, organizational resources that can be used to reward activists, and legitimacy stemming from the widespread popularity of the social insurance programs (Palier 2006: 111).

The construction and administration of French minimum benefits gave the social partners and the insurance funds a vested interest in their development and the possibility to influence them. Once French minimum benefits were in place, the social partners, and especially the unions, criticized the use of insurance funds to finance minimum benefits. They argued that the existing system of funding violated the insurance principle and was a cause of the deficits of the insurance funds (Palier 2006: 112). They have encouraged the extension of state responsibility for welfare benefits under the banner of defending the insurance schemes. In several instances, cuts in insurance benefits were sweetened by expanding state funding responsibilities or introducing new minimum benefits financed by the state, such as new minimum benefits created for those who had exhausted their insurance benefits (ASS) and for new labor market entrants without insurance (AI). The new benefits were financed by the state and not by contributions and thus eased the pressure on the insurance funds (Palier 2005: 220–1). Likewise the 1993 reform of private sector pensions resulted in major cuts but also larger state responsibility for financing non-contributory pension benefits (Palier 2006: 115).

German unions have had a closer relationship with both the SPD and the CDU, and the unions have been part of a broader cross-party social policy coalition. This alliance long controlled the relevant parliamentary committees as well as the position of minister. Norbert Blüm, the CDU Minister of Labor and Social Affairs (1982–98), was himself a trade unionist, and in 1988 he promoted a member of the SPD to the top post of Permanent Secretary. Blüm was pivotal to the social policy faction of the CDU and the government that set the agenda as well as the broader cross-party policy coalition that existed until the late 1990s (Clasen 2005: 26).

A yardstick of the policy coalition's importance is the adoption of the 1993 long-term care insurance, which expanded the Bismarckian model. Already in the mid-1980s the Social Democrats advocated the introduction of a new social insurance scheme (*Pflegeversicherung*), while the Christian Democrats were initially negative to the idea, favoring the expansion of local services to the elderly and tax incentives to encourage families to provide more care (Alber 1986: 131). Pressure for change came from the municipalities that were financially responsible for social assistance and the growing number of nursing home patients who relied on assistance. On the eve of the 1990 federal election, and despite deep divisions in the government, Blüm pre-empted and pledged to introduce care insurance. After the election the Social Democrats presented their own proposal for care insurance, which basically backed up the minister's efforts to introduce care insurance (Morel 2006: 230–4). Thus the corporatist policy coalition in Germany not only defended the Bismarckian model but also extended it. By contrast, French corporatist politics were a factor in the expansion of non-contributory benefits and funding benefits through tax revenues, both of which broke with the Bismarckian model.

Immigrants' social rights and the territorial dimension

Because of sharp contrasts, the German–French comparison illuminates the importance of the territorial dimension in shaping immigrants' social rights. In the German case the responsibilities of the *Länder* and municipalities provided strong incentives for them to engage in the politics of rights contraction in the case of asylum seekers and co-ethnic immigrants. The *Länder* were also well placed to influence immigrants' social rights through their direct involvement in the federal legislative process.

In France the decentralization reforms introduced in the early 1980s during the first years of Mitterrand's presidency formally altered the centralized and hierarchical structure of the French state and thus the territorial dimension of

French politics. In the case of social policy, the reforms expanded the responsibility of the counties or departments for local social welfare programs (*aide sociale*), such as medical assistance and aid to children, families, and the elderly, and social services for children and the elderly. The municipalities or communes, through local welfare offices, have administered the programs.

The state retained responsibility for the functions related to "national solidarity," including the welfare of the immigrant population. The central government has determined the basic benefit levels and eligibility requirements of the programs, while the departments and communes could offer more generous benefits or create additional benefits (Schmidt 1990: 125–6, 330–1; Rocaboy 1999: 542–3, 545). State revenues have increasingly financed the various national social minimum benefits related to old age, disability, and unemployment as well as the minimum benefits paid to asylum seekers. In short, French subnational governments have had fewer incentives to target immigrants' assistance benefits for cuts than their German counterparts. Nor were asylum seekers evenly distributed across France so that they did not provide the subnational authorities with a common grievance.

The French departments have also much less political leverage against the central government compared to the German *Länder*. The political leverage of French subnational authorities has been highly personalized, informal, and elitist, occurring primarily through multiple office holding (*le cumul des mandates*). Most members of the National Assembly and even ministers in the government have been *cumulants*, simultaneously holding local and/or regional office as mayors, assistant-mayors, department or regional councilors. In this capacity, they have conveyed local grievances and demands. The vertical structure of this channel of influence provides little opportunity for horizontal coordination of recommendations compared to the possibilities in Germany. Contrary to the German case, French subnational officials have exerted little influence in formulating national policies affecting the social rights of immigrants. Equally important, the central government introduced legislation that prohibited subnational officials from barring non-citizens from local welfare benefits.

Conclusion

In the two conservative corporatist countries, immigrant rights have been influenced by several convergences in the major policy dimensions of their incorporation regimes and by commonalities in their welfare regimes as well as their differing policy responses to the defects of the Bismarckian system. Convergence in their incorporation regimes has primarily concerned citizenship acquisition, the permit system, family reunification, and growing emphasis on integration as a requirement for inclusion.

A closer examination of the politics behind these policies in France and Germany has disclosed the key role of political parties and left–right differences. In France their significance can be seen in the alternations in government and the resulting changes in legislation by the incoming government. Importantly, a left government reversed restrictive changes in the nationality code, thus largely reinstating the most inclusive feature of the French incorporation regime. Since 2002 mainstream right governments have increased the barriers of inclusion by increasing the permit requirements and naturalization requirements. Alternations in power have also affected immigrants' social rights. Left governments generally promoted immigrants' social rights; they advanced a vision of national solidarity that encompassed non-citizens, eliminated nationality as a requirement for minimum benefits, and made it illegal to exclude non-citizens from local benefits. Right governments eliminated the availability of nearly all benefits to undocumented immigrants and drastically shortened the duration of benefits to asylum seekers and in many cases terminated their benefits. They also worsened legal aliens' access to the safety net.

The fusion of inclusive and restrictive politics in Germany can easily obscure partisan differences. A dissection of the policy process has illuminated the influence of the political parties and left–right differences. The CDU-CSU has been largely responsible for the multiplication of requirements for inclusion, and a CDU Interior Minister strengthened the link between social benefits and the acquisition of settlement status and citizenship. The CDU-CSU has also blocked inclusive measures. After the 1992 asylum compromise the Kohl government stalled on citizenship reform, and the CDU-CSU obstructed the acceptance of dual citizenship in the 1999 nationality law reform. The Kohl government continued to maintain that Germany was not a country of immigration, and the CDU-CSU candidate for chancellor in the 2002 federal election opposed the new immigration law, claiming that newcomers would increase welfare costs. In contrast, the red-green government introduced the citizenship and immigration reforms improving immigrant rights.

Corporatist politics—a feature of the conservative corporatist welfare regime—have had major implications for immigrants' social rights. Corporatist politics contributed to France's and Germany's differing policy responses to the flaws of the Bismarckian model, and the dissimilar responses—non-contributory benefits versus insurance solutions—have affected immigrants' access to social benefits. Still corporatist arrangements have resulted in significant commonalities. In both countries corporatist politics have generated insider/outsider solutions that have provided core workers with more generous benefits than those outside the labor market or with weak attachments.

This sort of approach characterized the German and French retrenchment strategies and has continued relevance. Insider/outsider remedies and increased labor market segmentation through the growth of a-typical employment have led to a dualism in social entitlements—minimum benefits for a-typical workers and insurance benefits for core workers in the two countries (Palier and Thelen 2010). This dualism disproportionately affects both first and second generation immigrants who have had a weak attachment to the labor market.

The institutionalization of dualisms in the two conservative corporatist countries highlights the importance of the welfare state regime for immigrants' social rights. Also of significance, the policy venue over time has shifted from the ministry of labor and social affairs to the ministry of the interior in both countries. The shift has made policy dimensions of the incorporation regime more important to immigrants' social rights, and it altered the roster of participants. When the ministry of labor and social affairs was the policy venue, participants included the unions and welfare organizations that often spoke out for immigrant rights; labor legislation also extended participatory rights. By contrast, the interior ministry has usually introduced restrictions and measures affecting newcomers' access to benefits. These developments in the welfare and incorporation regimes have been decisive in shaping immigrants' rights and their prospects of inclusion in the 2000s.

10

Social Democratic Welfare States and the Politics of Inclusion and Exclusion

Several reforms during the past two decades largely consolidated the Swedish and Danish welfare states and strengthened the distinctive features of the social democratic welfare regime, while the entitlements and economic well-being of immigrants in both countries deteriorated during the 1990s. The Swedish economy was in serious trouble during the decade, and policy makers responded by making across the board cuts in social benefits. The downsizing of the Swedish welfare state, along with the poor performance of the economy, hit immigrants harder than the rest of the population. After economic recovery, several social reforms improved immigrants' entitlements. By contrast, Denmark experienced an economic upswing in the 1990s, hailed by some observers as the "Danish miracle" (Benner and Vad 2000). Despite a prospering economy, immigrants were targeted for sharp reductions in benefits. In effect, benefit cuts have become an integral part of Danish immigration policy with the aim of deterring unwanted newcomers.

The Swedish and Danish incorporation regimes have also moved in opposite directions. At the end of the 2000s the Swedish regime, along several policy dimensions, was the most inclusive of the countries in this book. Conversely, the Danish regime has become increasingly exclusionary, with very stringent requirements for citizenship acquisition, settlement status, and family reunification.

Sweden's and Denmark's differing approaches to immigrants' social rights and the growing gap between their incorporation regimes are especially puzzling because of the commonalities of the political institutions and welfare state policies of the Scandinavian countries. In fact, the similarities have led to conceptualizations of a model of politics and policies shared by the Scandinavian countries (Elder et al. 1982; Erikson et al. 1987; Einhorn and Logue 1989; Arter 1999; Goul Andersen and Hoff 2001; Kautto et al. 2001; Kangas and Palme 2005).

This chapter examines the politics behind the trajectories of immigrants' rights in Sweden and Denmark. It asks why Sweden and Denmark eventually adopted such different approaches. To understand the differences I trace and compare policy developments since the late 1960s. A closer look at the early immigrant policies in the two countries reveals interesting dissimilarities. There were important differences in the framing of immigrant policies and the impact of framing on policy venues, the positions of the parties and the structure of party competition, and the involvement of immigrants in the policy process. I deal first with the politics of rights extension and contraction in Sweden and then the Danish case. The final section sums up the major variations explaining the policy differences.

Sweden: The inclusive turn and beyond

In several respects the politics of inclusion and the process of rights extension in Sweden contrast with the other European countries in this book. First, Swedish policy makers were quick to recognize the permanent character of immigration rather than believing or insisting that it was temporary (Geddes 2003b: 118). Recognizing that many immigrants would become permanent residents had major policy implications because of the emerging principle of domicile (*ius domicili*) prescribing that rights derive from residence. Equally importantly, the formulation of immigration policies and immigrant policies became compartmentalized, and the separation facilitated an inclusive framing of immigrant policies. Finally, the introduction of immigrant policies amounted to bold inclusive policy reforms—a policy bang that has no counterpart in the other countries. The reforms of the mid-1970s simultaneously expanded immigrants' social, cultural, and political rights.

The 1970s legislation that improved immigrant rights represented an inclusive turn. Although the scope of inclusion has subsequently been questioned and contested, the inclusive impulse has remained relatively strong. Initially I discuss the politics behind the inclusive turn and its follow-up measures, and then the growing challenge to an inclusive approach.

The politics of rights extension: Equality, partnership, and the principle of residence

In 1968 the Social Democratic government officially acknowledged that Sweden was a country of immigration, and it affirmed that equality was the overarching goal of immigration policy (Prop 1968: 142, pp. 96–7). Eventually policy makers came to distinguish between immigration and immigrant policies. This distinction strengthened the frame of equality, and the distinction was decisive in determining the policy venue and the experts attached to the inquiry commissions, which play a major role in the Swedish policy process.

Nowhere is the importance of the distinction more evident than in the 1967 report of the commission on immigration policy and the 1974 report of the commission on immigrant policies, and the government bills based on the commission reports. The 1967 report was framed in terms of regulation and controls, whereas the frame of the 1974 report was equality and rights. Similarly, the 1968 government bill (Prop. 1968: 142) on immigration referred to newcomers as foreigners, and a foreigner policy consisted of measures to assist in adjusting to Swedish society (*anpassningsåtgärder*). The 1975 government bill spoke of newcomers as immigrants with equal rights, including the right to preserve their cultural heritage (Prop. 1975/76: 26). Despite the separation of immigration and immigrant policies, a crucial link between the two was the assumption that the goal of equality of all residents—newcomers, denizens, and citizens—required regulated immigration.

The distinction between immigration and immigrant policies developed from criticisms of the 1967 commission and the appointment of its successor. The 1967 commission had underscored that the state must take responsibility for formulation of immigration policy, and it recommended the establishment of a central administrative agency to deal with this policy area (SOU 1967:18, p. 243). Critics complained that the commission had scarcely dealt with immigrants, and that it seemed to assume they should assimilate rather than retain their cultural traditions. The critics called for a new commission to examine this issue. The trade union confederation (*Landsorganisationen i Sverige*, LO) urged the government to "formulate a clear objective for a minorities policy and that this objective entail explicit recognition of the cultural aspirations and activities of minorities." The Riksdag, the Swedish parliament, also requested a commission to examine the possibilities of immigrants to maintain their own linguistic, cultural, and religious traditions (*egenart*) (SOU 1974:69, p. 48).

In 1968 the government appointed a parliamentary commission, and the government's instructions specified that the commission was to deal with immigrant policy in the broadest sense rather than immigration policy. Its tasks included an inventory of not only the problems confronting immigrants and existing public measures to combat the problems but also the wishes of immigrants and minorities organizations. On the basis of the inventory, the commission was to consider policy measures to eliminate conditions that put immigrants and minorities in a worse position compared to the rest of the population (SOU 1974:69, pp. 33–4, 447–52).

POLICY GOALS AND RECOMMENDATIONS

In its 1974 report, the commission recommended a comprehensive immigrant policy with equality, freedom of choice, and partnership or co-participation (*samverkan*) as its goals. The goal of *equality* contained both a socio-economic and a cultural dimension. Socially and economically, immigrants were to have living conditions that were equivalent to the rest of the population. Culturally, the report stated that to achieve the goal of equality a minority policy ought to accord the possibility to maintain and create respect for one's language and cultural identity. It underlined that the goal was equal rights for immigrants irrespective of their land of origin. *Freedom of choice* involved immigrants' decisions about the extent to which they wanted to maintain their language and culture and/or embrace Swedish values and norms. *Partnership* or cooperation focused on immigrants' participation; minority groups were regarded as equal partners in the development of society, and they should receive necessary support to form associations of their own. This goal also encompassed mutual tolerance and solidarity (SOU 1974:69, p. 19, 25, pp. 94–6).

The commission's recommendations ranged from social provision, labor market measures, housing, education, media and information, formal consultative arrangements for immigrants, subsidies for immigrant associations and religious congregations, and strengthening the political influence of immigrants. The commission endorsed four approaches to increase immigrants' political influence and thus co-participation: (1) measures to encourage immigrants' participation and election to decision making positions in the political parties and unions, (2) immigrant councils with co-determination functions in the area of public services, (3) the right to vote and stand in local and regional elections, and (4) making it easier to become a citizen (SOU 1974:69, p. 328).

Many commission recommendations were translated into legislation. In 1975 the Riksdag declared its unanimous support of the guidelines and goals of immigrant policy. The same year, it granted non-citizens local political rights. The constitutional rights of non-citizens were strengthened; the protection of their fundamental liberties and rights was written into the Swedish constitution, the Instrument of Government, along with guarantees of the cultural rights of ethnic, linguistic, and religious minorities. The 1974 Instrument of Government also prohibited denaturalization (the withdrawal of citizenship of naturalized citizens). Other inclusive measures were reducing the residence requirement and eliminating the economic self-sufficiency test for naturalization, removing the citizenship requirement for many jobs in the public sector, subsidies to immigrant associations, and improving immigrants' social rights where there were differences between newcomers and citizens.

POLITICAL PARTIES AND IMMIGRANTS

The arrival of immigrant policies on the political agenda coincided with a radicalization of the Social Democratic Party (*Socialdemokraterna*). In 1969 the party adopted the Towards Equality Program that signaled a major offensive in several policy areas, including social measures. Among the inequalities targeted for reform were those between Swedish citizens and immigrants (Jämlikhet 1969: 44, 53, 121–2). This form of inequality was eclipsed by other inequalities, but equality was marshaled as a major argument for the extension of immigrants' social, political, and cultural rights. The Towards Equality Program also highlighted equal influence in a participatory democracy, which resurfaced in the goal of partnership and co-participation in the commission's report.

Immigrants were among the agenda setters in formulating the immigrant and minority policies of the 1970s. They raised the issue in the mid-1960s, bringing the perspectives of immigrants and minorities to the debate, and the debate involved immigrants across ethnic groups, denizens, and newcomers. Immigrants criticized an assimilation or Swedification (*försvenskning*) approach, and the debate then focused on two alternatives: a melting pot versus a multicultural strategy. In 1968 internal working groups were set up in the Social Democratic party, the People's party (*Folkpartiet*), and the conservative party (*Högern*, the Right, but since 1969 *Moderaterna*, the Moderates). They all issued reports that were positive toward multicultural policies actively supported by the state (Schwarz 1966, 1971; Hansen 2001: chapter 6), but opinions within the parties remained divided. Internal party differences were ironed out, and in the early 1970s the three parties supported multicultural policies, but they framed the policy intentions differently. The center-right parties emphasized immigrants' freedom of choice to retain and develop their culture on a Swedish foundation. The Social Democrats stressed that ethnic equality was a precondition for immigrants and minorities to achieve social and economic equality (Hansen 2001: chapter 7).

Immigrant associations mobilized during the appointment of the commission, asking that representatives of minorities be involved in the commission's work as experts. The associations also participated in the consultation or remiss procedure, expressing their views on commission recommendations. Prior to the appointment of the commission on immigrants they had used the remiss procedure to criticize assimilationalist tendencies in existing policies, and their demands had also contributed to the appointment of the commission (Hansen 2001: 136–42, 194–6).

Of key significance, first generation immigrants were experts of the commission, that is, they had insider influence. Sven Reinans of Estonian descent and Sulo Huovinen of Finnish origins served as experts. In this capacity, they drafted substantial parts of the main report. Reinans was responsible for

217

minority issues and Huovinen for cultural and educational issues (SOU 1974:69, pp. 36, 40). These issues were of central concern to the Estonian and Finnish communities respectively. The Estonians, as Second World War refugees, furnished a model of integration. They had successfully integrated into Swedish society, while establishing their own ethnic community organizations and newspapers. For the Finnish population a major issue was home language instruction in the schools.

The issue of political rights also had high priority among the Finns both in Sweden and Finland, and Nordic cooperation provided a transnational arena to promote political rights. In 1973 Finnish representatives introduced a proposal in the Nordic Council to grant Nordic citizens the right to vote in local and regional elections in all the Nordic countries. In Sweden voting rights for immigrants had first been discussed in parliament when a Social Democratic bill in 1968 requested that the commission revising the constitution examine the issue. The constitutional commission rejected voting rights for non-citizens in local elections because of the close connection between local and national politics. Since the law on local elections was not part of the constitution, the issue was kept alive. All parties, except the Moderates, introduced bills supporting immigrant voting rights in 1973 and 1974, and the Social Democratic government appointed a commission to work out the details of the reform (Hammar 1979; Bäck and Soininen 1996).

The commission on immigrant voting rights included two members with immigrant backgrounds—the first immigrants appointed to an inquiry commission. Again Sven Reinans served as an expert (SOU 1975:15). The commission on voting rights recommended that immigrants who had resided in Sweden for three years be granted the right to vote and to run for office in local and regional elections. Besides justifying the reform as strengthening democracy and the interests of immigrants in politics, and thereby promoting their integration, the commission argued that residence had de facto become the fundamental basis for the public regulation of rights (SOU 1975:15). The reform extended the principle of residence, which had determined social rights, to political rights.

In sum, the Swedes adopted a profoundly political strategy of integration that entailed extending the right to vote and the right to hold office to foreign citizens—and its radical variant, which was not implemented, included parliamentary voting rights for non-citizens. The rationale behind the strategy consisted of three arguments: first, political rights would encourage newcomers to take an interest and become involved in community affairs; second, immigrants' political rights would mean that the political parties could not afford to ignore the concerns and issues of non-citizens; and, third, immigrant collaboration was a prerequisite in formulating effective and fair immigrant policies (SOU 1975:15, pp. 102–4; Prop. 1975/76: 23).

POLICY MACHINERY AND ADMINISTRATIVE POLITICS

Immigrant policies were institutionalized through the creation of a new central administrative agency and later in 1973 the appointment of a minister responsible for immigration and immigrant policies. The National Board of Immigrant Affairs (*Statens invandrarverk*, SIV) came into operation in 1969. The establishment of the Board represented an upgrading of immigrant issues; it also created a stronger institutional platform for pro-immigrant activists, and its staff included immigrants.

The Board's main functions were to coordinate policies affecting immigrants, to continuously monitor and call attention to the special needs of immigrants, and to provide information to immigrants. Tasks of other administrative units—granting asylum and permanent residence status, along with naturalization—were transferred to the agency. In others words, although the distinction between immigration policies and immigrant policies had been important in policy formulation, the two types of policy were combined as tasks of the minister and the Board. On the other hand, the Board's tasks with regard to immigrant policy were defined in residual manner because of the universal nature of the welfare state. To the greatest possible extent, measures to aid immigrants were to be part of universal social provision. This definition of responsibility diminished the policy functions of the SIV in comparison to the National Labor Market Board, the National Board of Education, and the National Board of Health and Welfare. Instead the SIV had an important watchdog function vis-à-vis the other agencies.

The National Board of Immigrant Affairs became a key administrative actor in this policy area. Through the remiss system of consultation it exerted influence, for example, in the case of voting rights for immigrants (Hammar 1979); its staff served as members, experts, and in the secretariats of inquiry commissions dealing with immigration and immigrant policies. The existence of the Board encouraged administrative solutions and administrative politics. Important administrative solutions included the simplification of application procedures, which eased permit requirements and even citizenship requirements in the 1970s and early 1980s. Later the modifications were codified in law. In the area of reforms, the clearest examples of administrators' input were the 1985 refugee reception reform (Soininen 1992) and anti-discrimination legislation.

Although administrative politics have been important in shaping immigrant policies and administrative procedures improved immigrants' rights, their weight should not be overstated, as Tomas Hammar's (1985: 277–81) conclusions tend to do. It is true that immigration and immigrant policies were not issues in electoral politics, especially at the time his book was written, but immigrant policies have largely been products of the parliamentary political process, and both administrative and party arenas have been influential in the preparatory stage of legislation. This was the case of the immigrant policy reforms of the mid-1970s and subsequent inclusive measures. Furthermore, the government has been pivotal in appointing inquiry commissions and introducing reform bills. Nor have governments always adopted commission recommendations.

SUBSEQUENT INCLUSIVE MEASURES

A legacy of the inclusive turn has been the emphasis on rights and co-partici-pation. Pro-immigrant activists in the political parties, parliament, and the SIV continued to promote inclusive reforms. The most important were efforts to extend national voting rights to immigrants, introducing dual citizenship, tackling discrimination against immigrants, and eliminating inequalities in social rights.

National voting rights and dual citizenship

Following the local voting rights reform, MPs from the left parties repeatedly introduced bills to give non-citizens the right to vote in parliamentary elec-tions. When the Social Democrats returned to power with a left parliamentary majority in 1982, the Riksdag requested that the government appoint a par-liamentary commission to propose legislation to grant immigrants national voting rights. Arguing that place of residence—not citizenship—should deter-mine the right to vote in parliamentary elections, the commission's left majority recommended a constitutional amendment that would (1) give Nor-dic citizens national voting rights after three years of residence and (2) remove the right to vote of Swedes living abroad after ten years.

The party consensus on immigrant voting rights of the 1970s evaporated as the center-right parties defended Swedish citizenship as the foundation of voting rights. The intensity of the conflict was reinforced by tactical calcula-tions of the left and the right. Introducing national voting rights for immi-grants favored the left parties, and the removal of voting rights of Swedes abroad disadvantaged the center-right parties. Fearing that the left majority in the Riksdag would enact the recommendations, the center-right members of the commission pointed to the norm of broad consensus in amending the constitution. To underscore their opposition, they issued a joint reservation rejecting the principle of residence and the commission's recommendations. Ultimately the government did not go ahead with a constitutional amend-ment (SOU 1984:11, pp. 11–40; Bäck and Soininen 1996: 30–2). The amend-ment procedure made it likely that non-citizens' parliamentary voting rights would become an election issue, politicizing immigration and immigrants. Constitutional amendments require that parliament adopts the proposal twice with an election intervening.

After the abortive attempt to introduce national voting rights, Social Democratic governments supported a reform allowing dual citizenship. Already in the mid-1980s a Social Democratic government appointed a commission on dual citizenship (DsA 1986: 6), and the issue resurfaced in 1991. However, the question was not resolved until the 1997 appointment of an inquiry commission to consider a modernization of the citizenship law, which resulted in the 2001 reform on dual citizenship. Ironically, the commission directives declared that dual citizenship should be avoided and instead emphasized examining the pros and cons of introducing *ius soli* for Swedish born children whose non-citizen parents were permanent residents. This proposal came onto the agenda through a 1996 Social Democratic party bill, co-sponsored by Nalin Baksi Pekgul of Kurdish extraction, and she was also a member of the commission. The commission's work changed dramatically when the 1997 European Convention on Nationality abandoned its opposition to multiple nationality, and the government issued new instructions to consider dual citizenship. The commission recommended the general acceptance of dual citizenship. A chief argument was that it would remove an obstacle that prevented many immigrants from becoming citizens, and it would enhance the possibilities of immigrants to participate in the political process (SOU 1999:34). All the parties supported the reform, except the Moderates who voted against the government bill, arguing that it devalued Swedish citizenship (RP 2000/2001: 70, pp. 3–26, 120).

Anti-discrimination legislation and positive measures
Legislation banning discrimination on the basis of ethnicity developed haltingly. In the early 1980s an expert commission, headed by the former director general of the National Board of Immigrant Affairs, presented draft legislation for a law against ethnic discrimination on the labor market. It prohibited both direct and indirect discrimination and placed the burden of proof on the employers (SOU 1983:18). Many years lapsed before such legislation was on the statute books. A law prohibiting direct discrimination was first enacted in 1994, indirect discrimination in 1999, and a reversal of the burden of proof in 2008. The 2008 law also substantially broadened the spheres of its application, potentially strengthening immigrants' social rights. By contrast, positive measures to promote ethnic equality were adopted in the mid-1980s. The major concrete result of the commission was the establishment of an anti-discrimination commissioner (DO), whose main tasks were to combat ethnic discrimination and adopt positive measures to promote ethnic equality on the labor market.

The politics of anti-discrimination were plagued by disagreement, as political actors pulled in different directions, and the divisions made for incremental solutions. Left governments preferred positive measures and initially corporatist solutions, but the LO was first among the employee organizations to support anti-discrimination legislation. Center-right governments, and especially ministers from the liberal party, favored legislation to protect individuals against discrimination instead of relying on collective bargaining. The major steadfast proponent of a corporatist solution was the employers' organization, which generally opposed anti-discrimination legislation. Judicial experts in the commissions were at times hesitant toward indirect discrimination and positive measures (SOU 1992:96; SOU 2006:22). Instead administrative officials, the general director of SIV, and the anti-discrimination commissioner actively promoted strengthening anti-discrimination legislation and positive measures.

Equal access to social benefits
In presenting the 1975 immigrant policy bill, the Minister of Immigrant Affairs noted that differences in the rights of citizens and non-citizens still existed, but she declared that efforts to eliminate the differences between the rights of permanent residents and citizens would continue (Prop. 1975/76: 26). The policy aspiration of equal rights influenced the social rights of immigrants on at least four scores. First, it was important to the reforms that improved immigrants' access to the citizen pensions and welfare benefits in the late 1970s and early 1980s, and again in the early 2000s when benefits were introduced for persons who were ineligible for the minimum pension. Second, when special benefits were introduced for asylum seekers in the late 1980s, the benefit levels were linked to the social minimum determining regular assistance benefits, thus providing equal benefits for asylum seekers. Third, the income and accommodation requirements for family reunification were officially removed in a revision of the aliens law during the late 1970s. The 1996 government bill on asylum rejected the introduction of such requirements for elderly parents on the grounds that Swedish citizens were not required to support their elderly parents, and the introduction of such a requirement for non-citizens would conflict with the goal of equality laid down by immigrant policy (SOU 1995:75, p. 164). A decade later a commission, weighing the pros and cons of a maintenance requirement, concluded it was incompatible with the universal principles of the Swedish welfare state (SOU 2005:103, p. 138). Fourth, citizens from EU member countries after the eastward enlargements of 2004 and 2007 gained equal access to social benefits.

The emerging challenge to inclusion

The challenge to inclusion and immigrant rights gained momentum during the 1990s. The decade witnessed the first contraction of immigrants' social rights. The conservative and liberal parties also began to call for a re-evaluation of Swedish citizenship through raising the requirements of naturalization and introducing the possibility to withdraw the citizenship of naturalized citizens. Finally anti-immigration opinion peaked in the early 1990s and new right-wing anti-immigration parties began to campaign for office.

RIGHTS CONTRACTION

The outcome of the 1991 election represented a rightward shift among the voters. The New Democrats (*Ny Demokrati*), the Moderates, and the Christian Democrats (*Kristdemokraterna*) made gains. The center and left parties experienced losses, and the Social Democrats suffered their worst defeat since 1928. A minority right-center government headed by Carl Bildt (1991–4) came into office. The Moderate Prime Minister, whose party had campaigned on welfare state rollback, interpreted the election results as a mandate for change.

Neoliberalism, prescribing a narrower role of the state and celebrating the market, strengthened an economic perspective on rights and integration. The liberal Minister of Immigrant Affairs in the new right-center government underlined the economic nature of integration, emphasizing that "the ultimate proof on integration is that one can support oneself" (Demker and Malmström 1999: 85). This signaled the beginning of a tougher approach to immigrant policies and integration often shared by the liberals and the conservatives. The rise of neoliberalism also led to increased competition between the liberals and the conservatives, as they vied to be its chief standard bearers. The Moderates toned down their conservative tenets and emphasized their newfound liberalism. The liberals changed their official name to the People's Party—the Liberals. A further consequence was the weakening of the social or reform liberal fraction of the party over time, which had implications for the party's traditional pro-immigrant stance.

The government's aspiration of welfare state rollback specifically affected the social rights of asylum seekers as increasing attention was on the costs of the reception system, and the deepening recession added urgency to the need for cuts. The new government almost immediately appointed an inquiry commission to suggest solutions to the rising costs of asylum seekers. Before the commission delivered its report, however, the government lowered benefits for asylum seekers as part of a crisis package to deal with public finances in late 1992, and it also reduced asylum seekers' medical costs, cutting the costs of their medical examinations in half (Prop. 1992/93: 50). The commission's recommendations were to expand the loan component in assistance, terminate eligibility to regular social assistance, introduce fees for medical care, tighten means testing to include savings and income other than earnings, and introduce sanctions—lower benefits—for refusing to participate in reception activities (SOU 1992:133).

The government followed the commission recommendations with the exception of its proposal to increase the loan component in assistance, but it went farther than the commission in that it severed the link between asylum seekers' benefits and the social minimum. The bill also introduced the possibility of issuing temporary permits which limited access to regular medical care. On the other hand, the bill strengthened asylum seekers' rights by granting the right to work during the application process and promoting freedom of movement through a special housing allowance for those not living in reception centers or municipal housing (Prop. 1993/94: 94).

In 2010 the right-center government led by Moderate Fredrik Reinfeldt (2006–) introduced an income test for family reunification and utilization of assistance precluded family reunion. The rationale for the income test was that it would create a work incentive for newcomers and thus promote their integration. The Moderate Immigration Minister was a chief advocate of income and adequate accommodations requirements for family reunification, and the government appointed a commission to work out the details. The commission's instructions specified that the requirements should have as broad application as possible but also listed several exemptions, including all immigrants who had lived four years in Sweden. This exemption meant that newcomers could apply for family reunification regardless of their income after four years (SOU 2008:114). Objections during the consultation phase of the policy process and the Christian Democrats' opposition within the government broadened the exemptions to include all families with children. The main argument was that a four-year separation would have detrimental effects on children—not equal rights or the universal principles of the welfare state.

TIGHTENING REQUIREMENTS FOR CITIZENSHIP AND PERMANENT RESIDENCE

When it came into office, the Bildt government (1991–4) shelved a Social Democratic government bill that recommended acceptance of dual citizenship (Prop.1990/91: 195). Instead it appointed a commission whose tasks included consideration of a stronger moral conduct requirement for citizenship acquisition and withdrawal of naturalization. The commission proposed to broaden the moral conduct requirement to include an assessment of the applicant's future conduct, introducing a discretionary element. The commission also recommended extending the waiting period for naturalization of persons who had a criminal record and considering a longer residence requirement for naturalization in order to better assess moral conduct. However the commission rejected withdrawal of citizenship (denaturalization) in cases where the applicant has made false statements. It argued for the principle of equality among citizens and that denaturalization would lead to two classes of citizenship (SOU 1994:33). Upon returning to power in 1994, the Social

Democratic government dealt with the commission's proposals. The government stiffened the moral conduct requirement but rejected the idea of lengthening the residence requirement (Prop. 1994/95: 179).

Importantly, a discursive shift occurred during the 1990s. It pitted inclusion against the re-evaluation of Swedish citizenship, which entailed raising naturalization requirements. The instructions to the 1997 commission on citizenship attached major weight to elevating the status of Swedish citizenship and spoke positively of a language requirement. Although the commission majority rejected a language requirement, the liberal member issued a dissenting opinion advocating that language proficiency be a requirement (SOU 1999:34). During the 2002 election, late in the campaign, the People's party launched a new tougher integration policy. The party argued that naturalization requirements were too lax, and it was joined by the Moderates. The liberals emphasized the language requirement, and the conservatives proposed the withdrawal of citizenship for naturalized citizens committing criminal acts (Boréus 2006). Prior to the launching of their tougher integration policy, support for the People's party had been sagging. In the election the party won 13.3 per cent of the vote compared to 4.7 per cent in the previous election (Madeley 2003), and its largest share of the vote since 1985.

The restrictive trend has also involved changes in the permit system. Temporary permits became more common in the 1990s in coping with mass asylum seeking and again with the resumption of labor immigration. In both instances it was right-center governments that introduced the temporary permits. Likewise the resource test, introduced by the Reinfeldt government, entailed new requirements for admission and residence for certain entry categories. The government also introduced a new requirement for a permanent residence permit for labor migrants—a work requirement of four years. The temporary permits of labor migrants increase insecurity; unemployment can jeopardize permit renewal.

The conservative Minister of Immigration also called for integration contracts, while the liberal Minister of Integration expressed skepticism. The Integration Minister appointed an expert commission to present the guidelines for a new civics course. The expert proposed a free civics course for all newcomers, irrespective of entry category, as a right, arguing that knowledge was a resource and precondition for participating in society and achieving equal rights. He also rejected making approved completion of the course a requirement for naturalization (SOU 2010:37).

NEW RIGHT-WING PARTIES

On a crest of anti-immigration opinion, a populist right-wing party, the New Democrats, won 6.7 per cent of the vote in the 1991 election and gained parliamentary representation. Many planks of the party's election platform echoed those of the mainstream right, such as tax reductions, privatization and the sale of public corporations, and the elimination of bureaucratic red tape and welfare fraud. More distinctively, the New Democrats campaigned on an overhaul of immigrant policies. They proposed temporary permits for refugees, loans instead of social benefits for newcomers, withdrawal of public funding for home language instruction, and deportation of foreign citizens who committed serious crimes (ND 1991). The election resulted in the New Democrats' holding a broker position since the right-center government did not have a majority in the Riksdag. However, the tactics of the mainstream parties and internal party disagreement limited the New Democrats' policy influence. In the 1994 election the party mustered only 1 per cent of the vote, marking its demise.

The Sweden Democrats (*Sverigedemokraterna*), much in the shadow of the New Democrats, also campaigned in the 1991 election and won two seats in local government. The party's long-term strategy has been to build up strength by gaining local office. By the 2006 election, the Sweden Democrats had won seats in over half of the municipalities. The party's finances were improved by municipal party subsidies, and it also received sufficient votes in the 2006 parliamentary election to qualify for national party subsidies (Fryklund et al. 2007: 74–82). Although anti-immigration opinion has gradually weakened since the early 1990s, a large reservoir of dissent existed in the late 2000s; nearly 50 per cent endorsed a policy resulting in fewer newcomers (Demker 2010: 110). In the 2010 parliamentary election, the Sweden Democrats finally entered the Riksdag, winning 5.6 per cent of the vote.

On two counts the Sweden Democrats represent a more formidable challenge to inclusive policies than the New Democrats did. As distinct from the New Democrats, the Sweden Democrats have their roots in a xenophobic and racist organization, Keep Sweden Swedish (*Bevara Sverige svenskt*, BSS). The overriding aim of the party is to stop immigration, and its program calls for altering the inclusive nature of the incorporation regime by making citizenship acquisition more difficult for non-ethnic Swedes (SD 2005, 2007, 2010). Second, the gradual build-up of the party's organizational strength means that the Sweden Democrats have potentially greater staying power than the New Democrats did.

The changing balance of political forces

The political forces for inclusion have weakened since the inclusive turn in the 1970s. The decade's euphoric belief in immigrant policies has given way to questioning their effectiveness and impact on integration. The party consensus of the 1970s that involved restricted admissions of workers, but a generous refugee policy including family reunification, combined with expansive immigrant rights has broken down.

The conservative and liberal parties have come to call for stricter requirements for citizenship acquisition and residence permits, while they have endorsed labor immigration, including unskilled workers. In other words, their position has become one of expansive admissions but restricted immigrant rights with emphasis on self-support. Accordingly the right-center government reinstated labor immigration in 2008 and later introduced support obligations for family reunification. In several respects, however, Swedish right-center governments have had a more inclusive approach than such governments in the other countries in this book. The mainstream right party has often had a moderate position, and its restrictionist policy aspirations have been tempered by the necessity of forming a coalition government with parties that have had a more inclusive approach—first the People's party and since the mid-2000s the Christian Democrats.

Since 1990 Social Democratic governments have introduced measures to limit admissions of asylum seekers and elderly family members. Despite these measures, their admission policy has been aptly described as "trying to be restrictive and generous at the same time" (Abiri 2000: 21), and a generous stance has reasserted itself at times. The governments reaffirmed their stance of expansive immigrant rights in promoting dual citizenship and rejecting support obligations for family reunions. The party has confronted divided opinions among its voters, making it more cautious. Differences have also been evident in the policy positions of members of Social Democratic governments since the mid-1990s. Simultaneously the Left party (*Vänsterpartiet*), formerly the Communists, and the Greens (*Miljöpartiet—de gröna*) have remained enthusiastic proponents of inclusion, advocating both expansive admissions and immigrant rights. A shared characteristic of the left parties has been their advocacy of expansive rights for newcomers.

Support for populist anti-immigration parties has been relatively weak, despite large numbers of voters endorsing immigration restrictions. The New Democrats sat in parliament for only three years (1991–4), and after nearly 20 years of campaign efforts, the Sweden Democrats finally secured parliamentary representation in the 2010 election and also a broker position. In response to the prospects of the Sweden Democrats entering parliament, all the mainstream parties vowed to reject the support of the Sweden Democrats in forming a government. In early 2011 the governing parties and the Greens reached an immigration policy agreement, which included improving undocumented immigrants' access to medical care and school attendance. Moderate Prime Minister Fredrik Reinfeldt declared that Sweden was at a crossroads and the agreement represented a continued humane policy and shut the door to exclusionary forces (RK 2011). This response, as we shall see, differed from the Danish mainstream right that embraced the support of the far right party and several of the party's policy proposals.

Denmark: From reluctant inclusiveness to exclusion

Although the rights extension process in Denmark and Sweden initially developed along similar lines, immigrant rights—both social and political rights—generated controversy in Denmark, and the Danes were more reluctant to extend rights to newcomers. For the most part, the effect of the early controversies was a delay in extending immigrant rights. The 1980s were a decade of contradictory trends in Denmark and formed a turning point. Although rights extension continued, the first reversals occurred in the 1980s. Restrictions grew in the 1990s but took on new proportions after the 2001 Danish election, substantially weakening immigrants' social rights and heightening the exclusionary nature of the incorporation regime.

The politics of inclusion: Shifting policy venues and disagreement

In 1969 the Danes appointed their counterpart to the commission on immigrant policy—an inquiry commission on foreign workers. The center-right government's instructions to the commission framed the issue as labor migration and the problems created by the growing numbers of non-Nordic foreigners in Denmark. More specifically, many foreigners did not follow the rules; they were often exploited on the labor and housing markets, and estranged from Danish society. The task of the commission was to propose changes in the work permit system and measures to alleviate the problems of foreign workers (Betænkning 589: 5, 7). Framing the issue in this way largely precluded a broader policy. Immigrants were defined as temporary workers and not as new members of the community or future citizens. Thus the Danes embarked on formulating a foreign workers policy (*fremmedarbejderpolitik*)— not a settlement policy. Nor did the Danes decouple immigrant policy from immigration policy. As long as the policy was framed as a foreign workers policy—and this was the frame until the late 1970s—labor migration remained a contentious issue between the unions and employers, diverting attention from other concerns and solutions. In short, this issue frame undermined the development of a comprehensive immigrant policy.

The framing of the issue also influenced the policy venue and the roster of participants. As an issue of labor migration the Danish commission had a corporatist tripartite composition with representatives of the employers, unions, and the state—the Ministry of Labor, along with social affairs, housing, foreign affairs, and justice, including the national police commissioner. The commission's main recommendations concerned the permit system; making membership in the sickness and unemployment insurance funds obligatory for foreigners; improving access to family benefits, subsidized housing, and vocational education; making Danish instruction available through evening classes; and providing leisure time activities and recreation centers. Two of the recommendations—temporary housing for foreign workers and family benefits—generated protests and disagreement (Betænkning 589).

After the first commission, critics claimed that there was no immigrant policy, only a series of ad hoc provisions in response to the social problems of foreign workers (Hjarnø et al. 1973). Nor were all the commission's recommendations enacted. In 1973 the Social Democratic government appointed a follow-up commission. Its mandate included suggesting improvements in the conditions of foreign workers, but the key ministry was now the Ministry of Social Affairs. The commission's report was more ambitious and focused on the social, cultural, and political rights of immigrants. The commission proposed giving foreigners access to educational allowances. It also repeated the recommendation to make family benefits available after six months' residence, but it was hesitant toward tax deductions for dependents, proposing that deductions be limited to two years. The first evidence of cultural rights for immigrants was in the commission's proposal that public libraries have books in the languages of the major immigrant groups. The political rights of non-citizens came onto the agenda via the 1975 recommendation of the Nordic Council that Nordic citizens be given the right to vote and stand in local and regional elections. As in the Swedish case, the commission recommended the rights be extended regardless of nationality (Betænkning 761).

Partisan disagreement again centered on family benefits and now also on tax deductions for foreigners. An additional source of dissension was local political rights for non-Nordic citizens. The proposal to grant these rights to all immigrants was delayed because of opposition within the Social Democratic–Liberal coalition government. After the 1979 election the Social Democrats formed a minority government and announced a review of immigrants' situation, including political rights and immigrants' tax allowances. When in 1981 the government introduced the bill granting all non-citizens the right to vote and stand in local and regional elections, the Conservatives (*Det Konservative Folkeparti*), nearly all the Liberals (*Venstre*)—a party which despite its name has been ideologically very close to the Conservatives—and the populist far right Progress Party (*Fremskridtspartiet*) voted against it (Togeby 2003: 50).

Gradually the focus of immigration *cum* immigrant policy shifted from foreign workers to refugees and the protection of aliens' legal rights. This shift brought changes in the policy goal and the policy network. The goal was a more humane immigration policy and improving the rights of refugees and legal aliens. The policy network now consisted of judges and lawyers, and it also included humanitarian groups, such as the Danish Refugee Council and the Danish Red Cross, along with organizations promoting international cooperation and human rights. The ministry in charge was the Ministry of Justice (Betænkning 882). This policy context was more auspicious because many Danes took pride in Denmark's international record of humanitarian aid to refugees, and a Dane, Poul Hartling, was the United Nations High Commissioner for Refugees (1978–85). Hartling had been Prime Minister in the Liberal government of 1973–75, so the shift in framing muted differences between the left and the right.

The 1977 aliens commission presented its final report in 1982, which led to the 1983 Aliens Law—model legislation in terms of its humanitarian approach to refugees. The law codified administrative practice by incorporating de facto refugees into the law and giving them the same status as convention refugees. It strengthened the legal rights to a residence permit and family reunification of both types of refugees. All asylum seekers could enter Denmark and stay while their application was processed, even if they did not possess a valid passport or visa. The law also eliminated the legal basis of the discretionary powers of the Minister of Justice and introduced procedural safeguards, along with the right to appeal (Pedersen 1999: 165). The newly created Directorate of Aliens rather than the aliens' section of the police was charged with the task of processing asylum applications and residence permits, and a board of appeals was established (Jensen 1999: 228).

Despite broad support for the law in the Folketing, the Danish parliament, controversy preceded and followed its adoption. The commission was deeply divided, and it issued a majority report written by the hardliners and a minority report drafted by the reformists. The minority right-center government, which came into office after the Social Democrats (*Socialdemokratiet*) resigned in September 1982, was split on the issue and confronted a parliamentary majority for reform. After several changes in the bill, the Conservative Minister of Justice put forward a compromise proposal and chose to negotiate with the Social Democrats. In the end, only the Progress Party voted against the law, charging that it was contrary to the will of the people (Højsteen 1992: 71–80; Jensen 1999: 227).

The move toward restrictions

The passage of the 1983 Aliens Law constituted the high-water mark in inclusive admission legislation, and nearly all subsequent changes to the law consisted of restrictions. The first revisions were aimed at curbing the number of asylum seekers, but restrictions spilled over to key policy dimensions of the incorporation regime. The first tightening of citizenship requirements occurred in 1983 through an ordinance issued by the new center-right government (Ersbøll 2006: 143), and in the 1990s restrictions affecting the incorporation regime gained new momentum.

Immediately after the adoption of the 1983 Aliens Law, the Conservative Minister of Justice began calling for its revision. The Progress party also kept up its opposition, claiming that the law violated the will of the people. The first of many revisions in 1985 was fueled by an all-time high in the number of asylum seekers and an increasingly acrimonious debate in the media with claims that the survival of Denmark as a nation-state was threatened. The 1985 revision, supported by the governing parties, the Social Democrats, and the Progress party, created a fast procedure for handling manifestly unfounded asylum applications and limited the right of appeal in these cases. The critics—the Radical Liberals (*Det Radikale Venstre*) and two parties to the left of the Social Democrats—charged that the revisions jeopardized the rights of asylum seekers, and they further objected that legislation contained no definition of manifestly unfounded cases (Jensen 1999: 229–48).

In the early 1990s the Conservative–Liberal government introduced a series of new restrictions affecting the incorporation regime. Residence requirements for permanent permits and naturalization were lengthened, and new requirements for family reunification were introduced. In 1990 the calculation of the residence requirement for citizenship was changed to seven years from the date of the applicant's permanent residence permit, and the following year the residence requirement for a permanent permit was raised from two to three years. In effect, the changes lengthened the residence requirement for naturalization to ten years. A 1992 amendment of the Aliens Law targeted family reunification; it increased the residence requirement to five years, required proof of an adequate income, and introduced stronger enforcement of obligations to support family members.

At the same time, advances occurred during the 1980s and the first half of the 1990s. Several improvements were facilitated by an administrative separation of immigrant and integration policies from immigration policies. Until 1993 immigrant and integration policies were located in the Ministry of Social Affairs. Besides local political rights, the main gains were the formation of an immigrant council to consult with the authorities (1983); better access to family benefits (1986), student benefits (1987), and minimum pensions; the first inclusion of persons with immigrant backgrounds on inquiry commissions (1993); the establishment of the National Council of Ethnic Equality (1993); and the passage of a law prohibiting discrimination on the labor market (1996) (Hammer 1995; Togeby 2003: 55, 128, 150).

INTEGRATION, IMMIGRANTS' SOCIAL RIGHTS AND EXCLUSION

In December 1994 the left-center government appointed a commission to formulate a comprehensive integration policy. It was a broad-based commission, including representatives of ethnic minority associations, humanitarian aid organizations, the labor market, and regional and local authorities. Several ministries were represented, with the Ministry of Internal Affairs providing the secretariat of the commission (Betænkning 1337, Bilag 1).

The Integration Law deviated markedly from the draft legislation recommended to the government in the commission's final report. The goals of the commission's version stressed the wishes, needs, and the capabilities of the individual immigrant and respect for his/her cultural identity. There were no traces of this in the law. Instead the individual alien was to gain an understanding of the basic values and norms of the Danish society. The other major goal of the law, but not mentioned by the commission, emphasized the speedy economic self-support of immigrants. The commission report had attached weight to strengthening the Council of Ethnic Minorities and incorporating persons with immigrant background and representatives for immigration associations in the administration through municipal integration councils composed of a majority of immigrants. The law did not include the commission's main recommendation to strengthen the Council of Ethnic Minorities, and it gave the municipalities considerable leeway in establishing and determining the membership of municipal integration councils. The law also lengthened the integration program to three years compared to 18 months proposed by the commission. A final difference was that the law created a new assistance benefit—the introductory allowance (*introduktionsydelse*)—pegged at a lower rate than the standard social assistance (Betænkning 1337: chapter 13; Lov 474/1998).

The divergences between the commission report and the Integration Law came about because of a press debate and party negotiations to secure a broad parliamentary majority. An editorial in the tabloid *Extra Bladet*, proposing lower assistance benefits for refugees, sparked a debate that eventually influenced the benefit levels of the integration program. The editorial argued that benefits led to passivity and served as a magnet to asylum seekers, and it won the immediate endorsement of an influential Liberal, Anders Fogh Rasmussen, who later became Prime Minister in the Liberal–Conservative government formed after the 2001 election. He was joined by the Conservatives and the Progress party. When the Minister of the Interior presented the government bill, it contained lower benefits for participants in the integration program. The justification was that reduced benefits would act as an incentive to enter the labor market more quickly. The Radical Liberals, the coalition partner of the Social Democrats, also favored a workfare orientation, which was criticized by the parties to the left of the Social Democrats. If workfare was to be included, a parliamentary majority for the Integration Law had to be secured through the right-wing parties. The Interior Minister also wanted wide agreement, including the support of the Conservatives and Liberals, to strengthen the people's respect for the Integration Law (Jensen 1999: 277; Ejrnæs 2001: 8–9).

Between the presentation of the government bill and the adoption of the Integration Law, the 1998 election took place, and immigration was a major issue. The Social Democrats and Radical Liberals remained in office, but the election signaled the breakthrough of the Danish People's party (*Dansk Folkeparti*), which had broken away from the Progress party. In the 2001 election the party won 12 per cent of the vote and a broker position in Danish politics. The Liberal–Conservative government formed after the 2001 election entered into policy negotiations with the Danish People's party on a regular basis. It was the policy packages coming out of these negotiations that altered the social rights of non-citizens and moved the Danish incorporation regime in an exclusionary direction.

The negative measures for immigrants included the 2002 lowering of the introductory allowance (*starthjælp*), requiring at least seven years of residence to be eligible for full assistance benefits, ending family reunion of elderly parents, tightening restrictions on reunification of spouses and requiring a bond of $7000, lengthening the residence requirement for an unlimited permit to seven years and for naturalization to nine years, introducing a loyalty oath for naturalization, and limiting acquisition of citizenship by declaration to Nordic citizens (MFII 2003b).

Neither the 2005 nor the 2007 election significantly altered the parliamentary constellation of power. The Liberal–Conservative minority government remained in office, backed by the Danish People's party. The party renewed its support of the government when the premiership changed hands in 2009. The slimmer vote for the governing parties in the 2007 election weakened their hand in negotiations with the Danish People's party.

Party negotiations in 2005 continued to undermine immigrants' social rights with respect to family benefits and regular assistance if both husband and wife received benefits. The parties agreed to stiffen requirements of language proficiency, economic self-sufficiency, and the civics test in 2008 (MFII 2005, 2008). The 2010 negotiations targeted immigrants' political rights and proposed a point system for a permanent residence permit. The parties agreed to raise the residence requirement from three to four years for local and regional voting rights (MFII 2010), and a point system was introduced in 2011. Overall, the policies of the government after 2001 dramatically increased the thresholds and conditions for inclusion.

Understanding the differences

Tracing the policy developments in Sweden and Denmark has helped us to identify several differences that have shaped dissimilar policy outputs. To gain a better understanding of the politics behind the policy differences, let us systematically compare framing, policy venues, the role of party politics and the structure of party competition, the territorial dimension, and ethnic mobilization and penetration.

Framing

The initial framing of immigrant policies was dissimilar. Defining newcomers as foreign workers or immigrants who were potentially permanent settlers affected the type of measures considered and the type of policy network involved. The Danish emphasis on labor immigration also influenced attitudes to family reunification, and the Danes strengthened support obligations in the late 1970s, while the Swedes abolished them even for elderly parents. Additional contrasts pertained to policy styles. The Swedes adopted a proactive approach; they formulated a comprehensive immigrant policy with visionary goals, and established new administrative machinery. Danish policy was characterized by an ad hoc approach, shifting in focus and ministerial responsibility for formulating policy; the first inquiry commission on foreign workers had a reactive stance, and explicit policy goals were conspicuous by their absence.

The emphasis on equality also differed. Less seldom was equality marshaled as an argument for change in Denmark. In the report of the first commission, equality primarily figured in the discussion of existing equal rights of immigrants and Danes, without invoking equality as a goal. The most explicit equality argumentation concerned political rights in the report of the second commission. However, it was as taxpayers that foreigners should have an equal say in determining the scope and uses of public revenues (Betænkning 761). At times the Danes used the equality argument against the social rights of immigrants. Besides arguing that the benefits of immigrants should be equal to those of the Danes, the commission stressed that the benefits of foreigners should not be different from those of Danes. On these grounds it expressed skepticism toward immigrants' tax deductions for dependents and special measures in the areas of housing and legal aid (Betænkning 761: 15). There has also been a Danish aversion to positive discrimination.

A final difference in framing was the Swedish emphasis on partnership and mutual tolerance, which stemmed from viewing newcomers as settlers. The Swedes declared that immigrants should be viewed as equal partners in the development of society, and they proposed measures to strengthen immigrant associations and consultative arrangements. This frame was missing in Denmark, and the Danes did not introduce consultative arrangements until the early 1980s.

Policy venues

Shortly after the immigration issue came onto the political agenda in the mid-1960s, the Swedes emphasized the necessity of greater state involvement to achieve a coherent policy, while the Danes were reluctant to assign more responsibility to the state, and they delayed setting up new policy machinery. The 1967 report of the Swedish commission on immigration underlined that the government (*statsmakterna*) had to take responsibility for policy formulation in this area, and the National Board of Immigrant Affairs was established in 1969. The establishment of a new central administrative agency was facilitated by the dualistic administrative structure of the Swedish state. As distinct from Denmark, which has a ministerial administration, Sweden has an organizational separation between the ministries responsible for policy making and preparation of legislation and the central administrative agencies responsible for implementation. Consequently, creating a new agency in Sweden was a much less dramatic step than setting up a ministry in Denmark. The establishment of the Board created a new policy venue, and the Board became a key administrative actor in this policy area, and its staff promoted immigrant rights. As head of the expert commission on anti-discrimination, the former director general of the Board was instrumental in the creation of the anti-discrimination commissioner, which has had no Danish counterpart.

The Danes tended to shun state involvement, preferring a larger role for civil society and local government. Indeed, it was a long and tortuous road before the Danes set up more effective state machinery for immigrant policies. Reliance on voluntary associations contributed to the delay. The Danish Refugee Council, founded in 1956 and made up of a dozen or so voluntary associations, became responsible for the reception of refugees and asylum seekers. The 1969 commission on foreign workers rejected assigning overall responsibility to a new state agency. It reasoned that state institutions should serve citizens and newcomers alike, without separate immigrant agencies. However, the commission recommended the establishment of an independent consultant to help immigrants; the position was created in 1970 and located in the Ministry of Social Affairs (Andersen 1979: 73). Instead the commission emphasized a stronger engagement of civil society and local governments, arguing that the small numbers of immigrants did not justify more state involvement (Betænkning 589). The follow-up commission in the mid-1970s reaffirmed this position, mainly calling for improvements in the existing coordination arrangements (Betænkning 761). At the end of the 1970s the Social Democratic Prime Minister, Anker Jørgensen, went on record against creating a separate immigration ministry (Jensen 1999: 220). From the 1990s onwards there was greater emphasis on the responsibilities of the central and local governments for a comprehensive immigrant policy, culminating in the 1998 Integration Law that launched the three-year introductory program. The Law transferred responsibility for the introductory program to local government, diminishing the role of the Refugee Council. In 2001 the government established the Ministry of Refugees, Immigrants, and Integration.

Another feature, regarded as typical of the Scandinavian countries, has been the consultative nature of the policy process through inquiry commissions and the remiss procedure that bring together state and societal actors. Although inquiry commissions play an important role in the policy making of both countries, Swedish inquiry commissions have been more important policy venues than in Denmark. In this policy area, the recommendations of the Swedish commissions have often been incorporated in government bills, and usually adopted with large parliamentary majorities. In Denmark several recommendations of the inquiry commissions went unheeded or were postponed for long periods. A major difference between the commissions was their corporatist composition in Denmark and their parliamentarian composition in Sweden. In the latter case partisan differences could often be resolved or reduced during commission deliberations, whereas in Denmark party positions blocked further action on commission proposals or substantially modified them. Expert commissions in Sweden have sometimes met a similar fate, as exemplified by the expert commission on anti-discrimination legislation.

The territorial dimension

The territorial dimension consisting of the pattern of immigrant settlement and the divisions of responsibilities between the central and local governments has played out differently in the two countries, illustrating beautifully how policies create politics. In Denmark the territorial dimension fuelled divisions among the Social Democrats, driving the party to the right. During the first wave of asylum seekers, refugees were located in relatively few municipalities. Among the first prominent Social Democrats to call for restrictions were the mayors of municipalities with high concentrations of refugees. The mayors complained of the unwelcome extra costs of providing services and education for asylum seekers. Dissensions of this type continued to crop up, especially during peaks in the arrival of refugees. At times the mayors refused to accept more refugees in their municipalities, and they argued that there was an unfair distribution across local authorities. Furthermore, prior to the 1998

Integration Law, the national refugee council was responsible for the reception program for asylum seekers and received state funding for this purpose.

Internal party differences came to a head immediately before the 1987 election and again with the arrival of Bosnian refugees in 1992 and the decision to grant them permanent status. On the eve of the 1987 election, an internal Social Democratic report on refugee and immigration policies, chaired by a local politician, was hushed up. Its demands included greater assimilation of immigrants to Danish conditions and tighter rules on marriages between immigrants and spouses from their countries of origin. A new committee was appointed to draw up a coherent Social Democratic policy on refugees and immigrants, and the newly elected party leader mounted a campaign against racism and xenophobia. The discontent surrounding the Bosnians unleashed the so-called mayoral rebellion, once more exposing divisions in the Social Democratic Party. A central figure was the Social Democratic mayor of Århus, Thorkild Simonsen, who urged his party colleague, Prime Minister Poul Nyrup Rasmussen, to clarify what the government had done to promote integration (Jensen 1999: 235–6, 254–6, 260–84). It was against this backdrop that the Social Democratic government appointed the commission on integration, and eventually Simonsen became the minister who introduced the 1998 Integration Law with its concessions to the right.

In Sweden the territorial dimension has revolved around conflicts between the national government and municipalities over resources to cover the costs of immigrant policies, which overshadowed divisions between the local party organizations and the party leadership. The "Entire Sweden Strategy" led to a wider dispersion of newcomers across the country; the municipalities were responsible for reception services, and they received state funding for accepting asylum seekers. Responsibility for the reception of refugees was shouldered by most local governments by the late 1980s (SOU 1996:55, pp. 54–5). A consequence was a perception of a fair distribution of responsibilities, even if a few municipalities, generally run by the conservatives, opted out of the reception program.

Still there have been high concentrations of immigrants in the three major metropolitan areas, and the proportion of immigrants in all three has grown since 1990. Local politicians from the metropolitan areas have primarily called for more resources or measures to ease the pressure on their communities rather than major changes in immigration or integration policies. A major grievance, however, was the housing allowance for asylum seekers which encouraged chain immigration to areas with a large immigrant population, and local politicians lobbied for a change. In 2005 the allowance was modified so that it could only be used when it was necessary to move in connection with a new job (Borevi and Myrberg 2008; SOU 2009:19). This was the closest parallel to the influence of the rebel mayors on integration policy.

In short, the territorial dimension, especially the funding arrangements for carrying out local responsibilities, created major dissatisfaction among the Danish mayors. In attempting to resolve their frustrations the mayors primarily operated through the Social Democratic party, moving it toward the right. In Sweden, dispersal of asylum seekers and funding arrangements at least initially muted municipal discontent, but increasing concentrations put more pressure on local and national politicians.

Party politics

The most obvious answer to the policy differences is the existence of an anti-immigration party since the late 1970s in Denmark and its pivotal position after the 2001 election, whereas there has been no far right anti-immigration party at the national level in Sweden apart from 1991–4 and after the 2010 election. In Denmark the Progress party was a permanent fixture of the party landscape until it was eclipsed by the Danish People's party in 2001.

The continuous existence of an anti-immigration party has influenced Danish politics in several ways. The Progress party offered an institutional base for opponents to immigration and foreigners, transforming amorphous views into a political force. From the outset the party tapped into existing negative popular opinions (Togeby 1998: 1145), but it also constantly nurtured anti-immigration sentiments. Furthermore, Danish popular opinion has been ambivalent, even contradictory. As an illustration, an overwhelming majority in the mid-1990s believed that the large numbers of immigrants and refugees increased Denmark's economic problems, at the same time as they thought that Denmark ought to accept and help persons fleeing persecution (Gaasholt and Togeby 1995: 47–8). Ambivalences such as this can be mobilized in favor of either exclusion or inclusion, highlighting the significance of the political parties and their messages to the electorate.

The extreme proposals of the Progress party and the Danish People's party have shifted the center of gravity in the policy debate and altered the political agenda. Since 1990 the two parties repeatedly called for the disenfranchisement of non-Nordic citizens in local elections, the introduction of annual quotas for naturalization, tighter requirements to become a Danish citizen, no home language instruction in the schools, and lower social benefits for foreigners (Nielsen and Pihl 1998, Bilag 1). The Progress party advocated the removal of all foreign citizens who could not support themselves (except Geneva Convention refugees) and the deportation of all Muslims. It demanded limited economic assistance for Convention refugees (which is in violation of the Geneva Convention) and no public assistance for other foreigners (Goul Andersen 2003: 189; Boréus 2008: 24).

However, the far right party has been only one component of the political equation in introducing stringent policy measures since 2001. Equally important have been the governing mainstream right parties' willingness to collaborate with the Danish People's party. What explains the cooperation of the Liberals and the Conservatives with the far right anti-immigration party and the Moderates' position of shunning such collaboration?

Differences in the structure of party competition and its effects on the prospects of holding office have been of central importance (Green-Pedersen and Krogstrup 2008). Although Denmark and Sweden have had strong Social Democratic parties and minority governments have been the rule in both countries, a crucial difference has been that a left parliamentary majority has been much more likely in Sweden, and this in turn strengthened the dominance of the Social Democratic party over the executive. In the 1960s the center-right parties began to cooperate in order to dislodge the Social Democrats from executive power, and they succeeded in the 1976 election. In the process the parties played down their differences in order to present themselves as a credible alternative to the Social Democrats. Moreover, the period from 1968 to 1973—important years for the inclusive turn—represented a nadir in the conservatives' polling strength, weakening their position vis-à-vis the centrist parties. In the 1991 election and the 2006 election the right-center parties largely avoided immigration and immigrant issues.

A left majority in the Danish parliament has been a rare phenomenon, and when the Social Democrats have been in government, they have usually had to rely on the support of the centrist parties. In addition, there has been the much stronger vote for the two Danish mainstream right parties—the Liberals and Conservatives—(ranging from 20 to 40 per cent) compared to the single Swedish mainstream right party—the Moderates—(between 12 and 30 per cent). The strength of the Danish mainstream right has approached that of the Social Democrats but neither had a parliamentary majority. In this situation the centrist parties became critical to forming a government. From the early 1980s right-center coalition governments existed, followed by left-center governments from 1993 to 2001. Christoffer Green-Pedersen and Jesper Krogstrup (2008: 622) point out that the centrist parties have only changed their position slowly, typically being in coalition with the right or the left for a decade. This provided a powerful incentive for the mainstream right to seek a majority through a rapprochement with the far right party, especially when opinion polls showed the possibility of a parliamentary majority consisting of the Liberals, Conservatives, and the Progress party. Once in opposition, the Liberals and to a lesser extent the Conservatives began to campaign on restrictive immigration and immigrant policies (Green-Pedersen 2002: 124).

The 2001 election produced a right parliamentary majority for the first time since 1920 and led to the formation of a Liberal–Conservative government based on the support of the Danish People's party. This type of government existed until the 2011 election, and a Liberal was the Minister of Refugees, Immigrants and Integration. In election campaigns the governing parties pointed with pride to the changes in immigration and immigrant policies during their period in office.

Ethnic mobilization and penetration

An additional striking difference between the policy processes in the two countries has been the input of immigrants and persons with immigrant backgrounds in Sweden. Refugees who had come during the Second World War were active in formulating the immigrant policies of the 1970s. They, together with more recent immigrants, were among the main agenda setters, and they participated in party affairs. Immigrants were also experts or members of the commission on immigrant policy and the commission on voting rights, exercising insider influence. Immigrant penetration of the parties and inquiry commissions was accompanied by ethnic mobilization at various stages of the policy process.

The 1974 immigrant policy commission set a precedent in providing access to immigrants that influenced subsequent commissions in this policy area. During the past four decades immigrants served on several parliamentary inquiry commissions dealing with major policy dimensions of the incorporation regime, such as the commissions on citizenship law, immigrant and integration policies, anti-discrimination, the reception of refugees, and family reunification.

In the Danish case none of the commissions working in 1970s included immigrants. Only occasionally were individual foreigners or organized immigrants consulted. Not even the 1977 commission that strengthened the legal rights of aliens conferred with immigrant organizations (Højsteen 1992). Nor were there immigrant voices in the public debate during the decade (Jensen 1999). Instead the advocates of pro-immigrant policies were the consultant in the Ministry of Social Affairs and human rights activists and organizations.

The lack of consultation sparked immigrant protests and was a mobilizing force. There were sporadic protests by foreign workers during the first commission in the early 1970s. In the mid-1970s the follow-up commission's recommendations also caused immigrants to protest. They opposed the commission's proposal to eliminate tax deductions for maintenance responsibilities and formed the first multiethnic immigrant organization in an attempt to influence the issue (Togeby 2003: 126).

The situation changed as immigrants became better organized. To strengthen the case for political rights for non-citizens, immigrant organizations publicly declared that immigrants wanted the right to vote (Togeby

2003: 50, 127). The need for consultation and inclusion was formally recognized in 1983 when the government established a national advisory body, the immigrant council, later the National Council of Ethnic Minorities. In the 1990s immigrants were finally included in inquiry commissions. They were members of the commission on integration, and they left an imprint on the commission's recommendations. Most of these recommendations were not incorporated into the 1998 Integration Law or they were diluted. Since 2001 immigrants have largely been excluded from the policy formulation process affecting their rights.

Conclusion

In two respects, the preconditions for a politics of exclusion have been quite similar in Denmark and Sweden. In both countries, large sections of the population have been negative to immigration, and the media have been filled with derogatory stories about immigrants (Green-Pedersen and Krogstrup 2008: 616–18). The differing policy outputs in the Swedish and the Danish cases underline the significance of politics, and through process tracing we have identified key differences in framing, policy venues, and the nature of the policy machinery; the political parties, the structure of party competition, and the partisan composition of governments; and immigrant organizing and penetration of the policy process.

Importantly the initial drive for inclusion was weaker in Denmark, and from the outset the politics of inclusion was characterized by partisan differences, in part because of how immigrant policies were framed. Shifting policy venues contributed to the lack of policy continuity, as did frequent changes in government during the 1970s. In Denmark the overall polling strength of the right parties has been stronger than in Sweden, and the parties pushing for inclusion made up a smaller portion of the political spectrum compared to Sweden. The most enthusiastic Danish champions of pro-immigrant policies were the parties to the left of the Social Democrats and the Radical Liberals. The Danish Social Democrats were divided on immigrant policy and more skeptical toward positive measures, viewing them as a contradiction of equality and universalism. The territorial dimension contributed to a deepening of divisions within the party. At the same time the Social Democratic party was crucial to the introduction of inclusive measures during the 1970s and early 1980s, and during these years there was a parliamentary majority for such measures. From the mid-1980s onwards the forces favoring exclusionary policies gathered strength as the Progress party made anti-immigration its raison d'être and warned of a Muslim peril in 1984, and new anti-immigration and anti-Islam organizations formed. The Liberals and Conservatives also became increasingly restrictionist. Still until 2001 there were shifting parliamentary majorities for inclusive and exclusionary policies.

A major contrast between the two countries has been the continuous existence of an anti-immigration party in Denmark since the late 1970s, and its existence has had major repercussions for Danish politics. Nevertheless the Danish far right anti-immigration party is not sufficient in explaining the increasingly exclusionary incorporation regime and the worsening of immigrants' social rights. One of the main conclusions of this chapter is the importance of the responses of the mainstream parties. The Danish mainstream right parties decided to enter an alliance with the far right party. By itself the party, which has won less than 15 per cent of the vote, could not produce the paradigmatic shift in the incorporation regime and immigrant rights. Moreover, the decision to collaborate with the Danish People's party was in line with the two parties' earlier policies. A Conservative–Liberal coalition government (1990–3) had introduced measures changing key policy dimensions of the incorporation regime in an exclusionary direction. Long before, in the 1970s and early 1980s, the two parties had opposed inclusive measures.

In the Swedish case international migration literature has categorized the Swedish incorporation regime and immigrant policies as inclusive, but there has been little analysis of the politics behind this development. Instead inclusiveness has been relegated to a concomitant of the egalitarian social democratic welfare state (Geddes 2003b). This chapter has documented the multiple sources and dynamics of the politics of inclusion. The distinction between immigration and immigrant policies strengthened an inclusive frame—one that emphasized equality, rights, partnership, mutual respect, and tolerance. The frame dovetailed into a larger participatory discourse on greater democracy, equality, and co-determination, which had reinforcing effects for immigrants to participate in the policy process that extended their rights. Party consensus eventually emerged on state measures to strengthen immigrant associations and religious congregations, on aiding immigrants who wanted to maintain their cultural traditions, and on granting immigrants political rights at the local and regional level. All the parties endorsed the inclusive goals of immigrant policies. The creation of a new central administrative agency furnished an institutional platform for pro-immigrant policy activists, as did the 1974 commission on immigrant policies. The measures it recommended amounted to a paradigmatic shift in the Swedish incorporation regime.

Even though the 1970s consensus on inclusion has been under mounting pressure, an inclusive approach so far has generally persisted. At several critical junctures, shifting parliamentary majorities for inclusive measures have crystallized. The initial response to the parliamentary presence of the Sweden

Democrats was to create an alliance between the governing parties and the Greens on immigration and immigrant policies to limit the influence of the party. Ironically, the formation of this alliance strengthened the forces for inclusion compared to the situation before the election victory of the Sweden Democrats. The alliance proposed to improve the social rights of undocumented immigrants and to make major improvements in the permit system even for unskilled workers (SOU 2011:26)—contrary to trends in the other European countries. Admittedly, the major mainstream right party has not had the option of securing a parliamentary majority through collaboration with the far right party. Just as important, however, the Moderates' strong stance on labor immigration militated against such collaboration even if the option had existed. On the other hand, the Moderates' holding the position of Immigration Minister offers the possibility of introducing restrictive regulations, as occurred during the Reinfeldt government's first term in office (2006–10).

In summation the examination of the Swedish and the Danish cases underscores that inclusive outcomes were not merely an offshoot of the Swedish and Danish welfare state regimes. Policies have been determined by the balance of political forces pushing for inclusion or alternatively exclusion and restrictions.

11

The Politics of Inclusion
and Exclusion Compared

Moving beyond paired comparisons, this chapter compares the politics of inclusion and exclusion across the six countries. Through process tracing we have examined the politics of policy formation in each of the countries and compared the politics by welfare regime type. A shortcoming of this type of comparison is its focus on two countries, which limits the possibilities of generalizing. A further weakness of paired comparisons is that the particularities of the two selected countries can determine the nature of the puzzles the analyst tries to unravel—in this case puzzles concerning policies affecting immigrant rights. Comparing across all six countries offers the prospect of new insights and wider generalizations. Such a comparison also exposes the limits of existing generalizations and theoretical claims, shedding light on their traveling capacity or wider applicability in comparative analysis.

What do our cases tell us more generally about the importance of actors and contexts for inclusive or exclusionary policy outputs across the six countries? And to what extent do our cases confirm or differ from the results of earlier research? Again the discussion is structured by the components of my analytical framework. I also return to the research questions, formulated in the Introduction to Part II, to illuminate the components' importance. The individual cases have shed light on their importance but here I provide a more systematic and comprehensive discussion across the six countries.

Framing

What have been the major frames of immigrants' social rights and immigrant policies more generally? What impact has framing had on immigrant rights? How has framing influenced the policy venues?

Two aspects of framing have been particularly important in shaping immigrant rights. First, framing is at the heart of the politics of justification, and the impact of frames on immigrant rights is reflected in their justifying various policy proposals that have been translated into legislation. Second, framing involves problem construction, and this has also had major consequences for immigrant rights.

The politics of justification

The single most important set of frames promoting immigrants' social rights and inclusion across the six countries has revolved around equality. Equality frames, in a variety of forms, have justified legislation and court decisions extending immigrant rights. Equality before the law and equal protection underpinned the US Supreme Court's ruling that the states could not bar legal permanent residents from welfare benefits, a decision that contributed to triggering the welfare rights extension process. The equalization of refugee rights was a key frame of the 1980 Refugee Act. The social rights of New Commonwealth immigrants were first framed in terms of full and equal citizenship but eventually this framing was supplanted by equal opportunities and racial equality. The French invoked the constitutional principles of equality in extending rights to national minimum benefits to non-citizens but also in justifying anti-discrimination legislation. Such legislation was required to ensure the equality and equal treatment of citizens, an argument also made in the UK during the 1960s. Equal rights and equal treatment of co-ethnic and non-German immigrants were pivotal to the counterframe challenging the ethnic model of citizenship with its highly differential consequences for immigrant rights. In expanding labor migrants' rights to participate in unions and corporatist bodies, the French and the Germans emphasized equality among workers. In the two Scandinavian countries, equality and equal rights were master frames of the reform legislation of the 1970s and early 1980s.

Frames of deservingness have also enhanced immigrant rights, and two specific frames have had major relevance. First, the most significant frame of this type across the six countries, although not very prominent in the UK, has been the deservingness of politically persecuted persons. Persecution by communist regimes increased their deservingness in the US and Germany. This framing contributed to strengthening the social rights of refugees in comparison to those of other entry categories in the US. The deservingness of the politically persecuted was reinforced by the German and French constitutions through the right of asylum. In Denmark and Sweden this frame was fused with international solidarity, and solidarity with Third World countries called for the rich countries to adopt a generous policy.

The second major frame of deservingness has been contributions to the nation, which has been a dominant frame in the US. In the heyday of labor migration, the frame of contributions was also prominent in France and Germany. Immigrants contributed to the economic recovery and growing postwar prosperity of the two countries. With the resumption of labor immigration in the European countries during the 2000s this frame has gained new currency.

Central to the politics of rights contraction and exclusion has been framing immigrants negatively to undermine their deservingness. Among the most common disparaging frames have been immigrants as fakes, free-riders and welfare scroungers, criminals, and security threats. In Germany persons applying for refugee status were increasingly framed as fake asylum seekers (*Schein-asylanten*) who were abusing the right of asylum, and co-ethnic immigrants were accused of being fake Germans from the late 1980s and onwards. Bogus asylum seekers abusing social benefits has been a shared frame across many European countries, but British government officials have excelled in characterizing most entry categories as guilty of welfare fraud. These frames justified German and British laws that worsened the social rights of asylum seekers and in Germany also the social rights of co-ethnic immigrants. In Denmark the frame of welfare abuse was decisive to the provisions of the 1998 Integration Law that introduced lower benefits for newcomers (Ejrnæs 2001: 8–9). *Les clandestins* served as a frame of undeservingness in France, paving the way for measures that eliminated undocumented immigrants' access to insurance benefits even when they had paid contributions. More generally, across the countries the illegal entry of undocumented immigrants has been marshaled as an argument against granting them residence and social rights. The subtext of all these frames is dishonesty, casting doubt on the trustworthiness of newcomers.

Another form of negative framing has been to portray immigrants as a problem. Especially damaging as a justification for exclusion has been the problem of non-assimilation, and the premise that non-European immigrants were incapable of assimilation. Such claims figured prominently in France, Germany, and Denmark, and they were often accompanied by insinuations that non-European immigrants posed a threat to the nation. Eventually this frame came to impinge on newcomers' social rights, often as sanctions for failing to meet requirements of integration or assimilation. Immigrants have also been framed as the source of social problems. A key example was the "threshold of tolerance" thesis, which held that concentrations of immigrants led to a deterioration in public housing, schools, and services. Frames of this sort have put the onus on immigrants. They have caused or exacerbated social problems, and they have failed to integrate, thus forfeiting their deservingness.

Refashioning frames of deservingness has also played a major role in the politics of rights contraction and disentitlement. Neoliberal proponents of contract liberalism have sought to alter the understanding of rights by emphasizing that they are conditional upon the fulfillment of obligations and responsibilities, thus downplaying the view that rights derive from the equal worth and dignity of the individual. This frame has weakened the social rights of citizens and non-citizens alike, but its impact across the countries has varied, having much stronger resonance in the liberal regime countries. Finally the politics of disentitlement have also entailed devising new frames of deservingness, which have excluded immigrants. One of the most influential frames of this type has been citizenship. It was at the core of the US welfare act of 1996, and the frame has gradually gained ground in other countries, and of our six countries, notably in the UK where the Borders, Immigration and Citizenship Act of 2009 reserved full social rights for citizens.

Problem construction

Framing entails problem construction, and how a problem is constructed has several political consequences. First, problem construction can favor certain solutions and block consideration of other remedies. Second, the construction of problems and their solutions can determine who are affected by the policies, that is, whether they include or exclude immigrants. Third, the definition of a problem can influence the policy venue, the range of relevant actors and supportive coalitions. Fourth, the initial framing of the problem can also have effects on how a policy is institutionalized.

The ways in which problem construction can influence the range of solutions are demonstrated in the dissimilarities of problem construction in France compared to those in several other countries. We have already discussed the differences in problem construction between the French and the Germans concerning the major defect of the Bismarckian social protection system, how the differences influenced their policy responses, and the policies' differing ramifications for immigrants' social rights. Extending the comparison to the liberal regime countries further highlights the importance of framing and problem construction. In the US and the UK, welfare dependency was the problem, and the Americans and British viewed individual responsibility as the solution to welfare dependency. Individual responsibility was equated with the obligation to become economically self-sufficient, and the focus was on workfare measures. By contrast, the French defined the problem as social exclusion and the solution was inclusion. They emphasized "participation in the life of the community in the name of the right of citizenship," and insertion measures had a broader ameliorative scope than workfare (Morel 2004: 94–101, quotation, p. 97). Finally, the New Labour government made combating social exclusion a top priority, but the British defined the excluded quite narrowly. Measures were targeted to the most excluded or deprived groups (Burchardt 2005), and the definition did not include immigrants. The broader French conception of social exclusion encompassed long-term unemployment, the erosion of social bonds, especially family instability, social isolation, and marginalization (Silver 1994), and immigrants were among the ranks of the excluded.

Two of our cases—the UK and Sweden—provide insights into the long-term importance of problem construction through the initial framing of integration or immigrant policies. In the UK, integration policies were initially cast in dual frames of public order and full citizenship. The public order frame, along with the existing duties of the Home Office, promoted it as the key policy venue. The second frame underlined the problem of the emergence of second-class citizens, and the solutions were anti-discrimination legislation and special welfare measures for immigrants (later minorities)—tasks that did not fit with the other duties of the Home Office. The uneasy relationship between policing and immigrant policies was partially broken first in the mid-2000s when the tasks of combating discrimination and minority welfare measures were moved from the Home Office to other departments (Somerville 2007: 76, 78), but the Home Office retained responsibility for services and benefits for asylum seekers.

The Swedes conceived of immigration as the arrival of potentially permanent residents, and they defined the problem as newcomers' adjusting to Swedish society and conditions that disadvantaged immigrants and minorities compared to the rest of the population. The solution was immigrant policies that aimed at facilitating settlement in Sweden and creating equivalent living conditions for all residents. Immigrant policies were framed in terms of equality and equal rights. A new central administrative agency was established to deal with immigration and immigrant issues, and it fell under the Ministry of Labor Affairs. Responsibility for equivalent living conditions rested with the existing welfare authorities at the state, regional, and local levels. Thus, despite a shared concern about preventing unequal outcomes for newcomers in both countries, dissimilar frames set their settlement policies on quite different trajectories.

In summing up the influence of framing in determining the appropriate policy venues, we find cases where framing can be quite important in establishing the policy venue, and even institutionalizing the administration of policies. Frequently, however, the relationship between framing and policy venues is of a routine nature; it involves defining an issue as belonging to a particular policy area. For example, social legislation generally has a specific set of policy venues. Once an issue is defined as social policy its assignment to these venues is largely a matter of convention. The experiences of our six countries reveal several cases of strengthening or weakening immigrants' social rights because their eligibility or restrictions on their eligibility, without much fanfare, were folded into social reform legislation. Political controversy centered on the main features of the reform, diverting attention away from the issue of immigrant rights, and this could be of enormous advantage or have disastrous results.

Policy venues

What policy venues have been in charge and what impact do policy venues have on immigrant rights?

Policy venues, as authoritative sites of decisions, privilege specific sets of actors and shape the policy network. The significance of policy venues in determining immigrants' social rights can be easily grasped by examining different venues within a specific national context because many factors are more or less held constant. Such an examination reveals how a change in venue alters the roster of participants, the lines of conflict, policy coalitions, and the scope of support for various measures, all of which affect policy outputs.

Two illuminating examples of the consequences of different policy venues are provided by the experiences of the US and Denmark. Their experiences also illustrate the importance of institutional arrangements. In the US the separation of powers has often entailed the involvement of several policy venues for any issue area. As we have seen, different venues played an influential role in shaping the social rights of specific entry categories, but multiple policy venues have had contradictory effects on immigrant rights.

In the Danish case a single venue has been in charge of formulating policies, but the venue has changed over time. The importance of the policy venue is best illustrated by the contrast between the Ministry of Labor Affairs and the Ministry of Justice. When the Labor Ministry was the policy venue, the roster of participants reflected tripartite corporatism: state representatives together with the unions and employers. Divisions between labor and management, reinforced by partisan differences between the left and right, blocked the enactment of several recommendations. With the shift to the Ministry of Justice, the roster of participants comprised legal experts, rights activists, and humanitarian organizations. The lines of conflict were altered, making possible a broad coalition of support that included a parliamentary majority, resulting in legislation that strengthened immigrants' legal rights.

The effects of a change in policy venues can also be observed in the conservative corporatist countries. During the years of labor immigration, the ministries of labor and social affairs were the main policy venues. Because of the jurisdictions of the ministries, immigrants' social rights were a matter of concern, and major improvements in their rights took place. The termination of labor migration entailed immigration controls, involving the interior ministry. Gradually the interior ministry became the dominant policy venue, and this site has largely operated to the disadvantage of immigrant rights. Immigration legislation drafted within the interior ministry has often eroded the social rights of immigrants.

Integration policies have experienced a parallel shift in venues. Both the French and German governments have assigned responsibility for integration and immigration policies to the same ministry since the mid-2000s. As in France and Germany, the Danes amalgamated ministerial responsibility for integration and immigration policies, and in the UK the Home Office from the beginning was in charge of both policies. When ministerial responsibility for the two policy areas has been combined, integration runs the risk of becoming subordinate to immigration policy goals, affecting integration measures and the requirements that newcomers must meet to demonstrate successful integration.

Still there are limitations of this line of reasoning, and exceptions, such as the Swedish case, bring them into focus. In the early 1970s the Swedes appointed a minister of immigrant affairs, who was in charge of both immigrant and immigration policies. Similarly the responsibilities of the National Board of Immigrant Affairs spanned both types of policies. This did not lead to a contraction of immigrant rights but to an expansion. Why was this the case? Over the years (1973–95)[1] the ministers, members of the left and center parties, believed that Sweden ought to pursue a generous policy (Demker and Malmström 1999: 76–88). The Board's role in easing permit and naturalization requirements also contrasts with administrative developments in the other countries. The Swedish agency was staffed by pro-immigrant activists, including several immigrants. France also provides an exception; during the Jospin government (1997–2002) immigration legislation expanded the social rights of immigrants.

In summary, several countries display a similar pattern regarding policy venues and immigrant rights. When a policy venue has immigration as its main responsibility, immigrant rights have often taken a back seat or become secondary to admissions policies, frequently leading to rights contraction. Policy venues that have other tasks than controlling immigration generally have a better record in extending and defending immigrant rights. Nevertheless, exceptions suggest that types of policy venues are not sufficient conditions in promoting or contracting immigrant rights.

---

[1] Since the mid-1990s the tasks have often been divided between a minister of immigration and a minister of integration.

The policy venue thesis revisited

The policy venue thesis argues that bureaucratic and judicial policy venues are systematically biased in favor of immigrants' social rights (Guiraudon 2002: 139). Two merits of the thesis are (1) it directs attention to the role of institutional arrangements in determining policy outputs and (2) it brings policy venues, and especially administrative politics, into the analysis. To what extent do our six cases confirm the thesis?

BUREAUCRATIC VENUES

Of the six countries, the British case provides the most dramatic contradiction to the thesis with regard to bureaucratic venues. Administrative measures and wide discretionary powers have been crucial in curtailing immigrants' social rights. The bureaucratic venues worsening immigrants' social rights were both the Department of Social Security and the Home Office. Neither stealth nor politics behind closed doors shielded their social rights.

Additional exceptions are encountered in the experiences of several other countries where restriction-minded administrators and agencies have attempted or succeeded in circumscribing immigrants' rights. Both the French and German cases reveal instances of bureaucrats, either independently or on the orders of ministers, acting to limit immigrants' rights. In France administrators and technocrats were first to claim that non-European immigrants could not be assimilated, and the director of the immigrant welfare agency was a keen advocate of the "threshold of tolerance" thesis, which weakened immigrants' social rights (Freeman 1979; Schain 1999: 207). German administrators and street-level bureaucrats have exercised substantial discretion in denying asylum seekers' benefits (Minderhoud 1999: 142; Bosswick 2000; Morris 2002: 32–50). In the US a bureaucratic agency—the General Accounting Office—was first to call for restrictions on newly arrived immigrants' access to welfare benefits in the mid-1970s, and it continued to be a player in the contraction of immigrants' social rights. Bureaucratic officials in the Reagan administration also tightened the eligibility rules for the legalization of undocumented immigrants (Tichenor 2002: 263–5). In sum, even bureaucratic venues responsible for immigrant incorporation have deviated from the claims of the policy venue thesis.

JUDICIAL VENUES

The importance of judicial politics in extending immigrants' social rights is particularly evident in the United States, but even here there are limits to the policy venue thesis. The Supreme Court has primarily declared state legislation curtailing immigrants' social rights unconstitutional, but it has upheld the prerogative of Congress to introduce special requirements for immigrants' eligibility to social entitlements and thus unequal social rights. Tellingly, federal judges nullified the 1994 California initiative restricting undocumented immigrants' access to schools and services, but the 1996 welfare act passed by Congress survived legal challenges (Fix and Passel 2002: 184).

Ironically, given the standard picture of a traditionally weak judiciary in the service of the state (Wright 1999: 92), the French courts have been quite active in expanding and protecting immigrants' social rights. The 1990 constitutional court ruling granted immigrants equal rights to national assistance benefits, and court decisions overturned local measures that excluded immigrants from social benefits. On the other hand, the Constitutional Court has upheld residence requirements for social benefits, and eligibility for the major safety net benefit has been founded on a residence requirement that has excluded newcomers (HCI 1998).

In his monumental comparative study of judicial politics and immigration, Joppke emphasizes the poor record of British courts in expanding immigrant rights, arguing that "parliamentary sovereignty and common law restraints have neutralized the courts as effective opponents of the executive, resulting in Home Office absolutism in immigration policy" (1999: 137). He contrasts the docile British courts with the activist courts in the US and Germany.[2] Admittedly, early court decisions in discrimination cases affecting social rights went against immigrant and minority complainants (Griffith 1977: 87–93), and the rulings of the law lords in the area of social provision have been characterized as a "trust the authorities" approach (Robertson 1998: 339–70, quotation p. 370). However, since the mid-1990s a series of rulings have overturned restrictions on asylum seekers' social benefits (Morris 2007: 52–3; Somerville 2007: 96–7). The courts have become more assertive and can hardly be described as docile. Still the government has had the final say, and it has introduced statutes that have reversed the high court's decisions.

The record of the German courts in promoting immigrants' social rights is also mixed. Rulings that have advanced their rights include the 1979 Federal Constitutional Court decision that foreigners could not be barred from assistance benefits even when no bilateral agreement existed (Guiraudon 2002: 137). In early 2010 the Court ruled that the unemployment assistance benefit (ALG II), utilized by many non-citizens, did not provide a socially acceptable minimum and its low level was especially damaging to children, undermining their life chances. To the detriment of immigrants' social rights, the courts have ruled that discrimination on the basis of nationality was constitutional, thus upholding laws and regulations that denied equal treatment of foreign

---

[2] Using a comparative data set on claims making over immigration in Britain, France, Germany, and Switzerland during 1990–2004, Paul Statham and Andrew Geddes (2006: 254–5) have questioned Joppke's conclusion about the wide gap between courts in the UK and Germany.

citizens, such as the labor law and the social insurance law (Wilpert 2003: 259). Court decisions also confirmed the legality of restrictions imposed on the late resettlers during the 1990s, including disentitlement to welfare benefits (Joppke 2005; Klusmeyer and Papademetriou 2009: 124). Nor have the German courts always adopted an activist stance. Rulings of the Constitutional Court have deferred to the federal government and to the *Länder* (Bosswick 2000: 52; Klusmeyer and Papademetriou 2009: 172–3, 123). There are also instances of court rulings having little impact. In response to the Constitutional Court's ruling on unemployment assistance's inadequate social minimum, the federal government proposed negligible changes.

Finally, Denmark and Sweden lack activist courts, and the expansion of immigrant rights has not been driven by judicial politics. Still both countries accorded extensive social, political, and cultural rights to newcomers until Danish policy makers embarked on an increasingly restrictionist course in the 1990s. Accordingly, the explanation of rights extension in these two countries lies elsewhere than in judicial policy venues. Furthermore, several Swedish legal experts as the heads of inquiry commissions hardly distinguished themselves as promoters of immigrant rights or stronger anti-discrimination legislation, and the judicialization of asylum decisions since the mid-2000s has led to fewer cases of acceptance.

To sum up, bureaucratic policy venues may share a number of overarching norms distinguishing them from other types of venues, but individual bureaucratic agencies develop specific cultures. The previous chapters have documented the significance of discretionary administrative cultures in the British case but also in the French and German cases. The policy venue thesis needs to take greater stock of recruitment and staffing procedures. As indicated by the Swedish experience, differences in *who* is in charge can be as significant to policy outputs as the rules of the game that are typical of bureaucratic venues. Just as important, bureaucratic policy venues are often susceptible to the wishes and instructions of restrictionist executives (Joppke 2001). Nor do judicial policy venues always trump restriction-minded executives. In short, activist courts are not a necessary condition or a sufficient condition for the extension of immigrant rights. Courts across the countries have engaged in both the politics of expanding and contracting immigrant rights.

The territorial dimension

When and how does the territorial dimension promote the extension or contraction of immigrants' social rights? Has decentralization adversely affected their social rights?

Across the six countries, funding arrangements have been important in shaping actors' incentives to engage in the extension or contraction of immigrants' social rights. A neglected factor in theorizing how the cost–benefit calculus determines expansive versus restrictive policy outputs is the level of government that pays the bill. Subnational governments' perceptions of unfair financial burdens because of many immigrants have often sparked local opposition. Of further significance are the channels and political leverage of subnational units in federal systems compared to unitary states. However, local and regional opposition has played a role in restrictive policy outputs in both federal and unitary states—the United States and Germany but also Denmark.

In the United States the territorial dimension contributed to both expanding and reducing immigrants' social rights. The high concentration of newcomers to relatively few states made immigrant entitlements a principal concern to politicians in those states. Members of Congress from high immigration states promoted the entitlements of immigrants when proposals entailed federal funding, but they often sought restrictions when state and local revenues financed services and benefits. The legislative process also provided ample opportunities for them to influence policy outcomes.

The German case is of special interest for several reasons. First, developments were contrary to the proposition that the diffusion of costs promotes expansiveness. Rather, the fairly even distribution of asylum seekers combined with the states' and municipalities' financial responsibilities for their reception and welfare benefits provided a common grievance and incentives for restrictions. Institutional arrangements—representation of the *Länder* in the Bundesrat, the powers of the Bundesrat, the conferences of *Länder* ministers, and the association of local governments—facilitated a mobilization to exert pressure on the federal government. Of the six countries, German subnational governments have had the most direct impact on national policy worsening immigrants' social rights.

Sweden and Denmark are unitary states with relatively strong municipal and regional governments responsible for the delivery of welfare benefits and services, but politics of the territorial dimension developed differently. A crucial difference was the initial financing and organization of reception programs for asylum seekers. Simultaneously with the rising numbers of asylum seekers in the 1980s, the Swedish municipalities became increasingly responsible for their reception, and the state funded asylum seekers' introductory period. The distribution of asylum seekers was not as even as in Germany, but the "Entire Sweden Strategy" meant that most of the municipalities received asylum seekers. In Denmark high concentrations of immigrants and the perception of unfair burdens led to a rebellion of the mayors who became frustrated over increasing costs for services and education for immigrants. Since immigrants were concentrated in left strongholds, the mayors' criticism was channeled through the Danish Social Democratic party, putting pressure on the party leadership. Eventually the Social Democratic Prime Minister appointed one of the rebel mayors as the minister in charge of integration reform, and the 1998 Integration Law transferred responsibility for introductory programs to the municipalities, provided state funding for the programs, and lowered assistance benefits for newcomers during the three-year introductory period. That the central government paid roughly half the costs for assistance benefits also furnished it with an incentive to reduce the availability of these benefits to new arrivals.

Although French decentralization reforms in the early 1980s expanded the departments' and communes' responsibility for local welfare programs (*aide sociale*), the central government has checked the influence of subnational authorities on immigrants' social benefits in a variety of ways. Importantly, the central government has been responsible for minimum benefits related to "national solidarity," and it has determined the basic benefit levels and eligibility requirements of these programs. National minimum benefits, including the minimum benefit paid to asylum seekers, were primarily funded by central government revenues. Thus the funding of benefits available to immigrants created fewer economic incentives for French subnational authorities to restrict immigrants' assistance benefits compared to the systems of funding in several other countries in this book. However, immigrants' welfare benefits were not completely insulated from local influence. The local authorities could bar immigrants from benefits through the establishment of local schemes. In areas with high concentrations of immigrants, such as Paris and the south of France, restrictions on immigrants' eligibility were introduced. The central government countered by passing legislation that prohibited them from disqualifying immigrants from benefits provided by local schemes. Central control can, of course, also worked in a negative direction, as demonstrated when the central government limited asylum seekers' benefits and when it abolished FAS, the immigrant welfare agency, despite many protests.

The UK has been renowned for its centralized state, and subnational authorities have had little influence in formulating policies. Devolution has introduced a territorial dimension to social provision, but the central executive has been pivotal in formulating social and integration policies before and after devolution. The central government has also had major responsibility for assistance benefits since the early postwar years, and its involvement has exceeded that of our other countries. Both funding and administration have been at the national level, and benefit rates and eligibility requirements have been determined centrally. As in the Danish case but to a greater extent, central funding creates financial incentives to reduce spending on assistance benefits. Perhaps this helps account for the zeal of British government officials in emphasizing that newcomers abuse the welfare system. Nationally administered social assistance benefits have meant little subnational influence on immigrants' access to benefits, but the centralized system also facilitated the verification of immigration status in determining applicants' eligibility for benefits.

To what extent do the experiences of the six countries confirm the conventional wisdom that centralization promotes the social rights of immigrants and ethnic minorities, while decentralization has adverse effects? In line with the claims about decentralization, subnational authorities have worsened immigrants' access to benefits, primarily in the US and Germany—the most decentralized systems of our six cases—while in France such measures were reversed by central government legislation. Statutory rights, centrally established benefit levels, and nationwide administrative rules have prevented subnational authorities from curtailing immigrant rights but they are not sufficient conditions guaranteeing favorable outcomes for immigrants' access to benefits. Central control can have favorable or unfavorable consequences for immigrants' social rights. Most strikingly, it has been central governments that have been responsible for the major deterioration in the social rights of immigrants through legislation or changes in regulations in all six countries. Again much depends upon who is in control.

Political parties

What evidence do we find for the anti-populist norm thesis that mainstream parties do not politicize immigration and immigrant issues in election campaigns? How important are left–right differences in politicizing these issues in elections and in shaping policies affecting immigrant rights?

Two strands of thinking about political parties have figured prominently in the international immigration literature. The first, guided by Freeman's "anti-populist norm" thesis, has emphasized the role of mainstream parties in keeping immigration and immigrant policies out of the electoral arena in order to avoid intensifying ethnic or racial conflict in their societies. By default this view assigns major weight to the rise of right-wing anti-immigrant parties in politicizing immigration and immigrant policies in elections. A common denominator of many far right anti-immigration parties has been welfare chauvinism, that is, the demand for full entitlements for the native population and lower or no benefits for newcomers.

The second strand has argued that immigration politics straddles the left–right divide. This view has nurtured the assumption of few or no major party differences in this policy area and in turn the view that parties and the partisan composition of governments are not a key variable in determining policy outputs. This view has also spilled over to immigrant rights. Looking first at electoral politics and then at the policy process, what role have parties played in our six countries?

Parties and elections

The mainstream parties have not made immigration and immigrant policies a perennial campaign issue, but there have been several deviations from the anti-populist norm thesis and the assumption that mainstream parties prefer a closed or insulated arena. Nor are the deviations confined to the European countries. Indeed, it has been very tempting for the mainstream right parties to make immigration and immigrant policies an election issue since popular opinion, as noted by Freeman in his paradox of expansive immigration policies, has generally favored restrictions. Mainstream parties in *all* the countries have played the immigration card in courting voters, and in Britain, the US, and Germany, these issues have been fused with claims of welfare abuse and higher welfare costs for taxpayers. Thus the presence of a populist party has not been a necessary condition for politicizing immigration and immigrant policies and the social rights of immigrants.

In the three countries with no or weak anti-immigration parties at the national level, it has generally been the mainstream right parties that have politicized immigration and immigrants' social rights in election campaigns. The US represents a clear-cut case of no influence by a far right party. However, in the 1996 US presidential election, the Republican candidate tried to capitalize on anti-immigration sentiments among the voters, and the party platform condemned immigrants' utilization of welfare. In the next three presidential elections, neither immigration nor immigrants' welfare benefits was a campaign issue. Although this can be interpreted as a return to normalcy, it was not the anti-populist norm that dictated the removal of immigration from presidential elections but vote-winning considerations— appealing to the Latino vote or downplaying an issue dividing the Republican party.

The British mainstream right party has played the immigration card in elections much more frequently than the US party, but only in the run-up to the 1979 general election can Thatcher's emphasis on immigration possibly be interpreted as a response to a small far right anti-immigration party. Instead, a decade earlier, the drive for an increasingly restrictive approach to immigration policy came from the right wing of the Conservative party and Enoch Powell, then a member of the shadow cabinet. Powell attacked the existing immigration policy and the 1968 Race Relations Act, and he contributed to making immigration policy an issue in the 1970 general election (Studlar 1978). Since voters have repeatedly viewed the Tories as better equipped to deal with immigration than Labour (Saggar 2003), it is not surprising that the Tories or individual party candidates have brought up the immigration issue in several elections (1970, 1979, 1992, 2001, 2005, and 2010). In elections during the 2000s the Tories exploited the immigration issue, and New Labour responded by stressing its tough stance (Solomos and Back 1993; King 2002: 2–14, 24; Kavanagh and Butler 2005: 73, 88–90; Somerville 2007: 127–9).

On several occasions the German mainstream right (CDU-CSU) has acted in contradiction of the anti-populist norm thesis, perhaps most blatantly in the early 1980s. After losing the 1980 federal election, the mainstream right politicized the immigration issue and immigrant policies as public opinion became increasingly negative. It mounted a massive attack on the government for not controlling immigration, and CDU politicians called for return immigration, claiming that non-European immigrants could not be assimilated. In state elections during the early 1980s the CDU campaigned on reducing the number of foreigners and a rotation system (Joppke 1999: 80–1). In the late 1990s the CDU made citizenship reform an issue in a state election, and the CDU-CSU candidate for chancellor in the 2002 federal election came out against the new immigration law, arguing that immigrants increased welfare costs and integration measures were an extra burden to taxpayers (MN 2002). Again in the 2008 Hessen state election the CDU reverted to the claim that Germany "was not a country of immigration" and stressed that there were "too many criminal young foreigners" (MN 2008).

In Sweden immigration and immigrant policies have seldom been a campaign issue. Even here, however, a mainstream party made immigration and immigrant policies an election issue when no national anti-immigration party existed. In the 2002 election the People's party–the Liberals campaigned on a new tougher integration policy and stricter requirements for citizenship acquisition (Boréus 2006). A major explanation of the low salience of immigration in Swedish elections has been the parties' office-winning strategies. The Moderates have not politicized immigration or immigrant policies because it would damage the possibilities of forming a right-center government (Green-Pedersen and Krogstrup 2008). Significantly the right-center parties that won the 2006 election said much less about immigration and immigrant policies than in the 2002 campaign (Boréus 2006, 2010: 152). Rather than conformity to the anti-populist norm, strategic considerations have accounted for non-politicization of immigration and immigrants issues in Swedish elections.

FAR RIGHT PARTIES AND MAINSTREAM PARTIES

In the Danish and French cases, far right parties have campaigned on immigration and immigrant issues since the mid-1980s, often making outlandish claims and election promises. In effect, the parties have kept the issue on the political agenda and eliminated the possibility of the anti-populist norm coming into play. Nevertheless these two cases highlight the importance of the mainstream right parties.

A difference between France and Denmark is that Le Pen and the FN have campaigned on the issue of immigrants' social rights but with comparatively little support of the other parties. In Denmark once the issue of immigrants' social rights was raised, several parties eventually chimed in. Part of the difference is related to dissimilarities in the structure of party competition in Denmark and France. In both countries party competition has been between a left and right block of parties, but two contrasts have been crucial. The first is the polling strength of the right, which has been much stronger in France compared to Denmark. Second, the prize of government in Denmark was long influenced by centrist parties which could back either the parties of the right or the left. With no immediate prospects of forming an alliance with the centrist parties, the two mainstream right parties began to campaign on restricted benefits for immigrants with the goal of a right parliamentary majority that included the far right anti-immigration party (Green-Pedersen and Krogstrup 2008: 621–3).

The structure of party competition in France has involved a polarization between the left and the right. The office-winning strategies of the French parties have focused on strengthening the prospects of their own block, building electoral alliances and holding party factions together. The FN has succeeded in siphoning off voters from both the left and the right, but as a rightist party, it has posed a serious electoral challenge to the mainstream right. The challenge has been aggravated by the two ballot majority electoral system for the National Assembly and the importance of electoral alliances. When the FN has passed the threshold for participating in the second round of voting and no electoral alliance existed between it and the mainstream right, the result has been triangular contests, making it easier for a united left block to win office.

In coping with the challenge, the mainstream right has been divided over whether or not to collaborate with the FN. Since 1988, however, the official policy of the mainstream right has been not to enter electoral alliances with the FN in national elections. The right parties have alternated between an accommodative strategy of policy convergence hoping to wean away voters from the FN (the 1993 legislative election) and an adversarial strategy of policy divergence (the 2002 presidential election) (Meguid 2008). I would add that their refusal to enter electoral alliances has constituted a third strategy of isolation. Importantly, the strategy of isolation, together with the electoral system, has consigned the FN to infinitesimal or no representation in the National Assembly.

Thus in France and Denmark, the mainstream right parties have diverged in their responses, but both cases underline the key role of the mainstream right vis-à-vis far right parties. The Danish mainstream right adopted an accommodative strategy, which enhanced the influence and legitimacy of the far right anti-immigration party whose polling strength continued to grow in the 2005 and 2007 elections. The response of the mainstream left parties in France and Denmark has also differed. In France the Socialist party frequently adopted an adversarial election strategy (Meguid 2008), while the Danish Social Democrats have vacillated between an accommodative and adversarial strategy since the late 1990s.

In conclusion, there have been important instances of mainstream parties conforming to the anti-populist norm. However, mainstream right parties have also converted their restrictive stances on immigration and immigrant rights into campaign issues, and this has occurred regardless of whether they had to compete with far right parties. In Britain and Germany the conservative parties campaigned on these issues prior to the breakthrough of such parties, and there has not been a far right party in the US. Nor can the removal of immigration and immigrant policies from the campaign agenda always be attributed to the anti-populist norm; their removal has also come about because of tactical considerations to win votes. In countries with an electorally successful far right party, the mainstream parties can criticize, emulate, or ignore its election promises. Mainstream right parties have often campaigned on restrictive policy positions, while left parties have tended to criticize the proposals or remain silent but campaign on alternatives.

To the extent that mainstream right parties have targeted immigrants' rights and social entitlements for cuts in election contests and left parties have not, the left–right divide has manifested itself in electoral politics. The rise of small parties on the right and left has further reinforced the importance of the divide. Finally, immigrant voters have overwhelmingly supported left parties; left voting among immigrants in the six countries has often been over 60 per cent and as high as 80 per cent (Wihtol de Wenden 1994: 104; CFMB 2000: 341; Leal et al. 2005; Aytar 2007: 143; Messina 2007: 209–10; Bird et al. 2011: chapter 3). Although exceptions exist, the broad contours of a left–right pattern in electoral politics emerge across the countries.

Parties and policies

Even more important in my analysis are parties in their capacity as office holders and policy makers or policy brokers. Holding office ensures that parties are central actors in the policy process, but a prerequisite for parties to determine policy variations is the existence of party differences on policies. A further precondition for parties making a difference is holding executive power or being in a position to influence policies. Accordingly, the partisan composition of governments and patterns of office holding comprise a key variable. Policy outcomes are additionally shaped by the dynamics between actors and the institutional features of the policy process; party policy differences can be diluted when the process is characterized by widespread power sharing and multiple veto or opportunity sites. Lastly in considering the importance of parties in policy formation, I examine not only policy areas marked by party strife but also those where left and right governments have distinctive records of policy improvements or inaction.

A shared trait of many single country studies and several comparative analyses has been emphasis on either party consensus or the importance of cross-party alliances in shaping immigration and immigrant policies (Hammar 1985; Guiraudon 1998, 2000b; Gimpel and Edwards 1999; Hansen 2000: 228; Tichenor 2002; Dahlström 2004; Schain 2007). Party lines have been fuzzy on immigration policy. Governments of the left and right have introduced entry restrictions, in several instances with pan-partisan support. In explaining the expansive thrust of US admission policies, analysts have pointed to the importance of left–right alliances (Tichenor 2002). This observation also has relevance for Europe. For example, left governments in Britain (Blair) and Germany (Schröder), joined by business, promoted the resumption of labor immigration in the 2000s (Green 2004: 112; Somerville 2007). In Sweden the lack of restrictions on the citizens of the EU members after the eastward enlargement was the result of the opposition parties of the left and right joining forces against the Social Democratic government (Arvidsson 2009). Generalizations about party consensus and left–right alliances have considerable merit with regard to admission policies.

LEFT–RIGHT DIFFERENCES

The assessment of party consensus, however, requires qualification with regard to issues involving immigrant rights. A pattern of left–right policy differences that has shaped legislation appears across all six countries. In some instances similar left–right policy differences have crystallized in several countries, while in others the pattern of differences has been specific to the country. Overall, however, left–right policy differences have revolved around inclusive versus exclusionary measures. In addition to social rights, the issues generating left–right policy differences have been citizenship acquisition, immigrants' political rights, the right of domicile and requirements for permanent residence, and legalization and the rights of undocumented newcomers—issues related to key dimensions of a country's incorporation regime. Increasingly these issues have become intertwined with immigrants' social rights.

Citizenship acquisition

Perhaps the best bellwether of inclusion or exclusion is the ease or difficulties of immigrants becoming citizens, since citizenship is emblematic of membership in the community. Left–right differences on citizenship acquisition have influenced legislation in five of the countries. As we have seen, citizenship acquisition in Germany and France was a source of protracted partisan controversy during the 1980s and 1990s, with rightist parties favoring restrictive legislation and the left advocating inclusive measures. In Germany a Social Democratic–Liberal coalition government already in 1981 introduced a bill granting second generation foreigners the right to naturalization, but the bill was rejected by the CDU-CSU majority in the Bundesrat (Green 2001: 32). During negotiations of the 1992 asylum compromise, the Social Democrats secured major concessions improving foreigners' possibilities to become citizens, and it was a Social Democratic–Green coalition government that introduced the landmark 1999 nationality reform. The CDU-CSU obstructed the acceptance of dual citizenship, and a CDU Interior Minister was responsible for the 2007 amendments to the Nationality Law, introducing new restrictions. In France the Jospin government (1997–2002) largely reversed the stiffer requirements of the 1993 nationality code, put in place by the right government. In Sweden the introduction of dual citizenship was a drawn-out affair, and the Social Democrats were instrumental in moving the issue forward. Already in 1991 a Social Democratic government bill approved the principle of dual citizenship (Prop. 1990/91: 195). However, a right-center government came into office, and it shelved the bill. Later a Social Democratic government appointed the inquiry commission that led to the 2001 reform permitting dual citizenship. Only the conservative party voted against the reform. In the 2000s the conservative and liberals have argued for stiffer naturalization requirements. Danish mainstream right governments (2001–11), with the support of the far right party, dramatically tightened citizenship requirements so that they were the most stringent of our six countries in the late 2000s. The left and center parties voted against the 2004 amendment of the Danish nationality law that incorporated many of the harsher requirements (Ersbøll 2006: 130).

In three countries, the right parties have linked citizenship acquisition to social rights. In the US the House Republicans proposed that non-citizens who utilized welfare should be ineligible for naturalization. At the insistence of President Clinton this proposal was deleted from the congressional bill that he signed into law. The Republicans also wanted to alter the principle of *ius soli* so that undocumented immigrants' children born in the US would no longer become citizens at birth. As non-citizens they would be ineligible for welfare benefits and their parents would not be able to claim benefits on their behalf. The 2007 amendments to the German Nationality Law disqualified foreigners born in Germany from becoming citizens if they received social or unemployment assistance. The most extreme case has been Denmark where the conservative government tightened the economic self-sufficiency requirement so that it has included both current and previous participation in welfare programs. In 2005 the government first barred immigrants whose use of assistance benefits exceeded one year during the five years prior to naturalization, and in 2008 it shortened the period to six months during the past five years. In sum, left–right differences are set in sharp relief on the issue of citizenship acquisition and in three cases parties of the right have tied the issue to social rights.

Political rights

The left–right divide has also pervaded the issue of immigrants' political rights, which has been influenced by conceptions of citizenship. German and French parties of the left endorsed local voting rights for immigrants, and in Germany two left-led *Länder* passed legislation granting non-German immigrants local voting rights in 1989. The CDU-CSU parliamentary party brought the matter to the Constitutional Court, which struck down the legislation (Joppke 1999: 194–5). Besides supporting local voting rights, the French socialist government removed restrictions on immigrants' right of association and provided subsidies to immigrant organizations in the early 1980s. Socialist governments also included (1984) and extended (1990) immigrant representation on the governing council of FAS, the French agency for immigrant welfare, and set up the National Council of Immigrant Populations, a consultative body of the minister of social affairs. By contrast, conservative governments in the 2000s first reduced the budget of FAS, which had become a platform of immigrant organizing, and later abolished the agency. In the Danish case, a Social Democratic government extended the right to vote and stand for office in local and regional elections to non-Nordic immigrants in 1981, and the Conservatives, Liberals, and far right party voted against the bill. The far right kept the issue alive, demanding disenfranchisement. In 2010 the conservative government raised the residency requirement to four years. The Swedish mainstream right party, although reluctant, did not oppose granting local and regional political rights to non-citizens during the parliamentary vote in 1975. However, a sharp left–right cleavage developed when the left parties recommended giving non-citizens the right to vote in national elections in the early 1980s. The fierce opposition of the center-right parties removed the issue from the agenda. Notably, neither citizenship acquisition nor immigrants' voting rights have been left–right issues in Britain, and immigrants' voting rights in the US have been a non-issue.

Residence rights

The right of abode (settlement) and requirements for a permanent resident permit have caused disputes between the parties of the left and right in France. From the 1970s into the 2000s French conservative governments have sought to tighten permit requirements. Conversely socialist governments have introduced several measures to strengthen the right of domicile, such as a single permit (*le titre unique de séjour et de travail*) that replaced residence and work permits and disassociated the right of abode from having employment in the mid-1980s. Although the mainstream right supported the introduction of the single permit, the Chirac government (1986–8) almost immediately tightened the requirements for the single permit. In 2003 the rightist government made assimilation a requirement for a permanent permit, and it increased the minimum residence requirement for a permanent permit from three to five years. The changes in requirements for a permanent permit also affected newcomers' access to the basic safety net benefit since immigrants who have a permanent permit are eligible even if they do not meet the work test. In Germany the multiplication of requirements for a permanent residence permit has been an incremental output of party negotiations that eased the severe requirements for naturalization, but the CDU introduced and codified demanding conditions for a residence permit as part of the compromise. The permit requirement of paying social insurance contributions for five years linked the social protection system to the incorporation regime, and the requirement of a secure livelihood strengthened the link. In Denmark the right government of Anders Fogh Rasmussen (2001–9) raised the residence requirement for a permanent permit from three to seven years and multiplied permit requirements. As in France and Germany, Denmark has stiffened its requirements for a permanent residence permit so that they resembled earlier requirements for naturalization. Right governments in the three countries have also tightened the requirements for family reunification and made permit requirements for spouses more rigorous. The Swedish right-center government (2006–) introduced temporary work permits, and for those with this type of permit, employment became a requirement for acquiring a permanent residence permit. The government also introduced support obligations for family reunification.

The issue of legalization has long been on the policy agenda in France and the United States, and left–right differences have influenced policies. French socialist governments sponsored large-scale legalization programs in the early 1980s and the late 1990s, while conservative governments have favored the review of applications on an individual basis, resulting in many fewer successful applicants. The Jospin government made legalization automatic after ten years of residence, but the mainstream right government later eliminated this possibility. French conservative governments also consolidated the link between social rights and legal status by making entitlement of most social benefits, including social insurance benefits, dependent upon a residence permit. In the US the Reagan administration and congressional Republicans succeeded in, first, barring undocumented immigrants who had been on welfare from acquiring legal status and, second, in banning legalized immigrants from welfare benefits for five years. Verification procedures to prevent undocumented immigrants from receiving benefits were strengthened under Presidents Ronald Reagan and George W. Bush, and the Bush administration eliminated the possibility of undocumented immigrants receiving social security benefits.

Social rights

So far we have seen that parties of the right have increasingly sought to strengthen the linkage between social rights and acquisition of permanent residence, citizenship, and legal status with varying degrees of success. The sanctions for utilization of welfare benefits have included disqualification from legal status, a permanent residence permit, and naturalization. An additional trend has been the introduction of unequal social rights for newcomers, again frequently but not always at the suggestion of parties on the right. This has entailed either barring immigrants from benefits during their first years in the country—as in the US, the UK, France, and Denmark—or pegging their benefits at a lower rate than regular benefits—as in Germany, France, the UK, and Denmark. In Sweden it was a right-center government that severed the link between asylum seekers' benefits and the social minimum.

Conservative governments have also introduced restrictions through social legislation. In a major overhaul of the safety net, the French government introduced a work test of five years for immigrants not coming from the European Economic Area (primarily the EU member states) in 2009. Similarly in the mid-2000s the Danish government tightened eligibility rules for social assistance, and immigrants were the target of the changes (MFII 2005).

In the US and France left–right differences on immigrants' social rights have been quite sharp. During the past three decades the Democrats and Republicans have periodically been at odds over the social rights of newcomers, and Congressional votes on a series of bills affecting immigrants' social rights have largely followed party lines. The Republicans opposed the institutionalization of refugees' social rights in 1980, and argued for making immigrants who had utilized welfare benefits ineligible for legal status in the mid-1980s. Furthermore, it was the House Republicans who initially came up with the idea to bar permanent legal residents from federal welfare benefits, introducing a differentiation in the social entitlements of citizens and non-citizens, which underpinned the 1996 welfare act. In France left governments were responsible for making national minimum benefits available to non-citizens and for safeguarding their access to local social benefits, while right governments have weakened the social rights of immigrants, both undocumented and legal aliens.

Finally, the British case appears to be an exception at first glance. It is hard to find left–right differences on immigration and asylum policies, citizenship acquisition, and immigrants' political and social rights. Nonetheless, Labour has distinguished itself from the Tories by introducing milestone legislation in the area of minority rights, such as the 1965, 1968, 1976, and 2000 Race Relations Acts and the 1998 Human Rights Act. Anti-discrimination legislation has also strengthened the social rights of minorities and immigrants. Conversely, the record of the Thatcher and Major governments was one of inaction. Thus the British case highlights the importance of considering policy areas where left and right governments have distinctive policy records of improvements or inertia—not just looking at policy areas characterized by partisan strife.

An examination of policies affecting immigrant rights across the six countries reveals importance of the partisan composition of government, but several factors operate to mute the translation of party positions into legislation. Within parties, especially large parties, and blocks of parties, divisions of opinion exist. The mainstream right contains politicians with liberal views, just as the left has its restrictionists. Multiparty governments and minority governments have also militated against clear-cut differences finding their way into legislation, as have power sharing features of the policy process. Nor have left governments always undone restrictive legislation introduced by right governments.

Despite these countervailing influences, the left–right divide has been integral to the politics of inclusion and exclusion in shaping encompassing and restrictive policies across the countries. Left–right differences have often been sharper in policy proposals than in actual legislation that has emerged from party negotiations, but even many of these laws have been marked by party policy differences. Parties in executive office are vested with the power of initiation and responsibility for formulating policies, and this authority outweighs the prerogatives of bureaucratic and judiciary policy venues. In short, the partisan composition of government is too important a factor to be ignored, which has long been the case.

Immigrant organizing and penetration of the policy process

To what extent and how have immigrants penetrated the policy process and to what effect?

Immigrants' political participation has been a growing area of research, and increasingly in a comparative perspective. Seldom, however, has immigrant organizing and penetration of the policy process been conceived of as an explanatory variable shaping policies. The failure to do so has several explanations. Among them, newcomers are generally assumed to be negligible in the policy process or primacy has been assigned to systemic factors as determinants.

Despite the tendency to downplay immigrants as political actors, they have come to occupy key political posts in all six countries during the past two decades, holding positions as legislators, cabinet ministers, junior ministers, advisors to ministers, governors, or party leaders. An additional change is the rise of first generation immigrants to these positions in several countries. Furthermore, in spite of the growing scholarly emphasis on their transnational activism, immigrants' political mobilization has frequently revolved around immigration and immigrant rights in their countries of settlement (Koopmans et al. 2005: chapter 3).

Mapping out immigrants' positions in the political process indicates that there is considerable variation in immigrants' political organizing and their penetration of the policy process across the six countries. Only in three countries—the US, Sweden, and Germany—have immigrants been directly involved in formulating policies affecting their rights. In these countries, immigrants or persons with immigrant backgrounds have exerted insider influence on policies. Consultative arrangements involving immigrant and minority groups have been common in the European countries. In some instances, consultation has concerned implementation of integration or social policies, that is, the administration of existing policies. Still, consultative arrangements have provided opportunities for influencing the policy agenda or the distribution of resources as well as lobbying. The policy machinery of immigrant policies has also served as an arena of immigrant participation and activism in the UK, France, and Sweden. A final aspect of immigrant organizing has consisted of penetrating politically significant organizations, such as political parties. Penetration of the parties can make the party leadership more appreciative of immigrant needs and concerns, resulting in indirect policy influence.

The US: A nation of immigrants and immigrant politics

In the United States, a "nation of immigrants" with an inclusive incorporation regime, one would expect immigrant and ethnic penetration of the policy process and the political mobilization of immigrants and minorities. Indeed, since the late 1960s their organizational resources have grown; an impressive rise in ethnic minority representation in Congress has occurred; and immigrant organizing and strategies have often followed the lead of African Americans. For example, ethnic minority representatives have formed congressional caucuses to monitor the effects of legislation on members of their constituencies—first African Americans (1969), then Hispanics (1976), and finally Asians and Pacific Islanders (1994). Gradually minority and immigrant congressional members have strengthened their positions in the House subcommittees dealing with social welfare and immigration. Because of fragmentation, penetration of the policy process provides the possibility of influence but no guarantee of determining outcomes. A fundamental weakness has been that immigrant and ethnic minority penetration has been largely confined to the House of Representatives and the Democratic party. In addition, even in the subcommittee on immigration where minority representation has been strong, ardent restrictionists have also been members.

Although minority members of Congress either failed or effected only minor changes favoring immigrants during the many twists and turns in the passage of the 1996 welfare act, they have influenced immigration legislation as part of a larger policy coalition both inside and outside of Congress. A major accomplishment was the defeat of provisions in the 1996 immigration act (IIRIRA) to reduce legal immigration. Likewise the Hispanic lobby together with its allies in Congress left an imprint on the 1986 immigration act (IRCA) in expanding eligibility for the amnesty program, prohibiting discrimination on the basis of immigration status, and establishing a new office in the Justice Department charged with investigating cases of discrimination. Even earlier, minority members of Congress joined forces to support the 1980 Refugee Act. The piecemeal restoration of immigrants' access to Food Stamps in 1998 and 2002 depended on the forging of a broad coalition—immigrant organizations, the welfare lobby, nutrition groups, farmers' associations, and officials from states with high concentrations of immigrants.

Comparatively speaking, immigrants in the US arguably have more political clout than immigrants in several of our cases. A growing number of members of Congress have become spokespersons for ethnic minorities and immigrant groups; through them, immigrants have access to the legislative process. Immigrant organizations have pursued successful lobbying and litigation strategies, and they can point to several victories. Since the 1996 presidential election, immigrants' votes have assumed greater importance; in particular candidates have vied for the Latino vote. Political power, however, is relational and must be assessed in terms of the power resources of other actors in the national context—not merely compared across countries. In the US immigrants faced a formidable challenge to their social rights in the mid-1990s, with House Republicans bent on cutting non-citizens' benefits, the Republicans in control of the House and the Senate, and the President committed to welfare reform. Divided and without allies, the minority status of ethnic representation in the policy process was laid bare.

In conclusion, two points need to be underscored. First, the fragmentation of the policy process means that minority influence often requires participation in broad policy coalitions. Second, veto sites simultaneously function as opportunity sites, and failure in one site can be reversed or mitigated by success in another. An instructive illustration is immigrant organizations' use of the courts that overturned (1) the denial of undocumented newcomers' social rights at the state level and (2) the restrictive procedures of the Reagan administration in the legalization of undocumented aliens.

Sweden: Immigrants as political insiders and agenda setters

As distinct from their US counterparts, immigrants in Sweden had no parliamentary representatives in the early 1970s—when the inclusive turn occurred. Nevertheless, as we have seen, immigrants were insiders in the policy process. As experts in the inquiry commissions on immigrant policies and local voting rights, they authored several of the recommendations that became new laws.

The inclusion of experts and members with immigrant backgrounds on the commissions established a precedent. Since the mid-1970s persons with immigrant backgrounds have been included on many inquiry commissions dealing with immigrant issues as experts and members. This inclusive practice conforms to the longstanding constitutional norm of consulting interested parties directly affected by the legislation under consideration. The norm has primarily opened the possibility to influence policy dimensions of the incorporation regime but much less frequently social policies per se. However, the recommendations of the commissions have influenced immigrants' social rights when incorporation regime policy dimensions and social policies have intersected.

Besides their role in the preparatory stage of the legislative process, immigrants were agenda setters. In this capacity, immigrants contributed to reframing policy so that it no longer was a foreigner policy consisting of adjustment measures but an immigrant policy whose goals included equal rights and mutual respect. Again in the 1990s debate, persons with immigrant backgrounds voiced new criticisms, which had an impact on legislation. They criticized the term "immigrant," stressing that its use demarcated immigrants and Swedes, highlighting them versus us. The term was removed from several laws, and immigrant policies were renamed integration policies.

During the 1960s immigrants also joined unions and political parties, and as members they began to voice immigrant demands in internal debates and worked to get immigrant issues on the agenda. First generation immigrants gained positions on the governing boards of left parties in the 1980s, and non-European immigrants began to enter positions of leadership in the parties during the 1990s, first as officers in the party youth organizations, and later as party officers. The unions and parties have also served as springboards to parliamentary and executive office. The first "immigrant" candidates were elected to parliament in 1979. Over the years their numbers increased and their ethnic backgrounds became more diverse, with major breakthroughs in the 1994, 2002, and 2010 elections. Foreign born persons also advanced to ministerial posts.

In conclusion, immigrant penetration illustrates the accessible nature of the Swedish policy process. Its openness is reflected in the number of first generation immigrants who have been members or experts in inquiry commissions, MPs, and cabinet ministers. Through their inclusion in inquiry commissions they have participated in shaping immigrant policies and in some cases the social rights of immigrants. Admittedly immigrant representatives and experts have been a minority, and critics would argue they have been hostages of the majority. Nevertheless, immigrant views have been represented in the preparatory stage of the policy process, and in some cases they have been decisive to policy outputs. MPs with immigrant backgrounds have also influenced the policy agenda, continuing the tradition of agenda setters, and an immigrant cabinet minister was in charge of integration policy during 2006–10.

Germany: Co-ethnic immigrants as insiders and foreigners as outsiders

The German incorporation regime's diametrically opposed treatment of resettlers and foreigners has set the parameters of immigrants' political participation and mobilization, creating political insiders and outsiders. Historically, co-ethnic immigrants, as Germans and thus citizens, had almost immediate access to the political process, and they wielded profound influence in configuring the status and social rights of the *Aussiedler*. Immigrants of German origin, who were expellees (*Vertriebene*) and refugees from the former territories of the Third Reich, became a political force the new Federal Republic of Germany. By the early 1950s German immigrants had penetrated the corridors of power as members of the civil service, MPs, and even ministers. In the first Bundestag election in 1949, 77 returnee MPs (18 per cent) were elected, representing all the political parties. Immediately after his election victory, the CDU Chancellor, Konrad Adenauer, established the Ministry for Expellees. The new ministry was headed by an expellee from Poland, Hans Lukaschek. He oversaw the 1953 legislation that introduced the status of *Aussiedler*, establishing the principle of social parity between resettlers and Germans—the foundation of co-ethnic immigrants' social rights (Schindler 1999: 1031–45, Levy 2002: 20–3, 29; Joppke 2005: 170, 286).

By contrast, the political activities of foreigners were initially suppressed and generally viewed with suspicion. The political mobilization of foreigners was circumscribed by the retarded development of political rights and low naturalization rate of non-German immigrants. Although the Basic Law guarantees the rights of assembly and association, foreign citizens first gained the right to establish their own associations in 1964. While co-ethnic immigrants could form compatriot associations to champion their rights, foreigners' participation in associations related to their homelands was discouraged. Such participation was seen as running counter to loyalty or lasting commitment to Germany, a requirement for naturalization. Since 1967 foreign citizens have been allowed to join a political party, but not to form a political party, as the expellees did. Legislation also prohibited foreigners from becoming the majority of a political party (Hammar 1990: 79; Neuman 1998: 265; Green 2004: 17). Equally important, non-German immigrants have had little access to the federal policy process that formulates measures directly affecting them.

To sum up, at a critical policy juncture, co-ethnic immigrants through insider representation significantly influenced the social rights attached to *Aussiedler* status. Although the Ministry of Expellees was abolished in the late 1960s, it was not until the 1990s that a fundamental policy reorientation occurred. *Aussiedler* status was redefined and gradually phased out of existence, and policy decisions eroded the privileged social rights of co-ethnic immigrants. Parallel with the policy changes, the political influence of the most recent wave of resettlers (*Spätaussiedler*) deteriorated (Münz and Ohliger 1998: 180, 194; Klekowski von Koppenfels 2003: 310–12, 315, 318). In the 2000s both German newcomers and non-German immigrants were poorly represented in political decision making bodies at the federal and state levels (Wüst 2011), and their advances during the decade remained dwarfed compared to the first wave of resettlers' penetration of the policy process.

The resettlers' policy legacy survived into the 2000s. Even after the erosion of co-ethnic immigrants' social rights, they continued to be net beneficiaries of social provision. By comparison, the impact of foreigners' political marginalization on their social rights is brought sharply into focus on two counts: first, the failure to solve the "problem of foreigners' utilization of social assistance," identified as a problem as early as 1979 and, second, foreigners, whose economic needs have often exceeded those of the German population, remained net contributors to the social protection system.

The UK: Involvement in the Labour party and racial equality policy machinery

In the UK immigrants' penetration of the policy process has been a gradual and spotty affair; it has mainly consisted of involvement in the Labour party and gaining positions in the racial equality policy machinery. Already in the 1960s New Commonwealth immigrants had established a modest presence in the Labour party, and immigrant activists participated in the policy coalitions behind the 1965 and 1968 race relation acts. Immigrants also pointed to the shortcomings of the local race relations committees; their criticisms, along with research reporting widespread discrimination, aided in putting race relations back on the policy agenda and the introduction of the 1968 Race Relations Act.

Although the first New Commonwealth immigrant stood for Parliament as a Labour candidate in the 1964 election, it was not until the late 1980s that candidates who were visible minorities succeeded in getting elected to Parliament. Since their breakthrough in the 1987 election when four minority Labour candidates were successful, minority representation continued to inch upwards with a total of 15 MPs (13 Labour and two Conservative) in the 2005 election (Layton-Henry 1992: 163–9; Solomos 2003: 199–202; Criddle 2005: 160). Ethnic minorities and immigrants have some electoral clout because of their concentration in a number of constituencies and their strong vote for Labour.

Parallel with their growing presence in the Labour party, ethnic minorities consolidated their positions in the racial equality policy machinery and the key organizations lobbying on racial issues. In the 1960s and 1970s the commission members were almost exclusively white notables, whereas two decades later they represented a broad cross-section of ethnic and racial minorities. Just as important, the policy machinery both at the national and local levels was strengthened over the years. Armed with a mandate of continuous review of legislation and suggesting improvements, the Commission for Racial Equality adopted an activist stance and its authority in this policy area grew.

When New Labour came to power, the government introduced measures accommodating the concerns of ethnic minorities and immigrant communities. In response to complaints from the constituency offices, the government removed the primary rule that often entailed arbitrariness preventing family reunions, and it also passed a law stiffening the penalties for racial harassment and assault. Subsequently Labour introduced the 2006 Racial and Religious Hatred Act, legislation long favored by Muslim advocates (Bleich 2003: 197–9; Somerville 2007: 20, 58). The most far-reaching change was the introduction of the 2000 Race Relations Act designed to combat institutional racism.

In conclusion, immigrants and ethnic minorities have indirectly influenced the flagship of British integration policy—anti-discrimination policies—and anti-discrimination measures are important in transforming formal social rights into effective rights. By contrast, immigrants and ethnic minorities had little access to the policy process formulating immigrants' social rights, as the process increasingly became the domain of administrative politics in the Home Office and the Department of Social Security.

Denmark: Delayed access and mobilization against exclusion

Immigrants' in Denmark have not exerted much influence over immigrant policies or the social rights of immigrants either directly or indirectly. As brought out previously, immigrants were not included in the major Danish inquiry commissions dealing with immigrant policies until the 1990s. Although the first commissions with immigrant members led to positive legislation for newcomers and ethnic minorities (creating the Council of Ethnic Equality—disbanded in 2002—and improving immigrants' adult education), the government disregarded or modified many recommendations of the commission on integration.

Immigrants have also been slow to gain parliamentary and executive office, although they have succeeded much better in getting elected to local office. The first immigrants entered the Folketing in 2001, and none had held a cabinet position at the end of the 2000s. In comparison with Britain and Sweden, the major left party in Denmark did not provide much of a platform for immigrants to advance to parliamentary office. The first time an immigrant on a Social Democratic ticket entered parliament was in 2007. At the local level, however, the party's record is much better. The Social Democrats have fielded the largest number of immigrant candidates for local office, and their success rate has been much higher than those of immigrant candidates from the other parties (Togeby 2003: 183, 185). Nevertheless, immigrant and ethnic voters and activists have not constituted as influential a constituency in the Danish Social Democratic party, as they did in the Labour party. Instead it appears that the clout of the Social Democratic mayors in communities with high concentrations of immigrants has outweighed immigrant and ethnic voters as a constituency in the Danish party.

Not only was immigrant access to inquiry commissions and parliamentary office delayed; their organizing was halting, and initially characterized by confrontation rather than collaboration. In fact, exclusion sparked immigrant protests and was a mobilizing force in the 1970s. As immigrants became better organized, the need for consultation and inclusion was formally recognized with the establishment of a national advisory body. The advisory council has allowed for a form of consultation with immigrants and ethnic organizations that is hived off from the legislative process. However, formal hearings on policy proposals, which have been much more prevalent than participation in inquiry commissions, have given immigrant and minority organizations a chance to make their views known. Moreover, the Council has provided a forum that can influence the policy agenda (Togeby 2003: 153–4, chapter 9).

After 2001, when the Danish People's party became a broker party, immigrants were largely shut out of the policy process that affected them. The politics of exclusion, producing a deterioration of noncitizens' social rights, has also been reflected in immigrants' claim making. Compared to immigrants in the UK, Germany, and France, Danish immigrants' claims have concentrated on integration issues, and especially the social rights of newcomers (Togeby 2003: 151–2, 143).

Finally, immigrants' exclusion and political isolation help explain the emergence of a new party, New Alliance, headed by Naser Khader, in the 2007 election. Khader, a first generation immigrant who came to Denmark as a young child, stressed that the party was to serve as a bridge between the immigrant population and Danes, and that its purpose was to put an end to the broker position of the anti-immigration party. The New Alliance almost succeeded. It won five seats in the Folketing but then fell apart. Worse, one of its elected MPs swung her support to the far right party, dealing a fatal blow to the strategy of neutralizing the Danish People's party. A year and a half later, the new party was in shambles. Naser Khader, no longer party leader, left the party and joined the Conservative party. Negotiations between the government and the far right party that worsened immigrant rights continued to be the order of the day until the 2011 election.

France: Protest, consultation, and appointed office

In France immigrant organizing faced major constraints due to restrictions on their right of association until 1981, and immigrants' activism during the early postwar period was often channeled into unions and parties, especially the Communist party and communist-dominated unions that organized branches where many immigrants worked (Schain 1999). Migrant workers also engaged in protest activities; they staged rent and labor strikes. After the 1981 legislation granting immigrants the equal right of association, along with subsidies, immigrant organizations flourished. The emergence of ethnic associations was accompanied by greater consultation of the immigrant community. During the 1980s immigrants and persons with immigrant backgrounds were key activists in the human rights and the anti-racist movements and during the 1990s in the *sans papiers* movement (Waters 2003). Immigrant partisan activism shifted from the communist to the socialist party in the 1980s as immigrants and their children pinned their hopes on Mitterrand, but disillusionment set in during the 1990s. The left parties and the unions no longer fulfilled the function of aiding in immigrants' socialization as they once had (Schain 1999).

This pattern of organizing has affected the potential policy influence of immigrants and ethnic minorities. Direct actions have influenced both immigration *cum* immigrant policies and social policies. On several occasions demonstrations and mass mobilization have resulted in the removal of the most controversial proposals from legislation or a delay in adopting contested proposals. Demonstrations contributed to the withdrawal of the government's proposal to revise the nationality law in the mid-1980s and stopping the most draconian measures of the 1980 Bonnet law as well as similar proposals in the mid-1990s. From the late 1970s to the mid-2000s, sporadic but recurrent protests and unrest have prompted the formulation of new community action plans and the allocation of additional resources to immigrant suburbs.

It is more difficult to find traces of immigrant influence in the regular policy process. Consultation *à la française* frequently ends in the ministry making its own decision, contrary to the views of those consulted and triggering protests. Consultation with immigrant organizations has been no exception. Immigrant consultation in France has primarily pertained to implementation of social welfare and integration projects. The dismantling of the immigrant welfare agency in 2006 eliminated a formal channel of consultation. It represented a facet of Sarkozy's emphasis on assimilation, terminating official sanction of immigrant status as a basis for organization and removing an important arena of immigrant organizing.

Immigrant penetration of the policy process via elected office presents a contradictory picture. On the one hand, persons of immigrant origins from European countries have advanced to high political office—president, prime minister, members of the government, or MPs. Furthermore, the National Assembly has long had members of color but they have been elected by the overseas territories, not metropolitan France. On the other hand, no comparable ascendancy to elected office exists for politicians of African or Arab origins representing the communities of current immigrant populations. The major parties fielded few immigrant candidates with a non-European background in the 2002 and 2007 legislative elections, and none was elected. Of the countries in this book, France's national parliament displayed the largest gap in representation of non-European ethnic minorities as MPs in relation to the electorate (Messina 2007: 215; Brouard and Tiberj 2011: 164–5).

Although parliamentary office has been elusive for persons of non-European origins, appointed office has gradually opened up to them. Socialist Prime Minister, Edith Cresson (1991–2), appointed a junior minister of integration of Togolese origin (Weil 2004: 287), and during the 2000s there was a further increase. Under President Sarkozy the Fillon government appointed the first second generation immigrant of North African origins to a major ministerial post, Minister of Justice. However, short terms of office and posts as junior ministers have weakened possibilities of influencing policies. Despite advances, non-European immigrants have yet to gain a lasting presence in the inner circles of the policy process, which is highly centralized and insulated.

In conclusion, the pattern of immigrant organizing and penetration of the political process has varied across the six countries, and the variations provide insights into policy variations. Immigrants have been more successful in influencing directly or indirectly immigration and immigrant or integration policies than social policies. The most important exception is the German case, where a co-ethnic immigrant was responsible for introducing legislation that strengthened the social rights of *Aussiedler* so that they were on a par with those of other Germans. In the US, Hispanics and African Americans were part of the coalition that institutionalized refugees' social rights as well as the alliance that partially restored immigrants' social rights after the 1996 welfare act.

Irrespective of their mode of political incorporation, immigrants across the countries have become politically engaged. They have exercised their rights collectively or individually. Instances have ranged from the mass demonstrations across the US in 2006 against stiffer sanctions against undocumented immigrants, so far the largest organized by Latinos/as (MN 2006: 2 and 3), to individual legal challenges to adverse decisions on public housing by British officials. Immigrants have become more and more involved in the political process but their penetration of the policy process has been much more uneven across the six countries.

Conclusions

By drawing on comparative welfare state studies and international migration literature, the analytical framework used here provides considerable leverage in understanding policy outputs and policy variations affecting immigrant rights. I would argue that the framework has been more fruitful than utilizing only the theoretical perspectives in either the welfare state literature or the migration literature. The analysis has also furnished new insights into the importance of the interface between social policies and immigration policies. As we have seen, immigrants' social rights have been increasingly influenced by immigration laws and regulations as well as integration measures in some cases. Across all six countries there are instances of serious erosion in new-comers' social entitlements when they have become intertwined with admission policies or the policy dimensions of the incorporation regime.

A further advantage of the analysis has been its examination of both rights extension and rights contraction, while many previous studies have dealt exclusively with the extension of immigrant rights. The inclusion of rights contraction has provided a test of the theoretical claims or explanations of the rights extension process. The results also differed substantially from descriptions of changes in rights that only look at immigrant rights without considering restrictions and rights contraction (Koopmans et al. 2005: 73).

Empirically my analysis has interrogated several theoretical assumptions and claims of previous research. Among them are the policy venue thesis, the anti-populist norm thesis, and hypotheses related to the cost–benefit calculus and the territorial dimension of immigration. In testing the claim that bureaucratic and judicial venues promote the extension of immigrants' rights, and in particular their social rights, my analysis points to the limits of bureaucratic and judicial politics. On the other hand, the analysis has demonstrated the importance of policy venues in shaping policies. As we have seen, different policy venues or a change in policy venues in the same country have had major implications for policy outputs and immigrant rights. Furthermore, administrative politics or bureaucratic venues have been decisive to immigrants' social rights but not in the way hypothesized by the policy venue thesis.

An empirical scrutiny of the thesis that mainstream parties prefer to keep immigration and immigrant policies out of the electoral arena has revealed that mainstream parties in all six countries have campaigned on these issues, and in four of the countries there was no national anti-immigration party that could explain the actions of the mainstream party. When mainstream parties have opted not to make immigration or immigrant rights election issues, they have frequently been motivated by tactical considerations to win votes and gain office rather than the anti-populist norm.

The analysis here also calls for a reconsideration of the territorial dimension and the cost–benefit calculus characterized by diffused costs and concentrated benefits for expansive or inclusive policy outputs. My examination of the relevance of this type of cost–benefit calculus has dealt with immigrant rights instead of admission policies. In theorizing the territorial dimension scholars have argued that the concentration of immigrants in specific localities is a driving force of restrictions (Money 1999; Freeman 2002). My analysis indicates that both geographic concentration in immigrant settlement, as in Denmark, and dispersion, as in Germany, can prompt restrictions and a contraction of social rights. Likewise high concentrations of immigrants promoted both the extension and contraction of rights, as in the US. Across the six countries a factor helping to make sense of these seemingly contradictory patterns has been a neglected component of the cost–benefit calculus: the level of government funding social benefits.

Finally, three points are worth stressing. The first point is the importance of framing, ideas, and ideological traditions across the six countries, although their implications are quite different in the paired comparisons. The two liberal regime countries represent polar opposites in terms of government institutions and the concentration of power. Their political parties also differ, and the nature of the politics of rights contraction was markedly different. Despite these dissimilarities, the US and the UK came up with quite similar policies that banned newcomers from means-tested benefits during their first years in the country. The single most important common denominator in the two countries was framing according to their liberal traditions. Substantial policy borrowing in the area of anti-discrimination measures during the 1960s and 1970s (Bleich 2003) and workfare measures during the 1990s was also facilitated by similar political traditions and the institutionalization of liberal ideas (King 1995, 1999).

Framing and ideological traditions are also crucial in explaining the dissimilar policy responses of the conservative corporatist regime countries to the Bismarckian model. Framing affected both problem construction and the politics of justification. Social exclusion, national solidarity, and rights, especially the right of inclusion (*le droit d'insertion*) were major ingredients in French framing, while German framing highlighted the changing nature of work, solidarity limited to members of social insurance schemes, and the principle of subsidiarity. Divergences in problem construction suggested different policy solutions.

The government institutions of the two social democratic regime countries are much more similar than in the case of the liberal and conservative regime countries. Despite many commonalities, disparities in their incorporation regimes have grown, and the Danes have also pursued a strategy of cutting newcomers' benefits. Differences in the initial framing of immigrant policies have been important on two counts. The first is the immediate impact of the framing on immigrant rights. The Danes framed newcomers as foreign workers who were temporarily in the country. This sort of framing was less conducive to the advancement of immigrant rights than the Swedish framing of immigrants as potential settlers with equal rights. An additional contrast that stemmed from framing immigrants as settlers was the Swedish emphasis on partnership and mutual tolerance, which had no counterpart in the Danish framing. The Swedish framing contributed to a policy that simultaneously improved the social, cultural, and political rights of newcomers. Second, the legacy of the initial framing has had continued relevance to the Swedish policy process. In refashioning immigrant policies as integration policies the Social Democratic government largely reaffirmed the visionary goals of equal rights, co-participation in the development of society, and mutual respect and tolerance. An example of the continuing resonance of the rights frame in shaping policies and the politics of justification has been integration policy. Attempts to introduce restrictions linked to an integration contract were thwarted using a rights argument. A rights frame and mutual respect have been missing in Danish politics, and integration policy has largely become a vehicle in curtailing immigrant rights.

The second point concerns the centrality of political parties and the left–right divide in shaping immigrant rights. Across the six countries left–right differences and partisan composition of governments have influenced policies affecting immigrant rights. In much of the previous literature, political parties were long a neglected factor in the study of immigration, integration policies, and immigrant rights. Recent efforts to bring parties into the analysis have tended to concentrate on the electoral dimension and office-seeking strategies rather than the office holding dimension. Attention has been given to parties of the far right and the mainstream right with less emphasis on left parties and the left–right divide. By concentrating on the office holding dimension and the full spectrum of political parties, the analysis here has documented the impact of parties and the left–right divide on policies affecting immigrant rights.

The third point involves immigrant politics. My focus on the politics of presence and penetration of the policy process represents a broader perspective in studying immigrant politics compared to most previous research. All too often immigrants' relation to the policy process has been viewed as one of policy takers rather than policy makers. In considering the possible influence of immigrants, earlier studies have primarily dealt with the political process and the agenda setting phase of the policy process with emphasis on immigrants' protests, mobilization, and claim making. By shifting focus and examining penetration of the policy process, the analysis has produced unexpected insights. In three of the countries immigrants had an input in the policy process as insiders, and they help to explain variations in policy outputs. The three cases suggest that the policy implications of immigrants' political inclusion are open-ended. Their penetration of the policy process does not necessarily result in inclusive policy stances and the adoption of inclusive policies, particularly when penetration privileges specific ethnic groups, as in the German case. Nevertheless, the incorporation of immigrants in the political process and the policy process can alter the balance in the political forces supporting inclusive or exclusionary measures and thus has crucial repercussions for the politics of inclusion and exclusion.

12

Conclusion: Immigrant Rights—a Challenge for Welfare States

This book began with a plea to turn around the debate on immigration and welfare states so that the focus was the impact of welfare states on immigrants' social rights, economic well-being, and social inclusion. This plea also involves rethinking the challenges to welfare states. Instead of viewing immigration and ethnic diversity as threatening the popular support of welfare state policies, we need to start thinking about immigrant rights and the social inclusion of newcomers and their children as a major challenge.

As a preliminary step in understanding the current challenge of newcomers' social inclusion, this book has analyzed immigrants' social rights across welfare states. A first conclusion is that there are considerable cross-national variations in immigrants' social rights and that the type of welfare regime matters. The individual chapters dealing with the three types of welfare states have brought out how regime attributes and retrenchment strategies distinctive to the welfare regime have affected immigrant rights. Most significantly, the decommodifying effects of welfare state policies for immigrants vary according to the welfare regime type. The social democratic regime countries have the highest levels of decommodification, that is, their policies have been more effective in reducing poverty and assuring that immigrants enjoy a socially acceptable standard of living than those of the conservative corporatist regime countries, and especially those of the liberal regime countries.

A second, equally important conclusion is that major discrepancies exist between the social rights of immigrants and those of native citizens. The focus on formal social rights and rights extension has nurtured the general assumption that there is little difference in the social rights of legal aliens and citizens, and this has precluded the idea that unequal rights or social inclusion might be a problem. However, an examination of substantive or effective social rights, as reflected in receipt of benefits, reveals a gap in the quality of citizens' social rights and those of immigrants across welfare states. Our analysis shows that in comparison to immigrants, native citizens were more likely to enjoy a socially acceptable standard of living; citizens were more likely to receive benefits in relation to their needs, and when they received benefits, they were more likely to be lifted above the poverty line. These results clearly refute claims that immigrants' access to benefits jeopardizes the quality of social rights enjoyed by citizens or impinges on the availability of benefits to citizens.

Parallel to the gap in citizens' and immigrants' rights we found differences between the social rights of the white population and those of visible minorities. Of major concern, benefits do a poorer job in eliminating visible minorities' risk of poverty than in the case of the white population. Immigration has introduced new patterns of stratification in social rights, and the lesser effective rights of immigrants and visible minorities across welfare states constitute the heart of the challenge.

An additional issue has concerned change in immigrants' social rights over time and the direction of the changes. Is the social inclusion of newcomers a growing challenge? We have seen that immigrants' social rights have tended to follow the vicissitudes of postwar welfare state expansion and contraction. Immigrants generally benefited from the growth of entitlements, while they have often been disproportionately affected by welfare state cutbacks and economic downturns.

It is tempting to view the mid-1990s as the beginning of a restrictive turn that has intensified across countries for several reasons. Welfare state restructuring accelerated in several countries. At the same time there has been little attention to how the changes influence immigrant rights or to the differential impact of reforms on immigrant rights. Across welfare states, one of the most obvious examples is pension reforms. In several respects, erosion in immigrants' social rights has gone unnoticed and unanalyzed.

In addition, reforms have deliberately sought to curtail immigrants' social rights during the past two decades. Perhaps the most fundamental change for immigrant rights has been a break with the territorial principle so that social rights are based on citizenship rather than legal residence. So far, however, this change has not occurred in all countries. Simultaneously there have also been major advances in immigrants' and non-citizens' access to benefits as well as measures that have sought to rectify immigrants' unintended disqualification from benefits since the mid-1990s.

Likewise, rival developments have characterized the social rights of different entry categories. On the one hand, specific entry categories have experienced a dramatic weakening of their social rights. Taking 1985 as a baseline and comparing the social rights of asylum seekers then and in the 2000s indicates a sea change in their rights across the countries. Serious deterioration has also occurred in the social rights of undocumented immigrants, with only sporadic signs of improvement. On the other hand, the rights of citizens and in some cases third country nationals permanently residing in the member states of the EU have improved over time. These contradictory trends have produced a growing differentiation in immigrants' social rights based on entry categories. The resumption of labor immigration in the European countries has further augmented the stratification of immigrant rights.

Changes in the policy dimensions of the incorporation regime have also been described as a restrictive turn. Several scholars argue that recent policy changes to promote immigrants' civic integration amount to utilizing illiberal means, and thus constitute a form of repressive liberalism (Joppke 2007; Guild et al. 2009). Christian Joppke further claims that the convergences in civic integration policies represent a major departure from national models or "the weakening of national distinctiveness" (2007: 1). Still of our six countries, two fall outside of this trend. A negative development in several but not all countries, identified earlier here, has been an increase in the requirements for a permanent residence permit so that they resemble naturalization requirements. On the policy dimension of family reunification, restrictions have multiplied, and since the mid-2000s several countries have introduced language proficiency as an entry requirement. Again, however, there are wide variations across our six countries concerning the requirements for family unification, with the strictest requirements in Denmark and the most lenient in Sweden. In the area of citizenship policies, different developments stand out across the countries. Major restrictions have been introduced in Denmark and the UK; attempts to make requirements more rigorous were abortive in France and the US; while citizenship requirements were eased in Germany and Sweden. In general a strengthening of anti-discrimination legislation has occurred, even if the improvements have been uneven.

Changes in the policy dimensions of the incorporation regime have not only made inclusion more difficult, they have also been of detriment to immigrants' social rights. Integration measures have been linked to social rights in two ways. In some countries, utilization of assistance benefits has made the non-citizen a candidate for participation in integration programs, and failure to comply involves severe sanctions, ranging from withdrawal of benefits and fines to disqualification from permanent residence status and naturalization. Finally, policy makers have tied social rights to admission policies in the belief that benefits are a magnet to immigrants and they could be deterred by eliminating access to benefits or reducing benefits. Even here there are variations between the countries.

Overall there has been a shift where rights contraction and differentiation outweigh rights extension. However, major policy variations affecting immigrant rights still exist, and policy developments have been neither unilinear nor uniform across countries. These irregularities, together with the rival trends in individual countries, underline the importance of politics. In meeting the challenge of newcomers' social inclusion and remedying the lesser social rights of immigrants and visible minorities, the politics of inclusion and exclusion will be decisive to the outcome.

References

Abiri, Elisabeth. 2000. "The Changing Praxis of 'Generosity': Swedish Refugee Policy during the 1990s," *Journal of Refugee Studies* 13 (1), 11–28.

Adema, Willem. 2006. "Social Assistance Policy Development and the Provision of a Decent Level of Income in Selected OECD Countries," *OECD Social, Employment and Migration Working Paper No. 38*. OECD: Paris <www.oecd.org/els>, accessed July 31, 2009.

Alber, Jens. 1986. "Germany," in Peter Flora (ed.), *Growth to Limits: The Western European Welfare States since World War II*, Vol. 2. Berlin: Walter de Gruyter, pp. 1–154.

Alber, Jens. 2003. "Recent Developments in the German Welfare State: Basic Continuity or a Paradigm Shift?" in Neil Gilbert and Rebecca A. Van Voorhis (eds.), *Changing Patterns of Social Protection*. New Brunswick, NJ: Transaction Publishers, pp. 9–73.

Alber, Jens and Gilbert, Neil (eds.). 2010. *United in Diversity? Comparing Social Models in Europe and America*. New York: Oxford University Press.

Aleinikoff, T. Alexander and Klusmeyer, Douglas. 2002. *Citizenship Policies for an Age of Migration*. Washington, DC: Migration Policy Institute.

Alesina, Alberto and Glaeser, Edward L. 2004. *Fighting Poverty in the US and Europe: A World of Difference*. Oxford: Oxford University Press.

Andersen, Karen. 1979. *Gæstearbejder, udlænding, indvandrer, dansker! Migration till Danmark 1968–78*. Copenhagen: Gyldendal.

Anttonen, Anneli and Sipilä, Jorma. 1996. "European Social Care Services: Is It Possible to Identify Models?" *Journal of European Social Policy* 6 (2), 87–100.

Armingeon, Klaus and Bonoli, Giuliano (eds.). 2006. *The Politics of Post-industrial Welfare States: Adapting Post-war Social Policies to New Social Risks*. London: Routledge.

Arter, David. 1999. *Scandinavian Politics Today*. Manchester: Manchester University Press.

Arts, Wil A. and Gelissen, John. 2010. "Models of the Welfare State," in Francis G. Castles, Stephan Leibfried, Jane Lewis, Herbert Obinger, and Christopher Pierson (eds.), *The Oxford Handbook of the Welfare State*. Oxford: Oxford University Press, pp. 569–83.

Arvidsson, Monika. 2009. "EU Labour Migration: Government and Social Partner Policies in Sweden," in Béla Galgóczi, Janine Leschke, and Andrew Watt (eds.), *EU Labour Migration since Enlargement: Trends, Impacts and Policies*. Farnham: Ashgate, pp. 87–100.

Ashford, Douglas E. 1982. *Policy and Politics in France: Living with Uncertainty*. Philadelphia: Temple University Press.

Ashford, Douglas E. 1991. "Advantages of Complexity: Social Insurance in France," in John S. Ambler (ed.), *The French Welfare State: Surviving Social and Ideological Change.* New York: New York University Press, pp. 32–57.

Aspinall, Peter and Mitton, Lavinia. 2007. "Are English Local Authorities' Practices on Housing and Council Tax Benefit Administration Meeting Race Equality Requirements?" *Critical Social Policy* 27 (3), 381–414.

Aytar, Osman. 2007. *Mångfaldens organisering: Om integration, organisationer och interetniska relationer i Sverige.* Stockholm: Department of Sociology, Stockholm University.

Bäck, Henry and Soininen, Maritta. 1996. *Invandrarna, demokratin och samhället.* Gothenburg: Förvaltninghögskolans rapporter, University of Gothenburg.

Baldwin-Edwards, Martin. 1991. "The Socio-Political Rights of Migrants in the European Community," in Graham Room (ed.), *Towards a European Welfare State?* Bristol: SAUS Publications, pp. 189–234.

Baldwin-Edwards, Martin. 2004. "Immigrants and the Welfare State in Europe," in Douglas S. Massey and J. Edward Taylor (eds.), *International Migration: Prospects and Policies in a Global World.* Oxford: Oxford University Press, pp. 318–34.

Baldwin-Edwards, Martin and Schain, Martin A. 1994. "The Politics of Immigration: An Introduction," in Martin Baldwin-Edwards and Martin A. Schain (eds.), *The Politics of Immigration in Western Europe.* London: Frank Cass, pp. 1–16.

Bale, Tim. 2003. "Cinderella and Her Ugly Sisters: The Mainstream and Extreme Right in Europe's Bipolarising Party Systems," *West European Politics* 26 (3), 67–90.

Bale, Tim. 2008. "Turning Round the Telescope: Centre-Right Parties and Immigration and Integration Policy in Europe," *Journal of European Public Policy* 15 (3), 315–30.

Bale, Tim (ed.). 2009. *Immigration and Integration Policy in Europe: Why Politics—and the Centre-Right—Matter.* London: Routledge.

BAMF 2007. *Integration in Zahlen 2006.* Nürnberg: Bundesamt für Migration und Flüchtlinge <www.bamf.de>, accessed December 20, 2007.

Banting, Keith. 2000. "Looking in Three Directions: Migration and the European Welfare State in Comparative Perspective," in Michael Brommes and Andrew Geddes (eds.), *Immigration and Welfare: Challenging the Boundaries of the Welfare State.* London: Routledge, pp. 13–33.

Banting, Keith and Kymlicka, Will (eds.). 2006. *Multiculturalism and the Welfare State: Recognition and Redistribution in Contemporary Democracies.* Oxford: Oxford University Press.

Barbier, Jean-Claude and Théret, Bruno. 2003. "The French System of Social Protection: Path Dependencies and Societal Coherence," in Neil Gilbert and Rebecca A. Van Voorhis (eds.), *Changing Patterns of Social Protection.* New Brunswick, NJ: Transaction Publishers, pp. 119–67.

Bauböck, Rainer, Ersbøll, Eva, Groenendijk, Kees, and Waldrauch, Harald (eds.). 2006. *Acquisition and Loss of Nationality: Policies and Trends in 15 European Countries. Volume 2. Country Analyses.* Amsterdam: Amsterdam University Press.

Baumgartner, Frank R. and Jones, Bryan D. 1993. *Agendas and Instability in American Politics.* Chicago: University of Chicago Press.

References

BBMFI. 2007a. "Änderungen durch Richtlinienumsetzungsgesetz (summary)" <www.beauftragtefuerintegration.de/staatsangehoerigkeitsrecht>, accessed February 8, 2008.

BBMFI. 2007b. *7. Bericht der Beauftragten der Bundesregierung für Migration, Flüchtlinge und Integration über die Lage der Ausländerinnen und Ausländer in Deutschland* <www.integrationsbeauftragte.de>, accessed December 20, 2007.

BBMFI. 2010. *8. Bericht der Beauftragten der Bundesregierung für Migration, Flüchtlinge und Integration über die Lage der Ausländerinnen und Ausländer in Deutschland* <www.integrationsbeauftragte.de>, accessed May 17, 2011.

BCIA. 2009. *Borders, Citizenship and Immigration Act of 2009* <www.legislation.gov.uk>, accessed August 16, 2011.

Beck, Ulrich. 1992 [1986]. *Risk Society: Towards a New Modernity.* London: Sage.

Beech, Matt. 2008. "New Labour and the Politics of Dominance," in Matt Beech and Simon Lee (eds.), *Ten Years of New Labour.* Basingstoke: Palgrave Macmillan, pp. 1–16.

Benner, Mats and Vad, Torben Bundgaard. 2000. "Sweden and Denmark: Defending the Welfare State," in Fritz Scharpf and Vivien A. Schmidt (eds.), *Welfare and Work in the Open Economy, Vol. II, Diverse Responses to Common Challenges.* Oxford: Oxford University Press, pp. 399–466.

Bergmark, Åke. 2000. "Socialbidragen under 1990-talet," in Åke Bergmark (ed.), *Välfärd och försörjning* (SOU 2000:40). Stockholm: Ministry of Social Affairs, pp. 129–69.

Bernitz, Hedvig Lokrantz and Bernitz, Henrik. 2006. "Sweden," in Rainer Bauböck, Eva Ersbøll, Kees Groenendijk, and Harald Waldrauch (eds.), *Acquisition and Loss of Nationality: Policies and Trends in 15 European Countries. Volume 2. Country Analyses.* Amsterdam: Amsterdam University Press, pp. 517–49.

Berthoud, Richard. 1998. *The Incomes of Ethnic Minorities.* Colchester: Institute for Social and Economic Research, University of Essex <www.essex.ac.uk>.

Betænkning nr. 589. 1971. *Betænkning om udenlandske arbejderes forhold i Danmark.* Copenhagen: Ministry of Labor.

Betænkning nr. 761. 1975. *Betænkning om udenlandske arbejderes sociale og samfundsmæssige tilpasning her i landet.* Copenhagen: Ministry of Social Affairs.

Betænkning nr. 882. 1979. *Betænkning om udlændingelovgivningen: administrative retningslinjer.* Copenhagen: Ministry of Justice.

Betænkning nr. 1337. 1997. *Integration, betænkning afgivet af det af indenrigsministeren nedsatte Integrationsudvalg.* Copenhagen: Ministry of the Interior.

Bird, Karen, Saalfeld, Thomas, and Wüst, Andreas M. (eds.). 2011. *The Political Representation of Immigrants and Ethnic Minorities.* London: Routledge.

Bleich, Erik. 2003. *Race Politics in Britain and France: Ideas and Policymaking since the 1960s.* Cambridge: Cambridge University Press.

Bleses, Peter and Seeleib-Kaiser, Martin. 2004. *The Dual Transformation of the German Welfare State.* Basingstoke: Palgrave Macmillan.

Blume, Kræn, Gustafsson, Björn, Pedersen, Peder J., and Verner, Mette. 2005. "A Tale of Two Countries: Poverty among Immigrants in Denmark and Sweden since 1984," in George J. Borjas and Jeff Crisp (eds.), *Poverty, International Migration and Asylum.* Basingstoke: Palgrave Macmillan, pp. 317–40.

BMAS. 2008. "'Riestern' lohnt sich fast 10,8 Millionen Verträge abgeschlossen" (February 7, 2008). Berlin: Federal Ministry of Labor and Social Affairs <www.bmas.de>, accessed February 12, 2008.

BMI. 2004. Act to Control and Restrict Immigration and to Regulate the Residence and Integration of EU Citizens and Foreigners (Immigration Act) of July 30, 2004. Berlin: Federal Ministry of the Interior <www.bmi.bund.de>, accessed May 11, 2006.

BMI. 2005. Nationality Act (Unofficial translation). Berlin: Federal Ministry of the Interior <www.zuwandrung.de>, accessed May 12, 2006.

Boeri, Tito, Hanson, Gordon, and McCornick, Barry (eds.). 2002. *Immigration Policy and the Welfare System*. Oxford: Oxford University Press.

Bonoli, Giuliano. 1997. "Classifying Welfare States: A Two-Dimensional Approach," *Journal of Social Policy* 26 (3), 351–72.

Bonoli, Giuliano and Palier, Bruno. 1996. "Reclaiming Welfare: The Politics of Social Protection Reform in France," *Southern European Society and Politics* 1 (3), 240–59.

Boréus, Kristina. 2006. *Diskrimineringens retorik: En studie av svenska valrörelser 1988–2002* (SOU 2006:52). Stockholm: Ministry of Justice.

Boréus, Kristina. 2008. "Making Natives 'Us' and Immigrants 'Them': A Study of Discrimination in Election Campaigns in Austria, Denmark and Sweden," paper presented at the Nordic Political Science Association, Tromsø, Norway, August 6–9, 2008.

Boréus, Kristina. 2010. "Including or Excluding Immigrants? The Impact of Right-Wing Populism in Denmark and Sweden," in Bo Bengtsson, Per Strömblad, and Ann-Helén Bay (eds.), *Diversity, Inclusion and Citizenship in Scandinavia*. Newcastle, UK: Cambridge Scholars Publishing, pp. 127–57.

Borevi, Karin. 2002. *Välfärdsstaten i det mångkulturella samhället*. Uppsala: Department of Government, Uppsala University.

Borevi, Karin. 2010. "Sverige: Multikulturalismens flaggskepp i Norden?" in Grete Brochmann and Anniken Hagelund (eds.), *Velferdens grenser*. Olso: Universitetsforlaget, pp. 43–130.

Borevi, Karin and Myrberg, Gunnar. 2008. "Välfärdsstaten och de nyanlända," paper presented at the XV Nordic Political Science Association Conference, Tromsø, Norway, August 6–9, 2008.

Borjas, George J. 1990. *Friends or Strangers: The Impact of Immigrants on the U.S. Economy*. New York: Basic Books.

Bosswick, Wolfgang. 2000. "Development of Asylum Policy in Germany," *Journal of Refugee Studies* 13 (1), 43–60.

Boswell, Christina and Geddes, Andrew. 2011. *Migration and Mobility in the European Union*. Basingstoke: Palgrave Macmillan.

Boswell, Christina and Hough, Dan. 2008. "Politicizing Migration: Opportunity or Liability for the Centre-Right in Germany?" *Journal of European Public Policy* 15 (3), 332–48.

Bowler, M. Kenneth. 1974. *The Nixon Guaranteed Income Proposal*. Cambridge, MA: Ballinger Publishing Company.

Bradley, Anthony. 2007. "The Sovereignty of Parliament: Form or Substance?" in Jeffrey Jowell and Dawn Oliver (eds.), *The Changing Constitution*. Oxford: Oxford University Press, pp. 25–58.

Brouard, Sylvain and Tiberj, Vincent. 2011. "Yes They Can: An Experimental Approach to the Eligibility of Ethnic Minority Candidates in France," in Karen Bird, Thomas Saalfeld, and Andreas M. Wüst (eds.), *The Political Representation of Immigrants and Minorities*. London: Routledge, pp. 164–80.

Brubaker, Rogers. 1989. "Citizenship and Naturalization: Policies and Politics," in Rogers Brubaker (ed.), *Immigration and the Politics of Citizenship in Europe and North America*. Lanham, MD: University Press of America, pp. 99–127.

Brubaker, Rogers. 1992. *Citizenship and Nationhood in France and Germany*. Cambridge, MA: Harvard University Press.

Brubaker, Rogers. 1995. "Comments on 'Modes of Immigration Politics in Liberal Democratic States'," *International Migration Review* 29 (4), 303–9.

Büchel, Felix and Frick, Joachim R. 2005. "Immigrants' Economic Performance Across Europe: Does Immigration Policy Matter?" *Population Research and Policy Review* 24 (2), 175–212.

Burchardt, Tania. 2005. "Selective Inclusion: Asylum Seekers and Other Marginalised Groups," in John Hills and Kitty Stewart (eds.), *A More Equal Society? New Labour, Poverty, Inequality and Exclusion*. Bristol: Policy Press, pp. 209–28.

Cameron, David R. 1991. "Continuity and Change in French Social Policy: The Welfare State under Gaullism, Liberalism, and Socialism," in John S. Ambler (ed.), *The French Welfare State: Surviving Social and Ideological Change*. New York: New York University Press, pp. 58–93.

Carmel, Emma, Cerami, Alfio, and Papadopoulos, Theodoros (eds.). 2011. *Migration and Welfare in the New Europe: Social Protection and the Challenges of Integration*. Bristol: Policy Press.

Castles, Francis G. 2004. *The Future of the Welfare State*. Oxford: Oxford University Press.

Castles, Francis G. and Mitchell, Deborah. 1993. "Worlds of Welfare and Families of Nations," in Francis G. Castles (ed.), *Families of Nations: Patterns of Public Policy in Western Democracies*. Aldershot: Dartmouth, pp. 93–128.

Castles, Stephen and Kosack, Godula. 1985. *Immigrant Workers and Class Structure in Western Europe*. Oxford: Oxford University Press.

Castles, Stephen and Miller, Mark J. 1993. *The Age of Migration: International Population Movements in the Modern World*. London: Macmillan.

Castles, Stephen and Schierup, Carl-Ulrik. 2010. "Migration and Ethnic Minorities," in Francis G. Castles, Stephan Leibfried, Jane Lewis, Herbert Obinger, and Christopher Pierson (eds.), *The Oxford Handbook of the Welfare State*. Oxford: Oxford University Press, pp. 278–91.

CFMB. 2000. Commission on the Future of Multi-Ethnic Britain, *The Future of Multi-Ethnic Britain*. London: Profile Books.

Clasen, Jochen. 1994. "Social Security: The Core of the German Employment-Centred Social State," in Jochen Clasen and Richard Freeman (eds.), *Social Policy in Germany*. New York: Harvester Wheatsheaf, pp. 61–82.

Clasen, Jochen. 2005. *Reforming European Welfare States: Germany and the United Kingdom Compared.* Oxford: Oxford University Press.

Cohen, Steve. 2001. *Immigration Controls, the Family and the Welfare State.* London: Jessica Kingsley.

CPR. 1999a. Schmidley, A. Dianne and Gibson, Campbell. US Census Bureau. Current Population Reports, Series P23–195. *Profile of the Foreign-Born Population in the United States: 1997.* Washington, DC: US Government Printing Office.

CPR. 1999b. US Census Bureau, Current Population Reports, Series 70–69, *Dynamics of Economic Well-Being, Participation in Government Programs, 1993–1994, Who Gets Assistance?* Washington, DC: US Government Printing Office.

CPR. 2001a. Tin, Jan and Castro, Charita. US Census Bureau, Current Population Reports, Series 70–77, *Dynamics of Economic Well-Being, Participation in Government Programs, 1993 to 1995, Who Gets Assistance?* Washington, DC: US Government Printing Office.

CPR. 2001b. Schmidley, A. Dianne. US Census Bureau. Current Population Reports, Series P23–206. *Profile of the Foreign-Born Population in the United States: 2000.* Washington, DC: US Government Printing Office.

CPR. 2002. He, Wan. US Census Bureau, Current Population Reports, Series P23–211. *The Older Foreign-Born Population in the United States: 2000.* Washington, DC: US Government Printing Office.

CPR. 2003. Mills, Robert J. and Bhandari, Shailesh. US Census Bureau, Current Population Reports, Series P60–223. *Health Insurance Coverage in the United States: 2002.* Washington, DC: US Government Printing Office.

CPR. 2004. Lester, Gordon H. and Tin, Jan. US Census Bureau, Current Population Reports, Series 70–94, *Dynamics of Economic Well-Being, Participation in Government Programs, 1996 to 1999, Who Gets Assistance?* Washington, DC: US Government Printing Office.

CPR. 2006. Loveless, Tracy A. and Tin, Jan. US Census Bureau, Current Population Reports, Series 70–108, *Dynamics of Economic Well-Being, Participation in Government Programs, 2001 through 2003, Who Gets Assistance?* Washington, DC: US Government Printing Office.

CQA. Various years. *Congressional Quarterly Almanac.* Washington, DC: Congressional Quarterly, Inc.

CQA+. 2002–3. *Congressional Quarterly Almanac Plus.* Washington, DC: Congressional Quarterly, Inc.

Craig, F. W. S. 1990. *British General Election Manifestos 1959–1987.* Aldershot: Dartmouth.

Craig, Gary. 1999. " 'Race,' Social Security and Poverty," in John Ditch (ed.), *Introduction to Social Security.* London: Routledge, pp. 206–26.

Craig, Gary. 2007. "Cunning, Unprincipled, Loathsome: The Racist Tail Wags the Welfare Dog," *Journal of Social Policy* 36 (4), 605–23.

Crepaz, Markus. 2008. *Trust beyond Borders: Immigration, the Welfare State and Identity in Modern Societies.* Ann Arbor: University of Michigan Press.

Criddle, Byron. 2005. "MPs and Candidates," in Dennis Kavanagh and David Butler (eds.), *The British Election of 2005.* Basingstoke: Palgrave Macmillan, pp. 146–67.

References

Dahlström, Carl. 2004. *Nästan välkomna. Invandrarpolitikens retorik och praktik.* Gothenburg: Department of Political Science, University of Gothenburg.

Delouvin, Patrick. 2000. "The Evolution of Asylum in France," *Journal of Refugee Studies* 13 (1), 61–73.

Demker, Marie. 2010. "Svenskarna långsiktigt alltmer positiva till invandrare," in Sören Holmberg and Lennart Weibull (eds.), *Nordiskt ljus.* Gothenburg: SOM-Institute, pp. 107–12.

Demker, Marie and Malmström, Cecilia. 1999. *Ingenmansland? Svensk immigrationspolitik i utrikespolitisk belysning.* Lund: Studentlitteratur.

Derthick, Martha. 1990. *Agency under Pressure: The Social Security Administration in American Government.* Washington, DC: Brookings Institution.

DF 2003. *Chronologie: histoire de l'immigration en dates.* La documentation française <www.ladocumentationfrancaise.fr/dossier_polpublic/immigration/chronologie>, updated July 2003, accessed December 9, 2003.

Diehl, Claudia and Blohm, Michael. 2003. "Rights or Identity? Naturalization Processes among 'Labor Migrants' in Germany," *International Migration Review* 37 (1), 133–62.

Dollé, Michel. 2004. "Income Support Policy in France," in Neil Gilbert and Antoine Parent (eds.), *Welfare Reform: A Comparative Assessment of the French and U.S. Experiences.* New Brunswick, NJ: Transaction Publishers, pp. 67–92.

Dörr, Silvia and Faist, Thomas. 1997. "Institutional Conditions for the Integration of Immigrants in Welfare States: A Comparison of the Literature on Germany, France, Great Britain, and the Netherlands," *European Journal of Political Research* 31 (4), 401–26.

Driver, Stephen. 2008. "New Labour and Social Policy," in Matt Beech and Simon Lee (eds.), *Ten Years of New Labour.* Basingstoke: Palgrave Macmillan, pp. 50–67.

Ds A 1986:6. *Dubbelt medborgarskap.* Stockholm: Ministry of Labor.

Ds 1991:79. *Introduktionsersättning till flyktingar och vissa andra utlänningar.* Stockholm: Ministry of Labor.

Dummett, Ann. 2006. "United Kingdom," in Rainer Bauböck, Eva Ersbøll, Kees Groenendijk, and Harald Waldrauch (eds.), *Acquisition and Loss of Nationality: Policies and Trends in 15 European Countries. Volume 2. Country Analyses.* Amsterdam: Amsterdam University Press, pp. 551–85.

Dummett, Ann and Nicol, Andrew. 1990. *Subjects, Citizens, Aliens and Others: Nationality and Immigration Law.* London: Weidenfeld & Nicolson.

Duvander, Ann-Zofie and Eklund, Stina. 2006. "Utrikesfödda och svenskfödda föräldrars föräldrapenningsanvändande," in Paulina de los Reyes (ed.), *Om välfärdens gränser och det villkorade medborgarskapet* (SOU 2006:37). Stockholm: Ministry of Justice, pp. 33–68.

DWP. 2007. *Opportunities for All: Indicators Update 2007.* London: Department for Work and Pensions <www.dwp.gov.uk/ofa>, accessed November 11, 2009.

DWP. 2008. *Employment and Support Allowance Equality Impact Assessment.* London: Department for Work and Pensions <www.dwp.gov.uk/docs/equalityimpactassessment.pdf>, accessed November 11, 2009.

Eardley, Tony, Bradshaw, Jonathan, Ditch, John, Gough, Ian, and Whiteford, Peter. 1996a. *Social Assistance in OECD Countries: Synthesis Report.* London: HMSO.

Eardley, Tony, Bradshaw, Jonathan, Ditch, John, Gough, Ian, and Whiteford, Peter. 1996b. *Social Assistance in OECD Countries: Country Reports*. London: HMSO.

ECRE. 2004. "Country Report 2004—France," European Council on Refugees and Exiles <www.ecre.org>, accessed December 18, 2007.

EI. 2010. *Erklæring om integration og aktivt medborgerskab i det danske samfund*. Copenhagen. Ministry of Refugees, Immigrants and Integration <www.nyidanmark.dk>, accessed March 15, 2010.

Einhorn, Eric S. and Logue, John. 1989. *Modern Welfare States: Politics and Policies in Social Democratic Scandinavia*. New York: Praeger.

Eitrheim, Pål and Kuhnle, Stein. 2000. "Nordic Welfare States in the 1990s," in Stein Kuhnle (ed.), *Survival of the European Welfare State*. London: Routledge, pp. 39–57.

Ejrnæs, Morten. 2001. "Integrationsloven—en case, der illustrerer etniske minoriteters usikre medborgerstatus," *AMID Working Paper Series 1/2001* <www.amid.dk>.

Elder, Neil, Thomas, Alistair H., and Arter, David. 1982. *The Consensual Democracies? The Government and Politics of the Scandinavian States*. Oxford: Martin Robertson.

Elmér, Åke. 1994. *Svensk socialpolitik*. Stockholm: Liber.

Engelen, Ewald. 2003. "How to Combine Openness and Protection? Citizenship, Migration, and Welfare Regimes," *Politics & Society* 31 (4), 503–36.

Enjolras, Bernard and Lødemel, Ivar. 1999. "Activation of Social Protection in France and Norway," in Dennis Bourget and Bruno Palier (eds.), *Comparing Social Welfare Systems in Nordic Europe and France*. Paris: MIRE-DREES (Centre of Research, Studies and Statistics), Ministry of Employment and Solidarity, pp. 469–503.

Erikson, Robert, Hansen, Erik Jørgen, Ringen, Stein, and Uusitalo, Hannu (eds.). 1987. *The Scandinavian Model: Welfare States and Welfare Research*. Armonk, NY: M. E. Sharpe.

Ersbøll, Eva. 2006. "Denmark," in Rainer Bauböck, Eva Ersbøll, Kees Groenendijk, and Harald Waldrauch (eds.), *Acquisition and Loss of Nationality: Policies and Trends in 15 European Countries. Volume 2. Country Analyses*. Amsterdam: Amsterdam University Press, pp. 105–48.

Esping-Andersen, Gøsta. 1990. *The Three Worlds of Welfare Capitalism*. Cambridge: Polity Press.

Esping-Andersen, Gøsta. 1992. "The Three Political Economies of Welfare Capitalism," in Jon Eivind Kolberg (ed.), *The Study of Welfare State Regimes*. Armonk, NY: M. E. Sharpe, pp. 92–123.

Esping-Andersen, Gøsta. 1999. *Social Foundations of Postindustrial Economies*. Oxford: Oxford University Press.

Esping-Andersen, Gøsta, Gallie, Duncan, Hemerijck, Anton, and Myles, John. 2002. *Why We Need a New Welfare State*. Oxford: Oxford University Press.

Esser, Hartmut and Korte, Hermann. 1985. "Federal Republic of Germany," in Tomas Hammar (ed.), *European Immigration Policy*. Cambridge: Cambridge University Press, pp. 165–205.

Eurobarometer. 2004. "Justice and Home Affairs," *Flash Eurobarometer 155*. Brussels: European Commission, pp. 19–21 <www.europa.eu.int/comm/public_opinion>, accessed April 6, 2005.

EUROSTAT. 2009. *European Union Labour Force Survey—Annual Results 2008*, 33/2009— Data in Focus <www.epp.eurostat.ec.europa.eu>, accessed September 20, 2009.

Evandrou, Maria and Falkingham, Jane. 2005. "A Secure Retirement for All? Older People and New Labour," in John Hills and Kitty Stewart (eds.), *A More Equal Society? New Labour, Poverty, Inequality and Exclusion*. Bristol: Policy Press, pp. 167–87.

Evans, Martin. 1998. "Social Security: Dismantling the Pyramids?" in Howard Glennerster and John Hills (eds.), *The State of Welfare: The Economics of Social Spending*. Oxford: Oxford University Press, pp. 257–307.

Faist, Thomas. 1995a. "Ethnicization and Racialization of Welfare-State Politics in Germany and the USA," *Ethnic and Racial Studies* 18 (2), 219–50.

Faist, Thomas. 1995b. "Boundaries of Welfare States: Immigrants and Social Rights on the National and Supranational Level," in Robert Miles and Dietrich Thränhardt (eds.), *Migration and European Integration: The Dynamics of Inclusion and Exclusion*. London: Pinter Publishers, pp. 177–95.

Favell, Adrian. 1998a. *Philosophies of Integration: Immigration and the Idea of Citizenship in France and Britain*. Basingstoke: Macmillan.

Favell, Adrian. 1998b. "Multicultural Race Relations in Britain: Problems of Interpretation and Explanation," in Christian Joppke (ed.), *Challenge to the Nation-State: Immigration in Western Europe and the United States*. Oxford: Oxford University Press, pp. 319–49.

Feldblum, Miriam. 1999. *Reconstructing Citizenship: The Politics of Nationality Reform and Immigration in Contemporary France*. Albany, NY: State University of New York Press.

Fennema, Meindert. 2000. "Legal Repression of Extreme-Right Parties and Racial Discrimination," in Ruud Koopmans and Paul Statham (eds.), *Challenging Immigration and Ethnic Relations Politics: Comparative European Perspectives*. Oxford: Oxford University Press, pp. 119–44.

Ferrera, Maurizio. 1996. "The 'Southern Model' of Welfare in Social Europe," *Journal of European Social Policy* 6 (1), 17–37.

Fielding, Steven. 2003. *The Labour Party: Continuity and Change in the Making of 'New' Labour*. Basingstoke: Palgrave Macmillan.

Fix, Michael and Passel, Jeffrey S. 1994. *Immigration and Immigrants: Setting the Record Straight*. Washington, DC: Urban Institute Press.

Fix, Michael and Passel, Jeffrey S. 2002. "Assessing Welfare Reform's Immigrant Provisions," in Alan Weil and Kenneth Finegold (eds.), *Welfare Reform: The Next Act*. Washington, DC: Urban Institute Press, pp. 179–202.

Fix, Michael and Zimmermann, Wendy. 1994. "After Arrival: An Overview of Federal Immigrant Policy in the United States," in Barry Edmonston and Jeffery S. Passel (eds.), *Immigration and Ethnicity: The Integration of America's Newest Arrivals*. Washington, DC: Urban Institute Press, pp. 251–81.

Fix, Michael and Zimmermann, Wendy. 2004. "The Legacy of Welfare Reform for U.S. Immigrants," in Douglas S. Massey and J. Edward Taylor (eds.), *International Migration: Prospects and Policies in a Global World*. Oxford: Oxford University Press, pp. 335–51.

FM. 2004. *Lavindkomstgruppen—mobilitet og sammensætning*. Copenhagen: Finance Ministry <www.fm.dk/1024/visPublikationesForside.asp?artikelID=6615&mode=hele>, accessed June 28, 2004.

FN. 2007. *2007 Programme de gouvernement de Jean-Marie Le Pen* <www.frontnational. com>, accessed April 22, 2007.

Freedman, Jane. 2004. *Immigration and Insecurity in France*. Aldershot: Ashgate.

Freeman, Gary P. 1979. *Immigrant Labor and Racial Conflict in Industrial Societies: The French and British Experience 1945–1975*. Princeton: Princeton University Press.

Freeman, Gary P. 1986. "Migration and the Political Economy of the Welfare State," *Annals of the American Academy of Political and Social Science* 485, 51–63.

Freeman, Gary P. 1995. "Modes of Immigration Politics in Liberal Democratic States," *International Migration Review* 29 (4), 881–902.

Freeman, Gary P. 2001. "Client Politics or Populism? Immigration Reform in the United States," in Virginie Guiraudon and Christian Joppke (eds.), *Controlling a New Migration World*. London: Routledge, pp. 67–95.

Freeman, Gary P. 2002. "Winners and Losers: Politics and the Costs and Benefits of Migration," in Anthony M. Messina (ed.), *West European Immigration and Immigrant Policy in the New Century*. Westport, CT: Praeger, pp. 77–95.

Freeman, Gary P. 2004. "Immigrant Incorporation in Western Democracies," *International Migration Review* 38 (3), 945–69.

Freeman, Gary P. 2006. "National Models, Policy Types, and the Politics of Immigration in Liberal Democracies," *West European Politics* 29 (2), 227–47.

Freeman, Gary P. and Betts, Katharine. 1992. "The Politics of Interests and Immigration Policymaking in Australia and the United States," in Gary P. Freeman and James Jupp (eds.), *Nations of Immigrants*. Melbourne: Oxford University Press, pp. 72–88.

Freeman, Richard and Clasen, Jochen. 1994. "The German Social State: An Introduction," in Jochen Clasen and Richard Freeman (eds.), *Social Policy in Germany*. New York: Harvester Wheatsheaf, pp. 1–17.

Frick, Joachim R. and Wagner, Gert G. 2001. "Living Conditions of Immigrant Children in Germany," in Koen Vleminckx and Timothy M. Smeeding (eds.), *Child Well-Being, Child Poverty and Child Policy in Modern Nations*. Bristol: Policy Press, pp. 275–98.

Fryklund, Björn, Kiiskinen, Jenny, and Saveljeff, Sigrid. 2007. *Populism and a Mistrust of Foreigners: Sweden in Europe*. Norrköping: National Board of Integration.

Fuchs, Lawrence H. 1990. "The Reactions of Black Americans to Immigration," in Virginia Yans-McLaughlin (ed.), *Immigration Reconsidered: History, Sociology, and Politics*. New York: Oxford University Press, pp. 293–314.

Gaasholt, Øystein and Togeby, Lise. 1995. *I syv sind—Danskernes holdninger til flygtninge og indvandrere*. Århus: Politica.

Gallie, Duncan and Paugam, Serge. 2000. "The Experience of Unemployment in Europe," in Duncan Gallie and Serge Paugam (eds.), *Welfare Regimes and the Experience of Unemployment in Europe*. Oxford: Oxford University Press, pp. 1–22.

GAO. 1975. "Need to Reduce Public Expenditures for Newly Arrived Immigrants and Correct Inequity in Current Immigration Law" (GGD-75-107). Washington, DC: General Accounting Office.

GB. 2004. *Green Book. Background Material and Data on Major Programs within the Jurisdiction of the Committee on Ways and Means*, US House of Representatives. Washington, DC: Government Printing Office.

Geddes, Andrew. 2003a. "Migration and the Welfare State in Europe," in Sarah Spencer (ed.), *The Politics of Migration: Managing Opportunity, Conflict and Change*. Oxford: Blackwell Publishing, pp. 150–62.

Geddes, Andrew. 2003b. *The Politics of Migration and Immigration in Europe*. London: Sage.

Geddes, Andrew. 2008. *Immigration and European Integration: Beyond Fortress Europe?* Manchester: Manchester University Press.

Gelatt, Julie and Fix, Michael. 2007. "Federal Spending on Immigrant Families' Integration," in Michael Fix (ed.), *Securing the Future: US Immigrant Integration Policy*. Washington, DC: Migration Policy Institute, pp. 61–80.

Gibney, Matthew J. 2004. *The Ethics and Politics of Asylum: Liberal Democracy and the Response to Refugees*. Cambridge: Cambridge University Press.

Giddens, Anthony. 1998. *The Third Way: The Renewal of Social Democracy*. Cambridge: Polity Press.

Gimpel, James G. and Edwards, James R., Jr. 1999. *The Congressional Politics of Immigration Reform*. Boston: Allyn & Bacon.

Ginn, Jay and Arber, Sara. 2001. "Pension Prospects of Ethnic Minority Groups: Inequalities by Gender and Ethnicity," *British Journal of Sociology* 52, 519–39.

Ginsburg, Norman. 1993. *Divisions of Welfare*. London: Sage.

Ginsburg, Norman. 1994. "Ethnic Minorities and Social Policy," in Jochen Clasen and Richard Freeman (eds.), *Social Policy in Germany*. New York: Harvester Wheatsheaf, pp. 191–206.

Givens, Terri and Luedtke, Adam. 2005. "European Immigration Policies in Comparative Perspective: Issue Salience, Partisanship and Immigrant Rights," *Comparative European Politics* 3 (1), 1–22.

Goodin, Robert E., Headey, Bruce, Muffels, Ruud, and Dirven, Henk-Jan. 1999. *The Real Worlds of Welfare Capitalism*. Cambridge: Cambridge University Press.

Gordon, Paul. 1985. *Policing Immigration: Britain's Internal Controls*. London: Pluto Press.

Gordon, Paul and Newnham, Anne. 1985. *Passport to Benefits? Racism and Social Security*. London: Child Poverty Action Group and Runnymede Trust.

Goul Andersen, Jørgen. 2000. "Welfare Crisis and Beyond: Danish Welfare Policies in the 1980s and 1990s," in Stein Kuhnle (ed.), *The Survival of the European Welfare State*. London: Routledge, pp. 69–87.

Goul Andersen, Jørgen. 2003. "The General Election in Denmark, November 2001," *Electoral Studies* 22, 186–93.

Goul Andersen, Jørgen. 2007. "Restricting Access to Social Protection for Immigrants in the Danish Welfare State," *Benefits* 15 (3), 257–69.

Goul Andersen, Jørgen. 2008. "Welfare State Transformations in an Affluent Scandinavian State: The Case of Denmark," in Martin Seeleib-Kaiser (ed.), *Welfare State Transformations: Comparative Perspectives*. Basingstoke: Palgrav Macmillan, pp. 33–55.

Goul Andersen, Jørgen and Hoff, Jens. 2001. *Democracy and Citizenship in Scandinavia*. Basingstoke: Palgrave.

Green, Simon. 2001. "Citizenship Policy in Germany: The Case of Ethnicity over Residence," in Randall Hansen and Patrick Weil (eds.), *Towards a European Nationality: Citizenship, Immigration and Nationality Law in the EU*. Basingstoke: Palgrave Macmillan, pp. 24–51.

Green, Simon. 2004. *The Politics of Exclusion: Institutions and Immigration Policy in Contemporary Germany*. Manchester: Manchester University Press.

Green, Simon. 2005. "Immigration and Integration Policy: Between Incrementalism and Non-decisions," in Simon Green and William E. Paterson (eds.), *Governance in Contemporary Germany: The Semisovereign State Revisited*. Cambridge: Cambridge University Press, pp. 190–211.

Green-Pedersen, Christoffer. 2002. *The Politics of Justification: Party Competition and Welfare-State Retrenchment in Denmark and the Netherlands from 1982 to 1998*. Amsterdam: Amsterdam University Press.

Green-Pedersen, Christoffer. 2007. "Denmark: A 'World Bank' Pension System," in Ellen M. Immergut, Karen M. Anderson, and Isabelle Schulze (eds.), *The Handbook of West European Pension Politics*. Oxford: Oxford University Press, pp. 454–95.

Green-Pedersen, Christoffer and Krogstrup, Jesper. 2008. "Immigration as a Political Issue in Denmark and Sweden," *European Journal of Political Research* 47 (5), 610–34.

Griffith, J. A. G. 1977. *The Politics of the Judiciary*. Manchester: Manchester University Press.

Griffith, J. A. G. 1997. *The Politics of the Judiciary* (5th edn.). London: Fontana Press.

Guendelsberger, John W. 1992–3. "Equal Protection and Resident Alien Access to Public Benefits in France and the United States," *Tulane Law Review* 67, 669–731.

Guild, Elspeth, Groenendijk, Kees, and Carrera, Sergio. 2009. *Illiberal Liberal States: Immigration, Citizenship and Integration in the EU*. Farnham: Ashgate.

Guiraudon, Virginie. 1998. "Citizenship Rights for Non-Citizens: France, Germany and the Netherlands" in Christian Joppke (ed.), *Challenge to the Nation-State: Immigration in Western Europe and the United States*. Oxford: Oxford University Press, pp. 272–304.

Guiraudon, Virginie. 2000a. "The Marshallian Triptych Reordered: The Role of Courts and Bureaucracy in Furthering Migrants' Social Rights," in Michael Bommes and Andrew Geddes (eds.), *Immigration and Welfare: Challenging the Borders of the Welfare State*. London: Routledge, pp. 72–89.

Guiraudon, Virginie. 2000b. *Les politiques d'immigration en Europe: Allemagne, France, Pays-Bas*. Paris: L'Harmattan.

Guiraudon, Virginie. 2002. "Including Foreigners in National Welfare States: Institutional Venues and Rules of the Game," in Bo Rothstein and Sven Steinmo (eds.), *Restructuring the Welfare State: Political Institutions and Policy Change*. Basingstoke: Palgrave Macmillan, pp. 129–56.

Guiraudon, Virginie. 2003. "The Constitution of a European Immigration Policy Domain: A Political Sociology Approach," *Journal of European Public Policy* 19 (2), 263–82.

Guiraudon, Virginie. 2005. "Immigration Politics and Policies," in Alistair Cole, Patrick Le Galès, and Jonah Levy (eds.), *Developments in French Politics 3*. Basingstoke: Palgrave Macmillan, pp. 154–69.

Guiraudon, Virginie. 2006. "Different Nation, Same Nationhood: The Challenges of Immigrant Policy," in Pepper D. Culpepper, Peter A. Hall, and Bruno Palier (eds.), *Changing France: The Politics that Markets Make*. Basingstoke: Palgrave Macmillan, pp. 129–49.

Hacker, Jacob S. 2002. *The Divided Welfare State: The Battle over Public and Private Social Benefits in the United States*. Cambridge: Cambridge University Press.

Hailbronner, Kay. 2006. "Germany," in Rainer Bauböck, Eva Ersbøll, Kees Groenendijk, and Harald Waldrauch (eds.), *Acquisition and Loss of Nationality: Policies and Trends in 15 European Countries. Volume 2. Country Analyses*. Amsterdam: Amsterdam University Press, pp. 213–51.

Hammar, Tomas. 1979. *Det första invandrarvalet*. Stockholm: Publica.

Hammar, Tomas (ed.). 1985. *European Immigration Policy*. Cambridge: Cambridge University Press.

Hammar, Tomas. 1990. "The Civil Rights of Aliens," in Zig Layton-Henry (ed.), *The Political Rights of Migrant Workers in Western Europe*. London: Sage, pp. 74–93.

Hammar, Tomas. 2003. "Einwanderung in einem skandinavischen Wohlfahrtsstaat: Die schwedische Erfahrung," in Dietrich Thränhardt and Uwe Hunger (eds.), *Migration im Spannungsfeld von Globalisierung und Nationalstaat*. Wiesbaden: Westdeutscher Verlag, pp. 227–52.

Hammer, Ole (ed.). 1995. *Håndbog om indvandrere og flygtninge*. Copenhagen: Forlaget Kommuninformation.

Hansen, Hans, Jensen, Helle Cwarzko, Larsen, Claus, and Nielsen, Niels-Kenneth. 2002. *Social Security Benefits in Denmark and Germany with a Focus on Access Conditions for Refugees and Immigrants*. Copenhagen: Rockwool Foundation Research Unit.

Hansen, Lars-Erik. 2001. *Jämlikhet och valfrihet: En studie av den svenska invandrarpolitikens framväxt*. Stockholm: Almqvist & Wiksell International.

Hansen, Randall. 2000. *Citizenship and Immigration in Post-War Britain*. Oxford: Oxford University Press.

Hayduk, Ron. 2006. *Democracy for All: Restoring Immigrant Voting Rights in the United States*. New York: Routledge.

Hayward, Jack and Wright, Vincent. 2002. *Governing from the Centre: Core Executive Coordination in France*. Oxford: Oxford University Press.

HCI. 1998. *Lutte contre les discriminations: faire respecter le principe d'égalité*, rapport au Premier ministre/Haut Conseil à l'intégration. Paris: La documentation française.

HCI. 2006. *Le bilan de la politique de l'intégration 2002–2005*, rapport par du Haut conseil à l'intégration. Paris: La documentation française.

HCI. 2009. *Études et intégration—Faire connaître les valeurs de la République, Les élus issus de l'immigration dans les conseils municipaux (2001–2008)*. Paris: La documentation française <www.ladocumentationfrancaise.fr/rapports-publics>, accessed December 28, 2009.

Heclo, Hugh. 1974. *Modern Social Politics in Britain and Sweden*. New Haven: Yale University Press.

Heinelt, Hubert. 1993. "Immigration and the Welfare State in Germany," *German Politics* 2 (1), 78–96.

Heinrich, Andreas. 2002. "The Integration of Ethnic Germans from the Soviet Union," in David Rock and Stefan Wolff (eds.), *Coming Home to Germany? The Integration of Ethnic Germans from Central and Eastern Europe in the Federal Republic*. New York: Berghahn Books, pp. 77–86.

Hendley, Alexa A. and Bilimoria, Natasha F. 1999. "Minorities and Social Security: An Analysis of Racial and Ethnic Differences," *Social Security Bulletin* 62 (2), 59–64.

Hero, Rodney and Preuhs, Robert R. 2006. "Multiculturalism and Welfare Policies in the USA: A State-level Comparative Analysis," in Keith Banting and Will Kymlicka (eds.), *Multiculturalism and the Welfare State*. Oxford: Oxford University Press, pp. 121–51.

Hill, Michael. 1990. *Social Security Policy in Britain*. Aldershot: Edward Elgar.

Hill, Michael J. and Issacharoff, Ruth M. 1971. *Community Action and Race Relations: A Study of Community Relations Committees in Britain*. London: Oxford University Press/Institute of Race Relations.

Hills, John. 2004. *Inequality and the State*. Oxford: Oxford University Press.

Hills, John and Stewart, Kitty. 2005. "A Tide Turned but Mountains yet to Climb?" in John Hills and Kitty Stewart (eds.), *A More Equal Society? New Labour, Poverty, Inequality and Exclusion*. Bristol: Policy Press, pp. 325–46.

Hinrichs, Karl. 2010. "A Social Insurance State Withers Away: Welfare State Reforms in Germany—Or: Attempts to Turn Around in a Cul-de-Sac," in Bruno Palier (ed.), *A Long Goodbye to Bismarck? The Politics of Welfare Reform in Continental Europe*. Amsterdam: Amsterdam University Press, pp. 45–72.

Hix, Simon and Noury, Abdul. 2007. "Politics, Not Economic Interests: Determinants of Migration Policies in the European Union," *International Migration Review* 41 (1), 182–205.

Hjarnø, Jan, Lundbæk, Torben, and Skovmand, Sven (eds.). 1973. *Fremmedarbejderpolitik*. Copenhagen: Mellemfolkeligt Samvirke.

HLR. 1983. "Developments in the Law: Immigration Policy and the Rights of Aliens," *Harvard Law Review* 96 (6), 1286–465.

HO. 2005. Home Office, *Controlling our Borders: Making Migration Work for Britain*. Five-year strategy for asylum and immigration <www.homeoffice.gov.uk>, accessed November 7, 2007.

HO. 2008. Home Office, Border and Immigration Agency, *The Path to Citizenship: Next Steps in Reforming the Immigration System* <www.homeoffice.gov.uk>, accessed February 4, 2009.

HO-UKBA. 2009. Home Office and UK Border Agency, *Reforming Asylum Support: Effective Support for Those with Protection Needs* <www.ukba.homeoffice.gov.uk>, accessed November 16, 2009.

Højsteen, Signe. 1992. "Dansk udlændingelovgivning med særligt henblik på perioden 1968–1986." Unpublished dissertation, Department of History, University of Copenhagen.

Howard, Christopher. 1997. *The Hidden Welfare State: Tax Expenditures and Social Policy in the United States*. Princeton: Princeton University Press.

Howard, Christopher. 2007. *The Welfare State Nobody Knows: Debunking Myths about U.S. Social Policy*. Princeton: Princeton University Press.

References

Howard, Marc Morjé. 2009. *The Politics of Citizenship in Europe*. New York: Cambridge University Press.

HR 4. US House, 104th Congress, "H.R. 4, Personal Responsibility Act of 1995." Full Text of Bills Available from: LexisNexis Congressional Online Service. Bethesda, MD: Congressional Information Service.

Huber, Evelyn and Stephens, John D. 2001. *Development and Crisis of the Welfare State: Parties and Policies in Global Markets*. Chicago: University of Chicago Press.

Hutchinson, Edward Prince. 1981. *Legislative History of American Immigration Policy*. Philadelphia: University of Pennsylvania Press.

IND. 2004. Immigration and Nationality Directorate, "Nationality, Immigration and Asylum Act 2002," Law and Policy <www.ind.homeoffice.gov.uk>, accessed May 1, 2004.

INSEE. 2005. *Les immigrés en France, édition 2005* <www.insee.fr>, accessed June 27, 2008.

Ireland, Patrick. 1994. *The Policy Challenge of Ethnic Diversity*. Cambridge, MA: Harvard University Press.

Ireland, Patrick. 2004. *Becoming Europe: Immigration, Integration and the Welfare State*. Pittsburgh: University of Pittsburgh Press.

Jackson, David C. 1999. *Immigration: Law and Practice* (2nd edn.). London: Sweet & Maxwell.

Jacobson, David. 1996. *Rights across Borders*. Baltimore, MD: Johns Hopkins University Press.

Jämlikhet. 1969. *Jämlikhet*. Stockholm: Prisma.

Jensen, Bent. 1999. "Thirty Years of Press Debate on 'Foreigners' in Denmark: Part I and Part II," in David Coleman and Eskil Wadensjö, with contributions by Bent Jensen and Søren Pedersen, *Immigration to Denmark*. Århus: Rockwool Foundation Research Unit/Aarhus University Press, pp. 191–289.

JO. 2006. Loi 2006–911 du 24 juillet 2006 relative à l'immigration et à l'intégration, *Journal officiel de la République Française*, <www.journal-officiel.gouv.fr>, accessed May 8, 2007.

Johansen, Lars Nørby. 1986. "Denmark," in Peter Flora (ed.), *Growth to Limits: The Western European Welfare States since World War II*, Vol. 1. Berlin: Walter de Gruyter, pp. 293–381.

Johnston, Richard, Banting, Keith, Kymlicka, Will, and Soroka, Stuart. 2010. "National Identity and Support for the Welfare State," *Canadian Journal of Political Science* 43 (2), 349–77.

Joppke, Christian. 1999. *Immigration and the Nation-State: The United States, Germany, and Great Britain*. Oxford: Oxford University Press.

Joppke, Christian. 2001. "The Legal-Domestic Sources of Immigrant Rights: The United States, Germany and the European Union," *Comparative Political Studies* 34 (4), 339–66.

Joppke, Christian. 2003. "Citizenship between De- and Re-ethnicization," *European Journal of Sociology* 44 (3), 429–58.

Joppke, Christian. 2005. *Selecting by Origin: Ethnic Migration in the Liberal State*. Cambridge, MA: Harvard University Press.

Joppke, Christian. 2007. "Beyond National Models: Civic Integration Policies for Immigrants in Western Europe," *West European Politics* 30 (1), 1–22.

Joppke, Christian and Morawska, Ewa. 2003. "Integrating Immigrants in Liberal Nation-States: Policies and Practices," in Christian Joppke and Ewa Morawska (eds.), *Toward Assimilation and Citizenship*. Basingstoke: Palgrave Macmillan, pp. 1–36.

Jowell, Jeffery. 2007. "The Rule of Law and its Underlying Values," in Jeffrey Jowell and Dawn Oliver (eds.), *The Changing Constitution*. Oxford: Oxford University Press, pp. 5–24.

Kangas, Olli and Palme, Joakim (eds.). 2005. *Social Policy and Economic Development in the Nordic Countries*. Basingstoke: Palgrave Macmillan.

Karapin, Roger. 2002. "Far-Right Parties and the Construction of Immigration Issues in Germany," in Martin Schain, Aristide Zolberg, and Patrick Hossay (eds.), *Shadows over Europe: The Development and Impact of the Extreme Right in Western Europe*. Basingstoke: Palgrave Macmillan, pp. 187–219.

Katzenstein, Peter. 1987. *Policy and Politics in West Germany: The Growth of a Semisovereign State*. Philadelphia: Temple University Press.

Kautto, Mikko. 2000. *Two of a Kind? Economic Crisis, Policy Responses and Well-Being during the 1990s in Sweden and Finland* (SOU 2000:83). Stockholm: Ministry of Health and Social Affairs.

Kautto, Mikko, Fritzell, Johan, Hvinden, Bjørn, Kvist, Jon, and Uusitalo, Hannu (eds.). 2001. *Nordic Welfare States in the European Context*. London: Routledge.

Kavanagh, Dennis and Butler, David. 2005. *The British Election of 2005*. Basingstoke: Palgrave Macmillan.

Kennedy-Brenner, Carliene. 1979. *Foreign Workers and Immigration Policy: The Case of France*. Paris: OECD.

King, Anthony. 2002. "Tony Blair's First Term," in Anthony King (ed.), *Britain at the Polls, 2001*. New York: Chatham House Publishers, pp. 1–44.

King, Desmond. 1995. *Actively Seeking Work? The Politics of Unemployment and Welfare Policy in the United States and Great Britain*. Chicago: University of Chicago Press.

King, Desmond. 1999. *In the Name of Liberalism: Illiberal Social Policy in the USA and Britain*. Oxford: Oxford University Press.

Klekowski von Koppenfels, Amanda. 2002. "The Decline of Privilege: The Legal Background to the Migration of Ethnic Germans," in David Rock and Stefan Wolff (eds.), *Coming Home to Germany? The Integration of Ethnic Germans from Central and Eastern Europe in the Federal Republic*. New York: Berghahn Books, pp. 102–18.

Klekowski von Koppenfels, Amanda. 2003. "Who Organizes? The Political Opportunity Structure of Co-Ethnic Migrant Mobilization," in Rainer Münz and Rainer Ohliger (eds.), *Diasporas and Ethnic Migrants: Germany, Israel and Post-Soviet Successor States in Comparative Perspective*. London: Frank Cass, pp. 305–23.

Klusmeyer, Douglas B. and Papademetriou, Demetrios G. 2009. *Immigration Policy in the Federal Republic of Germany: Negotiating Membership and Remaking the Nation*. New York: Berghahn Books.

Knapp, Andrew. 2004. *Parties and the Party System in France: A Disconnected Democracy?* Basingstoke: Palgrave Macmillan.

Kondo, Atsushi (ed.) 2001. *Citizenship in a Global World: Comparing Citizenship Rights for Aliens*. Basingstoke: Palgrave.

Koopmans, Ruud and Statham, Paul (eds.). 2000. *Challenging Immigration and Ethnic Relations Politics*. Oxford: Oxford University Press.

Koopmans, Ruud, Statham, Paul, Giugni, Marco, and Passy, Florence. 2005. *Contested Citizenship: Immigration and Cultural Diversity in Europe*. Minneapolis: University of Minnesota Press.

Korpi, Walter. 1980. "Social Policy and Distributional Conflict in the Capitalist Democracies: A Preliminary Comparative Framework," *West European Politics* 3 (3), 296–316.

Korpi, Walter. 1995. "The Development of Social Citizenship in France Since 1930: Comparative Perspectives," in *Comparing Social Welfare Systems in Europe*. Paris: MIRE, Ministry of Employment and Solidarity, pp. 9–47.

Korpi, Walter. 2002. *Velfærdsstat og socialt medborgerskab. Danmark i et komparativt perspektiv, 1930–1995*. Århus: Magtudredningen.

Korpi, Walter and Palme, Joakim. 1998. "The Paradox of Redistribution and the Strategy of Equality: Welfare State Institutions, Inequality and Poverty in Western Countries," *American Sociological Review* 63 (5), 661–87.

Koslowski, Rey. 1998. "European Union Migration Regimes, Established and Emergent," in Christian Joppke (ed.), *Challenge to the Nation-State: Immigration in Western Europe and the United States*. Oxford: Oxford University Press, pp. 153–88.

Ku, Leighton and Papademetriou, Demetrios G. 2007. "Access to Health Care and Health Insurance: Immigrants and Immigration Reform," in Michael Fix (ed.), *Securing the Future: US Immigrant Integration Policy*. Washington, DC: Migration Policy Institute, pp. 83–106.

Kurthen, Hermann. 1998. "Fiscal Impacts of Immigration on the American and German Welfare States," in Hermann Kurthen, Jürgen Fijalkowski, and Gert G. Wagner (eds.), *Immigration, Citizenship and the Welfare State in Germany and the United States, Part A: Immigrant Incorporation*. Stamford, CT: JAI Press, pp. 175–211.

Lahav, Gallya. 2004. *Immigration and Politics in the New Europe: Reinventing Borders*. Cambridge: Cambridge University Press.

Law, Ian. 1996. *Racism, Ethnicity and Social Policy*. London: Prentice-Hall/Harvester Wheatsheaf.

Law, Ian. 2009. "Racism, Ethnicity, Migration and Social Security," in Jane Millar (ed.), *Understanding Social Security* (2nd edn.). Bristol: Policy Press, pp. 75–92.

Layton-Henry, Zig. 1985. "Great Britain," in Tomas Hammar (ed.), *European Immigration Policy: A Comparative Study*. Cambridge: Cambridge University Press, pp. 89–126.

Layton-Henry, Zig (ed.). 1990. *The Political Rights of Immigrant Workers in Western Europe*. London: Sage.

Layton-Henry, Zig. 1992. *The Politics of Immigration*. Oxford: Blackwell.

Leal, David L., Barreto, Matt A., Lee, Jongho, and de la Garza, Rodolfo O. 2005. "The Latino Vote in the 2004 Election," *PS, Political Science and Politics* 38 (1), 41–9 <www.apsanet.org>, accessed December 2, 2008.

Legifrance. 2003. Loi n° 2003-1119 du 26 novembre 2003 relative à la maîtrise de l'immigration, au séjour des étrangers en France et à la nationalité, <www.legifrance.gouv.fr>, accessed December 19, 2003.

Legifrance. 2007. Loi n° 2007-1631 du 20 novembre 2007 relative à la maîtrise de l'immigration, à l'intégration et à l'asile <www.legifrance.gouv.fr>, accessed December 12, 2010.

Leibfried, Stephan. 1992. "Towards a European Welfare State? On Integrating Poverty Regimes into the European Community," in Zsuzsa Ferge and Jon Eivind Kolberg (eds.), *Social Policy in a Changing Europe*. Frankfurt: Campus Verlag, pp. 245–79.

Lenoir, Rémi. 1991. "Family Policy in France since 1938," in John S. Ambler (ed.), *The French Welfare State: Surviving Social and Ideological Change*. New York: New York University Press, pp. 144–86.

Lester, Anthony and Beattie, Kate. 2007. "Human Rights and the British Constitution," in Jeffrey Jowell and Dawn Oliver (eds.), *The Changing Constitution*. Oxford: Oxford University Press, pp. 59–83.

Levy, Daniel. 2002. "Integrating Ethnic Germans in West Germany: The Early Postwar Period," in David Rock and Stefan Wolff (eds.), *Coming Home to Germany? The Integration of Ethnic Germans from Central and Eastern Europe in the Federal Republic*. New York: Berghahn Books, pp. 19–37.

Levy, Jonah D. 1999. *Tocqueville's Revenge: State, Society and Economy in Contemporary France*. Cambridge, MA: Harvard University Press.

Levy, Jonah D. 2000. "France: Directing Adjustment?" in Fritz Scharpf and Vivien A. Schmidt (eds.), *Welfare and Work in the Open Economy, Vol. II, Diverse Responses to Common Challenges*. Oxford: Oxford University Press, pp. 308–50.

Levy, Jonah D. 2005. "Redeploying the State: Liberalization and Social Policy in France," in Wolfgang Streeck and Kathleen Thelen (eds.), *Beyond Continuity: Institutional Change in Advanced Political Economies*. Oxford: Oxford University Press, pp. 103–26.

Lieberman, Robert C. 2005. *Shaping Race Policy*. Princeton: Princeton University Press.

LIS. Luxembourg Income Study Database <www.lisdatacenter.org>.

Lister, Ruth. 1991. "Social Security in the 1980s," *Social Policy and Administration* 25 (2), 91–107.

Lochak, Danièle. 1992. "Discrimination against Foreigners under French Law," in Donald L. Horowitz and Gerard Noiriel (eds.), *Immigrants in Two Democracies: French and American Experiences*. New York: New York University Press, pp. 391–410.

Loescher, Gil and Scanlan, John A. 1986. *Calculated Kindness: Refugees and America's Half-Open Door, 1945 to the Present*. New York: Free Press.

Lov om integration af udlændinge i Danmark, nr. 474 af 1. juli 1998.

Luedtke, Adam. 2006. "The European Union Dimension: Supranational Integration, Free Movement of Persons, and Immigration Politics," in Craig A. Parsons and Timothy M. Smeeding (eds.), *Immigration and the Transformation of Europe*. Cambridge: Cambridge University Press, pp. 419–41.

Lundborg, Per. 2009. "The Dimensions and Effects of EU Migration in Sweden," in Béla Galgóczi, Janine Leschke, and Andrew Watt (eds.), *EU Labour Migration since Enlargement: Trends, Impacts and Policies*. Farnham: Ashgate, pp. 69–86.

Lundh, Christer and Ohlsson, Rolf. 1999. *Från arbetskraftsimport till flyktinginvandring* (2nd edn.). Stockholm: SNS.

Macdonald, Ian A. 1987. *Immigration Law and Practice in the United Kingdom* (2nd edn.). London: Butterworths.

Macdonald, Ian A. and Webber, Frances (eds.). 2005. *Immigration Law and Practice in the United Kingdom* (6th edn.). London: LexisNexis Butterworths.

Macridis, Roy C. 1987. "Politics of France," in Roy C. Macridis (ed.), *Modern Political Systems: Europe* (6th edn.). Englewood Cliffs, NJ: Prentice Hall, pp. 75–159.

Macridis, Roy C. 1990. "Politics of France," in Roy C. Macridis (ed.), *Modern Political Systems: Europe* (7th edn.). Englewood Cliffs, NJ: Prentice Hall, pp. 65–135.

Madeley, John T. S. 2003. "The Swedish Model Is Dead, Long Live the Swedish Model: The 2002 Swedish Election," *West European Politics* 26 (2), 165–73.

Mandin, Christelle and Palier, Bruno. 2005. "The Politics of Pension Reform in France: The End of Exceptionalism?" in Giuliano Bonoli and Toshimitsu Shinkawa (eds.), *Ageing and Pension Reform around the World*. Northampton, MA: Edward Elgar, pp. 74–93.

Mangen, Steen. 1991. "Social Policy, the Radical Right and the German Welfare State," in Howard Glennerster and James Midgley (eds.), *The Radical Right and the Welfare State*. Hemel Hempstead: Harvester Wheatsheaf, pp. 100–23.

Manow, Philip. 2005. "Germany: Cooperative Federalism and the Overgrazing of the Fiscal Commons," in Herbert Obinger, Stephan Leibfried, and Francis G. Castles (eds.), *Federalism and the Welfare State*. Cambridge: Cambridge University Press, pp. 222–62.

Manow, Philip. 2010. "Trajectories of Fiscal Adjustment in Bismarckian Welfare Systems," in Bruno Palier (ed.), *A Long Goodbye to Bismarck? The Politics of Welfare Reform in Continental Europe*. Amsterdam: Amsterdam University Press, pp. 279–99.

Marshall, Barbara. 2000. *The New Germany and Migration in Europe*. Manchester: Manchester University Press.

Marshall, T. H. 1950. *Citizenship and Social Class*. Cambridge: Cambridge University Press.

Martin, Claude. 2010. "Feminization of Poverty in France: A Latent Issue," in Gertrude Schaffner Goldberg (ed.), *Poor Women in Rich Countries*. New York: Oxford University Press, pp. 61–93.

Martin, Patricia P. 2007. "Hispanics, Social Security and Supplemental Security Income," *Social Security Bulletin* 67 (2), 73–100.

Maschke, Michael. 2003. "Immigrants between Labour Market and Poverty," in Peter Krause, Gerhard Bäcker, and Walter Hanesch (eds.), *Combating Poverty in Europe: The German Welfare Regime in Practice*. Aldershot: Ashgate, pp. 223–45.

Massot, Jean. 1990. "L'immigré et sa famille: le regroupement familial," in Elie Alfandari (ed.) *Immigration et protection sociale*. Paris: Sirey, pp. 81–9.

Mau, Steffen and Burkhardt, Christoph. 2009. "Migration and Welfare State Solidarity in Western Europe," *Journal of European Social Policy* 19 (3), 213–29.

McKay, Stephen. 2009. "Reforming Pensions: Investing in the Future," in Jane Millar (ed.), *Understanding Social Security*. Bristol: Policy Press, pp. 171–91.

McKay, Stephen and Rowlingson, Karen. 1999. *Social Security in Britain*. Basingstoke: Macmillan.

Meguid, Bonnie M. 2005. "Competition between Unequals: The Role of Mainstream Party Strategy in Niche Party Success," *American Political Science Review* 99 (3), 347–59.

Meguid, Bonnie M. 2008. *Party Competition between Unequals*. New York: Cambridge University Press.

Melnick, R. Shep. 1994. *Between the Lines: Interpreting Welfare Rights*. Washington, DC: Brookings Institution.

Menz, Georg. 2006. "'Useful' *Gastarbeiter*, Burdensome Asylum Seekers, and the Second Wave of Welfare Retrenchment: Exploring the Nexus between Migration and the Welfare State," in Craig A. Parsons and Timothy M. Smeeding (eds.), *Immigration and the Transformation of Europe*. Cambridge: Cambridge University Press, pp. 393–418.

Menz, Georg. 2009. *The Political Economy of Managed Migration*. Oxford: Oxford University Press.

Messina, Anthony M. 1989. *Race and Party Competition in Britain*. Oxford: Clarendon Press.

Messina, Anthony M. 2007. *The Logics and Politics of Post-WWII Migration to Western Europe*. Cambridge: Cambridge University Press.

Messu, Michel. 1999. "Solidarism and Familialism: The Influence of Ideological Conceptions on the Formation of French Social Protection," in Dennis Bourget and Bruno Palier (eds.), *Comparing Social Welfare Systems in Nordic Europe and France*. Paris: MIRE-DREES (Centre of Research, Evaluation Studies and Statistics), Ministry of Employment and Solidarity, pp. 113–25.

MFII. 2003a. *Vejledning om ydelser efter integrationsloven m.m.* 2003-06-30. Copenhagen: Ministeriet for flygtninge, indvandrere og integration <www.inm.dk>, accessed January 15, 2004.

MFII. 2003b. "Aftale mellem regeringspartierne og Dansk Folkeparti om udlændingelovgivning og indfødsret." Copenhagen: Ministeriet for flygtninge, indvandrere og integration <www.inm.dk>, accessed January 29, 2004.

MFII. 2003–4. *Forslag til Lov om ændring af indfødsretsloven*. Copenhagen: Ministeriet for flygtninge, indvandrere og integration, j.nr. 2003/300–36 <www.inm.dk>, accessed May 18, 2004.

MFII. 2004. *Udlændinge- og integrationspolitikken i Danmark og udvalgte lande—Baggrundsrapport*. Copenhagen: Ministeriet for flygtninge, indvandrere og integration <www.inm.dk>, accessed March 11, 2004.

MFII. 2005. "Aftale om 'En ny chance til alle.'" Copenhagen: Ministeriet for flygtninge, indvandrere og integration <www.inm.dk>, accessed July 18, 2005.

MFII. 2008. "Nye retningslinjer for meddelelse af dansk indfødsret træder i kraft 10. november 2008." Copenhagen: Ministeriet for flygtninge, indvandrere og integration <www.inm.dk/da-dk>, accessed December 9, 2008.

MFII. 2010. "Aftale mellem regeringen og Dansk Folkeparti, 15. marts 2010. Nye relger for at få permanent opholdstilladelse og serviceeftersyn af udlændinge- og integrationspolitikken" <www.nyidanmark.dk/da-dk/nyheder>, accessed March 16, 2010.

Millar, Jane (ed.). 2003a. *Understanding Social Security*. Bristol: Policy Press.

Millar, Jane. 2003b. "From Wage Replacement to Wage Supplement: Benefits and Tax Credits," in Jane Millar (ed.), *Understanding Social Security*. Bristol: Policy Press, pp. 123–43.

Millar, Jane. 2009. "Tax Credits," in Jane Millar (ed.), *Understanding Social Security* (2nd edn.). Bristol: Policy Press, pp. 233–51.

Miller, Mark J. and Martin, Philip L. 1982. *Administering Foreign-Worker Programs*. Lexington, MA: Lexington Books.

Minces, Juliette. 1973. *Les travailleurs étrangers en France*. Paris: Éditions du Seuil.

Minderhoud, Paul E. 1999. "Asylum Seekers and Access to Social Security: Recent Developments in The Netherlands, United Kingdom, Germany and Belgium," in Alice Bloch and Carl Levy (eds.), *Refugees, Citizenship and Social Policy in Europe*. Basingstoke: Macmillan, pp. 132–48.

Minkenberg, Michael. 2003. "The Politics of Citizenship in the New Republic," *West European Politics* 26 (4), 219–40.

MIPEX. 2011. *Migrant Integration Policy Index III* <www.mipex.eu>, accessed May 7, 2011.

MIRE. 1998. *Glossaire bilingue de la protection sociale*. Vol. 1: *Les termes français*. Paris: MIRE, Ministry of Employment and Solidarity.

MISSOC. 2007. *Social Protection in the Member States of the European Union, of the European Economic Area and in Switzerland*, Comparative Tables, Part 8: Finland, Sweden, United Kingdom, situation on January 1, 2007, <http://ec.europa.eu/employment_social/social_protection/missoc_tables_en.htm >, accessed March 23, 2009.

Mitchell, Deborah. 1991. *Income Transfers in Ten Welfare States*. Aldershot: Avebury.

MN. 2002–4. *Migration News* 9–11 <http://migration.ucdavis.edu/mn>, accessed May 23, 2006.

MN. 2006. *Migration News* 13 (3) <http://migration.ucdavis.edu/mn>, accessed November 14, 2009.

MN. 2007. *Migration News* 14 (3) <http://migration.ucdavis.edu/mn>, accessed December 11, 2007.

MN. 2008. *Migration News* 15 (2) <http://migration.ucdavis.edu/mn>, accessed February 3, 2010.

Modood, Tariq, Berthoud, Richard G., Lakey, Jane, Nazroo, James, Smith, Patten, Virdee, Satnam, and Beishon, Sharon. 1997. *Ethnic Minorities in Britain: Diversity and Disadvantage*. London: Policy Studies Institute.

Monéger, Françoise. 1990. "L'immigré et sa famille: l'incidence du statut personnel sur la protection sociale des immigrés," in Elie Alfandari (ed.), *Immigration et protection sociale*. Paris: Sirey.

Money, Jeanette. 1999. *Fences and Neighbors: The Political Geography of Immigration Control*. Ithaca: Cornell University Press.

Montanari, Ingalill. 1995. "Harmonization of Social Policies and Social Regulation in the European Community," *European Journal of Political Research* 27 (1), 21–45.

Montanari, Ingalill, Nelson, Kenneth, and Palme, Joakim. 2008. "Towards a European Social Model? Trends in Social Insurance among EU Countries 1980–2000," *European Societies* 10 (5), 787–810.

Morel, Nathalie. 2006. "Providing Coverage against New Social Risks in Bismarckian Welfare States: The Case of Long-Term Care," in Klaus Armingeon and Giuliano Bonoli (eds.), *The Politics of Post-Industrial Welfare States: Adapting Post-War Social Policies to New Social Risks*. London: Routledge, pp. 227–47.

Morel, Sylvie. 2004. "Workfare and *Insertion*: How the U.S. and French Models of Assistance Have Been Transformed," in Neil Gilbert and Antoine Parent (eds.), *Welfare Reform: A Comparative Assessment of the French and U.S. Experiences*. New Brunswick, NJ: Transaction Publishers, pp. 93–142.

Morissens, Ann. 2006a. "Immigrants' Socio-Economic Outcomes in Different Welfare States: How Do They Fare?" Ph.D. thesis, Department of Social Sciences, Roskilde University.

Morissens, Ann. 2006b. "Immigrants, Unemployment, and Europe's Varying Welfare Regimes," in Craig A. Parsons and Timothy M. Smeeding (eds.), *Immigration and the Transformation of Europe*. Cambridge: Cambridge University Press, pp. 172–99.

Morissens, Ann and Sainsbury, Diane. 2005. "Migrants' Social Rights, Ethnicity and Welfare Regimes," *Journal of Social Policy* 34 (4), 637–60.

Mörkenstam, Ulf. 2010. "Ekonomi, kultur och jämlikhet: Teman i svensk politik i invandrarfrågor decennierna efter andra världskriget," *Historisk tidskrift för Finland* 95 (4), 572–607.

Morris, Lydia. 1998. "Governing at a Distance: The Elaboration of Controls in British Immigration," *International Migration Review*, 32 (4), 949–73.

Morris, Lydia. 2002. *Managing Migration: Civic Stratification and Migrants' Rights*. London: Routledge.

Morris, Lydia. 2007. "New Labour's Community of Rights: Welfare, Immigration and Asylum," *Journal of Social Policy* 36 (1), 39–57.

MPI. 2004. "Global Data Center, United States: Estimates of the Net Number of Migrants." Washington, DC: Migration Policy Institute <www.migrationinformation.org>, accessed April 16, 2004.

Münz, Rainer and Ohliger, Rainer. 1998. "Long-Distance Citizens: Ethnic Germans and their Immigration to Germany," in Peter H. Schuck and Rainer Münz (eds.), *Paths to Inclusion: The Integration of Migrants in the United States and Germany*. New York: Berghahn Books, pp. 155–201.

Murray, Laura M. 1994. "*Einwanderungsland Bundesrepublik Deutschland*? Explaining the Evolving Positions of German Political Parties on Citizenship Policy," *German Politics and Society* 33, 23–56.

MV. 2009. Migrationsverket, tillståndsstatistik <www.migrationsverket.se>, accessed May 5, 2009.

Nannestad, Peter. 2004. "Immigration as a Challenge to the Danish Welfare State?" *European Journal of Political Economy* 20, 755–67.

ND. 1991. *Ny demokrati, partiprogram*. Stockholm: Ny Demokrati.

Nelson, Kenneth. 2008. "Minimum Income Protection and European Integration: Trends and Levels of Minimum Benefits in Comparative Perspective, 1990–2005," *International Journal of Health Services* 38 (1), 103–24.

Neuman, Gerald L. 1998. "Nationality Law in the United States and the Federal Republic of Germany: Structure and Current Problems," in Peter Schuck and Rainer Münz (eds.), *Paths to Inclusion: The Integration of Migrants in the United States and Germany*. New York: Berghahn Books, pp. 247–98.

Nielsen, Bodil Bjerg and Pihl, Louise. 1998. "På kanten af medborgerskabet—en analyse af dansk indvandrer/flygtningepolitik i ett medborgerskabsperspektiv." Master's thesis, Department of Political Science, University of Copenhagen.

Nielsen, Niels-Kenneth. 2004. "Social Transfers to Immigrants in Germany and Denmark," in Torben Tranæs and Klaus F. Zimmermann (eds.), *Migrants, Work, and the Welfare State*. Odense: University Press of Southern Denmark, pp. 245–84.

NOSOSKO. 2010. *Social tryghed i de nordiske lande 2008/09*. Copenhagen: Nordic Social Statistics Committee (NOSOSKO) <www.nososco-da.nom-nos.dk>, accessed July 28, 2011.

NS. 2007. Sarkozy, Nicolas. 2007. *Mon projet: Ensemble tout devient possible* <www.sarkozy.fr>, accessed May 7, 2007.

O'Connor, Karen and Epstein, Lee. 1988. "A Legal Voice for the Chicano Community: The Activities of the Mexican-American Legal Defense and Educational Fund, 1968–1982," in F. Chris Garcia (ed.), *Latinos and the Political System*. Notre Dame: University of Notre Dame Press, pp. 255–68.

OECD. 2004. *Trends in International Migration*. SOPEMI 2003. Paris: Organisation for Economic Development and Co-operation.

OECD. 2010. *International Migration Outlook*. Paris. Organisation for Economic Development and Co-operation <www.oecd-library.org>, accessed May 16, 2011.

OECD. 2011. *Employment Outlook 2011*. Paris: Organisation for Economic Development and Co-operation.

Offe, Claus. 1991. "Smooth Consolidation in the West German Welfare State: Structural Change, Fiscal Policies and Populist Politics," in Frances Fox Piven (ed.), *Labor Parties in Postindustrial Societies*. Cambridge: Polity Press, pp. 124–46.

Palier, Bruno. 2002. *Gouverner la sécurité sociale. Les réformes du système français de protection sociale depuis 1945*. Paris: Presses universitaires de France.

Palier, Bruno. 2005. *Gouverner la sécurité sociale. Les réformes du système français de protection sociale depuis 1945*. Paris: Quadrige/Presses universitaires de France.

Palier, Bruno. 2006. "The Long Goodbye to Bismarck? Changes in the French Welfare State," in Pepper D. Culpepper, Peter A. Hall, and Bruno Palier (eds.), *Changing France: The Politics That Markets Make*. Basingstoke: Palgrave Macmillan, pp. 107–28.

Palier, Bruno. 2010. "The Dualizations of the French Welfare System," in Bruno Palier (ed.), *A Long Goodbye to Bismarck? The Politics of Welfare Reform in Continental Europe*. Amsterdam: Amsterdam University Press, pp. 73–99.

Palier, Bruno and Thelen, Kathleen. 2010. "Institutionalizing Dualism: Complementarities and Change in France and Germany," *Politics & Society* 38 (1), 119–48.

Palme, Joakim. 1990. *Pension Rights in Welfare Capitalism: The Development of Old-Age Pensions in 18 OECD Countries 1930 to 1985*. Stockholm: Swedish Institute for Social Research.

Papadopoulos, Theodoros. 2011. "Immigration and the Variety of Migrant Integration Regimes in the European Union," in Emma Carmel, Alfio Cerami, and Theodoros Papadopoulos (eds.), *Migration and Welfare in the New Europe: Social Protection and the Challenges of Integration*. Bristol: Policy Press, pp. 23–47.

Parrott, Thomas M., Kennedy, Lenna D., and Scott, Charles G. 1998. "Noncitizens and the Supplemental Security Income Program," *Social Security Bulletin* 61 (4), 3–32.

Pavetti, Ladonna A. 2001. "Welfare Policy in Transition: Redefining the Social Contract for Poor Citizen Families and for Immigrants," in Sheldon H. Danziger and Robert H. Haveman (eds.), *Understanding Poverty*. New York: Russell Sage Foundation, pp. 229–77.

Pedersen, Søren. 1999. "Migration to and from Denmark during the Period 1960–97," in David Coleman and Eskil Wadensjö, with contributions by Bent Jensen and Søren Pedersen, *Immigration to Denmark*. Århus: Rockwool Foundation Research Unit/Aarhus University Press, pp. 148–90.

Pedersen, Søren. 2000. "Overførselsindkomster til indvandrerne," in Gunnar Viby Mogensen and Poul Chr. Matthiessen (eds.), *Integration i Danmark omkring årtusindskiftet*. Århus: Aarhus Universitetsforlag, pp. 160–207.

Pedraza-Bailey, Silvia. 1985. *Political and Economic Migrants in America: Cubans and Mexicans*. Austin: University of Texas Press.

Perlmutter, Ted. 1996. "Bringing Parties Back In: Comments on 'Modes of Immigration Politics in Liberal Democratic Societies'," *International Migration Review* 30, 375–88.

Perlmutter, Ted. 2002. "The Politics of Restriction: The Effect of Xenophobic Parties on Italian Immigration Policy and German Asylum Policy," in Martin Schain, Aristide Zolberg, and Patrick Hossay (eds.), *Shadows over Europe: The Development and Impact of the Extreme Right in Western Europe*. Basingstoke: Palgrave Macmillan, pp. 269–98.

Phillips, Anne. 1995. *The Politics of Presence*. Oxford: Clarendon Press.

Phillips, Coretta. 2005. "Ethnic Inequalities under New Labour: Progress or Entrenchment?" in John Hills and Kitty Stewart (eds.), *A More Equal Society? New Labour, Poverty, Inequality and Exclusion*. Bristol: Policy Press, pp. 189–208.

Pierson, Paul. 1994. *Dismantling the Welfare State?* Cambridge: Cambridge University Press.

Pierson, Paul (ed.). 2001. *The New Politics of the Welfare State*. Oxford: Oxford University Press.

Platt, Lucinda. 2003. "Social Security in a Multi-Ethnic Society," in Jane Millar (ed.), *Understanding Social Security*. Bristol: Policy Press, pp. 255–76.

Platt, Lucinda. 2007. "Child Poverty, Employment and Ethnicity in the UK: The Role and Limitations of Policy," *European Societies* 9 (2), 175–99.

Powell, Martin. 1999. "Introduction," in Martin Powel (ed.), *New Labour, New Welfare State? The "Third Way" in British Social Policy*. Bristol: Policy Press, pp. 1–28.

Prop. 1968:142. *Angående riktlinjer för utlänningspolitiken m.m.*

Prop. 1975/76:26. *Om riktlinjer för invandrar- och minoritetspolitiken m.m.*

Prop. 1987/88:80. *Om bistånd åt asylsökande, m.m.*

Prop. 1990/91:195. *Om aktiv flykting- och immigrationspolitik m m.*

Prop. 1992/93:50. *Om åtgärder för att stabilisera den svenska ekonomin.*

Prop. 1993/94:94. *Mottagande av asylsökande m.m.*

Prop. 1994/95:179. *Ändringar i utlänningslagen.*

Prop. 1997/98:16. *Sverige, framtiden och mångfalden: från invandrarpolitik till integrationspolitik.*

Prop. 2007/08:147. *Nya regler för arbetskraftsinvandring.*

References

Prop. 2009/10:60. *Nyanlända invandrares arbetsmarknadsetablering—egenansvar med professionellt stöd.*

Prop. 2009/10:77. *Försörjningskrav vid anhöriginvandring.*

PS. 2008. *A Detailed Guide to State Pensions for Advisers and Others.* The Pension Service, The Department for Work and Pensions <www.thepensionservice.gov.uk/pdf/np46/np46sept08.pdf>, accessed March 25, 2009.

Reimers, David M. 1985. *Still the Golden Door: The Third World Comes to America.* New York: Columbia University Press.

Ridge, Tess. 2009. "Benefiting Children? The Challenge of Social Security Support for Children," in Jane Millar (ed.), *Understanding Social Security* (2nd edn.). Bristol: Policy Press, pp. 151–69.

RK. 2011. Regeringskansliet, "Historisk överenskommelse om migrationspolitiken" <www.regeringen.se/sb/d/9863/a/162226>, accessed September 12, 2011.

Robertson, David. 1998. *Judicial Discretion in the House of Lords.* Oxford: Oxford University Press.

Rocaboy, Yvon. 1999. "The Decentralization of Welfare Policy in France: An Economic Perspective," in Dennis Bourget and Bruno Palier (eds.), *Comparing Social Welfare Systems in Nordic Europe and France.* Paris: MIRE-DREES (Centre of Research, Studies and Statistics), Ministry of Employment and Solidarity, pp. 541–60.

Rose, E. J. B. et al. 1969. *Colour and Citizenship: A Report on Race Relations in Britain.* London: Oxford University Press/ Institute of Race Relations.

RP. *Riksdagens protokoll 2000/2001: 70.* Minutes of the Swedish parliament.

S 269. US Senate, 194th Congress, "S 269, The Immigrant Control and Financial Responsibility Act of 1995." Full Text of Bills. Available from: LexisNexis Congressional Online Service. Bethesda, MD: Congressional Information Service.

Safran, William. 1998. *The French Polity* (5th edn.). New York: Longman.

Saggar, Shamit. 2003. "Immigration and the Politics of Public Opinion," in Sarah Spencer (ed.), *The Politics of Migration: Managing Opportunity, Conflict and Change.* Oxford: Blackwell Publishing, pp. 178–94.

Sainsbury, Diane. 1996. *Gender, Equality and Welfare States.* Cambridge: Cambridge University Press.

Sainsbury, Diane. 2005. "The Politics of Inclusion and Exclusion: Denmark and Sweden," Paper presented at the XIV Nordic Political Science Association Conference, Reykjavik, Iceland, August 11–13, 2005.

Sainsbury, Diane. 2006. "Immigrants' Social Rights in Comparative Perspective: Welfare Regimes, Forms of Immigration and Immigration Policy Regimes," *Journal of European Social Policy* 16 (3), 229–44.

Sainsbury, Diane and Morissens, Ann. 2002. "Poverty in Europe in the Mid-1990s: The Effectiveness of Means-Tested Benefits," *Journal of European Social Policy* 12 (4), 293–306.

Sainsbury, Diane and Morissens, Ann. 2010. "Sweden: The Feminization of Poverty?" in Gertrude Schaffner Goldberg (ed.), *Poor Women in Rich Countries.* New York: Oxford University Press, pp. 28–60.

Sainsbury, Diane and Songur, Welat. 2001. "Invandrarna och det svenska trygghetssystemet i jämförande belysning," projektskiss.

Sales, Rosemary. 2007. *Understanding Immigration and Refugee Policy*. Bristol: Policy Press.

SAUS. Various years. *Statistical Abstract of the United States*. Washington, DC: Bureau of the Census.

SBD. 2009. Statistisches Bundesamt Deutschland, "Ausländische Bevölkerung in Deutschland nach aufenthaltsrechtlichem Status am 31.12.2008," *Bevölkerung und Erwerbstätigkeit: Ausländische Bevölkerung Ergebnisse des Ausländerzentralregisters*, version 1.07.2009 <www.destatis.de>, accessed December 11, 2009.

Schain, Martin A. 1985. "Immigrants and Politics in France," in John Ambler (ed.), *The French Socialist Experiment*. Philadelphia: Institute for the Study of Human Issues, pp. 166–90.

Schain, Martin A. 1996. "The Immigration Debate and the National Front," in John T. S. Keller and Martin A. Schain (eds.), *Chirac's Challenge: Liberalization, Europeanization and Malaise in France*. Basingstoke: Macmillan, pp. 169–97.

Schain, Martin A. 1999. "Minorities and Immigrant Incorporation in France," in Christian Joppke and Steven Lukes (eds.), *Multicultural Questions*. Oxford: Oxford University Press, pp. 199–223.

Schain, Martin A. 2007. "The Extreme-Right and Immigration Policy Making: Measuring Direct and Indirect Effects," in Virginie Guiraudon and Gallya Lahav (eds.), *Immigration Policy in Europe: The Politics of Control*. London: Routledge, pp. 70–89.

Schain, Martin A. 2008. *The Politics of Immigration in France, Britain and the United States: A Comparative Study*. New York: Palgrave Macmillan.

Schain, Martin A., Zolberg, Aristide and Hossay, Patrick (eds.). 2002. *Shadows over Europe: The Development and Impact of the Extreme Right in Western Europe*. Basingstoke: Palgrave Macmillan.

Scharpf, Fritz W. 1988. "The Joint-Decision Trap: Lessons from German Federalism and European Integration," *Public Administration* 16 (3), 239–78.

Scharpf, Fritz W. and Schmidt, Vivien A. (eds.). 2000. *Welfare and Work in the Open Economy, Vol. I. From Vulnerability to Competitiveness*. Oxford: Oxford University Press.

Schierup, Carl-Ulrik, Hansen, Peo and Castles, Stephen. 2006. *Migration, Citizenship and the European Welfare State*. Oxford: Oxford University Press.

Schindler, Peter. 1999. *Datenhandbuch zur Geschichte des Deutschen Bundestages 1949 bis 1999*, Band I. Baden-Baden: Nomos Verlagsgesellschaft.

Schmidt, Manfred. 2003. *Political Institutions in the Federal Republic of Germany*. Oxford: Oxford University Press.

Schmidt, Vivien A. 1990. *Democratizing France: The Political and Administrative History of Decentralization*. Cambridge: Cambridge University Press.

Schuck, Peter H. 1998a. "The Re-Evaluation of American Citizenship," in Christian Joppke (ed.), *Challenge to the Nation-State: Immigration in Western Europe and the United States*. Oxford: Oxford University Press, pp. 191–230.

Schuck, Peter H. 1998b. *Citizens, Strangers and In-Betweens: Essays on Immigration and Citizenship*. Boulder: Westview Press.

Schuck, Peter H. and Münz, Rainer (eds.). 1998. *Paths to Inclusion: The Integration of Migrants in the United States and Germany*. Oxford: Berghahn Books.

References

Schultz-Nielsen, Marie Louise. 2000. "Integrationen på arbejdsmarkedet—og de sam-fundsøkonomiske forholds betydning," in Gunnar Viby Mogensen and Poul Chr. Matthiessen (eds.), *Integration i Danmark omkring årtusindskiftet*. Århus: Rockwool Foundation Research Unit/Aarhus Universitetsforlag, pp. 96–126.

Schuster, Liza. 2003. *The Use and Abuse of Political Asylum in Britain and Germany*. London: Frank Cass.

Schwarz, David (ed.). 1966. *Svenska minoriteter*. Stockholm: Aldus/Bonniers.

Schwarz, David. 1971. *Svensk invandrar- och minoritetspolitik 1945–1968*. Stockholm: Prisma.

SD. 2005. *Sverigedemokraternas principprogram 2005*. Antaget av Riksårsmötet den 4 maj 2003. Ändringar av programmet antogs vid riksårsmötet den 8 maj 2005 <http://sverigedemokraterna.se/vara-asikter/sverigedemokraternasprincipprogram-2005>, accessed May 6, 2010.

SD. 2007. *Invandringspolitiskt program*. Antaget vid Riksårsmötet den 19 maj 2007 <http://sverigedemokraterna.se/vara-asikter/invandringspolitisk-program>, accessed April 19, 2011.

SD. 2010. *99 förslag för ett bättre Sverige. Sverigedemokraternas kontrakt med väljarna 2010–2014*. Stockholm 2010-09-02 <http://sverigedemokraterna.se/files/2010709/valmani-fest_2010.pdf> accessed April 19, 2011.

Seddon, Duran, Fitzpatrick, Pamela, and Chatwin, Mick. 2002. *Migration and Social Security Handbook*. London: Child Poverty Action Group.

Seeleib-Kaiser, Martin (ed.). 2008. *Welfare State Transformations: Comparative Perspectives*. Basingstoke: Palgrave Macmillan.

SFS. 2008:884. Svensk författningssamling. *Lag om ändring i utlänningslagen (2005:716)*.

Silburn, Richard and Becker, Saul. 2009. "Life beyond Work? Safety Nets and 'Security for Those Who Cannot' Work," in Jane Millar (ed.), *Understanding Social Security* (2nd edn.). Bristol: Policy Press, pp. 55–73.

Silver, Hilary. 1994. "Social Exclusion and Social Solidarity: Three Paradigms," *International Labour Review* 133 (5–6), 531–78.

Silverman, Maxim. 1992. *Deconstructing the Nation: Immigration, Racism and Citizenship in Modern France*. New York: Routledge.

Södergran, Lena. 2000. *Svensk invandrarpolitik och integrationspolitik. En fråga om jämlik-het, demokrati och mänskliga rättigheter*. Umeå: Department of Sociology, Umeå University.

Soininen, Maritta. 1992. *Det kommunala flyktingmottagandet: genomförande och organisa-tion*. Stockholm: Centre for Research in International Migration and Ethnic Relations (CEIFO).

Solomos, John. 2003. *Race and Racism in Britain*. Basingstoke: Palgrave Macmillan.

Solomos, John and Back, Les. 1993. "Migration and the Politics of Race," in Patrick Dunleavy, Andrew Gamble, Ian Holliday, and Gillian Peele (eds.), *Developments in British Politics 4*. Basingstoke: Macmillan, pp. 321–31.

Somerville, Will. 2007. *Immigration under New Labour*. Bristol: Policy Press.

Songur, Welat. 2002. *Välfärdsstaten, sociala rättigheter och invandrarnas maktresurser. En jämförande studie om äldre invandrare från Mellanöstern i Stockholm, London och Berlin*. Stockholm: Department of Political Science, University of Stockholm.

SOU 1967:18. *Invandringen. Problematik och handläggning.* Utlänningsutredningens betänkande II. Stockholm: Ministry of Internal Affairs.

SOU 1974:69. *Invandrarna och minoriteterna.* Stockholm: Ministry of Labor Affairs.

SOU 1975:15 *Kommunal rösträtt för invandrare.* Stockholm: Ministry of Municipal Affairs.

SOU 1983:18. *Lag mot etnisk diskriminering i arbetslivet.* Stockhom: Ministry of Labor Affairs.

SOU 1984:11. *Rösträtt och medborgarskap. Invandrares och utlandssvenskars rösträtt.* Stockholm: Ministry of Justice.

SOU 1989:13. *Mångfald mot enfald. Slutrapport från kommissionen mot rasism och främlingsfientlighet.* Stockholm: Ministry of Labor Affairs.

SOU 1992:96. *Förbud mot etnisk diskriminering i arbetslivet.* Stockholm: Ministry of Cultural Affairs.

SOU 1992:133. *Mottagandet av asylsökande och flyktingar.* Stockholm: Ministry of Cultural Affairs.

SOU 1993:113. *Invandring och asyl i teori och praktik—en jämförelse mellan tolv länders politik.* Stockholm: Ministry of Cultural Affairs.

SOU 1994:33. *Vandelns betydelse i medborgarskapsärenden.* Stockholm: Ministry of Cultural Affairs.

SOU 1995:75. *Svensk flyktingpolitik i globalt perspektiv.* Stockholm: Ministry of Labor Affairs.

SOU 1996:55. *Sverige, framtiden och mångfald.* Stockholm: Ministry of Labor Affairs.

SOU 1999:34. *Svenskt medborgarskap.* Stockholm: Ministry of Cultural Affairs.

SOU 2000:41. *Välfärd, ofärd och ojämlikhet.* Stockholm: Ministry of Social Affairs.

SOU 2005:103. *Anhörigåterförening.* Stockholm: Ministry of Foreign Affairs.

SOU 2006:22. *En sammanhållen diskrimineringslagstiftning.* Stockholm: Ministry of Justice.

SOU 2008:114. *Försörjningskrav vid anhöriginvandring.* Stockholm: Ministry of Justice.

SOU 2009:19. *Aktiv väntan—asylsökande i Sverige.* Stockholm: Ministry of Justice.

SOU 2010:16. *Sverige för nyanlända. Värden, välfärdsstat, vardagsliv.* Stockholm: Ministry of Integration and Gender Equality.

SOU 2011:28. *Cirkulär migration och utveckling.* Stockholm: Ministry of Justice.

Soysal, Yasemin Nuhoglu. 1994. *Limits of Citizenship: Migrants and Postnational Membership in Europe.* Chicago: University of Chicago Press.

S-P. 2010. "Conditions particulières d'attribution aux étrangers du revenu de solidarité active (RSA)" <http://vosdroits.service-public.fr/particuliers/F15553.xhtml>, accessed January 20, 2010.

Spicker, Paul. 1991. "Solidarity," in Graham Room (ed.), *Towards a European Welfare State?* Bristol: SAUS Publications, pp. 17–37.

SS. 2007. *Ekonomiskt bistånd för inrikes och utrikes födda 1998–2005.* Stockholm: National Board of Social Welfare.

SSB. 1995. *Social Security Bulletin, Annual Statistical Supplement, 1995.* Washington, DC: Social Security Administration.

SSB. 2007. *Social Security Bulletin, Annual Statistical Supplement, 2007.* Washington, DC: Social Security Administration.

SSI. 2008. *SSI Annual Statistical Report, 2007*. Washington, DC: Social Security Administration <www.ssa.gov/policy/dpcs/statcomps/ssi_asr/2007/ssi_asr07.pdf>, accessed February 25, 2009.

SSPTW. 2010. *Social Security Programs throughout the World: Europe 2010*. Washington, DC and Geneva: Social Security Administration and the International Social Security Association <www.socialsecurity.gov/policy>, accessed August 25, 2010.

Statham, Paul. 2003. "Understanding Anti-Asylum Rhetoric: Restrictive Politics or Racist Publics?" *Political Quarterly* 74 (1), 163–77.

Statham, Paul and Geddes, Andrew. 2006. "Elites and the 'Organised Public': Who Drives British Immigration Politics and in Which Direction?" *West European Politics* 29 (2), 248–69.

Steck, Philippe, Rauber, Edith, Alfandari, Elie, and Chastand, Antoine. 1990. "L'immigré et sa famille: les prestations familiales des immigrés," in Elie Alfandari (ed.), *Immigration et protection sociale*. Paris: Sirey.

Stephens, John D. 1979. *The Transition from Capitalism to Socialism*. London: Macmillan.

Stewart, Kitty. 2007. "Equality and Social Justice," in Anthony Seldon (ed.), *Blair's Britain 1997–2007*. Cambridge: Cambridge University Press, pp. 408–35.

Stjernø, Steinar. 2005. *Solidarity in Europe: The History of an Idea*. Cambridge: Cambridge University Press.

Studlar, Donley T. 1978. "Policy Voting in Britain: The Colored Immigration Issue in the 1964, 1966 and 1970 General Elections," *American Political Science Review* 72 (1), 46–64.

Studlar, Donley T. 1993. "Ethnic Minority Groups, Agenda Setting, and Policy Borrowing in Britain," in Paula D. McClain (ed.), *Minority Group Influence: Agenda Setting, Formulation and Public Policy*. Westport, CT: Greenwood Press.

SV. 2007. *Barns omsorg 2005: Omsorgsformer för barn 1–12*. Stockholm: Swedish National Agency for Education <www.skolverket.se>, accessed January 28, 2008.

Taguieff, Pierre-André. 1996. "Un programme 'révolutionnaire'?" in Nonna Mayer and Pascal Perrineau (eds.), *Le Front national à découvert*. Paris: Presses de Sciences Po, pp. 195–227.

Taylor-Gooby, Peter (ed.). 2004. *New Risks, New Welfare*. Oxford: Oxford University Press.

Taylor-Gooby, Peter. 2005. "Is the Future American? Or, Can Left Politics Preserve European Welfare States from Erosion though Growing 'Racial' Diversity?" *Journal of Social Policy* 34 (4), 661–72.

Taylor-Gooby, Peter and Mitton, Lavinia. 2008. "Much Noise, Little Progress: The UK Experience of Privatization," in Daniel Béland and Brian Gran (eds.), *Public and Private Social Policy: Health and Pension Policies in a New Era*. Basingstoke: Palgrave Macmillan, pp. 147–68.

Thränhardt, Dietrich. 1999. "Germany's Immigration Policies and Politics," in Grete Brochmann and Tomas Hammar (eds.), *Mechanisms of Immigration Control: A Comparative Analysis of European Regulatory Policies*. Oxford: Berg, pp. 29–57.

Tichenor, Daniel J. 2002. *Dividing Lines: The Politics of Immigration Control in America*. Princeton: Princeton University Press.

Tienda, Marta and Liang, Zia. 1994. "Poverty and Immigration in Policy Perspective," in Sheldon H. Danziger, Gary D. Sandefur, and Daniel H. Weinberg (eds.), *Confronting Poverty*. New York: Russell Sage Foundation, pp. 330–64.

Titmuss, Richard M. 1968. *Commitment to Welfare*. London: Allen & Unwin.

Titmuss, Richard M. 1974. *Social Policy*. London: George Allen & Unwin.

Togeby, Lise. 1997. *Fremmedhed og fremmedhad i Danmark*. Copenhagen: Columbus.

Togeby, Lise. 1998. "Prejudice and Tolerance in a Period of Increasing Ethnic Diversity and Growing Unemployment: Denmark Since 1970," *Ethnic and Racial Studies* 21 (6), 1137–54.

Togeby, Lise. 2003. *Fra fremmedarbejdere til etniske minoriteter*. Århus: Aarhus Universitetsforlag.

UNHCR. 2007. *Statistical Yearbook 2005 Trends in Displacement, Protection and Solutions*. Geneva: UNHCR, The UN Refugee Agency <www.unhcr.or/statistics>, accessed December 19, 2007.

USDA. 1999. *Characteristics of Food Stamp Households: Fiscal Year 1997*. Washington, DC: Food and Nutrition Service, United States Department of Agriculture.

USDA. 2003. *Characteristics of Food Stamp Households: Fiscal Year 2001*. Washington, DC: Food and Nutrition Service, United States Department of Agriculture.

USDA. 2007. *Characteristics of Food Stamp Households: Fiscal Year 2006*. Washington, DC: Food and Nutrition Service, United States Department of Agriculture.

Vad Jønsson, Heidi and Petersen, Klaus. 2010. "Danmark: Den nationale velfærdsstat møder verden," in Grete Brochmann and Anniken Hagelund (eds.), *Velferdens grenser*. Olso: Universitetsforlaget, pp. 133–209.

Van Kersbergen, Kees. 1995. *Social Capitalism: A Study of Christian Democracy and the Welfare State*. London: Routlege.

Van Oorschot, Wim and Uunk, Wilfred. 2007. "Welfare Spending and the Public's Concern for Immigrants: Multilevel Evidence for Eighteen European Countries," *Comparative Politics* 40 (1), 63–92.

Verbunt, Gilles. 1985. "France," in Tomas Hammar (ed.), *European Immigration Policy*. Cambridge: Cambridge University Press, pp. 127–64.

Voges, Wolfgang, Frick, Joachim, and Büchel, Felix. 1998. "The Integration of Immigrants into West German Society: The Impact of Social Assistance," in Hermann Kurthen, Jürgen Fijalkowski, and Gert G. Wagner (eds.), *Immigration, Citizenship and the Welfare State in Germany and the United States, Part A: Immigrant Incorporation*. Stamford, CT: JAI Press, pp. 159–74.

Vourc'h, François, De Rudder, Véronique, and Tripier, Maryse. 1999. "Foreigners and Immigrants in the French Labour Market: Structural Inequality and Discrimination," in John Wrench, Andrea Rea, and Nouria Ouali (eds.), *Migrants, Ethnic Minorities and the Labour Market: Integration and Exclusion in Europe*. New York: St. Martin's Press, pp. 72–92.

Waters, Sarah. 2003. *Social Movements in France: Toward a New Citizenship*. Basingstoke: Palgrave Macmillan.

Weaver, R. Kent. 2000. *Ending Welfare as We Know It*. Washington, DC: Brookings Institution.

Weil, Patrick. 1991. "Immigration and the Rise of Racism in France: The Contradictions in Mitterrand's Policies," *French Politics and Society* 9 (3–4), 82–100.

Weil, Patrick. 2001a. "Access to Citizenship: A Comparison of Twenty-Five Nationality Laws," in T. Alexander Aleinikoff and Douglas Klusmeyer (eds.), *Citizenship Today: Global Perspectives and Practices*. Washington, DC: Carnegie Endowment for International Peace, pp. 17–35.

Weil, Patrick. 2001b. "The History of French Nationality: A Lesson for Europe," in Randall Hansen and Patrick Weil (eds.), *Towards a European Nationality: Citizenship, Immigration and Nationality Law in the EU*. Basingstoke: Palgrave Macmillan, pp. 52–68.

Weil, Patrick. 2004. *La France et ses étrangers* (2nd revised edn.). Paris: Gallimard.

Weil, Patrick and Spire, Alexis. 2006. "France," in Rainer Bauböck, Eva Ersbøll, Kees Groenendijk, and Harald Waldrauch (eds.), *Acquisition and Loss of Nationality: Policies and Trends in 15 European Countries. Volume 2. Country Analyses*. Amsterdam: Amsterdam University Press, pp. 187–211.

Wiesbrock, Anja. 2009. "Discrimination Instead of Integration? Integration Requirements for Immigrants in Denmark and Germany," in Elspeth Guild, Kess Groenendijk, and Sergio Carrera (eds.), *Illiberal Liberal States: Immigration, Citizenship and Integration in the EU*. Farnham: Ashgate, pp. 299–314.

Wihtol de Wenden, Catherine. 1994. "Immigrants as Political Actors," in Martin Baldwin-Edwards and Martin A. Schain (eds.), *The Politics of Immigration in Western Europe*. London: Frank Cass, pp. 91–109.

Wilensky, Harold. 1975. *The Welfare State and Equality*. Berkeley: University of California Press.

Wilkinson, Mick and Craig, Gary. 2011. "Wilful Negligence: Migration Policy, Migrants' Work and the Absence of Social Protection in the UK," in Emma Carmel, Alfio Cerami, and Theodoros Papadopoulos (eds.), *Migration and Welfare in the New Europe*. Bristol: Policy Press, pp. 177–94.

Williams, Fiona. 1995. "Race/Ethnicity, Gender and Class in Welfare States: A Framework for Comparative Analysis," *Social Politics* 2 (2), 127–59.

Wilpert, Czarina. 2003. "Racism, Discrimination, Citizenship and the Need for Anti-discrimination Legislation in Germany," in Zig Layton-Henry and Czarina Wilpert (eds.), *Challenging Racism in Britain and Germany*. Basingstoke: Palgrave Macmillan, pp. 245–69.

Wright, Vincent. 1999. "The Fifth Republic: From the *Droit de l'État* to the *État de Droit*?," *West European Politics* 22 (4), 92–119.

Wüst, Andreas M. 2011. "Migrants as Parliamentary Actors in Germany," in Karen Bird, Thomas Saalford, and Andreas M. Wüst (eds.), *The Political Representation of Immigrants and Ethnic Minorities*. London: Routledge, pp. 250–65.

Zimmermann, Wendy and Fix, Michael. 1994. "Immigrant Policy in the States: A Wavering Welcome," in Barry Edmonston and Jeffery S. Passel (eds.), *Immigration and Ethnicity: The Integration of America's Newest Arrivals*. Washington, DC: Urban Institute Press, pp. 267–316.

Index